Critical Acclaim for the authors' first volume, *Best Dives of the Western Hemisphere:*

"Don't plan a dive without it!...Concise and informative...one of the few bargains of the 90's."
Wendy Canning Church, President, Divers Exchange International

"It's a super book... I highly recommend it..."
Elizabeth Harriman, KABC Travel Radio, Los Angeles

"...for serious underwater enthusiasts who want to get in as much bottom time as possible...Best Dives is probably the only guide book they'll need."
Sharon Jaffee, *Caribbean Travel and Life Magazine*

"If water sports are your passion, look for Best Dives of the Western Hemisphere..."
Martin Rapp, *Travel & Leisure Magazine*

"Best Dives...covers the Caribbean quite well..."
Dan Coyle, Universal Press Syndicate

"...a truly useful and well-organized reference..."
Will Cantrell , *International Living*

"...a full library of Western Hemisphere destination guides—in a single indispensable book. What a terrific idea!"
Dee Scarr, Touch the Sea, Bonaire

"...opens a new world of discovery to anyone with a facemask and a desire to look beneath the water's surface."
Barbara Brundage , Pacific Stock, Hawaii

"A marvelously clear and vastly informative book. The best coverage of the subject matter I've seen, and incredibly easy to read—both in text and diagrams. Essential for the serious or beginning diver."
Dr. Susan Cropper, DVM, Society of Aquatic Veterinarians

"I highly recommend this well-written book for all divers."
Rick Sammon, President, CEDAM International

"...artwork and photography are outstanding..."
Bill Smith , *Dive Travel News*

"...details more than 200 of the finest dive sites in the Caribbean..."
The Retired Officer Magazine

"...this book does a very good job of picking the best few dives in a number of destinations..."
Rodale's *Scuba Diving Magazine*

ACKNOWLEDGEMENTS

The authors thank all of BEST DIVES' contributors, correspondents, photographers and researchers (identified throughout the book) for their enormous effort in preparing material for this edition.

A special thanks to our publisher, Michael Hunter, his assistant Kim André and contributors: Rick and Lisa Ocklemann, Alvin Jackson, Auston MacLeod, Mark Padover, Bob Di Chiara, Rick Sammon, Rose Abello, Marilyn Marx, Sue Cropper, Dee Scarr, Brenda Fine, Bill Smith, Beth Ann Molino, Karen and Dennis Sabo, Cathy Rothschild, Bill Tewes, Bill Wilson, Bruce Bowker, Castro Perez, Christopher Lofting, Maria Shaw, Daphne Moffat, Dave Farmer, Michel Angelo Harms, David Mac-Naghten, Derek Perryman, Diane Kegley, Dominique & Leroy French, Tom Mc Kelvey, Donna Oliver, Durand Berg, Efra Figueroa, Ellis Chaderton, Finn Rinds, Florence Marie, Gareth Edmonson-Jones, Gary Pereira, Bert and Gayla Kilbride, Gilbert Gjersvik, Guy Genin, H.V. Pat Reilly, Harry Ward, Iain I. Grummitt, James Abbott, Jeffrey Krames, Jennifer Woods, Jim Spencer, Joan Borque, John K. Darwent, John Yearwood, Jose E. Rafols, Julian Rigby, Karolin Kolcuoglu, Anita and Kenneth Liggett, Kenneth Samuel, Linda Fouke, Linda Jacobson, Luana Wheatley, Michael Young, Michelle Pugh, Mike Emmanuel, Mike Meyers, Mina & Bill Heuslin, Monica Leedy, Myron Clement, Raphael Legrand, Ray Jones, Scott Sunshine, Sean Robinson, Suzette Braun, Theo Smit, Thomas L.C. Peabody, Marilyn and Tim Benford, Ellis Chaderton, Tom Burnett, Walter Frischbutter, Erwin F. Eustacia, Ivan Englentina, and Eva Van Dalen.

BEST DIVES OF THE CARIBBEAN

Joyce Huber

Jon Huber

HUNTER
PUBLISHING INC

Hunter Publishing, Inc.
300 Raritan Center Parkway
Edison NJ 08818
(908) 225-1900

ISBN 1-55650-644-9

Maps by Joyce Huber
Cover photo: The Old Pier, Bonaire
by Jon Huber

CONTENTS

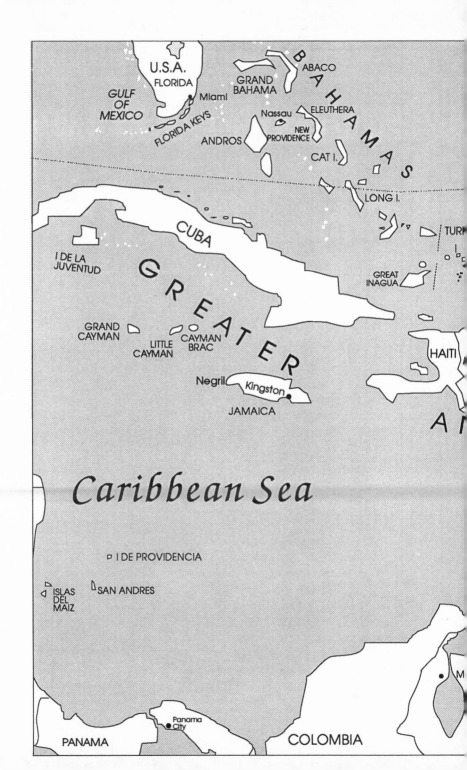

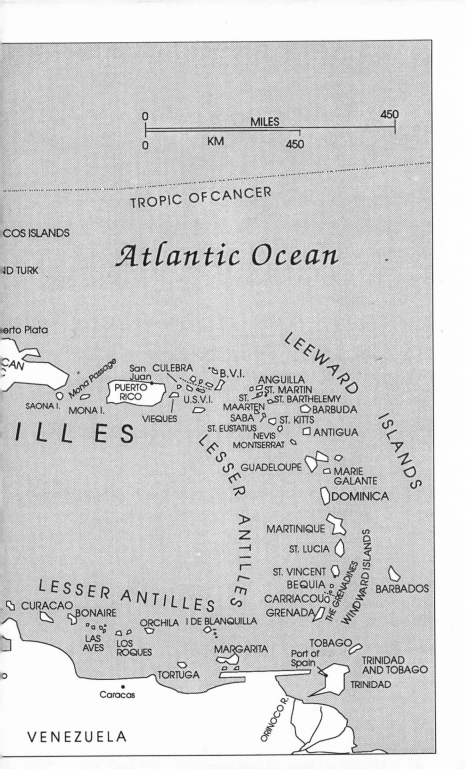

Starfish Ratings

Each dive and snorkeling site has been given a rating of from one to five starfish by prominent divemasters of the area.

☆☆☆☆☆ Five Starfish.

Best of the best diving; best visibility, best marine life, best wreck or reef dive.

☆☆☆☆ Four Starfish.

Fantastic dive. Outstanding in marine life or visual interest.

☆☆☆ Three Starfish.

Superb dive. Excellent visibility and marine life or wreck.

☆☆ Two Starfish.

Good Dive. Interesting fish and plant life; good visibility.

☆One Starfish.

Pleasant dive. Better than average.

Map Symbols

Dive site

Shipwreck

Snorkeling area

Airport

Introduction

Before the creation of underwater viewing equipment, early Caribbean travelers caught merely a glimpse of the world beneath the sea. But, once they did, the idea of subsea exploration really caught on. By the 1930's, rubber goggles with glass lenses and face masks became a standard part of many tropical travelers' wardrobe and a new wave of adventure travel began. And, though much has changed since those early days, the fascination of the sea and its splendid inhabitants are still romancing and captivating visitors the way they always have.

Dive vacations have since evolved into a major part of Caribbean travel. There are now resorts, travel agents, tour operators and yacht charters that cater exclusively to divers and snorkelers. Many all-inclusive resorts have added scuba lessons and tours. There is even a cruise ship with an all-dive itinerary. Sailing afficionados find hull-to-hull pick-up service offered by the dive shops. Novice sailor-divers can rent a yacht with a captain who doubles as a dive instructor and a reef-and-wreck tour guide. The biggest consideration left for the traveler is deciding where to go.

Best Dives of the Caribbean is designed to help you wade through this endless wonder of vacation choices. Whether you are a snorkeler, a novice diver or an experienced ocean explorer you'll find a unique choice of destinations, diver-friendly accommodations and dive services to pick from. We've added several adventure destinations to this edition and expanded others to include more dive and snorkeling sites, a wider choice of accommodations, eateries and après-dive activities.

You'll find suggestions for the best time of year to visit each island and where to write, call or fax for additional information.

Dive and snorkeling sites have been carefully described and rated for various skill levels by the top dive operators of each area and double checked by a member of our own U.S. based panel of dive-travel experts. Rules and etiquette for diving individual marine parks and reserves are listed throughout the guide.

If we've overlooked one of your favorite spots, write and tell us about it and we'll take another look for the next edition. In the meantime we hope you find *Best Dives of the Caribbean* a useful addition to your diver's book shelf.

Planning Your Trip

To plan your best dive vacation, consider first the type of trip that interests you most. It may be a stay at a luxury resort, a week's tour on a live-aboard yacht or an excursion into the wilderness. Then check the best time of year to go. A week of bad weather or rough seas can turn any vacation sour. With the exception of a few dependably dry spots near the equator—Aruba, Bonaire, and Curacao—most areas experience a predictable rainy season. And, though no one can guarantee the weather, each chapter discusses local weather patterns and suggests a best time of year to go.

Finally, consider your budget. You'll note a wide range of of live-aboards and land accommodations throughout this guide, plus the appropriate contact for additional listings at the end of each chapter. Families and groups may enjoy great savings by renting a private home or villa.

SCUBA CERTIFYING ORGANIZATIONS

Locations for SCUBA instruction near your home may be obtained from one of the following organizations.

UNITED STATES

IDEA, International Diving Educators Association, P.O. Box 8427, Jacksonville FL 32239-8427. ☎ 904-744-5554

NASDS, National Association of Scuba Diving Schools, 1012 S. Yates, Memphis TN 38119. ☎ 800-735-3483 or 901-767-7265

NAUI, National Association of Underwater Instructors, P.O. Box 14650, Montclair CA 91763. ☎ 800-533-6284 or 909-621-5801

PADI INTERNATIONAL, Professional Association of Diving Instructors, 1251 E. Dyer Rd., Suite 100, Santa Ana CA 92705-5605. ☎ 800-729-7234 or 714-540-7234

PDIC INTERNATIONAL, Professional Diving Instructors Corporation 1015 River Street, Scranton, PA 18505. ☎ 717-342-9434 or 717-342-1480

SSI, Scuba Schools International, 2619 Canton Court, Fort Collins, CO 80525. ☎ 800-892-2702 or 303-482-0883

YMCA, National YMCA Scuba Program, Oakbrook Square, 6083-A Oakbrook Parkway, Norcross/Atlanta, GA 30093. ☎ 404-662-5172

PACKAGE AND GROUP TOURS

Hundreds of dollars may be saved by choosing a package tour, offered by dive-tour operators, airlines, resorts and dive shops. For example, one package to Guadeloupe includes airfare and hotel for $100 less than the airfare alone. Package tours with diving are listed throughout this guide.

Off-the-beaten-track expeditions are offered by specialty organizations like **CEDAM** (Conservation, Ecology, Diving, Archaeology, Museums) which features programs as varied as an underwater archaeological dig on an ancient shipwreck or a mapping tour of the Galapagos. For information write to Membership Chairman at CEDAM International, 1 Fox Road, Croton NY 10520. ☎ 914-271-5365 or fax 914-271-4723.

Oceanic Society Expeditions, a non-profit, environmental group, offers sail/snorkel trips and dolphin swims. ☎ 415-441-1106 or 800-326-7491 or write to the Oceanic Society, Fort Mason Center, Bldg. E, San Francisto, CA 94123.

Be sure to read the fine print carefully when you are comparing tours. Transfers, sightseeing tours, meals, auto rentals, acceptable accommodations, taxes, tanks, and weights may or may not be included. Also ask whether extra airline weight allowances are included for dive gear.

Many dive clubs and dive shops across the U.S. are offering group trips. These provide an excellent opportunity for new divers, singles, and first-time travelers to get acquainted with new people and places.

BUDDIES

Divers' Exchange International, in Boston, maintains a computerized member list of divers and snorkelers around the world. A member seeking a buddy can easily be teamed up with one or more fellow divers living in a selected destination or with someone who is interested in traveling to that destination at the same time. Membership fees are $25 per year. This is a great idea for business travelers, singles, or couples where just one person dives. For additional information write to Divers' Exchange International, 37 West Cedar St., Boston, MA Box 2382; ☎ 617-723-2960. (DEI is owned and operated by Wendy Canning Church, author of "Aqua Expeditions".)

HANDICAPPED DIVERS

Handicapped divers will find help and information by contacting the **Handicapped Scuba Association** (HSA). The association has provided scuba instruction to people with physical disabilities since 1975. Over 600 instructors in 24 countries are HSA trained. HSA has developed the "Resort Evaluation Program" to assist handicapped divers select a vacation destination. They "check out" facilities and work with the staff and management to ensure accessibility. Once a resort is totally accessible it is "Certified" by HSA.

For a list of HSA certified resorts, group-travel opportunities and more information on HSA's programs, instruction and activities send $2.00 with a stamped, self-addressed legal size envelope to: Michelle Galler, HSA International, 7172 W. Stanford Ave., Littleton, CO 80213. ☎ 1-303-933-4864; fax 1-303-933-4583.

MONEY

Most large resorts, restaurants and dive operators will accept major credit cards, although you risk being charged at a higher rate if the local currency fluctuates. Traveler's checks are accepted almost everywhere and often you'll get a better exchange rate for them than cash. It's always a good idea to have some local currency on hand for cabs, tips and small purchases.

INSURANCE

Many types of travel insurance are available covering everything from lost luggage, trip cancellations and medical expenses. Since emergency medical assistance and air ambulance fees can run to several thousand dollars it is wise to be prepared. Trips purchased with some major credit cards include life insurance.

Divers Alert Network (DAN) offers divers' health insurance for $25 a year plus an annual membership fee of $15. Any treatment required for an accident or emergency which is a direct result of diving such as decompression sickness (the bends), arterial gas embolism or pulmonary baro-trauma is covered up to $15,000 with a 5 percent deductible. Air ambulance to the closest medical care facility, recompression chamber care and in-patient hospital care are covered. Non-diving travel-related accidents are NOT covered.

Lacking the ability to pay, a diver may be refused transport and may be refused treatment. For more information write to DAN, P.O. Box 3823,

3823,Duke University Medical Center, Durham NC 27710. ☎ 919-684-2948

International SOS Assistance is a medical assistance service to travelers who are more than 100 miles from home. For just $40 per person for 7 to 14 days or $70 per couple SOS covers air evacuation and travel related assistance. Evacuation is to the closest medical care facility which is determined by SOS staff doctors. Representative Michael Klein states that SOS has and will send out a private LearJet if necessary, to accommodate a patient. Hospitalization is NOT covered. Standard Blue Cross and Blue Shield policies do cover medical costs while traveling. For individual and group information write to International SOS Assistance, Box 11568, Philadelphia PA 19116. ☎ 800-523-8930 or 215-244-1500.

Lost luggage insurance is available at the ticket counter of many airlines. If you have a homeowner's policy, you may already be covered. Be sure to check first with your insurance agent.

Keep a list of all your dive equipment and other valuables including the name of the manufacturer, model, date of purchase, new price, and serial number, if any, on your person when traveling. Immediately report any theft or loss of baggage to the local police, hotel security people or airline and get a copy of that report. Both the list and the report of loss or theft will be needed to collect from your insurance company. Do not expect airlines to cheerfully compensate you for any loss without a lot of red tape and hassle. Regardless of the value of your gear the airline pays by the weight ($9 per pound) of what is lost. Be sure to tag your luggage with your name and address. Use a business address if possible.

(Note: We found particularly good care taken of our dive and camera gear by American Airlines and Air Aruba)

DOCUMENTS

Carry your personal documents on you at all times while traveling. Be sure to keep a separate record of passport numbers, visas, or tourist cards in your luggage.

SECURITY

Tourists flashing wads of cash and expensive jewelry are prime targets for robbers. Avoid off-the-beaten-track areas of cities, especially at night. Do not carry a lot of cash or wear expensive cameras or jewelry around your neck. Keep alert as to what's going on around you. Stay with your luggage until it is checked in with the airlines. Jewelry and other valuables should be kept in the hotel safe, when possible.

Rental cars have become a target for robbers, more so in the U.S. than the Caribbean, but a few incidents of "bump-'n-rob" crimes have been reported in the islands. To avoid problems, try to rent a car without rental agent markings. If someone bumps into your car, do not stop. Drive to a police staton and report the incident. Do not stop for hitchhikers or to assist strangers.

DRUGS

Penalties for possession of illegal drugs are very harsh and the risk you take for holding even a half-ounce of marijuana cannot be stressed enough. Punishment often entails long jail terms. In certain areas such as Mexico, your embassy and the best lawyer won't be much help. You are guilty until proven innocent. Selling drugs is still cause for public hanging in some areas.

CAMERAS

Divers traveling with expensive camera gear or electronic equipment should register each item with customs *before* leaving the country.

SUNDRIES

Items such as suntan lotion, aspirin, antihistamines, decongestants, antifog, or mosquito repellent should be purchased before your trip. These products are not always available and may cost quite a bit more than what you normally pay for them at home.

FIRST AID

Every diver should carry a small first aid kit for minor cuts, bruises or ailments. Be sure to include a topical antihistamine ointment, antihistamine tablets, seasickness preventive, decongestant, throat lozenges, band aids, aspirin, and diarrhea treatment.

SUNGLASSES

Tropical sunshine can damage your eyes. Sunglasses without a UV-filter coating will not protect against skin cancer to the sensitive skin surrounding the eyes. Both UV-filter sunglasses and a hat should be worn. Corning Glass has recently developed two lines of sunglasses that are particularly useful around water—*Serengeti Drivers* and *Serengeti Solar Barriers*. Both darken with exposure and are also useful on overcast days for driving, boating and fish spotting. We found Cabela's lower-cost fishing glasses equally effective, but less comfortable for long wear.

DIVER IDENTIFICATION

Most dive operations require that you hold a certification card and a logbook. A check-out dive may be required if you cannot produce a log of recent dives.

GEAR

Uncomfortable or ill-fitting masks, snorkels, and other personal diving gear can make your dive a miserable experience. You can greatly reduce the possibility of these problems by buying or renting what you'll need from a reliable dive shop or specialty store before departure. Snorkeling gear, especially, is often expensive to rent.

Packing Checklist

Snorkelers' Warm Water
Packing Check List

___ MASK
___ SNORKEL
___ FINS
___ FLOTATION VEST
___ REEF GLOVES
___ MESH CATCH BAG
(for wet gear or shell
collecting)
___ FISH ID BOOK OR CARD
___ SUNTAN LOTION

___ PASSBOOK OR
REQUIRED ID
___ SPARE STRAP
___ SPARE SNORKEL
___ RETAINER RING
___ PROTECTIVE CLOTHING
(against sunburn)
___ SUNGLASSES
___ U/W CAMERA & FILM
___ HAT

Warm Water Scuba
Packing Check List

___ MASK
___ SNORKEL
___ FINS
___ REGULATOR
___ DEPTH GUAGE
___ BOUYANCY
COMPENSATOR
(stab jacket)

___ SPARE SNORKEL
RETAINER RING
___ SPARE STRAPS
___ SUBMERSIBLE
PRESSURE GAUGE
___ WATCH/BOTTOM TIMER
___ WEIGHT BELT
(no lead)

__ WET SUIT, SHORTIE
   OR LYCRA WET SKIN
__ WET SUIT BOOTS
__ MESH CATCH BAG
__ U/W DIVE LIGHTS
__(PRIMARY AND BACK UP)
__ DRAMAMINE or other
   seasickness preventative
__ GEAR MARKER
__ DIVER CERTIFICATION
   CARD (C-card)
__ DIVER LOG BOOK
__ SUNGLASSES
__ SPARE MASK STRAP

___ DIVING KNIFE
___ DE-FOG SOLUTION
___ REEF GLOVES
   (not for use in marine parks)
___ CYALUME STICKS
   (chemical light sticks)
___ U\W CAMERA AND FILM
___ FISH ID BOOK
___ DIVE TABLES
___ PASSPORT or proof of
   citizenship as required
___ DIVE TABLES
___ SUNTAN LOTION
___ HAT (with visor or brim)

Anguilla

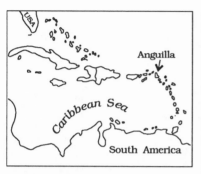

Anguilla (pronounced Ann-GWIL-A) is one of the Caribbean's best kept secrets. Though sailing buffs have enjoyed its secluded bays and coves for decades, divers are just discovering its rich coral walls, great wrecks and miles of shallow snorkeling gardens.

Sitting just five miles from St. Martin and 190 miles east of Puerto Rico, Anguilla is the northernmost of the Leeward Islands in the Eastern Caribbean. It is small, just 16 miles long and four miles wide with one main road that threads through picturesque villages, past small churches, rows of Indian cottages, and colorful fruit and vegetable stands. Scattered along its craggy coast are 30 white, sand beaches.

Delightfully tranquil, this crown colony is void of mammoth shopping centers, casinos, and crowds. Just 7,000 residents and a few thousand free-roaming goats comprise the local population.

Physically, Anguilla is predominantly low-lying, formed of limestone and coral with patches of mangrove and fresh-water ponds. Small cliffs on its north side are habitat to a variety of tropical birds as are nearby out islands where you can spot the Red-Billed Tropic bird, Royal Terns, Kingfishers, Laughing Gulls, Frigates and Blue-faced Boobies.

Anguilla's capital, The Valley is a tiny strand of pastel shops, government buildings and colorful houses.

Sandy Ground—just west of The Valley on the northwest end— is the main yacht and cruise-ship harbor. It is the location of the sole dive shop and the jumping-off point for sail-snorkeling cruises. Adjacent to Sandy Ground is Road Bay, a small strip of land with an ocean beach on one side and a maze of shallow salt ponds which attract a multitude of tropical birds on the other.

Contributors: Thomas L.C. Peabody, Iain I. Grummitt, Tamariain Watersports.

When to Go

The best time to visit Anguilla is from January to April. Tropical storms bringing an annual rainfall of 35 inches are a threat from late July till October.

Air and water temperatures are agreeable for diving year round. Average air temperature is 80° F. Water temperatures range from 78° to 90° F.

History

Until recently no one suspected that Anguilla had a long history, but some 23 aboriginal sites that date back as early as 2000 B.C. have been discovered by members of the Anguilla Archaeological and Historical Society.

The Fountain Cavern at Shoal Bay on Anguilla's north coast is the most impressive cave site. Thought to be a worship center, the rock walls contain numerous carvings of gods worshipped by the Arawak peoples. Three and one half acres of ground surrounding the Fountain Cave have been set aside as a national park to protect the cave and provide a sanctuary for Anguilla's native plants.

Scientists believe that during the last ice age Anguilla, St. Martin and Saba were one and provided a home for a varied mammal community. In 1883, the Smithsonian Institute published an account of the bones of a huge, pig-sized (now extinct) rodent, *amblyrlisa inundata*, found at Cavanna Cave on the north shore. Earlier this year a previously undisturbed pre-ceramic site was discovered at the east end of the island.

The Anguilla Archaeological and Historical Society is preparing a museum to display the artifacts collection.

Best Dives and Snorkeling Sites

Wreck diving and out-island snorkeling prevail over Anguilla's subsea activities.

Eight of the 25 sites regularly visited by Tamariain Watersports, the island's only full-service (PADI) dive shop, are wrecks that were intentionally sunk to create artificial reefs. Divemasters, Thomas Peabody and Iain Grummitt, boast the largest number of diveable wrecks in the eastern Caribbean—all in warm, clear water.

☆☆☆ The wreck of the *M.V. Oosterdiep* is one of the newest sites. It is a 130-ft freighter resting at 80 feet about three miles out from Road Bay. Intact and upright, it attracts schooling yellowtail, schoolmaster snapper,

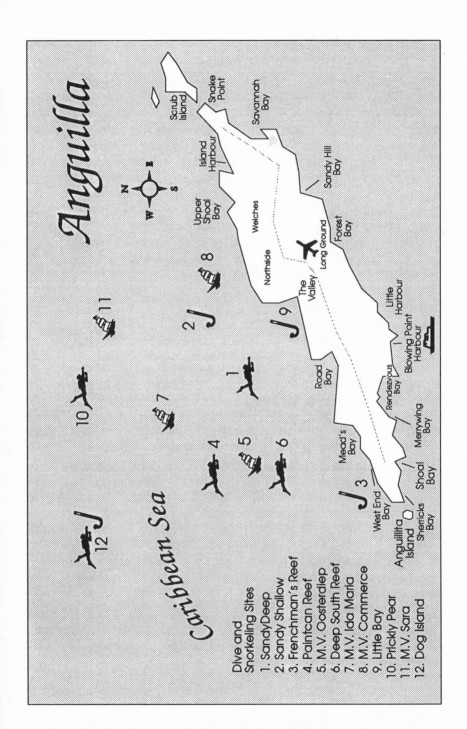

Atlantic spadefish, flying gurnard, stingrays and small fish. Penetration is not allowed without specialty certification and under the supervision of local divemasters.

☆☆☆ **Sandy Deep,** a mini wall and the favorite reef dive, is lush with hard and soft corals, gorgonians, and abundant fish life and lobster (no collecting). Not recommended for snorkeling, but good for the novice with depths from 15 to 60 ft. Sea conditions vary depending on the time of year.

☆☆☆ **Frenchman's Reef,** a collapsed, limestone cliff off the southern point of West End Bay, is Anguilla's best snorkeling and novice-diver spot. Depths are from the surface to 40 ft. The submerged terrain is mixed coral, boulders and sand. There are spectacular swim-throughs, ledges and caverns—a "Whitman's Sampler" of West Indies marine life. Seas are calm and visibility is good.

☆☆☆☆ The wall at **Dog Island,** ten miles northwest of Road Bay, is an outstanding dive with depths from 15 to 80 ft. The wall's rock and coral face is riddled with nooks and crannies where you'll find octopi, turtles, arrow crabs, basket sponges, slender tube sponges, shrimp and lobster. Seafans and gorgonians abound. Fish life includes horse-eye jacks, chub, parrotfish, huge grey and French angels, blacktip and nurse sharks. Stingrays bury themselves in the sandy bottom. The surface over the wall is usually too choppy for snorkeling, but other areas around Dog Island—Bay Rock, for example—are popular snorkeling spots when seas are calm. The boat ride is about 30 minutes.

☆☆ **Little Bay Reef** is a sheltered 15 to 25-ft reef, ideal for novice divers, students and snorkelers. The bottom is a mix of coral, sand and turtle grass. There is excellent micro life including nudibranchs and lettuce slugs, sea horses, turtles, octopi, barber shrimp and lobster. The reef is a stone's throw from shore but access other than by boat entails a rugged climb down a rocky footpath to the beach. Tamariain Water Sports offers snorkelers drop-off and pick-up service to the beach at Little Bay.

Noted underwater photographer Paul Humann shot extensively here for his famous book, *Reef Creatures.*

☆☆☆ **Shoal Bay East** is the best water-entry snorkeling and scuba site. There are two reefs, one directly off the beach that parallels the beach for some distance and another one a little further out. Depths range from the surface to 80 ft.

☆☆ The wreck of the *M.V. Commerce* is another freighter scuttled by divemasters Peabody and Grummitt. This 130-ft ship was sunk in 1986 off

Grunts

Limestone Bay on the northwest coast. Depth is 45 to 80 ft. Great for photography, dramatic remains of the ship are astir with schools of shimmering barracuda, golden sergeant majors, queen angels, green and spotted morays, sting rays and spiny lobster. Macro subjects proliferate. Seas are variable, usually a light chop with an occasional current. Bottom terrain is boulder coral and sand.

☆☆☆☆ Marine life is superb at **Deep South Reef**, a patch reef displaying beautiful pillar-, star- and brain-coral formations. A profusion of soft, pastel corals and gorgonians blend with the vibrant reds and oranges of the reef. Purple tube sponges, barrel sponges and sea fans are abundant. Triggerfish, trumpetfish, parrotfish, angels, jacks, southern stingrays, spotted drums, wrasses, blue tangs, crabs and lobster are in residence. Depths are 55 to 80 ft. Good visibility. Seas vary with winds. Deep South is a short boat trip, about a mile, from the south end of Road Bay.

☆☆☆☆ **Paintcan Reef** is named for colorful splashes of strawberry and vase sponges which adorn the magnificent hard-coral structures of this patch reef. Fish life, too, is excellent with glimpses of black durgon, blacktip and nurse shark, walls of grunts, morays, jacks, copper sweepers, barracuda, and schools of silversides and sergeant majors. Pink-tipped anemones, and iridescent tube sponges cluster along the walls of the reef. Hawksbill turtles are recurrent visitors. Paintcan is about three miles north of Road Bay, about a 15-minute boat trip. Depths are from 55 ft to 80 ft. Sea conditions vary. Recommended for experienced divers.

☆☆☆☆ The *M.V. Sara*, a freighter scuttled by the government to create an artificial reef, is impressive by size alone—over 230 ft. long. The *Sara* provides a fantastic backdrop for underwater photographs. Grunts, goatfish, barjacks, stingrays and small schooling fish frequent the area. Depth is 80 ft. It is about two miles north of Road Bay. Seas are usually choppy.

☆☆☆ Another favorite of macro photographers is the wreck of the *M.V. Ida Maria*. Scuttled in 1986 by divemasters Peabody and Gummitt, this 110-ft freighter sits on the sand at 60 ft. The deteriorating hull is overgrown with plate, pencil and clinging corals, anemones and sponges—home to sea horses, octopi, urchins, arrow crabs, banded cleaner shrimp, lavender shrimp and sea cucumbers. Huge green moray eels and lobster peek out from the cracks along the bottom. Fish life and visibility are outstanding. Seas vary with weather. The *Ida Maria* is about six miles north of Limestone Bay.

☆☆☆ **Prickly Pear Reef** is an underwater canyon characterized by ledges and caverns. One formation resembling a chimney is a beautiful backdrop for underwater portraits. There are schooling goatfish, crabs, lobster, barracuda, friendly angels and grouper, squirrel fish, longnose butterfly fish, tarpon, mangrove snapper and grunts. Nurse sharks rest on the sandy bottom under the ledges. Depths range from 40 to 70 ft. Prickly Pear is west of the *M.V. Sara*—about six miles out from Long Bay.

☆ **Sandy Shallow** is recommended for novice divers. A garden of soft corals and gorgonians slopes from 30 to 70 ft. Seas are usually calm. Small schooling tropicals and invertebrates populate this spot.

Catamaran and mono-hull sailboats leave Road Bay daily for snorkeling/picnic jaunts to: **Little Bay,** on Anguilla's northwest coast; **Prickly Pear Cays,** six miles out of Road Bay; **Shoal Bay,** on the south end of Anguilla; **Scilly Cay; Dog Island,** ten miles north of Road Bay and **Sandy Island,** the most popular out-island snorkeling destination. A tiny 650 ft by 160 ft, Sandy Island is surrounded by living reef ranging from waist-deep to ten ft.

Dive Operator

Tamariain Watersports is a PADI, five star dive center offering reef and wreck tours, certification and advanced training. Divemaster Thomas Peabody recommends use of a pony bottle and a safe second when diving the deep wrecks. Dive/accommodation package tours with any of the hotels can be arranged with Tamariain. ☎ 809-497-2020; fax 809-497-5125. Write to Tamariain Watersports Ltd. P.O. Box 247, The Valley, Anguilla, British West Indies.

Daily diving rates are $35 for a single tank; $60 for a two-tank dive; and $45 for a night dive.

Snorkeling cruises can be arranged through **Enchanted Island Cruises, Ltd.**, Road Bay. Enchanted Island operates a 50-ft catamaran, *Wildcat*, and a 31-ft monohull, *Counterpoint*. Local ☎ 497-3111. **Sandy Island Enterprises**, Road Bay has three *Shauna* power boats and a 26-ft sailboat, *Ragtime*. ☎ 497-6395. **Suntastic Yacht Services**, Road Bay, has a 37-ft yacht, *Skybird* and 30-ft powerboat, *Sunrise*. ☎ 497-3400/3699.

Accommodations

A 10% service charge is added to resort bills in lieu of gratuities, and eight percent government tax is added on rooms only.

Accommodations range from low- to mid-priced inns and cottages to luxurious resorts. Diving and snorkeling packages are offered through the dive operator (see above).

Syndans Apartments are clean, attractive studios overlooking the Sandy Ground beach and Road Salt Pond. Winter rates are $45 to $60 per day. ☎ U.S. 212-840-6636; U.K. 011 44-753 70087. Write to ITR 25 W 39th St., New York NY 10018.

Shoal Bay Villas is a small, intimate, beach-front condominium hotel. Units feature full kitchen, split-level bedroom/living room and a private patio with hammock. Restaurant, tennis, jacuzzi. Snorkeling and scuba off the beach. Fresh-water pool. Winter rates are $210 & $230 per night for two people. Boat and unlimited shore-dive packages offered. ☎ 800-722-7045; 809-497-2727; fax 809-497-3727.

The Mariners is a luxury, West Indian style, beachfront cottage complex at Sandy Ground. Choose from rooms or cottages, each with a veranda, refrigerator, ceiling fan, telephone and private bath. Winter rates for a double are $190-$220, summer, $125-$165. Dive packages, tennis, pool, restaurant. Romantic. ☎ 800-848-7938 or 809-497-2671. Write P.O. Box 139, Sandy Ground, Anguilla, BWI.

Anguilla Great House is a gorgeous new hotel built in the style of a West-Indian plantation house. It is situated on Rendezvous Bay where you can see the mountains of St. Martin on the nearby horizon. Features include an open-air restaurant, pool, beach bar and snorkeling off the mile-long beach. Suites have well-equipped kitchenettes. Winter rates per day for double occupancy are from $200 per day for a room to $475 for a two-bedroom suite. Summer: $115 for a room (double) to $295 for a two-bedroom suite. Money-saving packages available. ☎ 800-553-4939; 516-261-1234. fax 516-261-9606.

La Sirena is an intimate hideaway overlooking Mead's Bay, on the southwest portion of the island. Choose between individually-designed rooms and villas, all with ocean views, balcony, ceiling fans, phone & minibars. Restaurant, bar and two freshwater pools on site. Rates for a double are from $95 to $110 in summer; $180 to $215 in winter. Villas for one to four persons are from $160 in summer and from $290 in winter. Packages available. ☎ 800-331-9358 U.S. and Canada ☎ 800-331-9358 or 212-545-8435; fax 809-497-6829; in the U.K. 071-937-7725; fax 071-938-4793. Write to P.O. Box 200, Mead's Bay, Anguilla B.W.I.

The Ferryboat Inn is a small family-operated inn on the south side of the island. Snorkeling and swimming off the beach. Well-equipped apartments are adjacent to the beach. Restaurant. Rates are from $150 per day for a one-bedroom apartment, double occupancy. Rooms are clean, modern and attractive.

The most romantic and luxurious hotel on Anguilla is the **Malliouhana** which sits high on a rocky cliff over Meads Bay on the southwest shores surrounded by two miles of sand beaches. This tastefully-appointed resort features an exercise hall and massage room, three pools, close proximity to the dive shop, boutique, shops, hair salon, French gourmet restaurant, tennis courts with night lights, and impeccable service. Complimentary snorkeling and fishing gear, water skiing, cruises, windsurfing, sunfish and catamarans are included in the rates for rooms and suites. Doubles: Winter $480 to $1,080 per day. Summer $240 to $565 per day. $25 to $50 extra for child. ☎ 212-696-1323; fax 212-213-2297 or 809-497-6011; in the U.K. ☎ 272 732606; fax 272 237726. Write to P.O. Box 173, Anguilla, Leeward Islands, BWI.

Cinnamon Reef Beach Club in Little Harbour offers villa suites with spacious, split-level bedroom/living rooms, private patios and hammocks. Award-winning restaurant. Beautiful beach, tennis, jacuzzi. Winter rates, breakfast included, are from $250 to $325; Summer $150 to $225. ☎ 800-223-1108, 809-497-2727; fax 497-3727; Canada 416-485-8724, fax 416-485-8256; U.K. 0-45383 5801; fax 0-45383 5525.

The Inns of Anguilla are a group of 23 hotels, guests houses, apartments and villas offering attractively-priced accommodations from $65 to $150 per night. Week-long packages from $380. As with all Anguilla hotels, you can tie in a dive package for an extra $155 (three two-tank dives; $260 for five two-tank dives). Discount packages are available if paid in advance. For a list, description, brochures and rates of the inns write to Medhurst & Associates, 271 Main St., Northport, NY 11768; ☎ 800-223-9815; fax 212-545-8467. In Canada Ms. Cecile Jacobs, 801 York Mills Rd, Suite 201, Toronto, ONT M3B1X7 ☎ 416-299-4905; fax 416-445-9734. In the U.K. Anguilla Tourist Office, WINDOTEL, 3 Epirus Rd, London SW 67UJ, ☎ 01-937-7725; fax 071-938-4793.

Additional apartments, condos and resort listings are available from the Anguilla Tourist Board.

Other Activities and Sightseeing

Sailing, deep-sea fishing, sunset cruises, birdwatching at Little Bay and Crocus Bay, shelling and relaxing are the main activities on Anguilla. Plans for a movie theater and museum are in the works.

Anguilla's sightseeing spots are the Wallblake Historic House near the Roman Catholic Church; the prison at Crocus Hill; the old Warden's Place in the Valley; the Fountain Cave area, the Devonish Cotton Gin Gallery; Road Bay and Sandy Ground, where you'll find the dive shop and fishing boats.

Anguilla does not have a tourist-oriented nightlife, but a 15-minute ferry ride to St. Martin brings you to a wealth of duty-free shops, casinos and evening entertainment. Ferries leave Blowing Point for Marigot, St. Martin every forty minutes from 7:30 am till 11:00 pm. ☎ 6853.

For guided archaeological tours write to P.O. Box 252, Anguilla in advance of your trip. Deep sea fishing can be arranged at Road Bay and Island Harbor, glass bottom boat cruises are from Shoal Bay and Island Harbour (☎ 4155). Sunset cruises to out islands are offered by Enchanted Island Cruises, ☎ 3111. For bird-watching trips—best in September—at Little Bay and Crocus Bay call ☎ 2759.

Dining

Local lobster and fish dishes, plain and fancy, highlight Anguillan restaurant menus. Enjoy West Indian, French Creole, Mexican, European, Italian and fast food in a choice of romantic and rustic settings.

Anguilla's leading French eatery, **Hibernia** at Island Harbour offers dining on a huge veranda overlooking the sea. Choice menu picks are smoked Caribbean fish, grilled crayfish in lemongrass sauce, grilled snapper in honey & garlic, and home-made chestnut ice cream. Open for lunch and dinner. ☎ 4290. Major credit cards.

Uncle Ernie's in Shoal Bay is a laid-back beach bar and restaurant where you can get a beer for one dollar. Selections include barbecued chicken, fish or ribs with chips. ☎ 3520

Reefside, a friendly, beachfront complex adjacent to Shoalbay Villas, opens every day for breakfast, lunch and dinner. Offers grilled lobster, steaks, steamed shrimp and tropical drinks. Catch the beach barbecue on Wed, Fri & Sun from 12 to 3 pm. ☎ 2051. Major credit cards.

Fat Cat in George Hill packages hors d'oeuvres, entrees, salads, and desserts ready to heat in the oven or microwave. Call ahead for picnics, special entrees or special-occasion cakes. ☎ 2307. American Express.

Ships Galley on the beach at Sandy Ground features sumptuous West-Indian dishes—stewed whelks (shellfish) with sweet potatoes, scampi, grilled snapper and lobster. Open for breakfast, lunch and dinner. ☎ 2040. Major credit cards.

Vegetarian dishes with a Mexican flair are offered at **Que Pasa** in Sandy Ground where the chef whips up stuffed mushrooms, chili- potato soup, enchiladas in red chili sauce, quesadillas and burritos for lunch and dinner. Lobster, chicken, pork and beef are available for all dishes. Take-out and delivery service. ☎ 3171. Major credit cards.

Snorkel off the beach, then lunch under the seagrape trees at **La Fontana** in Shoal Bay. This garden of delights is open all day from 8 am till 10 pm and offers Caribbean and Italian specialties. Dinner favorites are *Rassa alla Zio Mario* (duck breast with blueberries and barolo wine) and *Lobster Conte Panuss* (lobster in fresh herbs and wine). ☎ 3492. Major credit cards.

For American food stop at the **Paradise Cafe** in Katouche, ☎ 3200, or enjoy luxurious Anguillian surroundings at **The Old House** at George Hill. **Brother's** in The Valley caters a wide variety of island and continental foods including conch and goat stew, fish, hot dogs, burgers—☎ 3550. **Cora's Pepper Pot** in The Valley specializes in curried dishes, seafood and soups. ☎ 2328.

Triggerfish

coast reefs where visibility is good, seas are dependably calm and currents mild, but new areas are continually opening up. Depths range from shallow to drop-offs of more than 2,000 feet. Dive shops offer both scuba and snorkeling tours. Scuba divers must show a certification card.

☆☆☆☆ **Shirley Heights**, off the south coast, is one of the island's most spectacular areas. Jagged cliffs, coral buttresses, huge boulders and shear drop-offs form the subsea terrain. Residents include eagle rays, schools of spade fish and turtles, with frequent sightings of mantas and dolphins. Huge mackerel and kingfish pass through. Depths are from ten to 100 ft.

☆☆☆☆ **Cades Reef**, a five-mile-long shelf off Antigua's southwest corner, is Antigua's largest reef structure. It has 25 or more different dive and snorkeling sites that vary in depth from 20 ft to 90 ft. such as **Lemon Ridge**, with depths from 20 to 45 ft; **The Chimney**, home to huge pillar coral formations inhabited by margate, squirrelfish, nurse sharks, morays; and the **The Pillars** at 50 to 80 ft where you'll see queen angel fish, triggerfish, black durgons, spotted and green moray eels.

Cades' ridges and valleys are shot through with small caves hiding lobster, crabs and small fish. Forests of elkhorn and staghorn coral provide shelter to an abundant fish population including huge grouper, eagle rays, throngs of grunts and sergeant majors, parrotfish, sting rays, snapper and barracuda. Visibility often exceeds 200 ft and seas are calm.

☆☆☆☆☆ **Monkshead** is a sandy coral passage in the center of Cades which is populated by garden eels, large stingrays and jacks. Spearfishing, shell, shellfish and coral collecting is prohibited.

☆ The **Wreck of the** *Andes*, an old freighter, lies in 20 ft of water off the west coast. She went down in 1905 when a cargo of cotton and pitch caught fire. The hull and scattered remains are overgrown with plate corals and red sponges. Visibility varies.

☆☆☆☆ **Sunken Rock**, just five minutes off the south coast is perhaps the islands' most popular dive when sea conditions permit. The dive

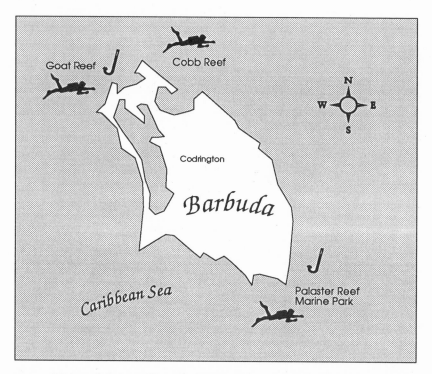

starts at 30 ft and drops off to 150 ft. Hundreds of coral crevices and ledges attract huge rays, amberjack, and barracuda. Recommended for experienced ocean divers.

☆☆☆ **Diamond Marine Park** located five miles off the north coast of Antigua is a large shallow barrier reef complex riddled with small caves, boulders, overhangs and canyons. Marine life is prolific with huge rays, nurse sharks, morays, lobster, queen helmuts, conch, and tropicals. Depths range from shallow to about 100 ft. Snorkeling and glass-bottom boat tours are offered by the local shops. Trips are weather dependent. Usually choppy.

☆☆☆ Shipwrecks abound all around the island, the favorite being the **Wreck of the *Jettias***, a 310-ft steamship that hit the reefs in 1917. The hull rests in 25 feet of water and offers dramatic photo opportunities.

Good shore snorkeling may be found off the beaches of the Galley Bay Hotel, Pineapple Beach Hotel, the Hawksbill Beach Resort and the Sandpiper Reef Hotel. (The Sandpiper Hotel is closed, but you can still use the beach).

BARBUDA

The dense reefs fringing Barbuda are largely unexplored. There are no dive shops on the island, but experienced snorkelers can swim to Palaster Reef, off Palmetto Point on the southwest tip of the island. More than 100 shipwrecks have been documented off Barbuda's coast. Charter day trips from Antigua can be easily arranged.

Antigua Dive Operators

Aquanaut Diving Centres are at the St. James' Club, ☎ 460-5000; Galleon Beach Club, ☎ 460-1024/1450 and Ramada Renaissance Royal Antiguan, ☎ 462-3733.

Or try: **Dive Antigua** at the Halcyon Cove Hotell, ☎ 462-3483; **Dive Runaway** Runaway Beach Club, ☎ 462-2626; **Dockyard Divers** at the Copper & Lumber Store Hotel, ☎ 460-1058/464-8591, VHF channel 68; **Jolly Dive** at the Jolly Beach Hotel, ☎ 462-0061; **Long Bay Dive Shop** at the Long Bay Hotel, ☎ 460-2005; **Pirate Divers** at the Lord Nelson Beach Hotel, ☎ 462-3094.

Several Antigua-based operators offer snorkeling jaunts to small out-islands. Check with individual dive operators for schedules.

Accommodations

Note: A 7% room tax and 10% service charge are added to accommodations. Some resorts include them in their package rates. Some do not. Check with individual operations.

Dive packages are offered at the **Royal Antiguan,** a Ramada resort. Rates start at $239 per person for three nights including one two-tank boat trip each morning. ☎ 800-SCUBA 4U (728-2248) or 201-934-6731. Write to Box 1322, Deep Bay, Antigua, WI.

The **St. James's Club** is an elegant resort set on a 100-acre peninsula. Guests choose from suites, villas, or rooms. Features: two pools, three restaurants, dive shop, horseback riding, fishing, yacht charters, exercise room, massage parlour. Dive packages start at $1,150 per person for accommodations for seven nights, breakfast and dinner daily, two two-tank dives per day for five days, all scuba equipment and full use of the club's sports facilities.Write to Box 63, St. John's, Antigua, WI ☎ 800-274-0008 or 809-460-5000.

Set on Antigua's southernmost tip, the **Galleon Beach Club and Hotel** offers one- and two-bedroom cottages and suites with fully-equipped kitchens. Rooms overlook Freemans Bay and English Harbour. Dive shop, restaurant and bar on premises. Winter rates for a one-bedroom suite start at $210 per night. Two-bedroom cottage for up to four people, $230 per night. Diving and meals are extra. ☎ 800-223-9815; or 809-460-1024.

The **Copper and Lumber Store Hotel** is a charming 17th-century brick building restored as an intimate 14-suite hostelry, located in Nelson's Dockyard. Each individually decorated room features beamed ceilings and dormer windows overlooking the harbour with luxurious Persian rugs, period antiques, four-poster beds and mahogany baths with brass fixtures. Ferry service to Galleon Beach for swimming and scuba. Dive shop on premises. Learn-to-dive packages offered at $985 (winter), $700 (summer) include seven nights accommodations, airport tranfers, a four-day certification course, equipment. For experienced divers: $885 (winter), $620 (summer) includes seven nights accommodations, airport transfers, five two-tank dives, dive-boat pickup, weights, belts, tanks. ☎ 800-633-7411 or 809-460-1058.

The lagoon off **The Galley Bay Hotel** is a favorite snorkeling spot. The resort does not offer scuba, but can arrange for reef trips through nearby shops. Galley Bay is a 30-room, all-inclusive resort set on 40 acres of landscaped grounds between a half-mile sandy beach and a lagoon. A variety of accommodations feature ceiling fans, refrigerator, cottages with grass roofs, and a gourmet restaurant. Rates per couple start at $275 per day and include all meals, drinks, and taxes. ☎ 800-223-6510; direct 809-462-0302.

Another snorkelers' favorite is **Jumby Bay**, an exclusive, yet accessible luxury resort on its own island, two miles north of Antigua. Off the beach are beautiful coral patches and throngs of tropicals. Jumby Bay offers 38 suites, all with ocean views and secluded beaches. Rates include three meals, afternoon tea, unlimited cocktails, laundry and picnic service. Three snorkeling trips are made to Bird Island each week. Facilities include tennis, water skiing and instruction, snorkeling, sunfish sailboats, bicycles, croquet and instruction, putting green, bar and laundry service. Rates include three meals, afternoon tea, unlimited cocktails, laundry and picnic service. For seven nights: winter, $5,370 per couple; spring $4,470 per couple; summer $3,570 per couple. Tax not included. ☎ 800-421-9016; 809-462-6000.

Pineapple Beach Club is an all-inclusive 125-room hotel located on Long Bay Beach. There is good snorkeling on a shallow coral reef off the hotel beach. Scuba can be arranged with local shops but is not included in the resort's all-inclusive package rates. Winter rates, per night, per couple start at about $400, including all meals, drinks, wind surfing, sailboats, snorkeling equipment, fishing, fitness center, tennis, beach, pool, nature trails and evening entertainment. Room tax is included. Reserve through travel agents or ☎ 800-966-4737; 809-463-2006.

Runaway Beach Club in St. John's is situated on a beautiful, palm-lined white-sand beach. Ten minutes from town. Choice of hotel rooms or one- and two-bedroom apartments. Pool, sailing, snorkeling and diving. Restaurant. ☎ 809-462-1318/4172 or write to Box 874, St. John's, Antigua, WI.

Palmetto Hotel, Barbuda. Located on Palmetto's Peninsula, to the southwestern side of Barbuda, this resort consists of a 63-room luxury hotel and 67 villas facing the ocean. The surroundings insure complete privacy and comfort, Two restaurants. Rates & reservations: ☎ 809-460-0326 (phone & fax).

For additional Antigua accommodations contact the Antigua & Barbuda Department of Tourism (see chapter end for listings)

Other Activities

A number of leisure cruises, most which last the better part of a day and include lunch, sightseeing, snorkeling and other entertainment, sail Antigua's jagged coast. The *Servabo Fun Cruise*, a 70-ft Brixham gaff-rigged ketch based off the shore of Dickenson Bay, departs from Antigua Village. The *Jolly Roger Pirate Cruise*, Antigua's largest sailing ship, is a two-masted schooner with daily and Saturday evening cruises, and the *Falcon*, an elegant catamaran, offers sunset and day snorkeling cruises to Barbuda and Bird Island, a tiny, uninhabited island that is a nesting ground to the red-billed tropic bird, sooty terns, brown noddies, and the brown pelican. Outstanding shallow, snorkeling reefs skirt Bird Island's beach. Most hotels can arrange for any of these cruises.

Antigua's northeast trade winds are ideal for windsurfers of all abilities. The island's sheltered west coast is perfect for beginners, while on the east coast, the giant "Atlantic rollers" are challenging even for advanced surfers.

Windsurfing lessons for novices, intermediate, and advanced board surfers are offered at several hotels including **Jolly Beach Hotel's Windsurfing Sailing School** and **Patrick Scales Water Sports** at Lord Nelson Beach Hotel.

Water skiing, jet skiing, and parasailing are offered at the **Wadadli Watersports Centre** at Buccaneer Cove and **Unlimited Hydro Sports** at Dickenson Bay and Jolly Beach.

Deep-sea fishing charters can be arranged through most hotels. Tennis courts are everywhere. **Viking Tennis Club** 809-462-2260 is a private club that offers temporary membership for visitors. **Temo Sports** 809-460-1781, a tennis and squash complex, has synthetic grass courts and tow glass-backed squash courts. Squash is offered at the **Bucket Club,** ☎ 809-462-3060.

Golf enthusiasts will enjoy Antigua's fine 18-hole, par-72 course at **Cedar Valley Golf Club,** ☎ 809-462-0161. This course has panoramic views of Antigua's northern coast and surrounding areas. Daily greens fees are $20 for 18 holes, $15 for nine holes; carts are $25 for 18 holes and $13 for nine.

Escorted horseback beach and cross-country tours are arranged at the **Wadadli Stables,** ☎ 809-462-2721 in St. John's.

The islands' exquisite scenery, varied terrain and well-preserved monuments make excellent walking and hiking territory. The capital of St. John's is filled with interesting attractions and shops, and the national park at Nelson's Dockyard provides historic sight-seeing opportunities. Mond's Hill, Boggy Peak, Fig Tree Drive, and Megaliths at Greencastel Hill are just a few of the hiking areas for adventurous souls.

Bicycles are another way to view Antigua's scenery. Mountain bikes can be rented for $10 per day from Sun Cycles, ☎ 809-461-0324.

Sightseeing

ANTIGUA

Two major sightseeing areas are the capital city of St. John's on the northwestern side of the island and English Harbour on the south side. St. John's, with a population of 35,000, is the center of business and visitor activity. More than half of the country's hotels surround the capital city.

Situated on a hilltop overlooking the center of town, **St. John's Cathedral** was originally constructed in 1683 and replaced in 1745. It was again rebuilt and reconsecrated in the 19th century, after a shattering earthquake. Its unusual architecture features two Baroque-style towers. The **Museum of Antigua & Barbuda**, located in the Old Courthouse, exhibits artifacts tracing the rich history of the sister islands, from prehistoric times through independence. **Government House** is the official residence of the Governor General for Antigua in St. John's. As such, it is not regularly open to the public, but is a fine example of 17th-century colonial architecture. **Fort James**, which once defended the entrance of St. John's Harbor, features weapons and other military details dating back to the American Revolution.

Other interesting things to see in and around St. John's include the **Public Market**, a semi open-air mart which provides much local color and the opportunity to sample native produce. The **Antigua Rum Distillery,** which may be toured with prior arrangement, is located at Deep Water Harbour. Cavalier and Old Mill Rums are made here. **Heritage Quay,** a shopping complex and cruise ship pier, offers a wide variety of duty-free shops, a casino, and a hotel. **Redcliffe Quay**, a restored arsenal, now houses shops and restaurants.

Many more historical buildings can be found on the other side of the island within the confines of **Nelson's Dockyard**. Built in 1784 at **English Harbour**, it served as the headquarters for Admiral Horatio Nelson, the commander of the Leeward Islands Squadron, during the days when a man's worth was measured in how quickly he could reload his musket.

Landmarks of the seamen's commitment to Antigua have been painstakingly restored and the area is now a national park. One landmark in particular is the **Copper and Lumber Store Hotel,** the former center of activity for purchasing construction materials. While the bottom served as a supply store, the upper floors were used as quarters for sailors whose ships were being hauled for repairs. Today, those early quarters are elegant rooms of a Georgian hotel, filled with period furnishings. Two other buildings, the old **Capstan House** and the **Cordage and Canvas Store** have been restored for additional hotel space by the Copper and Lumber owners. The **Admiral's Inn and Restaurant** also provides accommodations and the opportunity for leisurely investigation.

The complex has two museums. **Admiral's House,** with its bust of Nelson framing the doorway, is an original structure full of Nelsonian mementos reminiscent of his era. **Clarence House**, the former home of Prince William Henry, Duke of Clarence, who later became King William IV, is a graceful Georgian stone residence overlooking the Dockyard. Now home to Antigua's Governor General, when he is not in residence, it is open to the public, and the caretaker provides visitors with a lively lecture on the house's origins and history. In modern times, it has served as the vacation residence of Princess Margaret.

To the north are the stately ruins of Shirley Heights, named for General Thomas Shirley, the former governor of the Leeward Islands. The fortress includes extensive fortifications, barracks, and powder magazines which serve as great "lookout" points. On Sunday afternoons, Shirley Heights is a gathering spot where visitors can enjoy local reggae and steel bands and a tasty barbecue meal, as they watch the sun set over the dockyard area. On the southern side of the Harbour, about a ten minute walk from the dockyard, are the remains of **Fort Berkeley**, a small outpost with eight cannons.

Other restored chandleries include the **Master Shipwright's House,** the **Saw Pit,** the **Paint Store and Cells,** and the blacksmith's shop. One of the most authentic buildings is the old **Officer's Quarters,** now a combination art gallery, crafts workshop, gift shop, and restaurant. Looking out to sea, one can almost see the ghosts of sailors pointing their cannons at French ships battling to claim new bases in the Caribbean waters.

In the center of the island is Antigua's pioneer sugar plantation, **Betty's Hope Estate,** which introduced large-scale sugar cultivation and innovative methods of processing sugar. Founded in the 1650's by Governor Keynell and granted to Christopher Codrington in 1688, the Codrington family had interest in Betty's Hope for more than 250 years until 1920. Both Christopher Codrington and his son served as Governor General of the Leeward Islands, developing the plantation as the seat of government during the late 17th and early 18th centuries. Two old windmill towers still stand, together with the walls and arches of the plantation's boiling house. A conservation project was recently completed that has handsomely refurbished this historic site.

BARBUDA

Second to the magnificent reefs that surround the island, Barbuda's **Frigate Bird Sanctuary** tops the list of sightseeing favorites. It is located at the north end of Codrington Lagoon, and is only accessible by small boat. Here, the *Fregata Magnificens* brood their eggs in mangrove bushes that stretch for miles. In olden days, sailors called the frigate bird the "man-o-war bird" and the "hurricane bird," because their eight-foot wingspan gives them enough power to easily soar to 2,000 feet. Although visitors can see the birds throughout the year, the mating season, from September to February, is a brilliant spectacle when the male frigate inflates a crimson pouch at his throat and breast in an attempt to attract the female frigate. Chicks hatch from December to March and remain in the nest for up to eight months, until they are strong enough to fly.

A visit to the Sanctuary is a 45-minute trip in a wooden rowboat powered by a small outboard motor. The boats are piloted by Barbudians who cautiously navigate through the mangroves.

Barbuda's dry climate attracts many other species of birds including pelicans, warblers, snipes, ibis, herons, kingfishers, tropical mocking-birds, oyster catchers, and cormorants. Other wildlife found roaming the island are white-tailed deer, boar, donkeys, and red-footed tortoises. Unique to its marine life is the Barbudian lobster.

Besides snorkeling and bird watching, Barbuda offers some interesting attractions and activities. **Highland House** is the former estate of Sir William Codrington, the first lessee of Barbuda, where the annual rent to the crown was "one fatted sheep, on demand." **Dark Cave** is an underground cave with deep pools of clear water that extend approximately one mile underground, and at the **Caves at Two Foot Bay**, visitors can climb down into a circular chamber through a hole in the roof to view faded Arawak drawings on the walls.

Several Antigua-based companies offer day tours of Barbuda. Tour prices are approximately $120 per person, and include round-trip airfare, a tour and visit to the Frigate Bird Sanctuary and lunch.

Dining

The cuisine of Antigua and Barbuda is an evolution of the tastes and foods of the many groups that make up the islands' West Indian heritage: Carib Indians, French, English, African, Spanish, Portuguese, Indian, Lebanese, and Syrian. The influence of these cultures, and the diversity of locally grown fruits and vegetables, combine to create a cuisine to satisfy the most discerning palate. To showcase the islands' culinary diversity, resorts and local restaurants compete in the Annual Antigua Culinary Exposition, which takes place in May.

A trip to the public market in St. John's is a delectable opportunity to sample the real riches of Antigua and Barbuda. Visitors will find a variety of fruits and vegetables, some that are familiar to many in North America, but known by a different name. For instance, a *green fig* is a small green banana which must be cooked before eating. *Christophine*, a large type of squash with pale green flesh, is boiled and served hot. The *breadfruit* is rounded with a hard green skin and soft inside, and is cooked and served as a vegetable or made into bread, pie, or pudding. The islands' most famous fruit is the *Antigua black pineapple*, a smaller, sweeter version of the Hawaiian variety.

From the crystal waters surrounding the islands comes some of the most succulent seafood in the world. Local spiny *lobsters*, really langoustes, are delicious grilled with lime butter, as a cold salad, or a spicy curry. Conch, cockles (mollusks), grouper, and red snapper are other local seafood delights.

Other Caribbean specialties served are *Pepperpot*, a rich, thick stew containing beef, pork, vegetables and spices that is normally served with *fungee*, a dumpling made with cornmeal and okra. *Ducana* is a pudding made from grated sweet potato and coconut, mixed with pumpkin, sugar, and spices, and boiled in a banana leaf.

Besides local cuisine, restaurants scattered throughout Antigua and Barbuda offer French and Italian food, seafood, pizza, and fast food.

One can savor the taste of spiny lobster soup, codfish balls, Antiguan pineapple, or grilled lobster with lime butter at **Look Out Restaurant,** (☎ 463-1274) in Shirley Heights. This establishment has commanding views of Nelson's Dockyard, Falmouth Harbour, and, on a clear day, one can see the island of Montserrat across the Caribbean Sea. A lively steel band sets the festive mood on Sundays between 3 and 6 p.m. Entrees range from $10 to $15.

Coconut Grove Beach Restaurant (☎ 462-0806) sits beneath swaying palm trees at the water's edge on Dickenson Bay, and offers fresh lobster, seafood and Caribbean dishes. Open for breakfast, lunch and dinner.

In St. John's, **Brother B's** is an inexpensive spot for local dishes—dumpling and mackerel, curried conch, or fresh fish, hamburgers, or salads.

Tasty island dishes such as spicy land crab backs, saltfish balls and fish at reasonable prices are served at **18 Carat**, Lower Church Street, St. John's (☎ 462-0016), a porch and garden restaurant in the heart of town. Top it off with a piece of freshly made rum cake.

Situated high on a hilltop with a spectacular panorama view is Antigua's newest restaurant, **Jaws**. This lively spot features an indoor/outdoor dance floor with live entertainment. The kitchen, open 'til midnight, offers light fare.

Alberto's at Willoughby Bay offers dining in a giant gazebo cooled by the Caribbean breeze. Local seafood, prepared with an Italian accent, includes conch salad, lobster, and pasta dishes, and the wine list features many Italian favorites.

FACTS

Nearest Recompression Chamber: None on island

Getting There: American Airlines from the United States; Air Canada direct from Canada; British Airways direct from London; BWIA direct from the U.S. and Canada. Lufthansa direct from Frankfurt. LIAT flies inter-island. Bird International airport accommodates large aircraft, and passengers are served by a new and modern terminal.

Driving: British style, on the left. A valid drivers' license will secure a temporary license in Antigua at a nominal cost ($12 U.S.).

Island transportation: Taxis (expensive) are available at the airport, hotels, and harbor. Local bus service is also available for a nominal charge. Major rent-a-car companies have offices on Antigua. Arrangements for rentals can be made in advance of arrival.

Documents: Visitors from the U.S., Canada, U.K. and Germany require proof of citizenship such as a passport or birth certificate. Also required is an onward or return ticket.

Customs: Arriving passengers are allowed 200 cigarettes, one quart of liquor, and six ounces of perfume.

Currency: Antigua & Barbuda use the Eastern Caribbean dollar, also known as the "Bee Wee." The currency is tied to the U.S. dollar at an average exchange rate of E.C. $2.65 for U.S. $1.00 subject to fluctuation. Most major credit cards accepted.

Taxes: Airport Departure tax for stay-over visitors is U.S. $10. A 7% government tax is added to all hotel bills. There is a 10% service charge added to bills in lieu of tipping. Elsewhere tipping is discretionary.

Climate: Antigua's temperatures range from an average of 76°F in January/February to 83°F in August and September. Rainfall averages 45 inches per year with relatively low humidity. The rainy season is September, October and November, but there are usually only short showers.

Clothing: Casual light, loose-fitting cotton clothes are suggested. Generally informal, but some hotels and casinos require jackets at night. Ladies are requested to wear skirts or slacks rather than abbreviated shorts or swimwear while in the city. Light wetsuit or wetskin for diving during winter.

Electricity: Dual voltage available in major hotels, 220 and 110 AC, 60 cycles.

Language: English with an island lilt—"No big ting"

Religious Services: Protestant, Roman Catholic, Seventh-Day Adventist.

Additional Information: In the U.S., Antigua & Barbuda Department of Tourism, 610 Fifth Ave., Suite 311, New York NY 10020, ☎ 212-54-4117; or 121 S.W. First St., Suite 1001, Miami FL 33131, ☎ 305-381-6762.

In Canada, Antigua & Barbuda Department of Tourism and Trade, 60 St. Clair Ave. East, Suite 205, Toronto, Ontario, MT4 IN5, ☎ 416-961-3085.

In Europe, Antigua House, 15 Thayer St., London W1, England, ☎ 01-486-7073; Postfach 1147 Minnholzweg 2, 6242 Kronberg 1, Federal Republic of Germany, ☎ 06173-5011.

Aruba

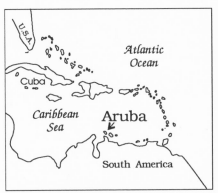

Vacationers discovered Aruba in 1957, when the first cruise ship, *Tradewinds,* arrived. The island has since developed into a top tourist destination. Easy to reach, it is just 18 miles from Venezuela's coast—yet far enough away to escape the hustle and bustle of civilization.

And, it is easy to explore, both above and below the sea. Just 20 miles long and six miles wide, its luxury hotels and dive boats line up neatly along the western (leeward) shore—minutes from popular reef and wreck dives. The shops and sights of the capital, Oranjestad, are nearby too.

Most visiting divers never venture beyond those two areas, but when the seas are calm, the waters off the rugged, northeastern coast become diveable, with dramatic coral ridges, wrecks, drop-offs, caves, overhangs, and superb marine life—eagle rays, huge groupers, turtles, coneys, and invertebrates. Here too, the above-water scenery is spectacular. A huge, natural coral bridge rises from the sea to 25 ft and stretches more than 100 ft long. On shore, windswept divi divi trees (*watapana*) beautymark the rocky cliffs and wind-sculpted sand dunes.

Inland, Aruba presents a unique Caribbean landscape of cactus, aloe, and rolling hills with gigantic boulders strewn about. Very low humidity and an average annual rainfall of only 20 inches explain the desert-like countryside. On the southeastern tip is Aruba's other major city, San Nicolas.

Arubans themselves may be their country's best advertisements. Long secure in a solid economy with good education, housing and health care, the island's population of about 71,000 regard tourists as welcome guests. Even the national anthem celebrates a high regard for hospitality. The line "Grandeza di bo pueblo ta su gran cordialidad" translates as "The greatness of our people is their great cordiality"—and thousands of visitors would agree.

Contributor: Castro Perez, Dive Specialist, Aruba Tourism

The native Aruban is a mixture of Dutch, Spanish, and Portuguese ancestry and so is his language, Papiamento. Dutch is the official language, but every Aruban child studies English from the age of 10 and most residents speak it well.

History

Aruba's history is a tale of varied influences. The Spaniards had relatively low regard for the land they discovered and claimed in 1499. Like its neighbors, Bonaire and Curacao, Aruba was officially declared an *isla inutil* (useless island). The Spanish found Arawak Indians of the Caiquetio tribe living there, just as they had in the Stone Age, and promptly shipped them off to Santo Domingo to work in the gold mines. About 11 years later, its discoverers turned Aruba into something of a large cattle ranch and some of the original inhabitants were brought back to work it.

For awhile the Indians regained control of their land, but in 1636 were taken over by the Dutch who have remained in power ever since. Through 300 years of changing economic fortunes and various immigrations, the ABC islands (Aruba, Bonaire and Curacao) were part of the Netherlands Antilles, whose governor reported directly to the queen.

Europeans began to immigrate to Aruba in the late 1700s. At this time, Oranjestad was founded and named after the reigning Royal House of Orange. During the 19th century, many Venezuelans arrived, adding a decidedly Spanish influence to the small country.

In 1824, gold was discovered in Aruba. Visitors can still see remains of the smelting works at Bushiribana and Balashi. When gold mining no longer proved profitable, Aruban aloe plantations flourished. Then, in the 1920s, the oil industry arrived. The Lago refinery, a subsidiary of Standard Oil, was established just outside San Nicolas and remained the island's most important employer until its closing in the spring of 1985. Its influence is likely to be permanent, however. The resulting influx of Americans and others has made English a prominent second language, and Aruba's main thoroughfare, L.G. Smith Boulevard, is named for Lago's one-time general manager.

Politically, Aruba has made quiet and peaceful change. On January 1, 1986, the nation left the Netherlands Antilles to become a separate entity within the Kingdom of the Netherlands. Now Aruba has its own governor, appointed by the queen. Local government is democratic, with an elected 21-member parliament and Council of Ministers.

Tourism in Aruba began in 1959 when the first hotel/casino, the Aruba Caribbean (recently restored to its former prominence by the Radisson company), opened its doors. However, the world truly began to discover the island in the mid-1960s. Hotels, casinos, restaurants, diveboats, shops and amusements have been popping up ever since.

Diving and Snorkeling Sites

Access to most of Aruba's dive and snorkeling sights is easiest by boat. All are a few minutes from shore. Many are close enough to swim to, but attempting to find the channels and cuts through the shallow reefs may be futile without a local guide.

☆☆ **Arashi Marine Park** , off the northwest corner of the island, is a pretty reef with throngs of juvenile fish, vase sponges, soft corals, sea plumes, sea fans, elkhorn and brain corals. Visibility is always 60 ft or better. Depths range from the shallows to 40 ft. Great for snorkeling and shallow dives. Seas are calm with an occasional light surge.

☆☆☆☆☆ Just south of Arashi is one of Aruba's most unusual sights and most popular dive, the wreck of the 400-ft German freighter, *Antilla*. The ship was scuttled when new in 1940, during WWII, when the Germans invaded Holland.

Locally referred to as the "ghost ship", it is covered by giant, tube sponges and brilliant, orange cup corals. Her twisted, rusting steelwork extends upward from the main section to above the surface, making for intriguing photo opportunities. The remains of the hull are surrounded by big lobsters and angelfish, moray eels and throngs of silversides. Octopus and puffers are common. Outside, schools of yellowtail and sergeant majors sway with the gentle current.

The wreck lies just north of Palm Beach in 60 feet of water. Visibility is between 60 and 90 ft.

☆☆☆ Snorkelers can circle the top section of the *Antilla*. But, the best shallow-reef snorkeling in Aruba is found at **Malmok.** You can reach Malmok by driving north from Palm Beach along L.G. Smith Boulevard, the main coast road. Park anywhere and walk down to the beach. Swim out from the shore about 70 yards where you'll find a lovely coral reef. If you look straight out to sea you'll spot the top of the *Antilla*. All the sail-snorkel boats stop at Malmok.

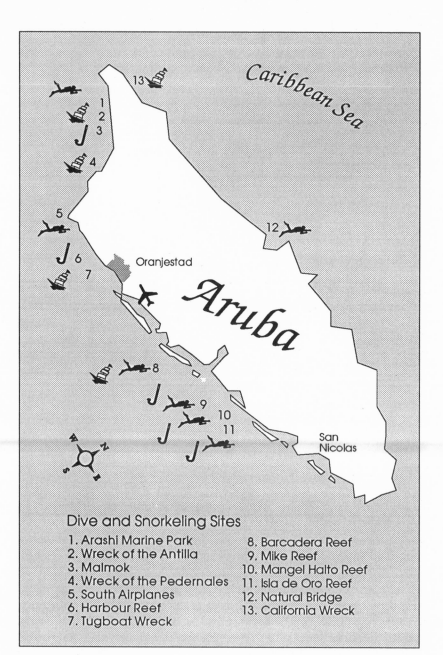

Caribbean Sea

Oranjestad

Aruba

San
Nicolas

Dive and Snorkeling Sites

1. Arashi Marine Park
2. Wreck of the Antilla
3. Malmok
4. Wreck of the Pedernales
5. South Airplanes
6. Harbour Reef
7. Tugboat Wreck
8. Barcadera Reef
9. Mike Reef
10. Mangel Halto Reef
11. Isla de Oro Reef
12. Natural Bridge
13. California Wreck

Blue Reef

Note: All of Aruba's beaches are open to the public, but a narrow strip directly behind the houses is private. Most homeowners have a sign marking where their back yard ends and the public beach begins.

☆☆☆ A short distance south of the *Antilla* is **Blue Reef**. This spot is usually a boat dive, but you can reach it by swimming out from Machebo Beach. The reef starts at 50 ft and drops to a sandy shelf at 90 ft. Large grouper, stingrays, wrasses, grunts, sergeant majors and trumpet fish swim amidst the elkhorn and staghorn corals.

☆☆ Just south of Oranjestad is the wreck of the *Pedernales*, an oil tanker torpedoed by a German sub during WWII. The U.S. military cut this wreck into three pieces. The bow and stern were salvaged, towed to the U.S. and welded together to create a new vessel which joined the Normandy invasion fleet of WWII. The center section was left behind and now rests at 25-40 ft off Palm Beach. A favorite of novice divers, the wreck is populated by barracuda, yellowtail, grunts, squirrel fish, trumpet fish, huge French angels and a profusion of silversides.

☆☆☆ **Barcadera Reef** is a two-mile-long reef, just south of Spanish Lagoon—four miles south of Oranjestad. Excellent for snorkelers and divers, the reef supports dense stands of elkhorn and staghorn corals, finger corals, vase sponges, wrasses, scorpion fish, huge parrot fish, French angels, lavender shrimp, damsel fish and pink-tipped anemones. The reef is 600 yards from the shore at Bacadera Harbor (boat dive). Depths range from 20 to 90 ft.

Barcadera Reef is also home to the wreck of the *Jane Sea,* a 200-ft freighter intentionally sunk by local divemasters to attract fish. *Jane Sea's* bottom rests upright in 45 to 90 ft of water.

☆☆ **Tugboat Wreck** is another super dive off Oranjestad. But the wreck is not nearly as interesting as the magnificent formations of brain, star and sheet corals growing from the bottom. Here too are spotted rays, eagle rays, moray eels, and unusual black and blue sponges. Depths are from 40 ft to 90 ft.

☆☆☆☆ Three-fourths of a mile south of Barcadera Harbor is **Mangel Halto** ("tall mangrove"). You can reach this site by swimming out from the Mangel Halto Beach for 60 yards. The reef slopes from 15 ft to 110 ft. Its ledges and ridges support an array of grooved brain coral, deep-water gorgonians, sea anemones, tube and basket sponges. Fish life includes copper sweepers, grunts, sergeant majors, lobsters, blue tangs, butterfly fish, queen angels, stingrays and jacks. At depth, green morays, grouper, nurse shark, tarpon and large barracuda inhabit small caves and overhangs.

☆☆☆ **South Airplanes** is the site of two vintage, twin-engine, aircraft wrecks—both unclaimed drug runners—sunk off Bucuti Beach to form an artificial reef and a fun dive. The wrecks, a Beech 18 and a DC 3 are intact and can be penetrated by four to six divers at the same time. Inside are octopuses, moray eels, lobsters and crabs. They are located outside of Sonesta Island at 35 ft and 60 ft. The rusting fuselages are great for video and still photography—both covered with a thin layer of clinging corals and hydroids.

☆☆ **Isla de Oro Reef** lies off Savaneta, an old Aruban fishing village, near the south end of the island. This site is close to the mangrove-lined shore and is challenging for novice and experienced divers. There is always some current running; visibility is usually excellent. Resident yellow sting rays, lobster, Spanish hogfish and French angelfish race the walls of star, brain and plate corals. At depth, sheet and leaf corals form ledges and caves—home to large morays and parrotfish. The reef begins at 60 ft and drops down to 125 ft.

☆☆☆ The *California* wreck off the northwest tip of the island is for experienced divers and then recommended only during periods of extreme calm. Resting at 40 ft, the scattered remains of the wooden ship are draped in orange and yellow sponges, plate corals and anemones. Huge grouper, jewfish, lobster, shark and barracuda frequent the area. A dense

Las Cabanas beach

reef of staghorn and pillar corals forms a breakwater beyond the wreck.

☆☆☆ Another north-shore adventure dive is the **Natural Bridge** where monster-size boulders adorned with black and soft corals will leave you in awe. Gigantic basket sponges rise from the bottom. Depths from 20 ft to 110 ft. Rough water and currents make this a choice for advanced divers only.

First-time snorkelers will find waist-high snorkeling outside of DePalm Island, located one-quarter mile offshore from the Water & Electricity Plant—four miles south of Oranjestad along L.G. Smith boulevard. Excellent scuba diving exists off the island too. A free ferry to DePalm leaves the mainland every half hour.

Dive Operators

Most Aruban dive shops offer scuba and/or snorkeling trips, certification and resort courses. One-tank dive trips start at $30; Snorkeling tours from $25. Mask, fins and snorkel rent for about $12 per day, but may be included at no extra charge on a sail tour.

Sail-snorkel cruises are offered by **DePalm Tours** (☎ 24545), **Red Sail Sports** (☎ 31603) and **Wave Dancers**, (☎ 25520).

Scuba courses and trips may be arranged through any hotel or direct through **Pelican Watersports** (☎31228/fax 32655), **Aruba Pro Dive** (☎ 25520/fax 37723), **Dax Divers** (☎ 21270/fax 34389), **S.E.A. Scuba** (☎ 34877/fax 34875), **DePalm Watersports** (☎ 24545), **Mermaid Sports Divers** (☎ 35546), **Mi Dushi** (snorkeling) (☎ 26034), **Native Divers** (☎ 34763), **Pelican Watersports** (☎ 31228), **Red Sail Sports** (☎ 24500), **Scuba Aruba,** (☎ 34142) or **Unique Watersports,** ☎ 23900.

Red Sail Sports also tempts guests with water skiing, jet skis and wave runners, tubbing, banana boat rides, Hobie Cat rentals, instruction and sailing with a captain, Sunfish and paddleboat rental and Sea Searcher floats. Their 35-ft catamaran, *Balia*, sets sail for morning snorkeling tours as well as sunset and dinner cruises. Red Sail is on the beach between the Americana Aruba Beach Resort and the Hyatt.

Accommodations

Known for its fabulous beaches, casinos and luxury resort complexes, Aruba is not a "divers island" and thus lacks any "dedicated dive resorts," but a growing interest in subsea sports has led to the merger of a few top resort communities with the island's watersports operators. The end result—convenient diving and money-saving packages. Prices are in U.S. dollars.

The 360-room **Hyatt Regency Aruba Resort & Casino** has teamed up with **Red Sail Sports** and developed the "Dive Into It" package. Summer prices start at $335 (double) for three nights/four dives. Seven nights/ten dives for $593.

Best Western's **Talk of the Town** and Machebo Beach hotel properties have created "Below Sea Level" dive packages. Prices start from $278 for three night/four dives to seven night/nine dives for $488—double occupancy. ☎ 800-223-1108.

Holiday Inn Aruba Beach Resort & Casino meets the needs of dive fanatics with an "Unlimited Dive Package" in cooperation with **Pelican**

Casibari Rocks

Watersports. The 600-room hotel management has developed an "Unlimited Dive Package"— three boat departures are scheduled daily and unlimited tank refills are available.

Bushiri Bounty is an all-inclusive resort which offers snorkeling and a scuba clinic (resort course) as part of the deal. Per-person, per-day, rates from $99 in summer and $129 in winter include three meals daily, unlimited liquor, midnight snacks, entertainment and a host of watersports and other activities. Tips are included. The beachfront resort features spacious rooms, a freshwater pool, beach bar, two restaurants, spa, jacuzzis and a white-sand beach. ☎ 800-462-6868; in Canada ☎ 203-266-0100.

Las Cabanas, a modern, 441-suite luxury resort complex offers packages with Pelican Watersports, on premises. Additional hotels with dive operations on the premises are the Port of Aruba Palm Beach Resort & Casino; the Aruba Caribbean Resort; Harbour Town Beach Resort & Casino (S.E.A. SCUBA); The Sonesta Hotel Beach Club & Casino (Dax Divers).

For a complete list of resorts contact your travel agent or The **Aruba Tourism Authority,** L.G. Smith Blvd. 172, Eagle, Aruba or ☎ 800-TO-ARUBA. In the U.S., 1000 Harbor Boulevard, Weehawken NJ. ☎ 201-330-0800; fax 201-330-8757.

Other Activities

Outdoor lovers will enjoy visiting Aruba's National Park—where flamboyant scenery, tropical foliage and even wild goats and donkeys await. The Arikok-Yamamoto National Park has two hiking trails. Free admission. Guided tours are through **DePalm Tours,** (☎ 24545); **Corvalou Tours,** (☎ 21149) and **Eco Destination Management,** (☎ 26034).

One of the island's newest sport attractions is **Aruba Sailcart**—landsailing which combines the sensation of sailing and the challenge of karting. Single and double carts are $15 and $20 for a half hour. Call **Mauries Tromp** at ☎ 36005 for reservations.

Board a glass bottom boat with **DePalm Watersports** (☎ 24545), **Pelican Watersports** (☎ 31288), **Red Sail Sports** (☎ 31603) and **Scuba Aruba** (☎ 34142).

Windsurfing board rentals and instruction are offered by **Sailboard Vacations** (☎ 21072), **Divi Winds** (☎ 35000), and **Roger's Windsurf Place** (☎ 21918). Prices start at $18.

Cave tours to view prehistoric Indian art may be arranged through **Aruba Transfer Tours and Taxi** (☎ 21149), **Tiny tours** (☎ 47449), **Sea & Sea Tours** (☎ 31228), and **Private Safaris Educational Tours** (☎ 34869). Archeologist **E. Boerstra** (☎ 41513) of Marlin Booster Tracking Inc. also offers tours that highlight Aruba's prehistoric Indian cultures. Tours start at $15 per person.

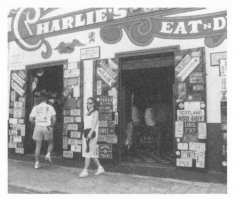

Charlie's, San Nicolas

Birdwatching, and nature tours are offered by **Julio Maduro, Corvalou Tours** (☎ 21149) or **Private Safaris Educational Tours** (☎ 34869).

Sunset cruises, deep-sea fishing, island tours, para-sailing, and sightseeing can all be easily arranged at your hotel.

Tennis is widely available and the **Aruba Golf Club** offers enthusiasts the chance to experience the most unusual golf course in the Caribbean with oiled, sand greens, the trade winds and an occasional goat as a live hazard. Equestrians can sign up for horseback riding at **Rancho El Paso.**

While nightlife to many divers equates with suiting up after sunset for yet another dive, others will find endless entertainment on shore in the form of casino gambling, limbo shows, reggae bands, and discos.

Those traveling with young children will enjoy a picnic at Baby Beach on the southwest tip of the island. This is a beautiful, natural lagoon with shallow, calm water. Baby beach is listed in many tour guides as a "great snorkeling beach" but, in fact, don't waste your energy carrying a mask or snorkel. There is absolutely nothing on the bottom but white sand, three juvenile yellowtails and an old sneaker. Outside the breakwater rough seas and strong currents pound a shallow coral reef, but access is narrow and unless you are in training to be a Navy Seal, pass it up. Boat diving in this area is fine as they anchor farther out and do it as a drift dive.

Sightseeing

A walking tour of Oranjestad would include the harborside fruit market; Fort Zoutman and King Willem III Tower, home to a Aruban heritage museum; the Numismatic Museum and the Archeology Museum. Shopping abounds.

If you are opposed to organized tours, grab a roadmap and rent a four-wheel-drive car to tour the island. Directly east of the high-rise hotel strip, on the north shore, you'll find the **Chapel of Alto Vista**, high above the sea on a most peaceful spot. It was built by Spanish missionary Domingo Antonio Silvester, and serves as a ceremonial center. Stations of the cross line the steep, cactus-lined road to the chapel. Driving east to Andicuri from Oranjestad will lead to the **Natural Bridge** (the largest of eight on the island) complete with huge gift and snack shops. The road is unpaved and bumpy in spots, but very scenic. Very photogenic at sunrise. Also worth a visit are the Casibari and Ayo rock formations, monstrous boulders which mystify geologists. Casibari is about halfway (three miles) between the Natural Bridge and Oranjestad. Ayo is approximately two miles from the Natural Bridge toward Casibari and Oranjestad. At Casibari stone steps give access to a viewing platform on top. At the entrance a formation resembling and named "Dragon Mouth" can be seen. You can climb on top and, on a clear day, see all of Aruba and the coast of Venezuela.

The California Dunes and California Lighthouse are at the northernmost tip of the island. The dunes are sand, but most of this is area is barren and rocky. High winds have carved some interesting shapes in the rocks. Views from the lighthouse ridge are magnificent.

Dining

All hotels have coffee shops and snack bars. Most also feature specialty restaurants which serve American, Continental and regional food. For outstanding native seafood dishes, don't miss **Brisas Del Mar Restaurant**, six miles south of Orangestad at Savaneta 222, ☎ 47718 (turn right after the Esso station). Additional country flavor is at **The Old Cunucu House Restaurant**, Palm Beach 150, which is set in a renovated 70-year old Aruban home. Or enjoy seafood or steaks inside a Dutch windmill at The **Mill Restaurant** (open from 6:00 pm to 11:00) ☎ 26300 or 22060—walking distance from the high-rise hotels.

Hotel meal plans are often accepted by outside restaurants. Check with your hotel.

The road to the Chapel of Alto Vista

An endless choice of fried foods and island drinks are offered by **Papa's & Beer**, 184 Palm Beach Road—Aruba's favorite "California" hang-out restaurant. Menu favorities are empanaditas (fried pastries filled with cheeses and meat), Filipino chicken wings, cheese nachos and chips with salsa & guacamole, deep-fried ice cream (very carefully). Entertainment nightly. It is a short walk from the hotel strip. Look for the big neon sign!

Great steaks are found at the **Holiday Inn Restaurant** and the **Manchebo Beach Hotel**. Other notable dining spots are: **El Gaucho,** Wilhelmastraat 80, ☎ 23677; **Gasparito**, Gasparito 3, ☎ 37044 and the **Moonlight Grill,** ☎ 23380 at the Talk of the Town Resort. Treat yourself to a light snack or lunch at the **"Seawatch" Restaurant** at the Aruba Palm Beach Resort. The tropical garden surroundings are magnificent.

Moderately priced meals are offered at the **Grill House** on Zoutmanstraat in Oranjestad (☎ 31611). Local bars dot the countryside.

One noticeable cultural influence on the island's restaurants has been the presence of Arubans who are of Indonesian descent—most from the Netherlands East Indies, with a few from Java. A well-known characteristic of Indonesians is their love of enticing dishes.

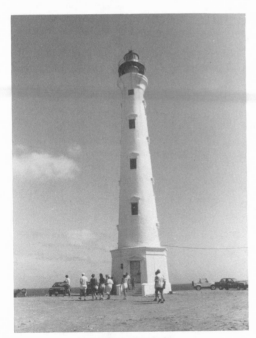

California Lighthouse

Indonesian restaurants feature a *rijsttafel*—a rice table which offers a buffet of many exotic dishes such as *nasi rames*, rice surrounded by meats; *edang kerrie*, curried shrimp; *daging smoor*, a meat stew; *pangsit goreng*, crispy, fried, minced meat in shrimp ball covered with dough and served with a sweet and sour sauce; *sate ajam*, chicken with a spicy peanut sauce; *ajam boemboe, chicken with ginger and red pepper;* and *ikan bali,* fish flavored in spices.

Sample these favorites at **Warung Djawa** on Boerhaavestraat 4 in Oranjestad (☎ 34888); the **Bali Sea Palace**, a floating restaurant on a Chinese house boat docked at the schooner harbor in Oranjestad or at **La Serre Restaurant** in the Aruba Concord Hotel (☎ 24470).

Fast foods are served at the **Steamboat**, across the street from the high-rise hotels; **Burger King** on Nassaustraat 81 in Oranjestad; **Charlies Bar** on Zeppelenfeldstraat 56, San Nicolas; and **Wendy's** on L.G. Smith Blvd. 90-92.

Helpful Phone Numbers

POLICE: ☎ 011-297-824-000

TAXI: ☎ 011-297-822-116 or 011-297-824-400

AIRPORT: ☎ 011-297-824-800

MEDICAL FACILITY: ☎ 011-297-826-034

Facts

Nearest Recompression Chamber: Curacao. None on Aruba.

Getting There: American Airlines (☎ 800-433-7300) offers direct flights from New York and two daily flights from Puerto Rico with connections from Boston, Philadelphia, New Jersey, Baltimore, Miami, Raleigh, Washington, Hartford, Providence, Chicago, Dallas, Detroit, Pittsburgh and other major U.S. cities. Air Aruba has direct flights from Newark and Miami. Aeropostal from Atlanta. From Venezuela, Maracaibo and Valencia; from Europe KLM; from Toronto and Montreal via Air Canada and Delta; from Georgia, Miami, Bonaire and Curacao via ALM.

Driving: Traffic moves on the right.

Language: The official language is Dutch, but residents speak Papiamento—a blend of Dutch, Spanish, Portuguese and English. English and Spanish are widely spoken.

Documents: Passport, official birth certificate, certificate of naturalization for U.S. and Canadian citizens. Return or continuing ticket.

Customs: If you have been out of the U.S. for 48 hours or more and have not claimed any exemption within 30 days, you may bring in $400 tax-exempt products including 100 cigars and 200 cigarettes and, for those 21 or older, one liter (33.8 oz.) of alcoholic beverages.

Canadians after 48 hours' absence may bring in goods to the value of $100. After seven days absence you may bring in goods to the value of $300. A person aged 16 or over may include up to 200 cigarettes and 50 cigars. If you meet the age requirements set by the province through which you reenter, you may include up to 40 oz of wine or liquor.

Currency: The Aruba florin = $1.77 U.S.

Credit Cards: Widely accepted.

Service Charges: There is an 11 ☎ service charge on room rates. The service charge on food and beverage is 10-15 ☎ in lieu of gratuities at hotels.

Climate: Dry and sunny with a year-round average temperature of 82 degrees F. Showers of short duration are during November and December. Aruba is outside the hurricane belt.

Clothing: Lightweight casual cottons. Informal for the most part, but dress-up clothes are advisable for a night out in one of the elegant restaurants, night clubs or casinos. Jackets are required for men at night in some casinos, night clubs and restaurants.

Note: Persons under 18 are NOT permitted in the casinos.

Electricity: 110-120 volts AC, 60 cycles (same as U.S.).

Time: Atlantic Standard Time. Same as Eastern daylight saving time, year round.

Tax: Airport departure tax, $10.

Religious Services: Roman Catholic; Protestant (Dutch Reformed, Anglican, Evangelican, Methodist, Seventh-Day Adventist, Church of Christ, Baptist); Jewish; Baha'i Faith.

Additional Information: Aruba Tourism Authority, L.G. Smith Blvd. 172, Eagle, Aruba ☎ 2978 or 23777; fax 2978 34702.

Aruba Tourism Authority, 1000 Harbor Boulevard, Weehawken, NJ 07047. ☎ 201-330-0800; fax 201-330-8757.

Barbados

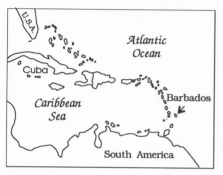

Barbados is a tiny island just 21 miles long by 14 miles wide rising bravely from the floor of the Caribbean Sea about 300 miles from Venezuela. It is the farthest east and the most isolated of the West Indian islands. Formed of ancient reef materials that have been compressed into rock and elevated to 1,000 ft above sea level, it is a paradise of rolling hills carpeted with forests of deep tropical foliage interrupted by cultivated fields of sugar cane, corn, sweet potatoes, and yams. Beyond the fields are lush groves of banana, mango, grapefruit, avocado, cherry and lime trees.

Set amidst this visual feast are first-rate resorts, vibrant nightlife, duty free shopping, and a full range of delightful dining spots. A well rounded selection of water sports and other leisure-time activities makes Barbados a best choice for couples and families.

Divers, both novice and experienced, are advised to visit Barbados between April and November when you can expect fabulous visibility on the barrier reef and calm seas. This changes during Dec thru March. A "North Swell" decreases visibility near shore and on the outer reefs.

During Spring, Summer and Fall the island's shallow shipwrecks offer a multitude of dive experiences. The best wrecks are found on the offshore barrier reef which extends along Barbados' windward or western, coast. The wrecks are camouflaged by soft corals, sea fans, and sponges, home to thriving communities of fish and other marine animals. Barbados offers snorkelers miles of white-powder sand beaches and shore-access coves with a wide range of corals and friendly fish.

Area Contributors: Dave Farmer, Jolly Roger Watersports; and Michael Young, dive guide.

Best Dive and Snorkeling Sites

☆☆☆☆☆ **Dottins Reef,** located a half-mile off the coast of St. James Parish on the west coast, stretches along the shore from St James to Bridgetown. It is the prettiest reef in Barbados with visibility at 100 ft or better. Basket sponges, sea fans, gorgonians, and thickets of staghorn and brain corals adorn the reef's canyons and walls. Depths start at 65 ft with some drop-offs to 130 ft. Reef residents include rays, turtles, barracuda, parrotfish, snapper and large grouper. Seas are generally calm.

☆☆☆ **Sandy Lane,** a deeper area off Dottin's Reef, is usually a drift dive. The walls, dotted with sponges and vibrant, clump corals, drop to 90 ft. Superb marine life abounds. A good spot for video photography. For experienced divers only.

☆☆☆ **Wreck of the** *Pamir,* located just 200 yds offshore, is easily accessible from the beach and is very open and uncluttered. This-150- ft ship was sunk in 30 ft of water by the Barbados dive shop operators to form an artificial reef. The ship's superstructure breaks the usually calm surface, making it perfect for snorkelers and snorkel-swimmers. Swarms of sergeant majors and butterfly fish inhabit the wreck. Nearby, about 60 yds out, is a small reef. Although visibility varies, seas are always calm. Dive operators request no spear fishing or collecting. An excellent dive for novices.

☆☆☆ **Bright Ledge Reef** is a narrow reef that wraps around the island's northern tip. Depths average 60 ft with deep dropoffs on either side. Unsuitable for novices but generally a safe dive and particularly good for photography. Encounters with gigantic pelagics, turtles and rays are frequent with dependable sightings of parrotfish, snapper, grouper, porgy, grunts, and glass eye snapper. The sea is generally calm unless there is a stiff wind or storm.

☆☆☆ **The** *Stavronikita,* a 360-ft freighter was gutted by a fire at sea fourteen years ago. After towing the sinking ship closer to shore, the government of Barbados sunk the smoldering mass where it would benefit divers and fishermen as an artificial reef. The wreck sits in 130 ft of water, the deck at 80 ft. Although the depth discourages most novice explorers, the ship is one of the island's most interesting dives. Its hull, covered with a colorful patchwork of small sponges and clinging corals, attracts schools of silversides and large pelagics. Very appealing to photographers.

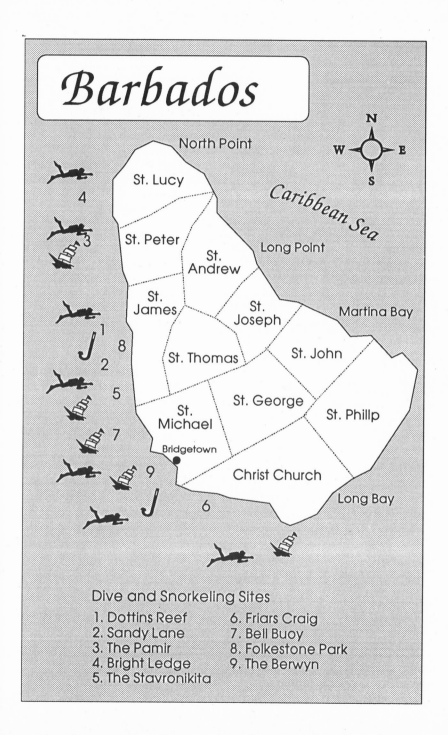

Barbados

North Point

N
W **E**
S

St. Lucy

Caribbean Sea

St. Peter

St. Andrew

Long Point

St. James

St. Joseph

Martina Bay

St. Thomas

St. John

St. George

St. Michael

St. Phillp

Bridgetown

Christ Church

Long Bay

4

3

1

8

2

5

7

9

6

Dive and Snorkeling Sites

1. Dottins Reef
2. Sandy Lane
3. The Pamir
4. Bright Ledge
5. The Stavronikita
6. Friars Craig
7. Bell Buoy
8. Folkestone Park
9. The Berwyn

☆☆ Nearby in shallow water lie the *Conimara,* an old P.T. boat, and the *Lord Combermere,* an old tug boat—both in 30-40 ft of water. Visibility varies. Good photo opportunities abound here as well. The wrecks can be reached from the shore after a 600-yard swim.

☆☆ *Friars Craig* is a good dive for the novice although strong current may be occasionally encountered. This is another purposely-sunken wreck. It lies in just 60 ft of water with the bridge at 30 ft, making it more accessible than the *Stavronikita.* A short 600-yd swim from the southwest corner of Christ Church Parish will put you over the wreck and an adjacent reef, **Castle Bank.** Exercise extreme caution and check the current before diving. Numerous fish and usually great visibility.

☆☆☆ **Bell Buoy Reef,** located off St. Michael's Parish on the island's southwest, is a wall dive with a shelf at 40 ft dropping off to a sandy bottom at 70 ft. The reef is alive with small critters amidst the shadows of large brain coral heads, sea fans and vase sponges. Schools of small reef fish, turtles, and an occasional ray are in residence. During windy periods this spot can be wiped out by strong currents.

☆☆☆ **Folkestone Park** is the favorite beach/snorkeling site in Barbados. An underwater trail has been marked around the inshore reef. It is also the favorite area for boaters and jet skiers so the swimming and snorkeling area has been roped off to insure safety. Snorkel with or near a group. A 200-yd swim from the sandy beach will take you to a raft anchored over the wreckage of a small barge sitting in 20 ft of water. During winter when the North Swell rises, visibility can drop drastically for as long as two days. During the rest of the year, Folkestone is the Number One snorkeling choice.

☆☆☆ The **Wreck of the *Berwyn*** is a 45-ft-long, French tug boat that sank in the early 1900s. It sits at the bottom of Carlisle Bay, 200 yards off the island's southwest shore at a depth of 25 ft. Encrusted with plate corals, the wreck is host to sea horses, frogfish, wrasses, arrow crabs and other small creatures. It is a favored snorkeling-photo site with good visibility and calm sea conditions.

Dive Operators

Dive shops are located along the west shores. **Exploresub** is located in a small cove on the edge of the Divi Southwinds Beach Hotel property on the Southwest coast of the island.

Beginning and advanced dive tours and certification courses are offered. Divemaster Michael Seale offers personalized reef and wreck tours for groups and individuals. Resort courses. St. Lawrence Gap, ☎ 809-428-3504. After six p.m., ☎ 428-4465.

Additional Dive Shops from north to south are **Heywoods**, in St. Peter Parish, **Blue Reef Watersports** at the Glitter Bay Hotel in St. James, ☎ 809-422-3133, **Les Wotton Diving School & Watersports** in Black Rock, St. Michael, ☎ 809 422-3215, **Sandy Lane Watersports, Village Watersports, Willies Watersports,** St Michael, ☎ 809-425-1060 or 809-422-4900, **Dive Shop Ltd.,** at the Grand Barbados Beach Resort, ☎ 809-426-9947; in St. Michael, **Dive Boat Safari** at the Barbados Hilton, ☎ 809-427-4350, **Scotch N Soda,** Christ Church parish, and **Marine Tours,** also in Christ Church parish.

Accommodations

Most hotels and nightlife are on the south and central western coast of the island. There are no dedicated dive resorts, but all will arrange for diving. Several guest houses, cottages and apartments may be rented for $30 per night and up. A list with current rates is available from the Barbados Board of Tourism. U.S., ☎ 800-221-9831; Canada ☎ 800-268-9122; U.K. 011-441-636-9448/9; Barbados ☎ 809-427-2623/4; fax 809-426-4080.

Divi Southwinds Beach Hotel sits on a half-mile of white sand beach near the St. Lawrence Gap. It is surrounded by 20 acres of tropical gardens and features 166 guestrooms and air conditioned suites, all having a patio and pool or ocean views. Beach-side restaurants offer local and international dishes. Pool-side bar and snackery. You are within walking distance of restaurants and nightlife. ☎ 800-367-3484, 607-277-3484 or write Divi St. James, 520 W. State St, Ithaca, NY 14850.

Pineapple Beach Club is an all-inclusive resort. Features are 131 air conditioned guestrooms and suites with ocean or pool views. Gourmet meals are served at the elegant beachside restaurant; refreshments are offered at a swim-up bar adjacent to the twin pools. ☎ 800-345-0356.

Grand Barbados Beach Resort is a luxury, beachfront resort with scuba facilities on the premises. Located in Carlisle Bay, the resort is just minutes from reef and wreck dives. Features are a fitness center, shopping arcade, coffee shop, restaurant, satellite tv, balconies, and meeting facilities.

"Atlantis" Submarine

Coral Reef is a luxury beachfront resort with its own dive shop (Les Wooten's Watersports) and featuring a nice pool, shops, and gardens. Reserve through your travel agent. For villas, apartments, and home rentals contact Villas and Apartments Abroad, 444 Madison Ave., NY, NY 10022. ☎ 212-759-1025.

Other Activities

Horseback riding can be arranged through the hotels. Stables are near Bridgetown. The **Sandy Lane Golf Course** at the Sandy Lane Hotel is a well maintained 18-hole course. Sunset sailing and deep-sea fishing can be arranged through the hotel. Submarining the reefs is offered aboard the 28-passenger, *Atlantis.* ☎ 809-436-8929. Cost is $70 U.S..

Sightseeing

Ride on an electric tram into **Harrison's Cave** to explore beautiful underground water falls, **Mirror Lake** and **The Rotunda Room** where the walls of the 250-ft chamber glitter like diamonds or view exotic tropical birds and native monkeys at the **Wildlife Reserve at Farley Hill**, St. Peter.

History buffs will delight in finding 17th-century military relics like antique cannons and signal towers around the island.

Shopping

Barbados abounds with boutiques, galleries and shops, with department stores such as **Harrison's** and **Cave Shepherd & Co.** offering goods from around the world. Island specialties include handmade puppets and clay and wood figures along with colorful silk screened prints and fabrics. Pepper sauce and Barbados rum are also high on the list of popular take-homes. Most shops are in or near Bridgetown.

Dining

West Indian specialties and native seafood dishes like grilled flying fish and lobster are featured throughout the island. Restaurants range from small home front rooms to large luxury hotel dining rooms. Many hotels—Sandy Lane for example—offer a barbecue served to the music of steel bands or open-air discos (The Carlisle). Fast food aficionados will not be disappointed; a **Kentucky Fried Chicken** (☎ 435-8185) and the **Barbados Pizza House** (Sunset Crest and Fontabell, ☎ 432-0227) are nearby.

Josef's, located in the St. Lawrence area, serves fabulous gourmet fish in a grand native home setting. ☎ 809-428-3379.

Pisces Restaurant, located in the St. Lawrence Gap, is noted for West Indian specialties and fabulous rum pie. ☎ 809-435-6564.

Witch Doctor, St. Lawrence Gap, offers innovative Caribbean dining in an attractive jungle setting. ☎ 435-6581.

"Nu-Bajan" cuisine is served at **Koko's** on Prospect, St James. Seating overlooks the ocean. Creole cuisine lovers be sure to try the **Brown Sugar Restaurant** in St. Michael. ☎ 809-426-7684.

FACTS

Recompression Chamber: Located in St. Annes Fort Garrison, St. Michael. Contact Dr. Brown or Major Gittens at ☎ 436-6185.

Getting There: British West Indian Airlines (BWIA) offer regular service from London, Frankfurt, Stockholm, Zurich, New York, Miami, and Toronto. American Airlines from New York. Barbados' Grantley Adams International Airport is modern and well kept.

Island Transportation: Taxi service is available throughout the island. (Note: cab fares should be negotiated before accepting service) Local auto-rental companies are at the airport. Motorbikes may be rented from Jumbo Vehicles ☎ 426-5689.

Driving: Traffic keeps to the left in Barbados.

Documents: Canadian and U.S. citizens require a birth certificate with a current photo I.D. or passport and return ticket in order to enter Barbados. Entry documentation is good for six months.

Customs: Personal effects of visitors, including cameras and sports equipment, enter duty free. Returning U.S. citizens may take back free of duty articles costing a total of $400 U.S. providing the stay has exceeded 48 hours in length and that the exemption has not been used within the preceding 30 days. One quart per person (over 21 years) may be carried out duty free. Canadians may claim up to $100 Can. each calendar quarter. After seven days they may claim up to $300 Can.

Currency: Barbados dollar (BD)= $1.98 U.S. or $1.43 CAN.

Climate: Temperatures vary between 75 and 85 ° F. Average rainfall is 59 inches.

Clothing Lightweight casual clothing is recommended. A jacket for men may be desirable for visiting nightclubs or dressy resort restaurants. Swim suits, bikinis and short shorts are not welcome in Bridgetown shops or banks.

Electricity: 110 AC, 50 cycles.

Time: Atlantic Standard (EST + 1 hr.)

Language: English with a local dialect.

Taxes: A ten percent tip is added to the bill at most hotels. A sales tax of 5 percent is also added to hotel and restaurant bills.

Religious Services: Anglican, Baptist, Catholic, Methodist, Moravian, Seventh Day Adventist, Jehovah's Witnesses.

For Additional Information: Barbados Board Of Tourism, 800 Second Ave., NY, NY 10017, ☎ 800-221-9831; in NY ☎ 212-986-6510.

Belize

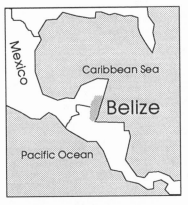

Fascinating and exotic, Belize offers a world of tropical adventure to divers and snorkelers. It is a preserve to the largest barrier reef in the western hemisphere, second only to the Great Barrier Reef in Australia; the magnificent Blue Hole, a 1000-ft ocean sinkhole; and three beautiful atolls—Lighthouse Reef, the Turneffe Islands and Glovers Reef. Within the reef system are hundreds of unchartered islands.

Just 750 miles from Miami, Belize lies on the Caribbean coast of Central America between Guatemala and Mexico. Populated by a mere 200,000 people, it is a country of approximately 9,000 square miles formed by inland mountain ranges with peaks over 3,500 ft and dense tropical jungles webbed by a coastline of mangrove swamps and 266 square miles of offshore coral islands. The 185-mile-long barrier reef parallels the shore from ten to 30 miles out, with prime diving locations around the out islands.

Tours to Belize are labeled "expedition" or "safari" rather than "vacation." Its offshore accommodations and facilities are considered primitive by Caribbean standards—few TVs, phones or automobiles on most of the islands—yet Belize's jungles and unspoiled reefs lure intrepid divers back again and again.

Visitors arriving in Belize City are best advised NOT to tour the inner city on foot as drugs are openly sold on the streets, and tourists sporting cameras, jewelry, or flashing money around may attract undesirable attention. By contrast the islands are lovely, sparsely populated and enjoyably safe. On the mainland outside Belize City one finds fairly rugged and varied terrain alive with yellowhead parrots, giant iguanas, monkeys and a curious creature called the gibnut—described by Belizean author, Robert Nicolait, as a cross between a fat rabbit and a small pig.

The heart of dive tourism is Ambergris Caye, a bustling resort and fishing community and the largest of the out islands or "cayes." Its main town,

San Pedro, is a few hundred yards from the Hol Chan Marine Preserve, the northernmost point of the Barrier Reef, and is the jump-off point to Belize's smaller cayes and atolls. Ambergris is just 20 minutes by air from Belize City or one hour, fifteen minutes by ferry (see end of chapter for transportation details). The northern portion of Ambergris is accessible by boat only, but plans for a road are under consideration. Transportation on Ambergris and the other islands is by golf cart or foot.

A new area for divers is Placencia, a quaint fishing village located on a 16-mile, coastal peninsula 100 miles south of Belize City. There are some coral heads off the beaches, but a half-hour boat ride will bring you to Laughing Bird Caye, a small island surrounded by pristine reefs, and the remains of old wrecks. Several Spanish galleons went down in this area over the years and occasionally a gold piece washes up on the beach. Placencia is an intriguing new place to explore.

Visit Belize during the dry season, from February to May. Annual rainfall ranges from 170 inches in the south to 50 inches in the north. Heaviest rainfall is from September to November.

The climate is sub-tropical with constant, brisk winds from the Caribbean Sea. Summer highs are rarely above 95° F, winter lows seldom below 60° F. Bug repellent is always needed as mosquitos and sand flies are a constant annoyance.

Belize has a long history of stable government. It is a member of the British Commonwealth, with a democratically-elected government. The people are Creoles (African-European), Garifuna (African-Indian), Mestizo (Spanish-Indian), Maya and European. English is the official language and is widely spoken, as is Spanish.

History

Early inhabitants of Belize were the Mayas whose territory also included Mexico, Guatemala, Honduras and El Salvador. They left behind great ceremonial centers, pyramids and evidence of a dynamic people with advancements in the arts, math and science. The Maya inhabited Belize as early as 9000 BC and flourished as a master civilization until most of them mysteriously disappeared about 1000 AD. Theories about their fate range from a guess of massive death by natural disaster to wild speculation about spaceship travel to other planets. Remnants of this ancient culture depict Belize as a major trading center for the entire

Mayan area. Today, a small population of Maya descendents inhabit the countryside.

At Altun Ha (30 miles north of Belize City), an excavated Maya center, spectacular jade and stone carvings have been unearthed including an ornately carved head of Kinisch Ahau, the Mayan Sun God. This head, weighing nine and three quarter pounds and measuring nearly six inches from base to crown, is believed to be the largest Maya jade carving in existence. Also uncovered was the Temple of the Green Tomb, a burial chamber which contained human remains and a wealth of jade pieces including pendants, beads, figures and jewelry. Side trips to this and other jungle archaeological sites are offered by most dive-tour operators.

During the 17th century, Belize was colonized by the British and the Spanish. In 1862, the settlement became an English colony known as British Honduras. It gained independence in 1981. Today, it is the only Central American nation where English is widely spoken.

Best Dive of Belize

THE BARRIER REEF

☆☆☆ **Hol Chan Marine Preserve** lies off the southern tip of Ambergris Caye. It is a five-square-mile reef area characterized by a natural channel or cut which attracts and shelters huge communities of marine animals. Maximum depth inside the reef is 30 ft, allowing unlimited bottom time. The outside wall starts at 50 ft, then drops to beyond 150 ft. Schools of tropicals line the walls with occasional glimpses of big turtles, green and spotted morays, six-foot stingrays, eagle rays, spotted dolphin and nurse shark.

A constant flow of seawater through the cut promotes the growth of large barrel and basket sponges, sea fans, and beautiful outcroppings of staghorn and brain corals.

Diving all along the barrier reef is extraordinary. There are caves, dramatic overhangs, and pinnacles, all with superb marine life, though commercial fishing has taken its toll on the really big grouper, shark and huge turtles that were commonplace ten years ago. The subsea terrain is similar throughout the area with long channels of sand running perpendicular to the overall reef system. These cuts run to seaward allowing a constant change of nutrient-rich seawater to cleanse and feed the coral.

The inner reef, that area facing land, is shallow, with coral slopes which bottom out between 20 and 40 feet. Amidst its forests of staghorn and elkhorn are throngs of juvenile fish, barracuda, invertebrates, spawning grouper, stingrays, conch, nurse shark and small critters.

Diving the outer reef brings a better chance to see mantas, permits, jacks, black durgons, tuna, dolphin, turtles and shark. Visibility is exceptional too. The reef profile outside is typically a sloping shelf to between 25 or 40 feet, which then plunges to 2,000 ft or more.

Live-aboard yachts which explore the entire coast are extremely popular in Belize, though local guides and tourist officials are working to attract more divers to their shore facilities and après-dive attractions.

The Atolls

Atolls are ring-shaped coral islands or island groups surrounding a lagoon. Most are in the South Pacific and are often the visible portions of ancient, submerged volcanos, but those in Belize are composed of coral and may have been formed by faults during the shifting of land masses.

All three, Lighthouse Reef, Glovers Reef and the Turneffe Islands are surrounded by miles of shallow reefs and magnificent, deep dropoffs. The sheltered lagoons are dotted with pretty coral heads and are great for snorkeling and novice divers. Outside, visibility exceeds 150 feet and marine life is unrivaled. Generally, the islands are primitive, remote and largely uninhabited, with the bulk of the population made up of free-roaming chickens, though each location has at least one dive resort and a resident divemaster.

☆☆☆☆ **The Turneffe Islands,** 35 miles from Belize City and beyond the barrier reef, are a group of 32 low islands bordered with thick growths of mangroves. The lower portion of the chain forms a deep V shape with Cay Bokel at the southernmost point. Reef areas just above both sides of the point are the favorite southern dive spots. Cay Bokel is where you'll find the Turneffe Island Lodge, a quaint resort offering dive services. West of the southern point are sheltered, shallow reefs at 20 to 60 ft depths. Along the reef are some old anchors overgrown with coral, a small, wooden wreck, the *Sayonara,* and a healthy fish population. Seas are rougher, currents stronger and the dives deeper to the east, but more impressive coral formations and large pelagics are found. The ridges and canyons of the reefs are carpeted by a dense cover of sea feathers, lacy soft corals, branching gold and purple sponges, anemones, seafans and luxurious growths of gorgonians. Passing dolphins and rays are the big attraction as they upstage the reef's "blue collar workers"—cleaning shrimp, sea cucumbers, patrolling barracuda, de-

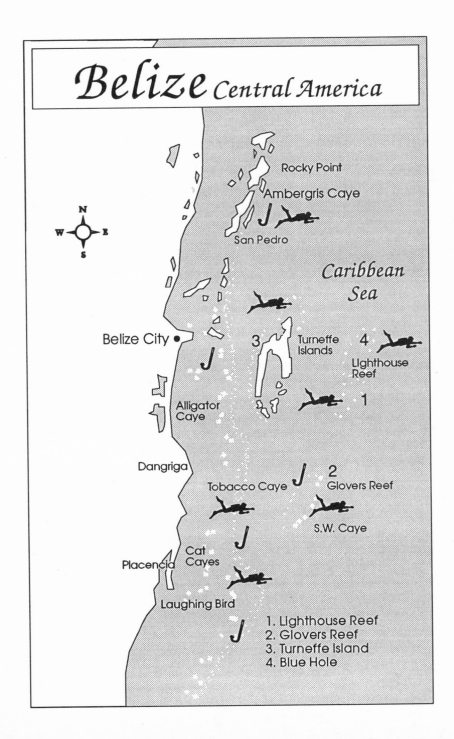

fensive damsel fish, schooling yellowtail, grunts and coral crabs. Snorkeling and diving are excellent, with outstanding water clarity, protected areas, and diverse marine life.

Rendezvous Point at the northernmost point is equal in sub terrain and diver interest, but is more often visited by fishermen. Much of the northern area is shallow mangrove swamp where tarpon, bonefish, shrimp and lobster proliferate

☆☆☆☆☆ The most popular atoll and that most visited by dive boats is **Lighthouse Reef**. It lies 40 miles from Belize City and is the outermost of the offshore islands within the Belize cruising area. Lighthouse is a circular reef system featuring several islands and small cayes. Located on its southeast boundaries is a beautiful old lighthouse and Half Moon Caye National Monument, the first marine conservation area in Belize and a bird sanctuary to colonies of the red-footed boobie.

Half Moon Caye has white-sand beaches with a drop-off on the north side and a shallow lagoon on the south end. A dock with a pierhead depth about six ft and an area for amphibious aircraft are on the north side of the island. Live-aboard dive boats are required to anchor in designated areas to prevent reef damage. All boaters must register with the lighthouse keeper upon arrival.

The lighthouse, situated on the tapering eastern side of Half Moon Caye, was first built in 1820. It was later replaced by another in 1848 and since reinforced by a steel-framed tower in 1931. Today the lighthouse is solar powered. A climb to the top offers a spectacular view.

To the north is the Lighthouse Reef Resort, an air-conditioned colony of English villas catering to divers and fishermen.

☆☆☆☆☆ Near the center of Lighthouse Reef is the **Blue Hole**, Belize's most famous dive spot. From the air it looks like an apparition. The cobalt blue of the Caribbean abruptly changes to an azure blue circle. The heart of the circle is an indigo blue.

Approaching by water is not as breathtaking, but beautiful nonetheless. You know you are somewhere special. It is an almost perfect circle, 1,000 ft in diameter in the midst of a reef six to 18 ft below the surface. Inside the shallow reef, the walls drop suddenly to a depth of 412 ft, almost completely vertical for the first 125 ft. Here they turn inward and slightly upward. At 140 ft you reach an awesome underwater "cathedral" with alcoves, archways and columns. It is a huge submerged cave with 12- to 15-ft-wide stalactites suspended 20 to 60 ft from the cavern ceiling. Formed thousands of years ago, perhaps during the Ice Age, the cave was once above sea level. This is always a guided dive and should be attempted only by experienced divers, but novice divers are as entertained by the shallows surrounding the crater's rim as are those venturing down to the cave. Note: The nearest recompression chamber is in Belize City.

Travel time to and from the Blue Hole and the cost of your trip will vary according to the location of your accommodations. If you are staying on Ambergris Caye the trip will take an entire day and cost about $125. From the Turneffe Islands travel time to and from is about half a day and the cost is included. If you are on a live-aboard, one of your stops will surely be the Blue Hole.

☆☆☆☆ South of the Turneffe Islands and Lighthouse Reef is the third and most remote atoll, **Glover's Reef**. It is a reef system formed by coral growing around the edges of a steep, limestone plateau. An almost continuous barrier reef encloses an 80-square-mile lagoon that reaches depths of 50 ft. The lagoon is an outstanding snorkeling spot, with over 700 coral heads. Outside, the reef starts at 30 ft and drops to more than 2000 ft Visibility exceeds 150 ft. Grouper, queen triggerfish and parrotfish are in abundance. Mantas, pods of dolphins, spotted eagle rays and sea turtles are occasionally spotted on the reefs. It is a spectacular diving and snorkeling spot with more than 25 coral species to be explored and thousands of sheltered spots. The reefs remain largely unexplored and are seldom visited by live aboards. Two dive/fishing resorts, Glovers Reef Resort and Manta Reef Resort offer experienced guides and services.

Dive Resorts

Rates listed are for winter, in U.S. dollars and subject to change. Most resorts and restaurants accept U.S. dollars, travelers checks, and major credit cards.

Note: Direct dial service is available between Belize and the U.S. and Canada. To call Belize, dial 011-501, drop the first zero from the local number, then dial the remaining numbers.

Ambergris Caye

Ramon's Village in San Pedro, offers 20 clean, thatched-roof bungalows with double beds and full baths. The resort has a decent pool-side bar and a fully-equipped dive shop offering reef trips and basic rentals. The atmosphere is relaxed and unhurried. Daily room rates are from $125 daily for a double, to $245 for a suite. For reservations ☎ 601-649-1990; fax 60-425-2411; or write P.O. Drawer 4407, Laurel MS 39441.

Victoria House, is on its own nine-acre beach. Day rates for standard rooms are from $110 for a double. Seven-night packages with airfare from the mainland included are from $1,142 for a room, $1,275 for a beach hut (casita), $1,342 for deluxe, and $1,657 for the ultra luxurious Windsor Suite. Kayaks, windsurfers, sunfish and a small catamaran may be rented. Restaurant. Glass-bottom boat trips, fishing trips, and excursions to jungle ruins and neighboring cayes are offered. ☎ 800-247-5159. Local 026-2067; fax 026-2429; or write to Victoria House, Ambergris Caye, Belize, Central America.

Matarocks South, (formerly House of the Rising Sun) a mile south of San Pedro, offers modern, beachfront apartments. Day rates for a double are from $100. Dive with Bottom Time Divers. Some units air-conditioned. Restaurant. Dive-travel packages through Ocean Connection. ☎ 800-365-6232; local 026-2336; fax 026-2349.

Paradise Resort Hotel, at the north end of San Pedro village, features a relaxing tropical atmosphere. Rooms have ceiling fans, air conditioning, TV and kitchenettes. Restaurant. Rates start at $150 for a double. A 25% tax and service charge is added. ☎ local, 026-2083.

Captain Morgan's Retreat is a thatched-hut village on the beach. Cabanas are private with ceiling fans and solid mahogany floors. Modern baths. Roomy. The resort is north of San Pedro reached by water taxi. Diving and fishing packages. Accommodations are from $155 for a double. Seven nights MAP with airfare from Houston are offered by Magnum Tours starting at $999. Add $50 per day for two tank dives. Snorkeling trips are $25 per person—your equipment.

Journey's End, is an outstanding, beachfront hotel just 500 yards from the Barrier Reef. The 50-acre resort is accessible by water taxi—ten minutes from the airstrip. Guests stay in luxurious, beach cabanas, pool-side villas, or waterfront rooms. Amenities include gourmet restaurant, tennis courts, beach bar, and freshwater, olympic pool with swim-up bar and grille. All watersports are offered. The 125-member staff caters to guests' every whim.

Rocks Inn is on the beach in walking distance of San Pedro. The hotel offers attractive, air-conditioned suites with modern appliances. Day rates are from $100 for a double. Dive-travel packages through Belize Tradewinds. ☎ 800-451-7776; fax 414-258-5336.

Caye Chapel

The Pyramid Island Resort sits on Caye Chapel, a three-mile, privately-owned island rimmed with miles of beautiful white beaches. This hotel has 32 beachfront, air-conditioned rooms each with private bath, two villas, a full-service marina on the leeward side, and a fantastic, circular restaurant and bar where you can see the coral reef and beyond. The resort's high performance boats are used for jaunts to the Blue Hole and for visiting other islands. In addition, the resort operates a 20-ft glass bottomed boat for snorkelers. Several skiffs are available for side trips to the jungle and Mayan ruins. ☎ 02-44409; fax 02-32405. Write to Pyramid Island Resort, Caye Chapel, P.O. Box 192, Belize City, Belize, C. A.

St. George's Caye

St. George's Lodge is the only commercial establishment on Saint George's Caye. The lodge, which is beautifully handcrafted of exquisite local hardwoods, houses a dining room, rosewood bar, secluded sundeck and 12 private rooms cooled by tradewinds. In addition, there are four new thatched cottages each with a private veranda overlooking the sea. All rooms and cottages feature private bath with shower, and windmill-powered electricity. (A 110-V A.C. converter is located in the lodge for recharging strobes etc.) Gourmet meals featuring fresh lobster, broiled native fish, and outstanding conch chowder followed by fabulous desserts created with local fruits are the fare of the day at this lodge. Diving takes place on a shallow wall ranging from 40 to 100 ft where there is a wide variety of corals and endless schools of fish. Visibility exceeds 100 ft. Rates, per person, per day, include round-trip ground and boat transportation from Belize International Airport, private bath, three meals daily, tanks, weights, full diving privileges, two trips daily, maid service, $257 (cottages); $228 (lodge). Non-divers $169.25 (lodge), $190 (cottage). Non-divers may swim from dive boats on a space-available basis. Instruction extra. ☎ 800-678-6871; local, 02-44190; fax 02-30461. St. George's Lodge, P.O. Box 625, Belize City, Belize, C. A.

The Turneffe Islands

Turneffe Island Lodge is the ultimate outpost for divers. Not for everyone, this lodge accommodates 16 guests in quaint bungalows with private baths and showers. (No phones). It is a private resort, American owned and operated, located approximately 30 miles from Belize

City. The entire island is surrounded by a sheer coral wall that starts at 40 ft and drops to more than 2,000 ft. On shore are miles of sandy beaches. Rooms have screened porches that face the Caribbean. Island specialties including lobster, fish, conch, and locally grown fruits and vegetables are served in the dining room. A two-hour boat ride—supplied by the lodge—from Belize City brings you to this heart of the outer reefs. Rates are $1,295 for six nights, seven days and include round-trip transfers, three meals daily, three-tank boat dives daily and lodging. Non-divers pay $900. Tanks and weights supplied. Bring your own personal gear. ☎ 1-800-338-8149 or fax 904-641-5285. Write to P.O. Box 480, Belize City, Belize, C.A.

Lighthouse Reef

Lighthouse Reef Resort offers luxury, air-conditioned rooms and villas. Tropic Air meets incoming flights at Belize International Airport to deliver guests to the resort's private airstrip. Flight time is 20 minutes. Diving packages, $1200 (non-divers $1050), run from Sat. to Sat. and include air-conditioned room with bath, three meals per day and snacks, three boat dives per day, night dives, tanks and weights. A fishing and diving package may be combined for $1400. ☎ 800-423-3114. Write: P.O. Box 26, Belize City, C.A.

Glovers Reef

Manta Reef Resort is on 12 palm-studded acres at the southern tip of Glovers Reef Atoll. It is conveniently perched atop a deep coral wall with easy beach entry. Guests stay in modern, tropical, mahogany cabanas with private baths and showers. The resort is self-contained with a spacious restaurant and bar built out over the water on an enormous pier and decorated with hand-rubbed native woods; dive boats, E6 photo lab and gift shop. Rates are $1295 per week, (Sat. to Sat.) per person, double occupancy and include round-trip transfers from the mainland, three meals and snacks daily, two, double-tank boat dives per day, unlimited beach dives. Flats- and ocean-fishing packages also available. ☎ 800-342-0052; local, 011-501-231895.

Placencia

Placencia Cove Resort, just north of the village, offers six beachfront cabins, each with two queen-sized beds, private bath (hot water), screened porches with deck furniture and hammock. A tennis court is on the premises. Winter rates start at $75 per day, per person and include three gourmet meals daily—American and Creole seafood specialties. The resort has a 1000-ft private beach, a 40-ft diesel-powered boat, a compressor and offers group trips to the reef. Smaller boats with local guides can be arranged for couples or individual trips to Laughing Bird Caye. ☎ 800-662-309; local 06-22024; or write P.O. Box 007, Placencia, Stann Creek, Belize, C.A. Major credit cards welcome.

The **Turtle Inn,** located a mile north of Placencia Village, features six thatched-roof, beachfront cottages, private baths, and offers guests a number of dive, snorkeling and jungle trips. Electricity is solar powered. Daily rates for a double are $93.50. Add $40 per person, per day, for three meals. ☎ U.S. 303-444-2555; local 06-22069. Write to Dr. Lois Kruschwitz, 2190 Bluebell, Boulder CO 80302.

Several low-budget hotels are located in the village such as **Ran's Travel Lodge** which offers diving and snorkeling trips. ☎ 06-22027 or write to Ran's, Placencia, Stann Creek, Belize, C.A.

Sightseeing

Day trips to Belize's archaeological sites, the rain forest and Belize Zoo are offered by local tour companies in Belize City and Ambergris Caye or can be arranged as part of your trip in advance. Day rates are from $65 to about $200 from Ambergris Caye to inland sites, depending on where you are headed.

Altun Ha is the most popular Maya Ruin and least expensive from Ambergris Caye. Tour operators include a picnic lunch, ground and sea transportation for about $65.

Xunantunich, (Maiden of the Rock) is on the west coast about 80 miles from Belize City. This is the largest ruin unearthed in Belize. Impressive views are had from the top of El Castillo, the main pyramid. Xunantunich is accessible only by ferry which runs from San Jose Succotz daily from 8 am to 5 pm. Trips often include a tour of the Belize Zoo and a drive around Belmopan, Belize's capital. Cost is approx. $135 U.S. including a Tropic Air flight, ground transportation, entrance fees and lunch.

Animals at the **Belize Zoo** are housed in naturalistic mesh and wood enclosures. The animals—jaguar, puma, toucan, spider and howler monkeys, and the "mountain cow"—are all indigenous to Belize. They were originally gathered for a wildlife film. The zoo is 30 miles west of Belize City.

From Belize City, driving up the Western Highway to Mile Marker 21 will bring you to **Gracie Rock,** one site of the movie "Mosquito Coast" where you'll find the remains of the huge icemaker blown up by Harrison Ford.

Guanacaste Park, about 50 miles southwest of Belize City is a 50-acre parcel of tropical forest located in the Cayo District at the junction of Western Highway and Hummingbird Highway. It is named for the huge guanacaste tree which can reach a height of 130 ft, with a diameter in excess of six ft. More than one hundred species of birds have been spotted.

The Blue Hole National Park & St. Hermans Cave are 12 miles southeast of Belmopan. This inland "Blue Hole" is a popular recreational spot where water, on its way to the Sibun River emerges into the base of a collapsed sinkhole about 100 ft deep and 300 ft in diameter. St Hermans Cave is about 500 yards from the Hummingbird Highway and is accessible via a hiking trail from the Blue Hole. The nearest of the three known entrances is impressive—a large sinkhole funneling to a 20 meter entrance. Mayan pottery, spears and torches have been found here.

Dining

Divers staying on Ambergris Caye, the main diver island, will find restaurants in the village of San Pedro offering fresh seafood and local dishes such as conch chowder, conch fritters, broiled snapper, shrimp, lobsters, and rice dishes often accompanied by home baked breads or soups. Chinese food is also extremely popular in Belize. Try the **Barrier Reef Restaurant** (☎ 026-2075), **The Palm Restaurant** (☎ 026-2249), **Lilly's** (☎ 026-2059). If you are staying at an out-island resort, meals are usually included in the price of the stay. Local fish, conch and chicken dishes are the usual.

Shopping

Small shops at the airport and resorts offer tee shirts, straw crafts and native carvings from mahogany, rosewood and ziricote, a two-toned wood indigenous to Belize.

Tours

The following tour companies offer diving and/or combination diving/jungle expeditions of Belize. There are pre-planned packages for groups and individuals or design your own and they will make all the

Maya ruin

arrangements. Most Belize tours from the U.S. depart Houston or Miami. Package rates for week-long trips are usually much lower than buying air, accommodations, diving, meals and transfers separately.

International Expeditions Inc. offers custom-guided trips for the naturalist. Tours are well organized to consider both skilled diver and novice snorkeler. ☎ 800-633-4734 or 205-428-1700; write to Number One Environs Park, Helena AL 35080.

Cedam (Conservation, Ecology, Diving, Archaeology, Museums) is a non-profit organization which offers scientific expeditions. ☎ 914-271-5365 or fax 914-271-4723. Write to 1 Fox Road, Croton NY 10520.

Scuba Tours' arranges for group or individual dive trips to Ambergris Caye or atolls. Choose from rooms, condos or live-aboard yacht. ☎ 800-526-1394 or 201-256-9115; fax 256-0591 or write to P.O. Box 366, Little Falls NJ 07424.

Ocean Connection is staffed by divers who know Belize well. They offer snorkeling, fishing & diving trips with a choice of islands and hotels. Beach & jungle treks, Mayan ruins & Belize national park tours are their specialty. Budget rates. Combination tours with Mexico are possible. ☎

800-365-6232 or 713-486-6991; fax 713-486-8362; or write 167 El Camino Real, Houston TX 77062.

Magnum's Belize, features dive and fishing packages to Ambergris Caye, Placencia, Corozal, Caye Caulker and Lighthouse Reef. ☎ 800-447-2931; write to 718 Washington Ave., Detroit Lakes MN 56502.

Belize Tradewinds takes divers and snorkelers on four- to seven-day expeditions to Ambergris or the out-islands with a choice of hotels. Travelers may combine a dive trip with horseback or canoe touring. ☎ 800-451-7776; fax 414-258-5336 or write 8715 W. North Ave, Wauwatosa WI 53226.

ICS Scuba and Travel has group and individual dive tours to Belize with accommodations at Journey's End on Ambergris Caye and a variety of side trips to Maya ruins, the rainforest, Jaguar preserve or river trips. Rates vary. ☎ 800-722-0205; fax 516-797-2132 or write 5254 Merrick Road, Suite 5, Massapequa NY 11758.

Sea Safaris arranges for scuba packages, archaeological tours and special interest trips. ☎ 800-821-6670 U.S. & Canada; fax 213-545-1672.

Best of Belize will create a custom package for divers or mainland visitors. ☎ 800-735-9520 or 415-663-8022; write to P.O. Box 1266, Point Reyes CA 94956.

Wilderness Southeast offers guided, educational expeditions to Belize's reefs. Groups formed by them or you. Guides are naturalists with a good knowledge of the area. ☎ 912-897-5108; write to 711 Sandtown Rd, Savannah GA 31410.

Out-Island Divers specializes in trips for groups and individuals on live-aboards. Tours depart from the U.S. ☎ 800-BLUE HOLE or 303-586-6020; local (San Pedro) 026-2151; or write P.O. Box 3455, Estes Park CO 80517.

Poseidon Venture Tours feature both live-aboard and island getaways with several out-island locations to choose from. ☎ 800-854-9334 or 714-644-5344; or write to 359 San Miguel Drive, Newport Beach CA. 92660.

Dive Operators

Bottom Time Dive Shop has reef and out-island tours for divers and snorkelers. In San Pedro, ☎ 026-2348.

Kingfisher Sports Ltd., Placencia, ☎ 062-310.

Adventure Coast Divers Belize City, ☎ 02-72957.

Caribbean Charter Services, Belize City, ☎ 02-45814.

Live-Aboards

Belize live-aboards offer access to these pristine diving areas and are popular among those who thrive on 24-hour diving.

Peter Hughes Diving operates the 120-ft *Wave Dancer*. ☎ 800-932-6237 or 305-669-9391; or write 1390 S. Dixie Highway, Waterway II, Suite 2213, Coral Gables FL 33146.

Belize Aggressor II is a 110-ft luxury yacht that carries 18 passengers. Offers all the amenities of a dive resort: air-conditioned private rooms, photo shop, film processing, mini movie theater, plus fast cruising speeds. ☎ 800-348-2628 or write Aggressor Fleet Ltd., P.O. Drawer K, Morgan City LA 70381.

Helpful Phone Numbers

POLICE: ☎ 90

HOSPITAL: ☎ 02-77251 or 90

TOURIST BOARD: ☎ 02-77213/73255; fax 02-77490

TROPIC AIR: ☎ 02-45671 for inter-island service

FACTS

Nearest Recompression Chamber: Belize City. Emergency helicopter service from atolls. Dial 90 for assistance.

Health: Anti-malaria tablets are recommended for stays in the jungle.

Airlines: Scheduled commercial service from the United States and Canada is by American Airlines (☎ 800-433-7300), Continental, SAHSA and TACA. Tropic Air flies from Cancun, Mexico.

In Belize, Tropic Air (☎ 02-45671) services major cities Ambergris Caye and the out-islands. Additional Belize cities are served by Island Air (☎ 02-31140 or 026-2435) or Maya Airways (02-72312).

Private Aircraft may enter Belize only through the Phillip Goldson International Airport in Belize City. Belizean airspace is open during daylight hours. Pilots are required to file a flight plan and will be briefed on local conditions. Landing fee for all aircraft.

By Car: Belize can reached from the U.S. and Canada via Mexico though reports of hold-ups on the roads deter most motorists. You must possess a valid drivers license and registration papers for the vehicle. A temporary permit will enable use of your vehicle without payment of customs. A temporary insurance policy must be purchased at the frontier to cover the length of stay in Belize. After three days, visitors must obtain a Belize driving permit for which you need to complete a medical form, provide two recent photos and pay $20.

Private Boats must report to the police or immigration immediately. No permits are required. You will need documents of the vessel, clearance from your last port of call, four copies of the crew and passenger manifest and list of stores and cargo.

Documents: Visitors are permitted to stay up to one month, provided they have a valid passport (and visa, if required). Travelers should demonstrate that they have sufficient funds for their visit (U.S. $50 per person, per day) and have a ticket to their onward destination. For stays longer than 30 days, an extension must be obtained from the Immigration Office, 115 Barrack Road, Belize City, at a cost of $12.50 U.S.

Transportation: Bus service around Belize City is readily available via Batty Brothers ☎ 02-72025; or Z-Line ☎ 02-73937/06-22211. Since few cars are available on the islands, transportation is usually arranged by the resort. On the mainland reservations can be made through National Car Rental (☎ 02-31586) or Avis (☎ 02-78367). Reserve prior to trip. Jeeps and four wheel drive vehicles are mandatory on back roads. Avoid local car rental companies or carefully check vehicles for scratches or dents and have them documented by the renter beforehand.

Ferries: Ambergris Caye and Caye Caulker can be reached by boat from Belize City. The *Andera* operates from Belize City to San Pedro leaving the docks of the Bellevue Hotel at 4 pm from Mon. to Fri. and 1 pm on Sat. returning to Belize at 7 pm. Also available to San Pedro is the *Miss Belize* which runs daily. Tickets may be purchased from the Universal Travel Agency in Belize City. *Miss Belize* departs from the docks behind the Supreme Court building. Travel time to San Pedro is one hour and 15 minutes. Non-scheduled service to Caye Caulker departs from the docks behind the Shell Gas Station on North Front St. Travel time to Caye Caulker is 45 minutes.

Departure Tax: U.S. $10.

Customs: Personal effects can be brought in without difficulty, but it is best to register cameras, videos and electronic gear with customs before leaving home. American citizens can bring home $400 worth of duty-free goods after a 48-hour visit. Over that purchases are dutied at 10%. Import allowances include 200 cigarettes or 1/2 lb. tobacco; 20 fluid oz alcoholic beverage and one bottle perfume for personal use. Note: removing and exporting coral or archaeological artifacts is prohibited. Picking orchids in forest reserves is illegal.

ry

ed for centuries by Arawak Indians, Bonaire was named after the
k word "bo-nah", or "low country" by Amerigo Vespucci who
ered the island in 1499.

ttempted to colonize the island between 1527 and 1633, but in 1634
tch claimed the island and established a military base to defend
t Spain. Later, in 1639 the Dutch West India Company developed
e for salt production, corn planting and livestock breeding. The
ny imported 100 African slaves and ran the island for the next 160

ritish occupied Bonaire briefly during the early 1800's, but the
regained control in 1816 and established a government plantation
based on commercial crops. With the abolition of slavery in 1863,
erations became unprofitable and the island was divided and sold.

he next 90 years, a severe economic recession forced many Bonaire-
migrate to Curacao and Aruba to work in the oil industry. By the
, however, Bonaire's economy recovered. The salt pans were modi-
use solar energy and became the most successful plants in the
. Tourism was introduced and divers have since come from around
obe.

aire Marine Park

79, the Netherlands Antilles National Parks Foundation (STINAPA)
ed a grant from the World Wildlife Fund for the creation of the
ire Marine Park. The park was created to maintain the coral reef
stem and ensure continuing returns from scuba diving, fishing
ther recreational activities.

park incorporates the entire coastline of Bonaire and neighboring
Bonaire. It is defined as the "seabottom and the overlying waters
the highwater tidemark down to 200 ft (60m)".

isitors are asked to respect the marine park rules—no sitting on
s; no fishing or collecting of fish; shells or corals, dead or alive.
rfishing is forbidden. Anchoring is not permitted. All craft must use
nanent moorings, except for emergency anchoring. Boats of less than
may use a stone anchor.

ular dive sites are periodically shut down to rejuvenate the corals.
rings are removed and placed on different sites.

United Kingdom citizens may bring in one liter of alcohol or two of wine; 200 cigarettes or 50 cigars; 250 cc of toilet water; 50 gms of perfumes.

Currency: Belize dollar = $.50 U.S.

Climate: Belize has a sub-tropical, humid climate. Average temperature 79 deg F. The rainy season is from April to December. Hurricanes form during late summer. Best time to visit is February through May though summer diving when weather permits (mid-August) often brings calm seas and excellent visibility.

Clothing: Lightweight clothing with long sleeves to protect against sunburn and a light sweater for evening wear. The dive resorts are extremely casual. Leave dress wear at home. For those who want to combine an expedition into the jungle with their diving vacation it is a good idea to check with the tour company. Bring mosquito repellent.

Gear: Divers' rental equipment is limited in Belize so be sure to bring all of your own personal equipment. The resorts do supply weights and tanks, but little else.

Electricity: 110/220V 60 cycles. Most island resorts run on generators which are out of service for at least part of the day. Air conditioning is limited.

Time: Central Standard Time.

Language: English

Additional Information: Belize Tourist Board, 415 Seventh Ave, New York NY 10001; ☎ 800-624-0686/ 212-268-8798; fax 212-695-3018. In Belize, 83 North Front St, P.O. Box 325, Belize City, Belize, C.A. In Canada, 112 Kent St., Suite 2005, Place de Ville, Ontario, Canada I1P 5P2, ☎ 613- 232-7389.

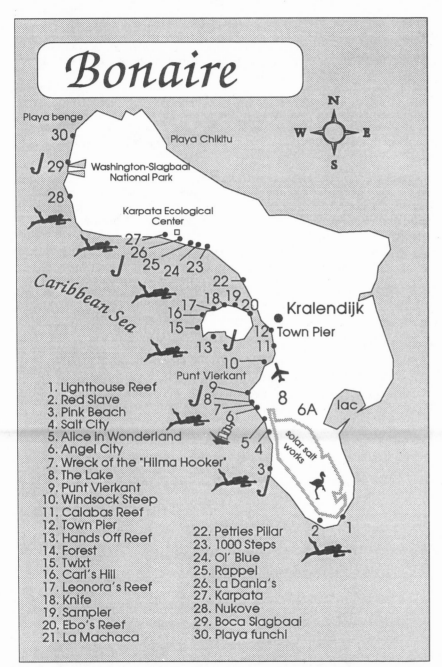

Bonaire

Note: Bonaire sites are periodically closed down for rejuvenation.
Check with local dive shops for availability before diving on your own.

Map labels:

Playa benge
30
J 29
28
Washington-Slagbaai National Park
Playa Chikitu
Karpata Ecological Center
27
26
25 24 23
J
Caribbean Sea
22
17 18 19
16 20
15
Kralendijk
13 12 Town Pier
11
10
Punt Vierkant
J 9
J 8
8
7
6
6A Iac
5
4
3
solar salt works
2 1

1. Lighthouse Reef
2. Red Slave
3. Pink Beach
4. Salt City
5. Alice in Wonderland
6. Angel City
7. Wreck of the "Hilma Hooker"
8. The Lake
9. Punt Vierkant
10. Windsock Steep
11. Calabas Reef
12. Town Pier
13. Hands Off Reef
14. Forest
15. Twixt
16. Carl's Hill
17. Leonora's Reef
18. Knife
19. Sampler
20. Ebo's Reef
21. La Machaca
22. Petries Pillar
23. 1000 Steps
24. Ol' Blue
25. Rappel
26. La Dania's
27. Karpata
28. Nukove
29. Boca Slagbaai
30. Playa funchi

BONAIRE

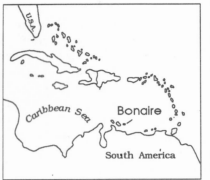

Both above and
aire is a colorful
flat, blessed wit
pink-sand beach
dent flamingos.
tal, sparkles w
buildings. To t
roads wind thro
tains and cactus-l
more than 190
birds reside. Ra
bright green, A
ruby-topaz hummingbirds, pearly-eyed thrashers, an
keets. At the island's southern tip, home of the Antille
Company, mountains of glistening, white salt offer a
the blue Caribbean. At days end a green flash follows

Beneath the sea a brilliant rainbow of marine life has
reputation as a world-class dive location. Strict cons
gether with calm waters protected by the crescent shape
preserved Bonaire's bountiful coral reefs and marine a

The second largest of the Netherland Antilles islands,
out of the hurricane belt—1,720 miles south of New Y
north of Venezuela—and therefore protected from reef
offers dependably dry weather and calm seas 365 days

With only 12 inches of rain annually, there is no fresh
water visibility is typically 100 feet or more. And becau
to shore, the water is calm and storms almost never oc
pick up a tank and dive anytime day or night, anywhe
Excellent snorkeling exists off all the south coast beache

Less than a mile from the south coast is Klein Bonaire
which acts like a barrier reef, creating calm leeward w
diving and snorkeling lies within this sheltered area. Th
coast, by contrast, is battered by strong waves that pound
coral cliffs.

Area contributors: Rose Abello, Harry Ward, Andre Nahr, S
& Photo; Dee Scarr, Touch the Sea.

Hist

Inhab
Araw
disco

Spai
the I
agai
Bona
com
year

The
Dut
sys
the

Ov
ans
19
fie
wo
th

B

In
re
B
e
a

T
f

Salt Pier

Dive and Snorkeling Sites

Hotels and dive shops offer daily trips to nearby offshore sites. Most are less than a ten-minute boat ride, but you don't need a boat or even a mask to see Bonaire's reefs; they grow to the surface in many areas and are visible from the shore. Excellent beach dives exist along the shores on the leeward side where channels have been cut allowing access to deeper water. These reefs slope down to a narrow ledge at 30 ft, then drop-off vertically to between 100 and 200 ft.

☆☆☆☆☆ One of the favorite boat dive areas is **Alice in Wonderland,** a double-reef complex, separated by a sand channel and extending from Pt. Vierkant south toward Salt Pier. There are a number of good dive sites within this reef system, all marked by dive buoys. The most popular is **Angel City** which starts at about 30 feet and drops off to a deep channel. Swim down the first reef slope to a narrow sand channel, keeping right. One of the largest purple tube sponges you will ever see is at the channel's northern end.

Scattered throughout the shallow terrace are stands of staghorn, star, giant brain, and flower corals—home to goatfish, jacks, groupers and trunkfish. Farther down is a garden-eel colony, queen conchs, and huge stingrays. Initially, the garden look like a bed of grass, but it will retract back into the sand if you wave your arm over them.

Off Klein Bonaire

Photo by Jon Huber

☆☆☆ Boat dives in Bonaire are inexpensive ($15 and up) and very convenient, but if you miss the boat, **Angel City** may be reached by swimming from shore. Drive to the Trans World Radio transmitting station, south of Kralendijk—its huge tower is easy to spot. Follow a track before the station entrance which leads to the shore. From there, enter opposite the Angel City buoy.

☆☆☆☆ **Salt City** is a boat or shore dive located at the southern end of "Alice in Wonderland." To reach Salt City, drive south from Kralendijk past the salt loading pier (very visible). You'll spot a large buoy south of the pier. Enter along the left "bank" formed by the large "sand river," a wide, sand stretch which eventually drops off the shallow terrace into a short, reef slope "island."

The terrace is landscaped with star, fire, mustard-hill, elkhorn and stag-horn corals. Sea life is superb, featuring scad, palometa, big groupers, snappers, garden eels, southern stingrays, tilefish and grey angelfish.

☆☆☆ The *Hilma Hooker*, a 250-ft freighter lies right off shore just north of Angel City Reef. Reached from the beach or by boat, this is Bonaire's most spectacular and notorious shipwreck. The ship was seized during a drug raid when a member of the Antillean Coast Guard discovered a false bulkhead. The crew abandoned the freighter and fled the island. Because of an unmanageable leak, Bonaire law enforcement agents were afraid that the ship would sink and damage the reefs, so they towed the ship

Diving the Cruise Ship Pier

out to where she now lies, creating an intriguing dive site. The wreck rests on a sandy bottom at 91 ft. Divers should stay outside the wreck and monitor bottom time.

☆☆☆☆ **The Lake** is yet another part of the "Alice in Wonderland" complex. Soft coral, purple tube sponges and a profusion of groupers, coneys, rock hinds and moray eels are in residence.

☆☆☆ **Punt Vierkant** is marked by the first buoy past the small lighthouse north of the "Alice in Wonderland" complex. To reach the site, drive south from Kralendijk past the Belnam residential area and toward the lighthouse. On the swim out you'll be joined by juvenile rays, trunkfish, groupers and snappers. As you descend, the fish are larger and the rays more numerous. Pastel gorgonians, and sponges decorate the wall.

☆☆☆ **Windsock Steep** is known for great snorkeling. This dive is off the small, sand beach opposite the airport runway. Watch out for fire coral as you explore the shallow terrace. The bottom is sandy, but stacked up with sergeant majors, angelfish, snappers, triggerfish, and barracuda.

☆☆☆☆ **Calabas Reef**, just off the beach in front of the Flamingo Beach Hotel, is reached by swimming over a sand shelf. Giant brain and star corals grow from the slope. Old anchors are scattered about. To the north

Bonaire's beach dive sites are marked by yellow "sign" rocks along the ocean road.

is a small sailboat wreck. The hotel pier is well lit after dusk, making it an easily accessible and attractive night-dive spot.

Reef inhabitants are parrotfish, French angels, damsels, Spanish hogfish and yellow snappers. Spotted, moray eels peek out from the crevices.

☆☆☆☆☆ **Town Pier** refers to the "old pier" in the center of town, between the customs office and the fish market. Town Pier is a popular site, especially for night dives. For safety reasons, the diving here is subject to permission from the harbormaster. All divers must check into the Harbormaster's office, located at the old fort with the cannon next to the main government building. Double-check with the tugboat captain on duty before entering the water.

Town Pier's main attractions are the submerged pillars which support a variety of marine life—octopi, seahorses, basket and tube sponges, Christmas-tree worms, orange-tube coral, arrow crabs. Walls of grunts, queen angels, spotted drums, blue chromis, morays, blue tangs, doctorfish and barracuda inhabit the area.

☆☆☆ **Lighthouse Reef** takes its name from the nearby Willemstoren Lighthouse and is located at the southernmost point of the island. It is a shore dive which can be entered at the Lighthouse or at most any point west. Due to the surf, this dive is only recommended to experienced, open-water divers. During calm seas, however, this site can also be dived by the novice if accompanied by a qualified dive master or instructor.

Lighthouse is aglow with sea plumes, sea fans, star, yellow-pencil, and brains corals. Marine life tends to be larger than at most other sites and includes parrotfish, schoolmasters, snappers, and sea turtles. Old anchors and chains rest in this area, the remains of ships wrecked prior to the lighthouse's 1838 opening.

☆☆☆☆ **Red Slave** is reached by driving south from Kralendijk, past the Solar Salt Works beyond the second set of slave huts. Strong currents limit this site to experienced, open-water divers.

The size and number of fish at Red Slave is spectacular. It is not unusual to spot four-foot tiger, yellowfin, or Nassau groupers. Gorgonians, orange crinoids, and black corals are found on the southern slope. Artifacts from pre-lighthouse wrecks rest on the slope such as anchors and ballast stones from the 1829 shipwreck *H.M.S. Barham.*

☆☆☆☆ **Pink Beach**, named for the unusual pinkish tint of the sand, is either a boat or shore dive. Drive south from Kralendijk, past the Solar Salt Works, to the abandoned salt barn on the right. Park by the barn or along the road and walk north of the barn to the beach. The mooring offshore marks the start of the dive.

Seaward of the mooring are clumps of staghorn coral and gorgonians. Schools of goatfish, porgies, and horse-eye jacks feed in this area with many large barracuda and stingrays.

☆☆☆☆☆ The dive sites surrounding Klein Bonaire are great for both diving and snorkeling. **Leonora's Reef**, on the north side is a snorkeler's paradise heavily covered with yellow pencil coral, fire coral, star coral and elkhorn stands on a narrow shallow terrace. West of the mooring are pillar coral formations. Expect to be greeted by masses of fish. "Attack" yellowtail snappers and tiny royal blue fish are joined at cleaning stations by tiger, yellowmount and rare yellowfin groupers.

☆☆☆☆ **Hands Off Reef** was named in 1981 when an experiment was conducted to determine whether inexperienced and camera-carrying divers do more damage to the corals than others do. "Hands Off," as the name implies, was not to be dived, designated solely as a control for later comparison to unlimited-access dives.

The reef slope is alive with black margate, grouper, rockhinds, and parrots. Some of the narrow valleys of the drop-off zone contain the remains of coral-head "avalanches" worth exploring.

☆☆☆☆ Nearby is **Forest**, another fabulous snorkeling and diving spot. The reef starts at 15 feet, dropping off to undiveable depths. This site is named for the abundant black coral "trees" growing at 60 ft from the wall. Two-ft queen triggerfish, friendly morays, filefish, sting rays, puffers and an abundance of small critters roam the "forest."

☆☆☆☆☆ **Twixt** is just north of Forest, around the southwest bend of Klein Bonaire. It provides excellent opportunities for wide-angle photography with huge basket sponges, sea whips, black coral, huge pastel fans, tube sponges, and star corals. Depths range between 15 and 100 feet. The coral wall slopes down to a sandy bottom. Seas are almost always calm and flat here.

☆☆☆☆ Large groupers frequent the pillar coral cleaning station at the upper edge of **Carl's Hill**. Named after photographer Carl Roessler, this spot is great for snorkeling and diving. The drop-off begins at 15 feet and drops sharply to 80 feet, creating a narrow precipice called Venus Mound. An occasional strong current cleanses the huge purple finger sponges on the slope. West of the mooring divers will find a buttress and sand valley, lined with coral rocks and cleaning stations—areas where fish line up to have barber or "cleaner" shrimp pick parasites from their mouths.

☆☆☆☆ **Ebo's Reef,** is superb for video and still photography. Shallow enough for snorkeling, the dropoff starts at 20 feet and slopes off to a sandy bottom at 150 feet. Dramatic overhangs of black coral grow in less than 30 feet of water. Masses of grunts, Spanish hogfish, groupers, sergeant majors, parrotfish, and yellowtail swarm the shelf. Small tunnels along the shelf are good hiding places for juvenile fish and small critters.

☆☆☆☆☆ **Knife Reef** is excellent for snorkeling and diving. A shallow half-circle of elkhorn coral creates a mini "lagoon" protecting star coral heads, gorgonians, and a multitude of fish. Bermuda chubs, peacock flounders, lizardfish and yellowhead jawfish rove the shallow terrace. The drop-off zone is fairly barren (the result of reef slides), but gorgonians, stinging coral, and yellow pencils thrive.

☆☆☆ Another snorkeler's delight is **Sampler.** Resident spotted eels and hordes of tamed, friendly fish will charm you as you investigate the lovely pillar- and staghorn-coral formations.

☆☆☆ Off the main island, in front of the Habitat dive shop is **La Machaca.** Ideal for night and warm-up dives this site is named after a small, wrecked fishing boat. Every variety of fish found in Bonaire's waters can be seen here by divers and snorkelers. An old tiger grouper, a spotted moray, and two black margates swim inquisitively throughout the wreck.

☆☆☆ **Petries Pillar** derives its name from the colony of pillar coral that grows atop the reef face. To reach Petries Pillar, travel north toward Gotomeer, turn left about half a mile past the last house onto an unpaved road. Follow that road down to the sea. Petries Pillar can be dived by boat or from shore.

☆☆☆☆☆ **1000 Steps (Piedra Haltu)** may be either a boat or a shore dive, though a boat dive may be easier and will definitely save you steps. To reach 1000 Steps, drive north from town along the scenic road towards Gotomeer until you reach the entrance of the Radio Nederland transmitting station. On your left are steep concrete steps leading down the mountainside to a sandy beach and the dive site.

Swim through the marked channel to s sandy shallow terrace. Gorgonians and flower corals are abundant. Lavender shrimp, barracuda, black durgons, yellowtail snappers, horse-eye jacks and schoolmasters populate the reef.

☆☆☆☆ **Ol' Blue** is a snorkeling paradise with mountainous star coral, swaying gorgonians, walls of reef fish, cleaning stations and calm waters. Get there by driving north along the scenic road to Gotomeer past the transmitting station to the white coral-rubble beach. The dive site is at the point where the road descends to the ocean and the cliff bends away from the road.

☆☆☆ **Rappel** is considered one of the best dives on the island. Named for its sheer cliff face, divers have been know to "rappel" down the wall. This is usually a boat dive, but may be reached by swimming out from Karpata.

Rappel's exceptional marine life includes, orange seahorses, green moray eels, spiny lobster, squid, marbled grouper, orange tube coral, shrimp, encrusting sponges, black coral and dense pink-tipped anemones.

☆☆☆☆☆ **Nukove** is off a little road that lies between Boca Dreifi and Playa Frans. It is a shore dive with a channel cut through the jungle of elkhorn coral which grows to the surface.

Numerous juveniles, shrimp and anemones may be seen in the cut. To the south are huge sponges, black coral, crinoids and sheet and scroll corals. Scrawled filefish, black durgons, grouper, wrasses and barracuda are in residence.

☆☆☆☆ **Boca Slagbaai** provides opportunity to see the best examples of buttress formations in Bonaire water. In addition, green morays, white spotted filefish, tarpon and barracuda are in abundance. Slagbaai boasts six concrete cannon replicas, halved and buried for the 1974 film, *Shark Treasure*.

To reach this dive, drive through the village of Rincon, into Washington/Slagbaai National park where you will follow the green arrows to Slagbaai. The center of the bay is barren, but a swim to the north brings across ridges and valleys of coral. Excellent snorkeling is to the south where two cannons may be viewed at the southern-most point of the bay.

☆☆☆ **Playa Funchi**, located in Washington/Slagbaai National Park, is another popular snorkeling area. From Rincon follow the green or yellow signs. Enter next to the man-made pier and swim north for the best snorkeling. Rays, parrotfish, rock hinds, jacks, groupers and angels swim through fields of staghorn coral.

Touch the Sea

Learn to pet moray eels, tickle sea anemones, get a manicure from a cleaner shrimp, massage the tummy of a "deadly" scorpion fish and befriend marine animals from which one normally keeps a safe distance. Diving with Touch-the-Sea creator, Dee Scarr, is an experience divers won't soon forget.

Ms. Scarr recommends that divers not try these antics without first participating in her program which includes classroom and underwater time. Bring or rent a camera—you'll enjoy shooting these normally hard-to-get-close-to creatures.

Arrangements to dive with Dee Scarr must be made prior to your trip to Bonaire by writing to her c/o Touch the Sea, P.O. Box 369, Bonaire, Netherlands Antilles, or calling 8529 on the island. From the U.S., 011-599-7-8529. A maximum of four divers may participate in one dive. Touch-the-sea programs close down for a few weeks during summer.

In the U.S., specialized land programs are offered for universities and groups.

"Touch the Sea" is a PADI Specialty Certification available to all certified divers. Dee Scarr is author of a book titled *Touch the Sea*, a children's book, *Coral's Reef,* and *The Gentle Sea.*

Dive Operators

Bonaire Scuba Center at the Black Durgon Inn offers reef and wreck diving trips by reservation. Resort and certification courses.

Carib Inn Dive Shop is a full service dive shop at the Carib Inn. Owner Bruce Bowker has been diving Bonaire for over 20 years and takes divers on his personalized tours of the south coast. Reef trips; resort, certification and advanced courses. Equipment sales, rental and repair. ☎ 011-599-7-5295 or write P.O. Box 68, Bonaire, NA.

Dee Scarr's "Touch the Sea" ☎ 011-599-7-8529 (see above)

Dive Inn is at three locations: Sunset Inn, Sunset Beach Hotel and Parnassia Apartments. Offers scuba packages, courses, reef trips, picnic trips. ☎ 011-599-7-8761; fax 011-599-7-8513 or write Kaya C.E.B. Hellmund 27, Bonaire, NA.

Neal Watson's Bonaire Undersea Adventures located at the Coral Regency Resort, offers dive training, shore and boat dives, night dives, equipment rental. ☎ 800-327-8150; in Bonaire, 011-599-7-5580; fax 305-359-0071 or write P.O. Box 21766, Ft. Lauderdale FL 33335.

Peter Hughes Dive Bonaire at the Divi Flamingo Beach Resort & Casino specializes in reef trips; resort, certification and advance courses; underwater photo and video courses. Daily E-6 and color print processing. Equipment sales, rental, and repair. Dive packages. ☎ 800-367-3484; in Bonaire 011-599-7-8285 or write Divi Resorts, 54 Gunderman Road, Ithaca, NY 14850.

Sand Dollar Dive and Photo at the Sand Dollar Beach Club offers certification, advanced, rescue, and divemaster courses. Reef trips, park trips, underwater photo and video courses. Same day E-6 and print processing. Equipment sales, rental and repair. Fishing, sailing, snorkeling, water skiing. ☎ 800-345-0805 or write P.O. Box 175, Bonaire, NA.

Great Adventures Bonaire offers certification and underwater photography programs, boat and shore dives, night dives and equipment rental. ☎ 800-424-0004; in Bonaire 011-599-7-7507.

Habitat Dive Center at Captain Don's Habitat is a PADI facility offering resort, certification and advanced courses; reef trips and 24-hour shore diving. ☎ 800-327-6709; in Bonaire 011-599-7-8240 or write P.O. Box 88, Bonaire, NA.

Accommodations

Bonaire's entire tourist trade revolves around its beautiful reefs. All but three of the island's hotels were built in the last 20 years and especially to accommodate divers. All have dive shops attached or nearby. Money saving dive/accommodation packages can be arranged through any listed below. Rates listed are winter prices.

Bruce Bowker's **Carib Inn** is one of Bonaire's most charming and intimate dive resorts. Oceanfront accommodations are air conditioned and have cable TV. Maid service, pool. Full service scuba facilities. Studio/ one-bedroom $59-89 daily. Two-bedroom suites, $119 daily. ☎ 800-223-9815 or 212-545-8469, or write P.O. Box 68, Bonaire NA.

Coral Regency Resort is a new all-suite ocean front resort. Each suite has a private balcony or patio with oceanview. Kitchens, cable TV, telephone, air conditioning and ceiling fans. Open-air restaurant and bar, pool. Neil Watson's Undersea Adventures full service dive facility. Packages.

Rooms, $45-$65 daily; one-bedroom suites, $160-$190 daily. Credit cards accepted. ☎ 800-327-8150 or write P.O. Box 21766, Fort Lauderdale FL 33335.

Divi Flamingo Beach Resort & Casino is a luxury resort on the beach overlooking Calabas Reef. A few have balconies directly over the water where you can view the reef and fish swimming by. All rooms are air-conditioned with private bath. Two pools, tennis, jacuzzi. Two excellent open air restaurants, casino, dive shop. Standard, $150 daily, deluxe, $185. Credit cards accepted. ☎ 800-367-3484 or write Divi Hotels, 2401 NW 34th Ave., Miami FL 33142.

Sunset Beach Hotel located on Playa Lechi Beach. New renovated rooms are air-conditioned with cable TV and telephone. Restaurant, beach bar, gift shop, tennis, dive shop. Laundry, dry-cleaning and babysitting services available. Private bath. Reef dives off the hotel beach. Very nice. Rooms are $100-130 daily; suites $160 daily. Credit cards accepted. ☎ 800-722-0205 or write ICS Scuba and Travel, 5254 Merrick Road, Suite 5, Massapequa NY 11758.

Harbour Village Beach Resort sits opposite Klein Bonaire on a powdery sand beach. Seventy two spacious, air- conditioned rooms, one- and two-bedroom suites with French doors leading to patios or terraces, cable TV, telephones, hair dryers. Pool, two restaurants, bar, marina, dive shop. Meeting and banquet facilities. Rooms are $205-265 daily; suites 365. Third person $25 per day. Credit cards accepted. ☎ 800-424-0004; fax 305-6690646 or write 1450 Madruga Ave, Coral Gables FL 33146.

Captain Don's Habitat offers deluxe, oceanfront cottages, cabanas, villas, studios. From $145 to $240 daily. Entire villas from $380-440 daily. Dive shop, restaurant, bar, pool, gift shop. Credit cards accepted. ☎ 800-344-4439; fax 305-225-0527 or write P.O. Box 115, Bonaire NA

The **Sunset Inn** overlooks Kralendijk Bay, next to Dive Inn. Five double rooms and two suites are air conditioned with refrigerator and remote cable TV. Suites and two rooms have kitchenettes ☎ 599-7-8291; fax 599-7-8118 or write Caradonna Caribbean Tours, P.O. Box 3299, Longwood FL 32779.

Sand Dollar Beach Club features luxurious oceanfront condominiums— all air conditioned, with kitchens, private baths, cable TV, balcony or terrace. Dive shop on premises with excellent diving off the beach. Tennis, pool bar, grocery store, sailing, babysitting. Studios, $145 daily, one-bedroom, $175 daily, two-bedroom, $225 daily. Credit cards accepted. ☎ 800-766-6016; fax 617-321-1568; or write Travel Marketing, 343 Neponset St., Canton MA 02021. Credit cards.

Other Activities

Exploring **Washington-Slagbaai Park** is a nice day's alternative to diving. One of the first national parks in the Caribbean, it is home to over 190 species of birds, thousand of towering candle cacti, herds of goats, stray donkeys, and lizards and more lizards. The park covers the entire northern portion of the island. Its terrain is varied and those who are ambitious enough to climb some of the steep hills are rewarded with sweeping views.

Cars can be taken through the park, and the two driving trails offer visitors the choice of a through tour of the park or a shorter excursion. A map, available at the entrance gate, indicates points of interest. The park is open from 8 am to 5 pm, though no one is permitted to enter after 3:30 pm. Entrance fee is $2. Visitors are advised to bring a picnic lunch, binoculars, a camera, sunscreen and plenty of drinking water. Opportunities for exotic bird photography are outstanding.

Driving south you'll pass roadside cliffs with 500-year-old Arawak Indian inscriptions. Just beyond is Rincon, the island's oldest village. A drive to the southern tip of the island will bring you past primitive stone huts which were once homes to slaves working the salt flats. It is hard to imagine how six slaves shared one hut when you see the small size of them. Nearby, 30-foot obelisks were built in 1838 to help mariners locate their anchorages. Further down is the island's oldest lighthouse, Willemstoren, built in 1837.

The salt ponds at Goto Meer are always occupied with resident flamingos, but flamingo watching is at its best at the solar salt flats on the southern end of the island. You can only watch from the road as the area is a sanctuary, but the huge bird population (10,000 to 15,000) en masse is an artful display. Every day at sunset, the entire flock flies the short trip to Venezuela. During Spring, a highlight is seeing the fluffy gray young. It is only after months of consuming brine shrimp that they attain their characteristic pink color. Since the birds are extremely shy, bring binoculars.

Guided bus tours of the national park or entire island are available through Bonaire Sightseeing Tours. ☎ 599-7-8778.

Boca Slagbaai, Washington/Slagbaai National Park

Ernest van Vliet's **Windsurfing Bonaire** features top-of-the-line equipment and classes for beginners to advance board sailors. Production or custom boards can be rented by the hours, day or week. He even provides transportation to and from island resorts twice a day.

Tours through the tiny capital city of Kralendijk ("coral dike" in Dutch) are highlighted by the colorful, well preserved buildings such as Fort Oranje, Queen Wilhemina Park, Government House and the miniature Greek temple-style fish market. The town pier makes for an interesting stop as do any one of the Kralendijk's open air bars and restaurants. Sunset watching is best at Pink Beach at the southeastern part of the island.

Dining

Restaurants in Bonaire offer a unique selection of local, creole and seafood dishes. Enjoy a delicious Cantonese dinner at the **China Garden Restaurant**,—an old restored mansion on Kaya Grandi; or Caribbean seafood and steak dishes at the **Chibi Chibi** open-air restaurant (located at the Divi Flamino Resort) or **Paul's Oceanfront Restaurant** in the Coral Regency Resort. A few miles north of Kralendijk on the coast road brings you to the **Bonaire Caribbean Club** for a cozy seaside and caveside lunch or dinner. Chefs at the **Beefeater Restaurant**, Playa Grande no. 3, will prepare a banquet of fish or steak dishes at your table. (☎ 8081 or 8773 for reservations).

On Thursdays **Playa Lechi Restaurant** at the Sunset Beach Hotel will shuttle you across the water to Klein Bonaire for a romantic and delicious beach barbecue. Sign up at the hotel's front desk before Wednesday, 6 pm—☎ 5300. Carry-out meals are offered by the **Green Parrot Restaurant** at the new Sand Dollar Beach Club (☎ 5454).

Local foods include *juwana*, a stew or soup made from local iguana; *piska hasa*, a fried fish dish served with funchi and fried plantains; *tutu*, funchi with frills—cornmeal mush with black-eyed peas; and goat stew made with onions, peppers, tomato, soy sauce and spices.

In Kralendijk, local dishes are served at the **Supercorner Playa** (☎ 8115); **Borinque Snack Bar** on Kaya Manuel Piar; **La Sonrisa** (☎ 5017); **Tom & Jerry Park**, behind the tourist office and **Julius' Place**, on Kaya L.D. Gerharts, (☎ 5544).

Helpful Phone Numbers

POLICE: ☎ 8000

TAXI: ☎ 8100

AIRPORT: ☎ 8500

MEDICAL FACILITY: ☎ 8900 (San Francisco Hospital)

FACTS

Nearest Recompression Chamber: San Francisco Hospital on the island.

Getting There: ALM Antillean Airlines offers daily service from Miami to Bonaire's Flamingo International Airport and Friday, Saturday and Sunday direct service from Atlanta's Hartsfield Airport. AVENSA has connecting flights from New York via Caracas, Venezuela with Servivensa, an affiliated carrier, on Wednesdays, Fridays and Sundays. AIR ARUBA offers direct service out of Newark International Airport on Fridays and Saturdays.

Driving: Foreign and international licenses accepted. Traffic to the right.

Language: The official language for Bonaire is Dutch, but residents speak Papiamento—a blend of Dutch, African and English. English and Spanish are widely spoken.

Documents: U.S. and Canadian citizens may stay up to three months providing they prove citizenship with a passport, birth certificate or a voter's registration card.

Flamingos at the Salt Flats

All visitors must have a confirmed room reservation before arriving and a return ticket. A visa is required for visits over 90 days.

Customs: U.S. citizens may bring home $400 worth of articles including 1 quart of liquor and 200 cigarettes. Canadian citizens may bring in C$300 of goods once each calendar year.

Currency: Netherland Antilles Florin or Guilder. U.S. $1.00 = NAfl 1.77.

Credit Cards: Widely accepted.

Climate: Mean temperature 82 °F year round; 22 inches rainfall annually.

Clothing: A wetsuit is not necessary, especially in summer, but adds comfort for repeated dives and night dives. Lightweight casual cottons. Informal.

Electricity: 127 volts, 50 cycles. Adapters are necessary.

Time: Atlantic (EST + 1 hr.)

Tax: Airport departure tax.

Religious Services: Roman Catholic, Adventist, Jehovah's Witness.

Additional Information: Tourism Corporation of Bonaire, Kaya Simon Bolivar #12, Kralendijk, Bonaire, Netherlands Antilles. ☎ 011-5997-8322 or 8649.

IN THE US: Tourism Corporation of Bonaire, The Carriage House at 201 1/2 E. 29th Street, New York NY 10016. ☎ 800-U BONAIRE or 212-779-0242.

Photo by Jon Huber

British Virgin Islands

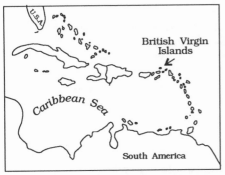

British Virgin Islands

Caribbean Sea

South America

Windswept and wildly beautiful, the British Virgins are a chain of 36 sparsely-inhabited islands and rocks lying 60 miles east of Puerto Rico. Most tourist activity centers around the four larger islands—Tortola, Anegada, Virgin Gorda and Jost Van Dyke. Except for Anegada, a flat coral slab surrounded by shallow reefs, the islands are mountainous and of volcanic origin. The highest point is Mt. Sage on Tortola at 1,781 ft.

The capital and chief port is Road Town on Tortola, the largest island and home to 80 percent of the BVI residents, with a population of 13,000. A toll bridge connects Tortola to Beef Island and the international airport which is being extended to accommodate large jets. Currently, international flights are through Puerto Rico or Antigua.

Save for a few clubs and discos that come to life on weekends, nightlife is quiet. The islands are devoid of casinos or high-rise hotels. Overall, BVI life is relaxed, yet retains some British formality in terms of dignity and manners. Crime is rare and nudity is not encouraged. Visitors are asked to respect the residents' wishes by covering up in town and dressing "appropriately" in restaurants and bars.

The BVI's prime attractions are hundreds of sheltered coves, isolated beaches and protected marine parks. Superb snorkeling and diving exists around the out-islands with towering coral pinnacles, underwater caves, canyons, lava tunnels and almost 200 different wrecks. Most areas have little or no surge and only gentle currents. Visibility may reach anywhere from 50 to more than 100 ft.

Clustered around the Sir Francis Drake Channel and protected from high wind and waves, the islands are enormously popular with sailors. In fact, half the BVI tourist "beds" are aboard the hundreds of yachts in Tortola's marinas.

Area Contributor: Gayla Kilbride, Kilbride Underwater Tours.

The best time to visit the BVI is between October and June. Reduced rates at hotels and on charter boats are available during July through September, hurricane season. Air temperature is 80 to 90° F year round.

History

In 1493 Christoper Columbus discovered the islands and named them *St. Ursula y las Once Mil Virgenes* (St. Ursula and the Eleven Thousand Virgins.) He found peaceful tribes of Arawak Indians on the larger islands. The Arawaks were the principal BVI residents until driven out by the Caribs, a warrior tribe, who dominated the area until 1955 when Emperor Charles V of Spain sent an invasion force to take over. By the turn of the 17th century most of the Caribs had fled or been killed.

During the 1500's, Dutch buccaneers and pirates held Tortola while preying on ships passing through Sir Francis Drake Channel. The pirates were finally driven out in 1672 by English planters who, with slave labor, developed the land for farming, and thrived on the export of bananas, sugarcane, citrus fruits, coconuts, mangoes and root crops until slavery was abolished in the early 1800's. Today, tourism has replaced agriculture as the islands' largest employer.

Politically, the islands are a British colony administered by an executive council with a governor appointed by the Crown.

Best Dive and Snorkeling Sites

☆☆☆☆☆ Wreck of the **R.M.S. Rhone**, featured in the movie *The Deep*, is by far the most popular dive in the BVI. Struck by a ferocious hurricane in October, 1867, the *Royal Mail Steamer, Rhone* was hurled onto the rocks at Salt Island as its captain, Robert F. Wooley, struggled desperately to reach open sea to weather the remainder of the storm.

The force with which the 310-ft vessel crashed upon the rocks broke the hull in two leaving two superb dive spots, a great snorkeling area at the stern, which lies in 30 ft of water amid rocks and boulders, and a good area for diving at the bow, at 80 ft on a sandy bottom. The top of the rudder sits just 15 ft below the surface. Its superstructure, encrusted with corals, sponges, and sea fans, provides a dramatic setting for underwater photography.

Fish greet divers and snorkelers as they enter the water. Living among the wreckage is a 300-pound jew fish, a very curious four-and-one-half-ft barracuda, named Fang, schools of snappers, grunts, jacks, arrow crabs,

British Virgin Islands

Caribbean Sea

Anegada

Virgin Gorda

Tortola

Jost Van Dyke

Sir Francis Drake Channel

St. John (U.S.V.I.)

Peter Island

Salt Island

Ginger

Cooper

Norman Island

11 ← (3 mi.)

5 ← (11 mi.)

Dive and Snorkelling Sites

1. The "RMS Rhone"
2. "Chikuzen"
3. Chimney
   (Great Dog Island)
4. Gary's Grottos
5. "Rokus"
6. Alice in Wonderland
7. P.O.S.
8. Joe's Cave
9. Van Ryans Rock
10. Invisibles
11. Paramatta
12. The Baths
13. Crawl National Park
14. The Caves
15. Manchioneel Bay

squirrel fish, and yellow tail. The *Rhone* is a boat-access dive. Sea conditions are usually calm; recommended for novices. Visibility is usually excellent, from 50 to more than 100 ft. Also, the *Rhone* is a national park and off limits to coral collecting and spear fishing. The wreck is located off Black Rock Point on the southwest tip of Salt Island.

☆☆☆☆ The *Chikuzen* is a 268-ft steel-hulled refrigerator ship that went down off Tortola's east end in 1981. Her hull, intact in 75 ft of water, has become a fish condominium with visibility so good that dive guide, Gayla Kilbride, tells how she can stand on the bow and see the stern.

Tenants of the *Chikuzen* are several large sting rays, occasional black tip sharks, schools of yellowtail, filefish, barracuda, octopus, drum fish, and jew fish. The ship rests on her port side allowing easy entry. Coral is just beginning to form on the hull. The *Chikuzen* is fine for novice divers. By boat access only. The outstanding visibility and large number of marine animals make for excellent photography.

☆☆☆ **The Chimney**, located at Great Dog Island, off the west end of Virgin Gorda is a spectacular coral archway and canyon covered with a wide variety of soft corals, sponges and rare, white coral. Hundreds of fish follow divers and snorkelers along the archway to a coral-wrapped, tube-like formation resembling a huge chimney. Inside the Chimney are circling groupers, crabs, brittle starfish, spiny lobster, banded coral shrimp, queen angels, tube sponges and schooling fish. This is a favorite spot for close-up photography. Maximum depth of the Chimney is 45 ft. The many shallow areas and protected-cove location make this a "best snorkel dive" as well as a good selection for the scuba diver. Boat access only. Some surge and currents when wind is out of the north.

☆☆☆ **Gary's Grottos** is near the shoreline, four miles north of Spanish Town on Virgin Gorda. It is a shallow reef characterized by three huge arches which give the feel of swimming through a tunnel. At the end of the "tunnel" divers find a cave guarded by a friendly moray. This rocky area is teeming with shrimp, squid and sponges. Protected from wind and waves, the cove is also a choice spot for a night dive. The average depth is 30 ft.

☆☆ **The Wreck of the Rokus.** On New Year's Eve, 1929, the Greek ship *Rokus* hit the reef on the southeast tip of Anegada. She sank in 40 ft of water with much of her hull remaining above the surface until hurricane Frederick struck in 1979. Remains of her cargo of animal bones can be found scattered around the wreckage. The reef surrounding the hull is pretty with large formations of elkhorn and staghorn as well as brain

Anemones

coral. An enormous eel has been spotted under the wreck by a number of divers. During the winter months, February through March, the song of migrating humpback whales can be heard from this site. This area is occasionally rough with small surges.

☆☆☆☆ **Alice in Wonderland,** a coral wall in the southwest bay off Ginger Island, slopes from 40 ft to a sandy bottom at 90 ft. Along this ornate wall awaits a fantasy of huge mushroom corals, villainous overhangs, and gallant brain corals which meld into a fairytale setting for longnose butterfly fish, rays, conch and garden eels. Visibility is good and seas are usually calm. Alice in Wonderland is a boat dive, good for photography, free diving, and novice through expert scuba diving.

☆☆☆☆ **P.O.S.** is named after "Project Ocean Search", a Cousteau project which is operational once a year. The reef, which follows the shoreline of Cockroach Island (one of the Dog Islands), is a must for every underwater photographer. Beautiful, towering pillar, staghorn, and elkhorn corals at 35 ft are swept by huge silvery tarpon, French angels, crabs, lobsters, and schooling fish. The "Keyhole," a hole in one of the coral walls, is just big enough to frame a diver for an underwater portrait.

☆☆☆ **Joe's Cave** is an underwater cavern located on the west side of West Dog Island. It can be explored by swimming from the entrance, at 20 ft, down to 75 ft where you'll find a magnificent opening to the sky. Outside the cave are many corals and rock formations. Eels abound. The bottom terrain is rough. Schools of gleaming copper sweepers live inside. This is a protected area with no current or surges. A good choice for divers of all levels.

☆☆ **Van Ryan's Rock** is a sea mount in the middle of Drake's Channel between Beef Island and Virgin Gorda. The top is at 16 ft and the bottom at 55 ft, with boulders and coral leading down to a sandy plain. Nurse sharks, eels, huge turtles, lobster, jacks, spade fish, and barracuda circle it. Divers and snorkelers should take care to avoid the huge clumps of fire coral. A current is occasionally encountered.

☆☆☆ **Invisibles**, a sea mount off Tortola's northeast tip, is a haven for nurse shark, eels, turtles and all types of reef fish from the smallest to the largest. Gayla Kilbride describes this area as a "Symphony of Fish." Depths go from three down to 65 ft, a nice range for both snorkeling and diving.

Snorkeling

Snorkeling gear may be rented or borrowed from most hotels and charter boats, although it is best to have your own to insure a comfortable fit. Be sure to bring your camera. Snorkeling trips are offered by the dive shops.

☆☆☆☆ **Wreck of the** *Paramatta* which ran aground on her maiden voyage in 1853, rests at 30 ft off the southeast end of Anegada. The ship is on a dense coral reef—perfect for snorkelers. If you stand on the ship's engine, you'll be shoulder deep. Enormous reef fish swim around the wreck, including a 200-pound jew fish, 30-pound groupers, butterfly fish, turtles, and rays. Still remaining are the stern and bow sections, long chain, port holes, and cleats of the wreck, all sitting amid beautiful elkhorn and staghorn coral formations, large sea fans, brain corals and red and orange sponges. This is a great spot for underwater portraits.

☆☆☆☆☆ **The Baths**, at the southern tip of Virgin Gorda, are where you'll find the islands' most famous beaches. The area is a natural landscape of partially submerged grottoes and caves formed by a jumble of enormous granite boulders. It is a favorite beach-access snorkeling area and one of the biggest tourist attractions in the BVI. The caves shelter a variety of tropical fish.

You can find this area by taking the trail which starts at the end of the Baths Road. A small bar just off the beach rents snorkel equipment. Beware of dinghies! The Baths is a favorite of cruise ship visitors.

☆☆ **Crawl National Park** is perfect for beginning snorkelers. Also on Virgin Gorda, it is reached via a palm lined trail from Tower Road. This is a bit north of the Baths. A boulder formation which has created a natural pond is good for children.

☆☆☆☆ **The Caves** at Norman Island are accessible only by boat. It is a favorite snorkeling-photo site, bright with sponges, corals and schools of small fish. The reef slopes down to 40 ft. Norman Island is rumored to have inspired Robert Louis Stevenson's *Treasure Island*

and the Caves are reputed to be old hiding places for pirate treasure. Moorings are maintained by the National Park Trust.

☆☆ **Manchioneel Bay,** Cooper Island has a beautiful shallow reef with packs of fish around the moorings. And **Anegada's** northern shores are fringed with shallow reefs.

Additional good snorkeling sites are found at Benures Bay, the Bight and Little Bight off Norman Island. At Peter Island, try the south shore at Little Harbor and the western shore at Great Harbor.

Note: A wetsuit top, shortie, or wetskin is recommended for night dives and winter diving. Snorkelers should have some protection from sunburn. The BVI reefs are protected by law, and no living thing may be taken. "Take only pictures, leave only bubbles."

Dive Operators

Kilbride's Underwater Tours. Bert Kilbride has been diving the British Virgin Islands since the 1950's—longer than anyone else. Well known as a treasure hunter, he has found 138 wrecks on Anegada Reef alone. Together with his wife Gayla and 14 others of the Kilbride clan, Bert operates a 42-ft dive boat named *Shah* at Norman Island and the *Sea Trek,* also 42 ft, out of the Bitter End Yacht Club. Their boats take you to 50 different dive locations. You may be escorted by any one of 16 diving Kilbrides. As personal friends of the "better mannered fish" the Kilbrides provide a diving tour that is educational as well as entertaining. Tours can be booked by writing to Box 40, Saba Rock, Virgin Gorda, BVI. ☎ 809-495-9638; fax 809-495-9369. Mail may take as long as six weeks so write early. Kilbrides serve the North Sound resorts and their tours cover all the islands. Resort courses through PADI certification and open water checkouts are available. Rates: $60 for a one-tank dive; $70-$90 for a two-tank tour— less 10% for bringing your own gear. Non-divers can join for a small fee.

Dive BVI Ltd., a PADI five-star shop, operates out of Leverick Bay, Virgin Gorda Yacht Harbour & Peter Island. Rates are $75 for a two-tank dive; $210 for three two-tank dives. Rendezvous. Snorkeling. Resort courses through certification are available. Write: P.O. Box 1040, Virgin Gorda, BVI ☎ 809-495-5513/800-848-7078.

Underwater Safaris, at the Moorings Mariner Inn on Tortola and Cooper Island offers fast 42- and 30-ft dive boats; full service, rendezvous with yachts, PADI certification. The Tortola shop is the largest retail dive shop in the BVI. Rates: $55 for a one-tank dive; $80 for a two-tank tour. Write: P.O. Box 139, Road Town, Tortola. ☎ 800-537-7032 or 809-494-3235.

Baskin In the Sun at the Prospect Reef Resort Marina has two dive boats which can accommodate 10 and 20 divers comfortably. Rates: $55 for a one-tank tour; $80 for a two-tank; $25 snorkel trip. Super service—never carry a tank or gear. PADI five-star dive center. Package tours can be booked through Baskin in the Sun, P.O. Box 826, St. Thomas, VI 00803, BVI ☎ 809-494-2858/9 or 800-233-7938

Blue Water Divers, located at Nanny Cay on the south side of Tortola, serves divers staying at Sugar Mill or the Windjammer. Blue Water Divers operates a 47-ft catamaran and a 27-ft dive boat. Dive tours are to the eastern sites in the BVI, such as Jost Van Dyke, as well as all the sites in the channel. ☎ 809-494-2847. Write: P.O. Box 846, Road Town, Tortola, BVI.

Caribbean Images Tours, Ltd. offers snorkeling excursions aboard a 34-ft boat. Half-day rate of $25 includes gear, refreshments, and instruction.

Island Diver Ltd at Village Cay Marina, Road Town offers reef and wreck tours, resort courses & snorkeling. ☎ 809-494-3878/52367.

Rainbow Visions Photography at Prospect Reef offers underwater still- and video-camera rentals. Processing. Custom videos and portraits. ☎ 809-494-2749. Write: P.O. Box 139, Road Town, Tortola, BVI.

Sailing And Scuba Live-Aboards:

Sail-dive vacations are an easy way for divers to enjoy a variety of sites and destinations. Live-aboard yachts are chartered with captain, captain and crew or "bare" to qualified sailors. Navigation is uncomplicated; you can tour most of the area without ever leaving sight of land. Most boats carry snorkeling gear as standard equipment; some of the large craft have compressors. And every dive shop offers some type of arrangement to accommodate seafarers.

With sailing almost a religion in the BVI, it is easy to customize a live-aboard dive or snorkeling vacation. If you are an experienced sailor and diver you can charter a bareboat and see the sights on your own. If you've never sailed before or have limited experience, you can "captain" a crewed yacht to find the best dive spots. If you've never sailed or dived, but want to learn both, you can charter a yacht with a crew that includes a divemaster (often the captains are qualified dive instructors) or arrange to rendezvous with a dive boat. Or you can book a week-long cruise on a commercial live-aboard where you'll meet other divers. Prices on private charters vary with the number of people in your party. With four to six people, a crewed yacht will average in cost about the same as a stay at a resort.

CUAN LAW

One of the world's largest trimarans (105 ft), *Cuan Law* was specifically designed with the scuba diver in mind. As with most live-aboards, you are offered "all the diving you can stand." Cuan Law accommodates 18 passengers in ten large, airy, double cabins, each with private head and shower. Rates from April through December start at $1200 per person for seven days and six nights. Transfers, tips, alcohol, scuba instruction are NOT included.

Cruises are booked up from three months to a year in advance. ☎ 800-648-3393 or write Trimarine Boat Company, P.O. Box 3160, Coos Bay OR 97420.

The Moorings Ltd. offers "Cabin ' N Cruise" tours for those wishing to enjoy a fully crewed sailing vacation without having to charter an entire yacht. Dive arrangements must be made separately. See listing below.

Conch Charters, Limited offers crewed sailing yachts from 30 to 50 ft. Prices range from $450 per person to $600 per person per week. (smaller boats carrying fewer divers are more expensive).

Bareboating

Private sailing yachts with diving guides and instructors are available from most of the charter operators listed below. You can arrange for your own personal live-aboard diving or snorkeling vacation. Be sure to specify your needs before going.

Bareboating can be surprisingly affordable for groups of four or more. Boats must be reserved six to nine months in advance for winter vacations and at least three months ahead for summer vacations.

Experience cruising on a similar yacht is required and you will be asked to fill out a questionnaire or produce a sailing resume. Instructor-skippers are available for refresher sailing. A cruising permit is required. For a complete list of charter companies contact the BVI Tourist Board at ☎ 800-835-8530 or write 370 Lexington Ave., Suite 511, NY, NY 10017.

The Moorings Ltd., Tortola, has been operating for 18 years. Their charter boats include Moorings 35, 38, 51, 50, 432 (43 ft), and 433 plus 39- and 42-ft catamarans. A Moorings 51, Morgan 60 or Gulfstar 60 may be chartered but with crew only. The Moorings' book "Virgin Anchorages" shows (aerial photographs) the best anchorages in the British Virgin Islands.

A three-day sailing vacation can be combined with a four-day resort/diving vacation at the Moorings Mariner Inn. Write to The Moorings, Ltd., 19345 US Hwy 19 North, Clearwater FL 34624-3193 ☎ 800-535-7289 or 813-535-1446.

Moorings dive-guide/boat captain, Jeff Williams has created a 62-page sailors' guide to dive and snorkeling titled *The Guide to Diving and Snorkeling in the British Virgin Islands*. You can pick up a copy at the Moorings or send $14.95 plus $1.50 (S & H) to DIVEntures, P.O. Box 115, Hopkinton, MA 01748.

Offshore Sailing School uses the Moorings boats and offers a "Learn to Sail" ($1200) package with the "Treasure Isle Hotel" and "Club Mariner" and an "Offshore, Live-aboard Cruising" Course in Tortola ($1,745 winter, $1,445 summer). The "Learn to Sail" course takes up half the day with plenty of time to make an afternoon dive or snorkel trip. The advanced course stops for snorkeling, but scuba is not possible. ☎ 800-535-7289.

B.V.I. Bareboats at the Inner Harbour Marina offers 32- to 50-ft yachts. Winter rates at $1,540 to $2,310; summer, $770-$1,225. ☎ 800-648-7240 or 809-494-4289. Write: P.O. Box 3018 Road Town, Tortola, BVI.

Discovery Yacht Charters at Nanny Cay has sailing yachts from 30 to 50 ft. Bareboat or crewed. ☎ 809-494-6026. Write: P.O. Box 281, Road Town, Tortola, BVI.

Accommodations

TORTOLA

Every type of accommodation is available in the BVI from tents to cottages, guesthouses, condos, luxury resorts to live aboard sailboats and motor yachts. Reservations can be made through your travel agent or the BVI Tourist Board at ☎ 800-835-8530 or in New York 212-696-0400.

Long Bay Beach Resort on Tortola's north shore has 82 deluxe hillside and beachfront accommodations. Beach, restaurant, tennis, pitch & putt gold. Rates start at $698 per person, per week for a seven-night, learn-to-dive vacation with breakfasts and four dinners. $160 refund for those who change their minds after a pool session. Dive packages with Baskin in the Sun. ☎ 800-729-9599. Write: P.O. Box 433, Road Town Tortola, BVI.

The Moorings-Mariner Inn, Tortola, is homeport to The Moorings charter boat operation. It has no beach. The poolside bar and restaurant are just a few steps from Underwater Safaris, the largest retail dive shop in the BVI.

The resort offers a new sail/dive vacation with three nights aboard a luxurious sailing yacht (snorkeling only) with your own skipper and provisions and four nights at the resort diving with Underwater Safaris. ☎ 800-535-7289, 809-494-2332 or write The Moorings Mariner Inn, 1305 US 19 S. Suite 402, Clearwater, FL 34624. Moderate.

Maria's By the Sea, Road Town, offers packages with Underwater Safaris. 20 rooms. Winter rates are $75 to $95 per day without diving. Write P.O. Box 206, Road Town, Tortola, BVI ☎ 809-494-2595.

Nanny Cay Resort & Marina, two miles southwest of Road Town, has 41 air-conditioned rooms from $125 per day in winter; $45 summer. TV, mini bars, phones, pool, restaurant, bar, tennis, windsurf school & dive packages. ☎ 800-786-4753. Write: P.O. Box 281, Road Town, Tortola, BVI.

Prospect Reef Resort is a sprawling ten-acre resort located on the west end of Road Town, Tortola, facing Sir Francis Drake Channel. The resort has over 130 rooms ranging from studios to standard rooms, full apartments, and luxury villas. This resort is the largest on Tortola and offers six tennis courts, miniature golf, two restaurants for casual food and drinks, and three pools. Rooms are cooled by ceiling fans and a breeze from the sea. An excellent buffet is served at the resort's Harbour Restaurant on Saturday nights. Scuba packages. ☎ 800-356-8937, 809-494-3311. Room rates, winter, from $130 per day. Write Box 104, Road Town, Tortola, BVI.

Treasure Isle Hotel, offering dive packages with **Sugarmill** on the northwest shore of Tortola, is a village of hillside cottages. Its proprietors Jeff and Jinx Morgan, are famous for their gourmet meals (they write for *Bon Apetit*). An old sugar mill houses the restaurant where you may dine by candlelight on conch stew, grouper salad, grilled swordfish and salads with lettuce from the Sugar Mill garden. Cooking classes available. Small beach. Rates for seven nights are from $966 per person including hotel, car rental, four gourmet dinners, six dives or resort course and two dives, day sail on schooner. ☎ 800-462-8834 or 809-495-4355. Write P.O. Box 425, Tortola, BVI. Moderate.

Treasure Isle Hotel has 40 rooms, pool, restaurant, air conditioning, bar. Dive packages with Underwater Safaris. package rates for diving and accommodations start at $683 per person, double. ☎ 800-537-7032 or 809-494-2501. Write: P.O. Box 68, Road Town, Tortola, BVI.

VIRGIN GORDA

The Bitter End Yacht Club is at John O'Point at Virgin Gorda's North Sound. Rooms are in luxury villas along the shore and hillside. The bar is a favorite story-swapping place for sailing and diving folk. Daily scuba trips arranged through Kilbride's Underwater Tours leave from the Bitter End Docks every morning. ☎ 800-872-2392, or 809-494-2746 or write P.O. Box 46, Virgin Gorda, BVI. Moderate.

Drake's Anchorage on Mosquito Island, just north of North Sound off Virgin Gorda, is a hideaway with ten beachfront units and two deluxe villas. The island has four lovely beaches, with snorkeling off shore and moorings for cruising sailboats. Scuba diving packages are arranged with Kilbride's Underwater Tours or Dive BVI. The dive shops pick you up at the dock. Mosquito Island can be reached by flying into Virgin Gorda and taking a cab to Leverick Bay where a Drake's boat will pick you up. ☎ 800-624-6651 or write Drake's Anchorage Resort Inn, P.O. Box 2510 Virgin Gorda, BVI. Expensive.

Biras Creek Estate has 34 luxury villas with garden & ocean views. Scuba packages, tennis, sailing. Packages for five nights in a suite and two nights on a 47-ft yacht, all meals, transfers, snorkeling equipment start at $1,250 per person (diving not included). ☎ 800-494-3557, 809-494-3555 or 914-763-5526. fax 914-763-5362. Write: P.O. Box 54, Virgin Gorda, BVI. ☎ 809-494-3555.

Other Activities and Sightseeing

Hiking and exploring are popular in the BVI. You will find deserted dungeons, sugar mills, pirate caves, rain forests and wooded trails. Tennis courts as well as horseback riding are provided by some of the hotels. Boardsailing and windsurfing equipment is available at many of the resorts.

TORTOLA

The three-acre **J.R. O'Neal Botanic Gardens** in the centre of Road Town feature a beautiful waterfall, lily pond and exotic tropical plants and birds. Nearby, on Main Street, is the **Virgin Island Folk Museum** which displays many artifacts from the *Rhone* and from early plantations. Hikers and botanists will find huge elephant-ear plants, and lush ferns under a

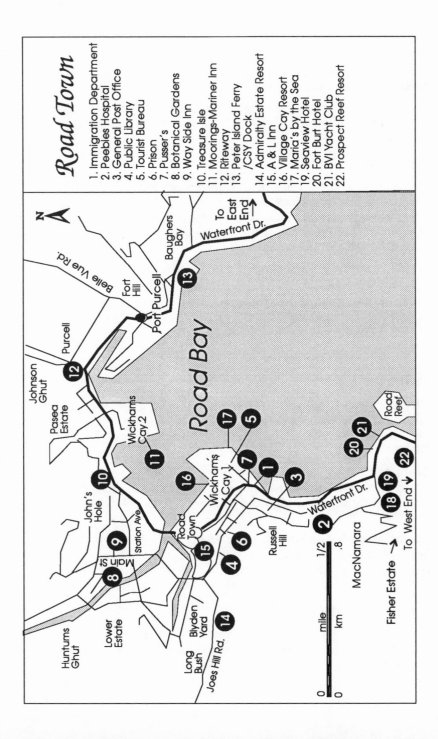

Road Town

1. Immigration Department
2. Peebles Hospital
3. General Post Office
4. Public Library
5. Tourist Bureau
6. Prison
7. Pusser's
8. Botanical Gardens
9. Way Side Inn
10. Treasure Isle
11. Moorings-Mariner Inn
12. Riteway
13. Peter Island Ferry /CSY Dock
14. Admiralty Estate Resort
15. A & L Inn
16. Village Cay Resort
17. Maria's by the Sea
19. Seaview Hotel
20. Fort Burt Hotel
21. BVI Yacht Club
22. Prospect Reef Resort

N

Belle Vue Rd.

Johnson Ghut

Pasea Estate

Purcell

Fort Hill

Baughers Bay

Port Purcell

To East End

Waterfront Dr.

Road Bay

Wickhams Cay 2

Wickhams Cay 1

John's Hole

Station Ave.

Road Town

Main St.

Huntums Ghut

Lower Estate

Long Bush

Blyden Yard

Joes Hill Rd.

Russell Hill

MacNamara

Fisher Estate

Waterfront Dr.

To West End

Road Reef

mile

km

1/2

.8

0

0

canopy of mahogany and manilkara trees at **Sage Mountain National Park.** Mt. Sage peaks at 1780 ft.

If you are cruising the BVI, be sure to visit **Stanley's** in Cane Garden Bay on the weekend where the steel band is reputed to be the best in the islands.

VIRGIN GORDA

Visitors will find the ruins of an 18th-century sugar mill at **Nail Bay** on Virgin Gorda's west coast. And just south of the Yacht Harbor at **Little Fort National Park** is some masonry from an old Spanish fortress. Monster granite boulders are at the **Spring Bay** beach between Little Fort National Park and the Baths.

Gorda Peak is a 265-acre national park with a wealth of mahogany trees and exotic plants.

There are small shops (NOT duty free) around Road Town, Tortola and Spanish Town, Virgin Gorda, specializing in local crafts and gifts.

Dining

TORTOLA

Rhymer's Beach Bar and Restaurant at Cane Garden Bay, Tortola, is a favorite among the locals. Serving fresh fish, lobster, it has Buffet Night on Tuesday and Saturdays. Open for breakfast, lunch and dinner. ☎ 54520.

Scatliffe's Tavern, another local favorite in Road Town, Tortola, specializes in local food such as fish soup made with coconut milk, conch fritters, ribs, and lobster dishes followed by fresh lime pie. Near the high school. ☎ 42797.

Carib Casseroles, on Tortola, has a "Meals on Keels" service for bareboaters experienced with boil-a-bags as well as sit down service. Food is a combination of Caribbean, French, Greek and Creole. Peanut Creole Soup, curry and casseroles are featured here. Moderate.

VIRGIN GORDA

The Bath & Turtle is a patio tavern in the Yacht Harbour serving breakfast, lunch, and dinner. Burgers, sandwiches, and homemade soups. ☎ 55239

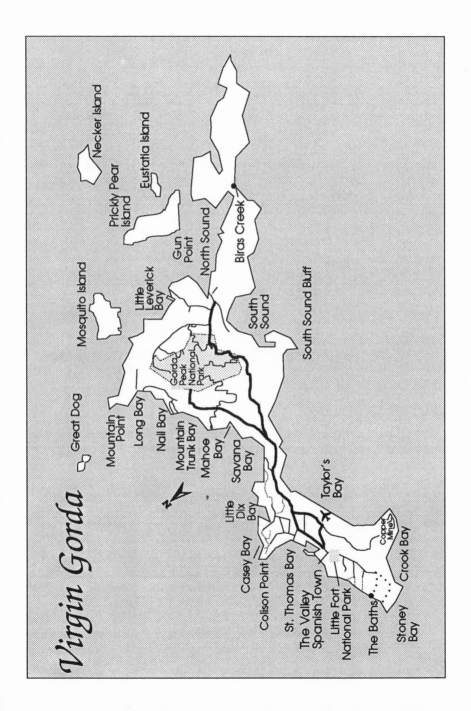

Mad Dog near the Baths specializes in sandwiches all day. Great view! ☎ 55830.

The Olde Yard Inn features a library and classical music. Homemade soups, local seafood, gourmet specialties. ☎ 55544. Reservations.

ANAGEDA

The Anegada Reefs Hotel serves lunch at their beach bar and specializes in barbecued lobster for dinner. Local fish or steak, chicken and ribs are also available. Moderate to expensive. ☎ 58002. VHF Ch 16.

MOSQUITO

Drake's Anchorage has been written up in Gourmet magazine for its fabulous Caribbean lobster, & local fish dinners. Meals include fresh baked bread, soup, appetizer, salad, dessert and coffee. Moorings are available for a low overnight charge. ☎ 42254. VHF Ch 16.

JOST VAN DYKE

Sandcastle at White Bay on Jost Van Dyke serves gourmet fish, lobster, rack of lamb, fresh breads and desserts for lunch and dinner in the open air restaurant on the beach. No credit cards. Reservations on channel 16 VHF. Moderate to High.

PETER ISLAND

Peter Island Hotel and Yacht Harbour offers lunch at the Beach Restaurant from 12:30 to 2:00 pm. Dinners are formal; men must wear a jacket and women, "cocktail" attire. ☎ 42561. Expensive.

FACTS

Nearest Recompression Chamber: The nearest chamber is located on St. Thomas in the neighboring USVI.

Getting There: San Juan, Puerto Rico is the airline hub for the Caribbean with frequent service to all parts of the United States, Canada and Europe. Beef Island is the major airport of Tortola and the BVI. Flights to San Juan with connections to the BVI from the United States on American (☎ 800-433-7300), Delta and Continental Airlines. Atlantic Air BVI, Sunaire Express or American Eagle fly from San Juan to Beef Island. Gorda Aero Services (☎ 5-2271) flies to Anegada from Tortola on Mon., Wed., and Fri. Inter-island ferry service is also available from St. Thomas to St. John & Tortola; or from Tortola to Virgin Gorda, Peter Island, Jost Van Dyke. Baggage can sometimes be delayed by a day on the small airlines. Divers carrying a lot of equipment should fly direct to St. Thomas and take a water ferry, to avoid having to change planes.

Island Transportation: Car rentals. TORTOLA: Airways, ☎ 4-4502; Avis, ☎ 4-3322; Budget, ☎ 4-2639; Alphonso, ☎ 4-1886; International, ☎ 4-2516. VIRGIN GORDA: Speedy's, 5-5240; Potter's, ☎ 5-5329. Scooters are also rentable from D.J.'s Scooters (Tortola) ☎ 4-5071 or Honda Scooter, ☎ 5-5212.

Taxi Service: Available from Beef Island Airport, Road Town Jetty, West End Jetty and from the dock on Virgin Gorda. TORTOLA: BVI Taxi, ☎ 5-2378 or 4-2875; Andy's Taxi, ☎ 5-5252; Style's Taxi, ☎ 4-2260. VIRGIN GORDA: Mahogany Taxi, ☎ 5-5542.

Driving: Valid BVI driving license required. A temporary license may be obtained from the car rental agencies for $10.00. Driving is on the left-hand side of the road. Maximum speed is 30 mph. Bicycles must be registered at the Traffic Licensing Office in Road Town. Cost of registration is $5.00. License plate MUST be fixed to the bicycle.

Fishing: The removal of any marine organism from B.V.I. waters is illegal for non-residents without a recreational fishing permit. ☎ 4-3429.

Documents: A valid passport is required to enter the BVI. For U.S. and Canadian citizens an authenticated birth certificate or voter registration card will suffice. Visitors may stay up to six months, provided they possess ongoing tickets, evidence of adequate means of support and pre-arranged accommodations. Visitors from some countries may need a visa. ☎ 809-494-3701.

Currency: U.S. Dollar. Personal checks not accepted.

Clothing: Casual, light clothing; some of the resorts require a jacket for dinner. Avoid exposed midriffs and bare chests in residential and commercial areas. Nudity is punishable by law. A wetsuit top, shortie, or wetskin is recommended for night dives and winter diving. Snorkelers should have some protection from sunburn.

Time: Atlantic Standard (EST + 1 hr.)

Language: English.

Climate: The BVI are in the tradewind belt and have a subtropical climate. Average temperatures are 75 to 85 deg F in winter and 80 to 90 deg F in summer. Nights are cooler. The hurricane season extends from July through September.

Taxes: There is a departure tax of $5.00 by air and $4.00 by sea. Also, a hotel accommodation tax of 7%.

Religious Services: Methodist, Anglican, Roman Catholic, Seventh-Day Adventist, Baptist, Jehovah's Witness, Pentecostal and Church of Christ.

For Additional Information: and a list of all guesthouses, apartments, hotels, campgrounds, charter operators, and restaurants contact the British Virgin Islands Tourist Board. *In Tortola:* P.O. Box 134, Road Town, Tortola, British Virgin Islands ☎ 809-494-3134. *In New York:* BVI Tourist Board, 370 Lexington Avenue, Suite 511, New York, N.Y. 10017. ☎ 800-835-8530, 800-232-7770 or 212-696-0400.

United Kingdom: BVI Tourist Board, c/o Intermarketing London, 82 Baker Street, London W1M 2AE. ☎ 071-935-6726.

Cayman Islands

Grand Cayman, Cayman Brac & Little Cayman

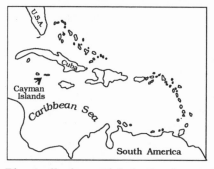

Dubbed "The Islands that Time Forgot" by the *Saturday Evening Post* in the early 1950s, the Cayman Islands—Grand Cayman, Cayman Brac and Little Cayman—today have become a top dive-travel destination. Located 480 miles south of Miami, this Caribbean trio entertains more than 200,000 visitors each year.

Physically beautiful, both above and beneath the sea, each island is blessed with an extraordinary fringing reef, superb marine life and long stretches of sparkling, palm-lined beaches.

Underwater Cayman is a submerged mountain range complete with cliffs, drop-offs, gullies, caverns, sink holes and forests of coral. The islands are the visible above-the-sea portions of the mountains. At depth, the Cayman Trench drops off to more than 23,000 ft.

Grand Cayman is the largest and the most developed of the three with world-class dive operations, restaurants and scores of luxury hotels and condominiums. The islands' no-tax status—enacted in the 1700's as a gift granted in return for the heroic action of Caymanians in saving the lives of passengers and crews of ten sailing ships—has attracted numerous corporations and banks. Its capital, Georgetown, ranks as the fifth largest financial center in the world, with nearly 600 international banks.

Cayman Brac and Little Cayman lie 89 miles northeast of the big island and are separated by a seven-mile-wide channel. Both wildly beautiful, each has its own special personality.

Little Cayman is VERY QUIET—virtually untouched by developers. The smallest of the three islands—only ten square miles—it has about 35 permanent residents. There are no shops, restaurants, movie theaters or

Area Contributors: Christopher Lofting, Mike Emmanuel, Mina Heuslein, Bill Heuslein, Anita and Kenneth Liggett, and Diane Kegley, Red Sail Sports.

traffic. Five phones service the entire island. Small resorts cater almost exclusively to divers and fishermen.

With daily, direct flights from North America and easy access from most other parts of the globe, most divers head first for Grand Cayman. Its famed Seven Mile Beach is headquarters for dive activity. More adventurous divers seeking a unique wilderness experience flock to the Brac and Little Cayman for superlative wall dives. Little Cayman is also noted for unsurpassed flats fishing.

When to go

Late summer and fall bring chance of a hurricane, but diving is possible year round. Conditions are generally mild, although steady winds can kick up some chop. When this happens dive boats simply move to the leeward side of the island and calmer waters. Air temperature averages 77°F. Water temperature averages 80°F.

History

As with many other Caribbean islands, the discovery of the Caymans is attributed to Christopher Columbus who discovered the islands on his second voyage while en route from Panama to Cuba in 1503. Amazingly, his primitive ships were able to negotiate the coral reefs with little trouble. He named these islands "Las Tortugas" for the countless marine turtles who came to Cayman beaches to breed. The turtles, which lived in captivity for long periods, became a source of fresh meat for the sailors, and the Cayman Islands became a regular stop for exploring ships.

Marine Regulations

With a dramatic growth in tourism and an increase in cruise-ship arrivals, the islands have enacted comprehensive legislation to protect the fragile marine environment. Marine areas are divided into three types: Marine Park Zones, Replenishment Zones and Environmental Zones.

The Marine Park Zones outlaw the taking of any marine life, living or dead, and only line fishing from shore or at and beyond the dropoff is permitted. Anchoring is allowed only at fixed moorings. (There are more than 200 permanent moorings around the islands.)

It is an offense for any vessel to cause reef damage with anchors or chains anywhere in Cayman waters.

Seven Mile Beach, Grand Cayman

In a Replenishment Zone, the taking of conch or lobster is prohibited, and spear guns, pole spears, fish traps and nets are prohibited. Line fishing and anchoring (at fixed moorings) are permitted. (Spearguns and Hawaiian slings are not allowed to be brought into the country)

Environmental Zones are the most strictly regulated. There is an absolute ban on the taking of any kind of marine life, alive or dead; anchoring is prohibited and no in-water activities of any kind are tolerated. These areas are a breeding ground and nursery for the fish and other creatures which will later populate the reef and other waters.

The Marine Conservation Board employs officers who may search any vessel or vehicle thought to contain marine life taken illegally. Penalties may include a maximum fine of CI$5,000 or imprisonment, or both.

Best Dives and Snorkeling

Grand Cayman

Grand Cayman is wall-diving country with steep drop-offs on all sides. The West Wall is a drop-off that runs parallel to Seven Mile Beach, thus offering the most convenient diving on the island. Most dive operators

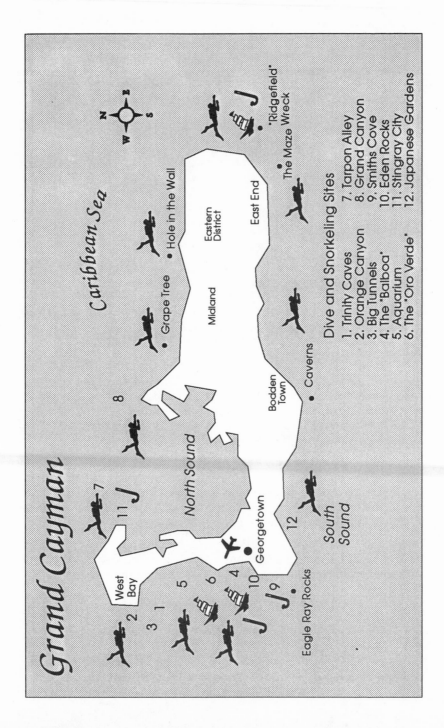

Grand Cayman

Caribbean Sea

N
W · E
S

North Sound

West Bay

South Sound

Georgetown

Bodden Town

Midland

Eastern District

East End

Eagle Ray Rocks

Caverns

Grape Tree

Hole in the Wall

The Maze Wreck

"Ridgefield"

Dive and Snorkelling Sites

1. Trinity Caves
2. Orange Canyon
3. Big Tunnels
4. The "Balboa"
5. Aquarium
6. The "Oro Verde"
7. Tarpon Alley
8. Grand Canyon
9. Smiths Cove
10. Eden Rocks
11. Stingray City
12. Japanese Gardens

Wreck of the Balboa *at night. "Lightning" is caused by a time exposure of a diver holding a light while swimming across the wreck.*

are located in this area, and many hotels offer dive and snorkeling trips to the sites—all five- to ten-minute boat rides. Flat-bottom dive boats attest to the calm seas. Several beach dives are possible. More sites along the South Wall have recently opened, particularly for experienced divers and photographers. This area is defined by a barrier reef that breaks the surface and serves as a coral fence. Conditions here are more demanding.

North Wall also lays claim to some of the most spectacular dive sites due to several unusual coral formations and passing pelagics.

Least explored is the East End Wall, often referred to as the last frontier.

Water temperature is a steady 82°F, visibility ranges from 100 to 150 ft and the coral reefs are exceptionally healthy, largely due to the conservancy measures enforced by the dive shops.

☆☆☆☆☆ **Stingray City** is the most photographed dive site in the Caymans, if not the entire Caribbean. Pictured in all the tourist board ads, the subject of endless travel articles and an Emmy-award film by Stan Waterman, this gathering of southern stingrays in the shallow area of North Sound is a marine phenomenon which has thrilled scuba divers and snorkelers since their discovery by two dive instructors, Pat Kinney and Jay Ireland, early in 1986.

After observing the normally solitary and shy rays gathering regularly at a shallow site where boats cleaned their conch and fish, Kinney and Ireland began hand taming exercises —carefully avoiding the razor-sharp, venomous spine in their whip-like tails. When safe hand feeding became a predictable event, they invited small groups of divers and snorkelers out to watch.

Today, the 20-member cast are big celebrities, luring curious visitors—as many as 150-200 per day—from across the globe. The location is shallow (12-20 ft), ideal for snorkelers as well as divers. Feeding time is whenever a dive or snorkeling boat shows up.

☆☆☆☆☆ **Trinity Caves**, located off the northern end of Seven Mile Beach is a maze of canyon trails between 60 and 100 ft. The trails are decked with gigantic barrel sponges, black coral, towering sea whips, sea fans, and a host of critters. Huge grouper and turtles, lobsters, squirrel fish, and schooling reef fish inhabit three cathedral-like caves for which the site is named. Their walls grasp clusters of pink anemones, vase sponges, and star corals. Sea conditions are generally calm with an occasional light current. Exceptional visibility. Some experience recommended.

☆☆☆☆ **Orange Canyon**, north of Trinity Caves is aglow with vibrant, orange, elephant-ear sponges. The reef starts at 45 ft, the edge of a deep wall also adorned with sea plumes, lavender sea fans and bushy corals— cover for shrimp, sea cucumbers, brittle stars, arrow crabs, file fish, turtles and small octopi. Calm seas.

☆☆☆☆☆ **Big Tunnels**, north of the Seven Mile Beach area, features a 50-ft coral archway linked to several tunnels and ledges bursting with rainbow gorgonians, sea fans, basket sponges, tube sponges, and branching corals. Eagle rays drift by the walls of sea urchins, anemones, grunts, puffer fish, bigeyes, and shrimp. Big morays peek out from the ledges. An occasional nurse shark is sighted. Average depth is 110 ft. Visibility is dependably excellent. Experience recommended.

☆☆☆☆ **The Wreck of the *Balboa*** is a 375-ft freighter at rest in 30 ft of water inside George Town Harbor—200 yards off the town pier. A favorite night dive, its twisted wreckage creates interesting video and still opportunities. Sea conditions are calm with good visibility, though several divers visiting the wreck at one time may kick up silt. Mingling about

Pool instruction by Red Sail Sports at the Hyatt Regency.

the hull are ever-present schools of sergeant majors, grouper, queen and French angels.

☆☆☆ **Aquarium** sits close to shore off the center of Seven Mile Beach. As the name implies, this is a grand meeting center for what appears to be every species of fish in the Caribbean. Count-and-name-the-fish is the favorite sport *du jour* at this 35-ft-deep coral grotto. Be sure to tote a waterproof fish ID card or book.

Spotted trunkfish, parrotfish, snappers, file fish, spotted morays, butter-flyfish, queen angels, queen triggerfish, puffers and schooling barracuda are just a few of Aquarium's residents. Though hard to see through the crowds of fish, the reef is very pretty with nice stands of staghorn coral, sponges and soft corals. Visibility superb. Calm seas make this a good choice for new divers.

☆☆☆ **The Wreck of the *Oro Verde*** lies 30 to 50 ft beneath the surface, straight out from the Holiday Inn on Seven Mile Beach. After running aground on the reefs in 1976, this 180-ft freighter was scuttled by local dive operators to create an artificial reef and new dive spot. The wreck, intact, is very photogenic. Divers are warmly greeted by its inhabitants— Spanish hogfish, French angels, snappers, butterflyfish, blue tangs and rock beauties. Seas are calm.

☆☆☆ **Tarpon Alley** is a canyon mirrored with schools of giant silvery tarpon, mammoth grouper and sting rays. Large pelagics flash by too. The "alley" is south of Orange Canyon and partially in the Seven Mile

Grand Cayman Snorkeling Spots

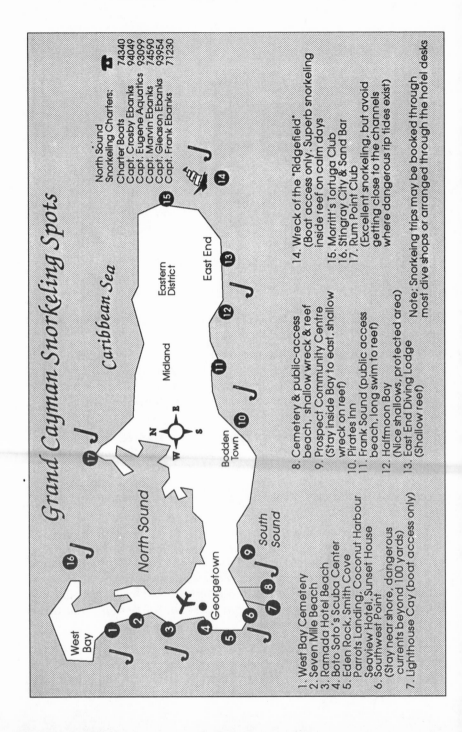

1. West Bay Cemetery
2. Seven Mile Beach
3. Ramada Hotel Beach
4. Boto Soto's Scuba Center
5. Eden Rock, Smith Cove
   Parrots Landing, Coconut Harbour
   Seaview Hotel, Sunset House
6. Southwest Point
   (Stay near shore, dangerous
   currents beyond 100 yards)
7. Lighthouse Cay (boat access only)

8. Cemetery & public-access
   beach, shallow wreck & reef
9. Prospect Community Centre
   (Stay inside Bay to east; shallow
   wreck on reef)
10. Pirates Inn
11. Frank Sound (public access
    beach, long swim to reef)
12. Halfmoon Bay
    (Nice shallows, protected area)
13. East End Diving Lodge
    (Shallow reef)

14. Wreck of the "Ridgefield"
    (Boat access only: Superb snorkeling
    inside reef on calm days
15. Morritt's Tortuga Club
16. Stingray City & Sand Bar
17. Rum Point Club
    (Excellent snorkeling, but avoid
    getting close to the channels
    where dangerous rip tides exist)

Note: Snorkeling trips may be booked through
most dive shops or arranged through the hotel desks

North Sound
Snorkeling Charters:
Charter Boats   74340
Capt: Crosby Ebanks   94049
Capt: Eugene Aquatics   93099
Capt: Marvin Ebanks   74590
Capt: Gleason Ebanks   93954
Capt: Frank Ebanks   71230

Caribbean Sea

North Sound

West Bay

South Sound

Georgetown

Bodden Town

Midland

Eastern District

East End

Beach replenishment zone. Top of the canyon walls are at 60 ft. Outside dropoffs leap down several thousand ft. Surface conditions are occasionally choppy.

☆☆☆☆☆ **Grand Canyon** is an enormous channel enclosed by jagged, perpendicular mountains. The walls are a cornucopia of sponges, sea whips, sea fans, hard corals and critters. This is the favored North Wall dive and is located off Rum Point. Depths start at 60 ft and drops off. Experience a must. Visibility is excellent. Boat access.

☆☆ **Japanese Gardens** is a series of long coral ridges off the south end of the island. The reef blossoms with a dense covering of elkhorn and antler corals, vase sponges and schooling fish. Depths start at 50 ft.

Snorkeling

Good snorkeling can be found by wading out from many swimming beaches on Grand Cayman. Just a few yards off shore you will find a bevy of beautiful reef fish darting in and out of clumps of living coral. Entry points to close-to-shore sites are Smith Cove, Ramada Treasure Island Hotel, Seven Mile Beach, West Bay Cemetery, Rum Point Club, Parrots Landing, Seaview Hotel, Coconut Harbour, Sunset House, Pirates Inn, Frank Sound Half Moon Bay, East End Diving Lodge and Morritt's Tortuga Club. Clearer water and more dramatic coral formations are found farther off shore and may be reached by boat. Snorkeling cruises, some with dinner or lunch, are offered by the hotels and dive shops. Snorkelers are urged to inquire about currents and local conditions in unfamiliar areas before attempting to explore on their own.

Snorkelers swimming off the Rum Point Club beach should stay clear of the channels which have rip tides.

A trail marked by a round blue and white sign with a swimmer outline denotes access through private property to the beach. All Cayman beaches are free for public use.

☆☆ **Smiths Cove,** south of George Town, is a shallow reef whiskered with an array of pastel sea fans and plumes. Trumpet fish, squirrel fish, schools of grunts and sergeant majors, butterfly fish, parrotfish and angels offer constant entertainment. The reef is a 150-ft swim from the beach on Southwest Point. Depths are from 15 to 45 ft.

☆☆ **Eden Rocks** is a favorite area for cruise ship groups. This area is less than 200 yds off shore from the Eden Rock Diving Center. Depths range from five to 40 ft. In addition to the beautiful coral grottoes, walls, caves and tunnels you'll find tame fish eagerly awaiting snorkelers. If you've yet to befriend a fish, this area offers the proper social climate. Good visibility and light currents are the norm here.

Dive Operators

Bob Soto's Diving Ltd. is a PADI Five Star facility with Seven Mile Beach locations at Holiday Inn, the Cayman Islander Hotel, and the Scuba Centre, near to Soto's Reef. The operation offers dive and snorkeling trips, underwater photo and video services, camera and gear rentals, open water PADI certifications, completion dives, and comfortable custom dive boats. Complete dive/accommodation packages with Grand Cayman hotels and condominiums available. ☎ 800-262-7686 or 809-949-2022; fax 809-949-8731. Write to P.O. Box 1801, Grand Cayman, BWI.

Red Sail Sports at the Hyatt Regency on Seven Mile Beach offers dive and snorkeling trips, PADI certification courses and daily resort courses. Snorkel and dive trips, dinner sails and cocktail cruises. Also, windsurfing, waterskiing and parasailing. ☎ 800-255-6425 or 809-947-5965; fax 809-947-5808. **Don Foster's Dive Cayman** is based at the Radisson Resort and Royal Palms on Seven Mile Beach. This full service facility offers certification and resort courses, rental and a photo center. Plus, snorkeling and glass bottom excursions, waverunners and sailboats. ☎ 800-83-DIVER or 214-437-0789. Fax 809-947-5133.

Eden Rock Diving Center is the shore entry point for Eden Rock reef. The shop rents and sells snorkel gear for children and grown ups, plus underwater cameras, tee shirts and gifts. PADI & NAUI courses. ☎ 809-969-7243.

Sunset Divers at Sunset House offers scuba instruction and dive packages, but is best known for its Underwater Photo Centre, operated by Cathy Church. The Centre offers 35mm and video camera rental, processing and photo instruction for all levels. Very informal and friendly with personalized service. Write to P.O.Box 479, Grand Cayman, BWI. ☎ 800-854-4767 or 809-949-7111.

Surfside Watersports, Ltd. has three locations on Grand Cayman, all offering dive and accommodation packages. ☎ 809-949-7330 or write P.O. Box 891, Grand Cayman, BWI.

Treasure Island Divers at the Ramada, offers instruction, shore dives, snorkeling trips, sail cruises. ☎ 809-949-4456. Write P.O. Box 1817, Grand Cayman, BWI.

Parrots Landing Watersports Park, a half-mile south of downtown Georgetown, has excellent shore diving on four beautiful, shallow reefs 30 yards from their dock and a wall dive 115 yards out. Six dive boats visit the South Wall, West Wall and Northwest Point. A 60-ft Catamaran, *The Cockatoo* sails from North Sound to Stingray City. Squid is provided for snorkelers to hand feed the rays. PADI and NAUI certifications. On shore, the park features water toys, picnic tables, barbecue grills, hammocks, sun deck and a half dozen friendly Cayman parrots. Park shuttle boats and busses will pick you up anywhere along Seven Mile Beach. ☎ 800-448-0428 or 809-949-7884. Write to P.O. Box 1995, Grand Cayman, BWI.

Snorkel sails, glass-bottom boat rides, submarines rides, dinner cruises, fishing and more are booked through **Charter Boat Headquarters** in the Coconut Place Shopping Center on West Bay Road. ☎ 809-947-4340, **Captain Eugene's Aquatics** at Morgan's Harbour Marina ☎ 809-949-3099 and **Crosby's Water Sport,** ☎ 809-947-4049 or 809-949-3372.

Atlantic Submarines takes up to 46 adventurous passengers wall diving in completely dry, air-conditioned, surface-pressure comfort. The 65-ft submarine plummets to depths of 100 ft. as it explores the reef. Children must be at least four years old. Cost is $70 per person, children (4-12) yrs, $34. ☎ 809-949-7700.

Dive Resorts and Accommodations

Grand Cayman has accommodations and packages for every budget and every need. Every dive shop listed above offers a money-saving, dive-accommodation package, some with air. For a complete list of guest houses, cottages and condos contact the Cayman Islands Department of Tourism. (see address end of chapter)

Seven Mile Beach Resorts

Ramada Treasure Island Resort is a 25-acre beachfront, luxury hotel with 290 spacious rooms. All are air conditioned, have ceiling fans, satellite TV, in-room safes, mini bars. Facilities include a well-equipped dive shop, gourmet restaurant, two freshwater pools, tennis and entertainment. Winter rates for a standard double room start at $220 per day. Summer, $155. Call for dive-package rates. ☎ 800-228-9898 or 809-949-7777, fax 809-949-8672.

Hyatt Regency offers 236 ultra-luxurious rooms, one- and 2-bedroom villas, three pools, tropical gardens, adjacent golf course, gazebo-style swim-up bar. Winter rates start at $260 per day for a double. Winter, double per day, $260. Summer, $170. Red Sail Watersports on premises. Handicapped accessible. ☎ 800-233-1234 or 809-949-8528; fax 809-949-8528. Major credit cards.

Holiday Inn allows children under 18 or an additional third or fourth person at no extra charge. Beachfront, dive shop on premises. Handicapped accessible. Winter, $188, Summer $148. Dive packages. ☎ 800-421-9999 or 809-947-4444. Major credit cards.

Radisson Resort is a huge, 315-room luxury resort, five minutes from town. Pool and beach bar, restaurant, nightclub. Handicap accessible. Don Foster's Diving on premises. All major credit cards. ☎ 800-333-3333 or 809-949-0088; fax 809-949-0288.

Georgetown area

Coconut Harbour, south of Seven Mile Beach, features suites with mini-kitchens, cabana bar & open air restaurant, shore diving on Waldo's Reef out front. Parrot's Landing Dive Shop on premises. Children under 12 free with parents. Rates include breakfast daily. Winter $162. Call for summer. ☎ 800-552-6281 or 809-949-7468; fax 809-949-7117.

North Side

Cayman Kai Resort Ltd. features luxurious cottages, villas, and town houses, all air-conditioned, on the north side of Grand Cayman. Lodges are complete with living-dining area, kitchen and patio. One bedroom with one bath for two divers rents for $135 per day. Four bedrooms with two bath villas for seven divers rent for $235 per day. Cayman Kai has a dive shop on the premises and offers rentals, and reef trips to the fabulous North Wall. ☎ 1-800-223-5427, or 809-947-9056.

Other Activities

Fishing, windsurfing, parasailing, and tennis are offered at most condos and resorts. An 18-hole, a nine-hole and a special Cayman course are located next to the Hyatt Regency Grand Cayman. On the latter, you use special lightweight balls which travel about half the distance of a normal ball. Grand Cayman's night clubs and larger hotels offer live entertain-

ment and dancing. The Cayman National Theater presents live perform-
ances of drama, comedy and musicals.

Sightseeing

The capital city George Town, has a well scrubbed look not always found
in the Caribbean. Visitors can tour the area by foot, taxi, moped or
rental car. Courtesy phones at the airport connect to the car rental
dealers. Driving is on the left. Along George Town's waterfront several
historic clapboard buildings have been lovingly restored and converted into souvenir shops, galleries and boutiques. Native crafts such
as black coral and turtle shell jewelry along with imported goods may
be purchased here.

Heading north along the famed Seven Mile Beach you come to the largest
congregation of hotels, condos, shopping malls and restaurants. Each
morning dive boats line up here and offer door-to-reef service to resort
and condo guests.

A side trip to the Cayman Turtle Farm is always fun as is a visit to Hell,
the town where visitors delight in having mail postmarked to send back
home.

Dining

Grand Cayman offers visitors an enormous variety of choices in dining.
Shopping centers along West Bay Road house several fast food eateries
such as **Burger King, Pizza Hut** and **Kentucky Fried Chicken** and **ICBY
Yogurt.**

For more formal dining—all seafood—try the **Wharf**, waterfront on West
Bay Road (☎ 9-2231) or **Seaharvest Restaurant** in front of Sunset House
(☎ 9-7111), **The Lobster Pot** above Bob Soto's Dive shop, **Ristorante
Pappagallo**, located in an exotic, modern thatched-hut-style building at
the end of West Bay.

CAYMAN BRAC

Often called the loveliest of the islands, this 12-mile strip of land is
rumored to be the resting place of pirates' treasure. Lying some 87 miles
east of Grand Cayman, Cayman Brac's (*brac* is Gaelic for bluff) most
striking feature is a 140-foot-high limestone formation covered by unusual foliage, including flowering cactus, orchids and tropical fruits such

as mango and papaya. Rare species of birds, including the endangered green, blue and red Caymanian parrot inhabit the island which is a major flyway for migratory birds. Resident brown booby birds soar the cliffs.

Cayman Brac is also known for its many caves where pirates in earlier centuries took refuge and, according to legend, buried their treasures. In fact, a peg-legged turtle pirate is the country's national symbol.

Native fir, palm and papaya trees shade the narrow streets. Fragrant thickets of bougainvilleas, hibiscus, periwinkle, and oleander surround the islander's houses, many of which were built with wood salvaged from the wreckage of ships that crashed on the reefs. A visit to the Brac Museum in Stake Bay offers a look at the history of ship building on the island.

Activities other than diving and snorkeling are limited. There are a few restaurants scattered along the main road which also features elevated caves with ladders for the tourists; Nims gift shop with fabulous hand-made woven bags, local crafts and post cards; and the main town area which has a convenience store, post office, gift shops and the island museum.

Best Dives of Cayman Brac

☆☆☆☆ **The Hobbit** dive site puts you in a living fairy tale of giant barrel sponges and brilliantly-colored corals. A flashing display of chubs, turtles, queen angels, octopi, grunts and queen trigger fish illuminate the reef. Located off the southeast tip of the Brac, average depth is 70 ft. Excellent visibility. Recommended for intermediate to advanced divers.

☆☆☆☆ **Radar Reef** is a series of coral pinnacles and canyons, each home to a splendid variety of elkhorn, star, and brain corals, lavender sea fans, tube and barrel sponges, feather dusters, and sea whips. Inhabitants are a lively community of turtles, sting rays, octopi, and swirls of tropicals. It is a great place for new divers with shallow depths—from 30 to 60 ft—and normally calm surface conditions.

Snorkeling

Excellent snorkeling in calm, shallow water exists all along the north shore. Several entry points are found at the boat launching areas where cuts through the dense coral have been blasted. Parking is available along side the north road.

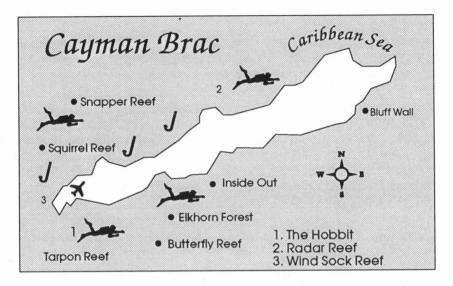

On the south shore try Sea Feather Bay which is located at the Bluff Road crossing. Small coral heads and juvenile tropicals abound.

Experienced snorkelers may want to dive on the barrier reef at the southwestern tip of the island. Water entry is best by boat but if you enjoy a long swim you can get out to the reef from either the public beach or one of the hotel beaches.

☆☆☆ **Wind Sock Reef,** which is off the now closed Buccaneer Inn, starts at about 25 ft dropping off to about 50 ft. This spur and groove reef offers a look at gardens of elkhorn, pillar corals, sea fans, orange sponges and gorgonians. Angels, barracuda, butterfly fish, file fish, trumpet fish and critters can be found hiding in the many crevices of the reef. Good visibility and usually calm seas.

Dive Operators and Accommodations of
Cayman Brac

Divi Tiara Beach Hotel and Dive Tiara caters almost exclusively to divers and snorkelers. The resort is first class with freshwater pool, Jacuzzi, tennis, 70 spacious, air-conditioned rooms, auto rentals, sailboards, bicycles and paddleboats. Snorkeling and diving can be found right off the Tiara Beach Hotel's palm-lined beach. The dive operation is exceptional with no effort spared to make every dive trip relaxing, safe and fun. Aboard six of their custom-designed dive boats, Dive Tiara visits the best dives of Cayman Brac as well as Little Cayman daily. The professional boat crew readily assists divers with gear set-ups and getting in and out of the water. There's no need to lug your gear back and forth to your room; it stays overnight in a gear storage room on Tiara's dive pier. ☎ 1-800-367-3484.

Brac Reef Beach Resort combined with **Brac Aquatics** offers comfortable, air conditioned rooms with satellite TV, a great beach, fresh water pool, whirlpool, beach bar and restaurant. Complete dive/accommodation packages start at $955 (summer) for five nights, three meals, two two-tank boat dives per day, ground transfers and bicycles. Unlimited diving off the beach. ☎ 1-800-327-3835 or 813-323-8727; fax 813-323-8827. Write P.O. Box 235, Cayman Brac, BWI.

There are other facilities such as "Soon Come," a charming two-bedroom, beachfront, reef-front, modern house for rent on the isolated south shore. (☎ 212-447-0337; fax 212-447-0335).

LITTLE CAYMAN

Little Cayman is rural, uncrowded and unhurried. This 11-mile-long island is populated by no more than three dozen people. Telephones are few and the roads are yet unpaved. The runway is grass. For a true get-away vacation this is the place. Activities are water sports and watching the iguanas. If you plan to visit Little Cayman, keep in mind that there are no stores. Items such as aspirin, mosquito repellent, decongestants, and suntan lotion must all be packed from home. Accommodations are not air conditioned.

Best Dives of Little Cayman

☆☆☆☆☆ **Bloody Bay Wall** is one of the top five dives in all the Caymans. The "Wall" peaks as a shallow reef at 15 ft and drops off to an unfathomed bottom. Bright orange and lavender tube sponges, pastel gorgonians and soft corals form a dense floral garden in the shallows. An extremely friendly six-foot barracuda named Snort may join your dive— flashing his pearly whites while cheerfully posing for videos and still photos. Eagle rays blast by the wall along with slower-moving turtles, spotted morays, and huge parrotfish. Sea conditions are usually calm although a stiff wind will churn the surface. Divers of all levels will find a good dive at Bloody Bay Wall.

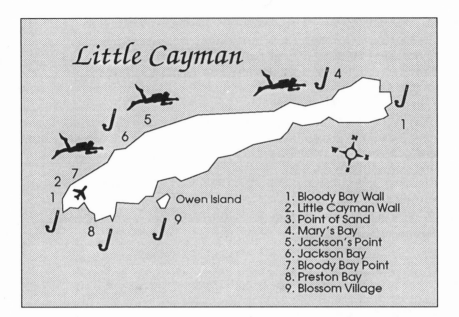

1. Bloody Bay Wall
2. Little Cayman Wall
3. Point of Sand
4. Mary's Bay
5. Jackson's Point
6. Jackson Bay
7. Bloody Bay Point
8. Preston Bay
9. Blossom Village

☆☆☆☆ **Little Cayman Wall,** off the island's west end, starts with a shallow blaze of exotic yellow, orange and blue sponges at 15 ft then drops off to unknown depths. Soft corals and big barrel sponges decorate the wall. Great for snorkeling and diving.

Snorkeling Little Cayman offers several superb snorkeling spots with visibility often exceeding 100 ft. Ground transportation to beach access sites is easily arranged through the dive operators. For the ultimate in free diving head out to Bloody Bay and Spot Bay off the north shore where the seas are calm, and the marine life spectacular. The boat ride takes about 25 minutes. Average depth on top of the North Wall is 25 feet.

Note: The Western half of the wall is called the "Bloody Bay Wall " and the eastern half "Jackson Wall."

☆☆☆ **Point of Sand,** off the southeast end of Little Cayman, is excellent for experienced and beginning snorkelers. A gentle current flowing from west to east maintains excellent visibility. The bottom is sandy with many coral heads scattered about. Marine life is fine and the site is accessible from the shore. Ground transportation can be arranged from the resorts.

☆☆☆ Good snorkeling for beginners at **Mary's Bay** starts 50 yards from the beach—inside the barrier reef. There is no current and visibility runs about 30 to 50 ft. A host of fish and invertebrates are found in the shallows. Depth averages three to eight ft. The bottom is turtle grass requiring booties or other submersible footwear. An old shack on an otherwise deserted shore marks the spot.

☆☆☆ **Jackson Point** (aka School Bus) is for experienced snorkelers only. Swim out about 75 yards from the beach where you'll see a small wall towering from a sandy bottom at 40 ft to 15 ft. Hundreds of fish, rays and turtles congregate in the shallows. Corals and sponges carpet the area. Swimming another 50 to 60 ft brings you to a much larger wall which drops off to extraordinary depths.

☆☆☆ **Jackson Bay** is similar to Jackson Point except the bottom of the mini wall drops off to a depth of 50 to 60 ft.

☆☆☆ **Bloody Bay Point,** recommended for seasoned snorkelers only, is well worth a visit. Beach access is difficult, requiring a long swim out to the reef located 100 yards from the shore. The bottom eases down to about 30 ft before the drop off to The Great Wall begins. The coral and marine life is spectacular.

☆ **Preston Bay** is another good choice for beginning snorkelers. Maximum depth is six ft; visibility 30 to 50 ft. Swarming fish and a white sandy bottom offer endless photo opportunities.

☆☆ **Blossom Village,** reachable by boat, is another great shallow spot. A light current keeps the visibility between 50 and 100 ft. A wide variety of exotic marine life around clumps of staghorn and brain corals will entertain you in depths ranging between four to eight ft.

Dive Operators and Accommodations of
Little Cayman

Little Cayman dive operations are smaller than those on Cayman Brac and Grand Cayman. Accommodations are not air conditioned.

Little Cayman Beach Resort is a new luxury hotel with air-conditioned rooms, private baths, fresh water pool, jacuzzi, cabana bar, tennis, restaurant, and a full-service dive/photo operation. Windsurfers, sailboats and bicycles offered. All-inclusive packages for diving, fishing and relaxing. ☎ 800-327-3835 or 813-323-8727. fax 813-323-8827.

Southern Cross Club is a ten-room fishing camp which warmly welcomes divers. Divemasters will take you to all the top dive and snorkel sites on Bloody Bay Wall or South Shore. Snorkelers mix with scuba groups. Resort courses are available. ☎ 809-948-3255 or in the United States 317-636-9501. Southern Cross Club, Little Cayman, Cayman Islands, BWI.

Sam McCoy's Diving and Fishing Lodge, a seven-room inn on the southwest shore offers rustic accommodations for up to 14 divers. Rooms in the main lodge are air conditioned with private bath. Twenty-ft fiberglass runabouts are used for reef trips. Rates per day start at $159 per person and include all diving, three meals per day, all transportation. Dive packages available. ☎ 800-626-0496 or 809-948-4526. Fax: 809-949-6821. Or write to Carl McCoy, P.O. Box 711, Georgetown, Grand Cayman, BWI.

Pirate's Point Resort features rustic guest cottages and a guest house. Owner Gladys Howard offers friendly service, all-inclusive dive packages from $180 per person, per day. Reef trips on comfortable inflatable run-abouts. ☎ 809-948-4210; fax 809-948-4610.

CAYMAN LIVE-ABOARD

See & Sea Travel Service operates the *Cayman Aggressor II* . Based in George Town, the luxury yacht features double staterooms and one quad which holds 18 passengers, along with a salon, carpeting, E-6 film processing, air conditioning, TV, video equipment and hot showers. Enjoyable meals including soups and salads, chicken, turkey, native fish and snacks are prepared on board. Packages include transfers, hotels, meals, diving, tanks, backpacks and weights. Prices are commensurate with those of Cayman land resorts. Write to See & Sea Travel Service, Inc. 50 Francisco St., Suite 205, San Francisco, CA 94133. ☎ Tel: 1-800-DIV-XPRT or 415-434-3400. Fax (415) 434-3409.

Facts

Nearest Recompression Chamber: George Town. This chamber is operated and staffed 24 hours a day by the British Sub-Aqua Club. Dial 555 for help.

Getting There: Cayman Airways provides scheduled flights from Miami, Houston, Atlanta, and Tampa to Grand Cayman with connecting flights to Cayman Brac and Little Cayman. Northwest, United, American and Air Jamaica fly nonstop from gateway cities into Grand Cayman. During peak season (Dec 15 -April 15) charter flights direct from many major snowbelt cities to Grand Cayman are available from Cayman Airways. Flight time from Miami is one hr. Grand Cayman is a regular stop on many cruise lines as well.

Island Transportation: Rental cars, motorbikes, and bicycles are available on Grand Cayman and Cayman Brac. Friendly and informative taxi drivers are stationed at hotels and other convenient locations.

Driving: Driving in the Cayman Islands is on the left. A temporary license is issued for a few dollars to persons holding U.S., Canadian or international licenses.

Documents: Proof of citizenship (birth certificate, voter's registration certificate) is required from U.S., British, or Canadian citizens. No vaccinations are required unless you are coming from an endemic area.

Customs: The penalties for trying to bring drugs into the Cayman Islands are stiff fines and, frequently, prison terms. No spearguns or Hawaiian slings permitted into the country.

Currency: The Cayman Island Dollar, equal to $.80 U.S.

Climate: Temperatures average about 80°F year round. The islands are subject to some rainy periods, but are generally sunny and diveable.

Clothing: Casual, lightweight clothing. Some nightclubs require that men wear a jacket. Wetskins or shorty wetsuits are useful to avoid abrasions when diving as are light gloves for protection against the stinging corals. Snorkelers should wear protective clothing against sunburn.

Electricity: 110 V AC, 60 cycles. Same as U.S.

Time: Eastern Standard Time year round.

Tax: There is a 6% government tax on accommodations. A service charge of 10 to 15 percent is added to several restaurant bills. Departure tax is $10.00 U.S.

Religious Services: Catholic, Protestant, Baptist, Mormon and non-denominational churches are found on Grand Cayman.

Additional Information: The Cayman Islands Department of Tourism, 6100 Blue Lagoon Drive, Suite 150, Miami FL 33126-2085. ☎ 305-266-2300; fax 305-267-2932. *New York:* 420 Lexington Ave, Suite 2733, New York NY. ☎ 212-682-5582; Fax: 212-986-5123. *United Kingdom,* Trevor House, 100 Brompton Road, Knightsbridge, London SW3 1EX. Write to Box 2066, Grand Cayman, Cayman Islands, BWI. ☎ 809-949-0623; fax 809-949-4053.

Cozumel

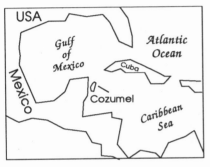

Cozumel, Mexico's largest island, is one of the top dive destinations in the western hemisphere and the best dive-travel bargain in the Caribbean. The island lies 12 miles off the Yucatan Peninsula, separated by a 3,000 ft-deep channel Most of the island's interior is dense jungle; its perimeter edged by an expanse of luxuriant, powder-sand beaches. Its cultural and commercial center, San Miguel, is a busy seaside city with a maze of shops, *cantinas* and restaurants. Just south of San Miguel is an ultra-modern cruise-ship terminal where daily-arriving ocean liners are greeted by a constant parade of dive boats. Dive resorts are scattered along the west coast where calm waters prevail and most sport diving is done.

A 1961 visit by Jacques Cousteau brought attention to Cozumel's spectacular diving and its incredible water clarity. Its fringing reef system is fed by warm, fast-moving Yucatan currents (a part of the Gulf Stream) as they sweep through the deep channel on the west side of the island. These currents bring a constant wash of plankton and other nutrients that support thousands of exotic fish. Immense rays, and jew fish populate the spectacular drop-offs and wrecks on the outer reefs; giant sea turtles nest along the beaches from May to September. And, visibility remains a constant 100 to 150 ft year round, often exceeding 200 ft.

Despite an onslaught of divers, Cozumel's reefs and marine life are better than ever. Once a mecca for spearfishermen, all of the reefs surrounding the island are now protected as a marine park. Those of you who may remember the dive operation's requests for qualifications being "You

Contributors: Scott Sunshine, Jim Spencer.

dive before?" will now be asked for C cards. A functional, free-to-divers recompression chamber is in operation.

When to Go

The best time to visit Cozumel is from November till June. Water and air temperatures average 80°F year round with hotter conditions in Summer. Summer and fall bring chance of heavy rains or hurricanes.

History

Cozumel was first inhabited by the Mayan Indians who settled as early as 300 A.D. They named it "Ah-Cuzamil-Peten," place of the swallows. Remains of their temples and shrines still can be found.

During the 1800s Cozumel was a busy seaport stopover for ships carrying chicle (used to make gum) from Central America to North America.

Best Dives of Cozumel

Most tours include a shallow dive on the inner reef and a drift dive along the outer wall. The dive boat drops you off at one end of the reef then follows your bubbles as you drift with the current to a predetermined point where you surface to rendezvous with the boat. Note: a maximum depth of 90 ft is enforced by the dive operators (this is expected to change to 130 ft). Novice divers may wish to avoid the strong currents associated with drift diving and stick to the inner reefs.

☆☆☆☆☆ The **Palancar Reef** complex, off the southwestern tip of the island, encompasses more than three miles of winding tunnels and coral canyons. Its most prominent feature is a 12-ft bronze statue of Christ created by sculptor Entique Miralda to commemorate the first Catholic Mass said on the island. The statue stands in 40 ft of water at the north end of the reef known as Big Horseshoe. Depths on the inner reef range from 30 to 60 ft. Visibility exceeds 100 ft. The drop-off on the reef's outer wall is laced with immense coral arches and tunnels—shelter to huge crabs, lobster and all types of morays.

Vibrant growths of tree-sized sea fans, yellow and lavender tube sponges, barrel sponges, giant sea whips and pink-tipped anemones adorn the wall.

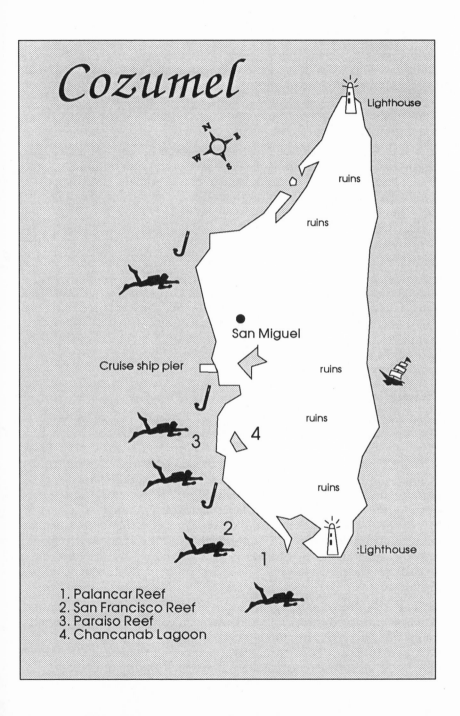

Cozumel

Lighthouse

ruins

ruins

J

San Miguel

Cruise ship pier

ruins

J

3

4

ruins

J

2

ruins

1

:Lighthouse

1. Palancar Reef
2. San Francisco Reef
3. Paraiso Reef
4. Chancanab Lagoon

Huge towering coral pinnacles on the south end of Palancar provide excellent photo and video opportunities. Fish are abundant, with gigantic parrotfish and groupers, schools of pork fish and grunts everywhere. Many of the groupers are tame and may be hand fed. At depth you'll find a profusion of black coral.

☆☆☆☆ **San Francisco Reef** offers underwater photographers a kaleidoscope of seascapes with an array of pastel gorgonians and sea fans, vase and barrel sponges, coral arches, caves and tunnels. Usually a drift dive, with huge angels, rays, groupers, and sea turtles greeting you along the way. Depths along the reef ledge are from 20 ft to 70 ft. The wall then drops off to channel depths. Visibility is excellent—usually 150 ft.

☆☆☆ **Paraiso Reef North** is a popular shallow dive just north of the cruise ship pier in San Miguel. The reef is accessible by swimming straight out 200 yds from the beach at the Hotel Sol Caribe or by dive boat. The remains of a twin engine airplane, sunk intentionally as part of a movie set, rests at 30 ft—creating a home for a vast array of fish life. Huge green morays, eagle rays, turtles, yellowtail, French angels, schools of porkfish, butterflyfish, and queen triggerfish may be found. The reef is a good choice for novice divers.

Snorkeling

Good snorkeling may be found all along Cozumel's east coast beaches. The reefs off the beaches at both the **Galapagos Inn** and **Playa San Francisco** have some nice stands of elkhorn and brain coral with a constant parade of juvenile tropicals and invertebrates. A side trip to neighboring **Isla Mujeres** where there is a magnificent shallow snorkeling reef along the southern shore is well worth the effort. Snorkelers head for Playa Garrafon, four miles from town. This area—*El Garrafon*, "the carafe"—is one of the finest snorkeling areas in the Caribbean. Just wade out from the beach with some cracker crumbs and you'll immediately be surrounded by crowds of friendly fish. Ideal for first time snorkelers. The beach has a dive shop, showers, refreshment stands & shops.

☆☆☆☆ **Chancanab Lagoon**, south of the cruise ship pier at Laguna Beach, is protected from wind and waves. Ideal for snorkeling, depths range from very shallow to about 30 ft. Schools of grunts, angel fish, damsel fish, trumpet fish, turtles, and snapper dart between the clumps of coral. Seafans and soft corals adorn the reef. Visibility runs about 75 ft,

Photo by Jon Huber

Drift Dive, Palancar Reef.

sometimes better. Snorkeling gear may be rented from shops on the beach. Changing rooms, freshwater showers and lockers are available.

Small admission fee. A botanical garden and a fast-food restaurant are on the premises.

Dive Operators

NOTE: To telephone or fax any of the Mexican listings from the U.S., dial 01152 + 987 + the five digit number.

Aqua Safari is on the ocean at 5th St. South. The shop offers drift dives, night dives, rentals and repairs. Custom dive boats can accommodate up to 20 divers. ☎ 20101; fax 20661. Write to: P.O. Box 41, Cozumel, Quintana Roo, Mexico 77600.

Blue Bubble Divers offers sunset dives, wreck and reef dives. Dive/accommodation packages from $400. ☎ 21865; fax 21865.

Del Mar Aquatics offers courses, trips, services. Dive accommodation packages offered. ☎ 21833 fax 21833. In the U.S. ☎ 1-800-877-4383. Write to P.O. Box 129, Cozumel, Quintana Roo, Mexico 77600.

Dive Palancar at the Diamond Resort has trips aboard a 44-ft custom dive boat to Palancar and Santa Rosa. Beach diving tours. English speaking guides. ☎ 23443 ext. 895.

Fantasia Divers specializes in small groups. Reef trips, videos, photo rentals. Hotel/diving packages.☎ 800-336-3483; fax 713-558-9687. For hotel/dive packages ☎ 800-336-3483. Write P.O. Box 79714, Houston TX 77079.

Pro Dive Cozumel offers packages with the Colonial Hotel. Features reef trips, handicapped-divers program, computer diving, night dives. ☎ 800-833-SEAS; fax 813-596-3891. Write to: 13393 Sorrento Dr., Largo FL 33644. In Cozumel, 20221; fax 22192. P.O. Box 56, Cozumel, Quintana Roo, Mexico 77600.

Scuba Cozumel visits Palancar National Park and offers dive/hotel packages. ☎ 800-847-5708; fax 713-783-3305. Write to Aquasub Tours, P.O. Box 630608, Houston, TX. In Cozumel, 20663.

Scuba Du at the Hotel Stouffer Presidente offers personalized dive tours. Dive/hotel packages. ☎ 21379; fax 24130. Write to: P.O. Box 137, Cozumel, Quintana Roo, Mexico 77600.

Scuba Shack offers unlimited shore diving and boat diving packages. ☎ 800-445-4716; fax 713-789-6772. In Cozumel, 20145; fax 20145. Write to: Scuba Shack Tours, 6750 Richmond Ave., Houston, TX 77057.

Scuba Tours of Cozumel offers courses, reef trips aboard fast, 42-ft custom dive boats. Dive/hotel packages starting at $250. ☎ 23656; fax 23046. Write to: Ave. Rafael Melgar #365, Cozumel, Quintana Roo, Mexico 77600.

Sea & Sun Divers features dive & snorkeling tours of the reefs and lagoon. Dive/hotel packages. ☎ 22915; fax 22915.

Accommodations

NOTE: To telephone or fax any of the Mexican listings from the U.S., dial 01152 + 987 + the five digit number.

Stouffer Presidente, two miles south of town at the Chancanab Lagoon, is a deluxe 253-room resort featuring a large pool, tennis, restaurants, entertainment and dive packages. Rates for hotel & diving for two start at $700 for three nights. Great snorkeling off the beach. ☎ 800-468-3571.

Casa Del Mar is an even less pricey dive resort, across the street from the beach, with air-conditioned rooms, telephones, on-site dive shop, snorkeling reef in front of hotel, sand beach, shopping arcade, gardens, pool, and restaurant. The hotel's bar is built from salvaged shipwrecks. Dive/accommodation rates start at under $300. Contact Tropical Adventures Travel, ☎ 800-247-3483; fax 206-441-5431.

La Ceiba, located just south of town, is a modern 115-room dive resort offering fast access to the reefs, beach diving, air-conditioned rooms, pool, swim-up bar, jacuzzi, snorkeling trail, two restaurants, cable TV and tennis. Near the cruise ship pier. ☎ 800-777-5873.

The Galapago Inn, is both casual and elegant, with thatch-roofed huts lining the beach, a pool with three mosaic sea turtles, air-conditioned rooms (each with a refrigerator and spacious closets), gourmet dining and an on-site dive shop. Right off shore is a nice snorkeling reef. The inn operates five roomy dive boats, and offers photography and scuba courses, E-6 film processing and professional service. Write to Aqua-Sub Tours, P.O. Box 630608, Houston TX 77263. ☎ 800-847-5708; fax 713-783-3305.

Plaza Las Glorias, just south of San Miguel, is a charming four-story, pueblo-style 170-room resort. Air-conditioned rooms have balconies or patios. Features include a dive shop, boutique, two restaurants, pool and ocean views. ☎ 800-342-2644.

The **Barracuda** caters almost exclusively to dive vacationers. (Their waterslide drops into the ocean.) Fifty units feature double beds, air conditioning, ceiling fans, and ocean views. Reservations through your travel agent or direct, ☎ 987-20002.

Sightseeing and Other Activities

Diving and sport fishing are the main activities on Cozumel, followed by wind surfing, jetskiing, and waterskiing which are offered by the resorts. The widest range of watersport rentals are at Playa San Francisco.

San Miguel's main tourist areas are **Plaza del Sol** where you'll find cafes, craft shops, jewelry stores, restaurants and fast food joints, and the *malecon,* Cozumel's seaside boardwalk. While touring the town stop in at the **Museum of the Island of Cozumel,** a two-story former turn-of-the-century hotel which features displays depicting island wildlife, anthropological and cultural history. Between May and September the museum offers marine-biologist-led tours to witness the sea turtles lay eggs on the eastern shore.

The **Chankanaab Lagoon Botanical Gardens,** two miles south of town, has 300 species of tropical plants and trees and an interesting Mayan museum.

Further south you'll come to the **Celarain Lighthouse** which you may climb for a spectacular view of the area. Be sure to first clear your visit with the resident caretaker.

Rent a jeep to explore the windward east coast of Cozumel. You'll find pounding surf and marvelous stretches of uninhabited beaches lined with mangroves and coconut palms. It may be wise to avoid swimming here because of the dangerous currents and strong undertow except at **Playa Chiquero,** a protected crescent-shaped cove and **Playa Chen Rio** which is protected by a rock breakwater.

Remains of Mayan temples and pyramids can be found at the northern end of the island. Guided tours to explore **San Gervasio** (once the Mayan capital), also on the north end, may be booked through most large hotels. Ferry trips to the larger, more impressive Mayan ruins on the mainland can be booked in town at the International Pier. Most dive packages include a side trip to **Tulum,** a Mayan walled city built in the late 13th century or to Isla Mujeres, a fabulous nearby snorkeling island.

Sightseeing flights around Cozumel, to neighboring islands, or the mainland can be arranged at the airport.

Dining

Local lobster, native grilled fish and a variety of Mexican dishes such as tacos, enchiladas or caracol (a giant conch) predominate at Cozumel's restaurants and road side stands. Several superb native eateries within a few blocks of the pier offer island specialties such as grilled turtle, grilled fish in banana leaves, conch cocktail and spicy steak strips. All in all, dining is quite good in Cozumel whether you choose romantic garden dining with strolling serenaders or a fast snack at one of the many stands.

Music is featured at most restaurants and hotel bars on Cozumel, and the island has a number of discos, including **Scaramouche** and **Neptuno.**

Pepe's Grill on Ave. Rafael Melgar features savory steaks, lobster and seafood. ☎ 20213.

Cafe Del Puerto, at the plaza is one of Cozumel's best spots for lobster and crab. You'll be entertained with live guitar music. ☎ 20316.

El Portal offers fabulous Mexican style spicy breakfasts. ☎ 20316.

Carlos' N Charlies and Jimmy's Kitchen, on Ave. Rafael Melgar 11, is a divers' favorite for Mexican steaks and seafood. ☎ 20191.

La Palmeras, at the pier (27 Rafael Melgar) is a good spot for breakfast and lunch. ☎ 20532.

La Laguna, on the beach restaurant at Chankanab National Park, serves up tasty shrimp, crabs and fish. ☎ 20584.

Pizza Rolandi on Ave. Melgar 22 specializes in Italian favorites.

Helpful Phone Numbers

POLICE: ☎ 20092

HOSPITAL: ☎ 20140

Facts

Nearest Recompression Chamber: Located in San Miguel, ☎ 22387.

Getting There: Direct flights from the U.S. are offered by Key Air, American, Continental, United, Mexicana and Aero Mexico. There are additional domestic flights from Acapulco, Cancun, Guadalajara, Mexico City, Merida, Monterey, and Veracruz. Cruise ships from Miami: Norwegian Caribbean Lines, Holland America, Carnival. The island also can be reached by bus ferry, car ferry and hydrofoil from Cancun. Isla Mujeres is reached by bus ferry, car ferry and air taxi from Cancun. Aerocozumel and Aerocaribe fly between the islands.

Island Transportation: Taxi service is inexpensive and readily available. Mopeds, cars and jeeps may be rented in town or at the airport. Book rental cars in advance of your trip.

Driving: On the right.

Documents: U.S. and Canadian citizens need a tourist card. To obtain one, you must show a valid passport or birth certificate. Citizens of other countries should contact their nearest Mexican consulate for regulations. The tourist card is necessary to leave the country as well and may be obtained from the Mexican consulate or your airline prior to departure.

Customs: Plants, flowers and fruits may not be brought into Cozumel. Persons carrying illegal drugs will be jailed. You may bring three bottles of liquor and one carton of cigarettes. Dogs and cats should have a current vaccination certificate. Divers carrying a lot of electronic or camera gear, especially video equipment, should register it with U.S. Customs in advance of the trip.

Water: Drink only bottled or filtered water to avoid diarrheal intestinal ailment. Also avoid raw vegetables and the skin of fruit and foods that sit out for any length of time.

Currency: The exchange rate of the Mexican peso fluctuates a great deal. At this writing $1 U.S. = 3000 pesos. Banks are open weekday mornings. Major credit cards and traveler's checks are widely accepted in Cozumel.

Climate: Temperatures range from the low 70's in winter to the high 90's in summer with an average of about 80° F. Winter months bring cooler weather; summer and fall, chance of heavy rain.

Clothing: Lightweight, casual. Wetsuits are not needed, but lightweight (1/8") short suits or wetskins are comfortable on deep wall dives.

Electricity: 110 volts; 60 cycles (same as U.S.).

Time: Central Standard Time.

Language: Spanish; English widely spoken.

For Additional Information: *In New York,* The Mexican Government Tourist Office, 405 Park Avenue, Suite 1400, New York, NY 10022.☎ 800-331-1100 or 212-755-7261. *In California,* 10100 Santa Monica Blvd., Los Angeles, CA 90067. ☎ 213-203-8191. *In Florida,* 128 Aragon Avenue, Coral Gables, FL 33134. *In Canada,* Mexican Government Tourist Office, Suite 1526, One Place Ville Marie, Montreal, Quebec, Canada H3B 2B5 ☎ 514-871-1052. *In the United Kingdom,* Mexican Government Tourism Office, 7 Cork Street, London, England, WIX 1PB.

Curacao

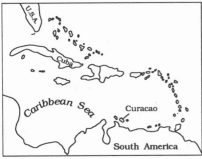

Curacao is the largest of five islands that make up the Netherlands Antilles, which include Bonaire, Saba, Saint Maarten and St. Eustatius. It is a dry and hilly island completely surrounded with rich coral reefs—many within a stone's throw of shore. Its coastline sparkles with beautiful sand beaches, secluded lagoons and snorkeling coves.

Willemstad, its capital, is delightfully Dutch with open-air markets, narrow streets and rows of shops offering imports from all over the world. It is best known for its colorful, Dutch-colonial architecture. According to legend, the first governor of Curacao suffered from migraine headaches due to glare from the white houses and ordered all residents to paint their homes pastel. The rows of pastel-colored town houses with gabled roofs, red tile and rococo-style facades in downtown Willemstad probably are the most photographed sights on the island.

St. Anna Bay, like an Amsterdam canal, divides the capital city in two parts—the Punda and the Otrabanda. A pontoon walking bridge, which opens several times a day to allow cruise ships to dock in town, connects the two sides of the city.

Christoffel Park in the northwestern sector of the island and marked by the island's highest peak (Mt. Christoffel is 1,250 feet high), displays the flora and fauna of desert-like Curacao. Undulating hills in this area are punctuated with the evergreen wayaca and huge cacti, reaching from the parched land like outstretched fingers.

History

Curacao's heritage and history is as long and multi-faceted as the 38-mile-long island itself. The Caiquetio Indians, a tribe of which were the "Indios Curacao," were the original inhabitants of Curacao. In 1499, when Alonso de Ojeda, a Spanish navigator who sailed with Columbus, discovered the island and the Indians. He named it for them.

Contributors: Erwin F. Eustacia, Michel Angelo Harms, Curacao Tourism Development; Ivan Englentina, Eva Van Dalen, Seascape Diving.

Later, in 1634, the Dutch captured Curacao, forcing the evacuation of the Spaniards and the Indian natives. By 1635, only 50 of the 462 inhabitants were native Indians and approximately 350 of the rest were Dutch soldiers. The island became one of the leading slave and salt trade centers for the Dutch West Indies Company.

For many years, England and France tried to conquer the island. The English were successful in 1800, but were defeated two years later by the Dutch. England eventually recaptured the island only to give it back as a result of the Treaty of Paris in 1815.

By the mid 1800s, Curacao's population was as varied as any found elsewhere in the world. One-time soldiers married Curacaoan women and established a livelihood on the island. Merchants from Europe stayed. Others were freed slaves who chose to remain on the island. All carried a part of their culture and tradition to this tropical paradise.

Curacao's harbor became the site of one of the world's largest oil refineries in 1914, following the discovery of oil in Venezuela.

Diving and Snorkeling

Like its sister islands, Aruba and Bonaire, Curacao lies far south of the hurricane belt and offers clear skies and good diving year round. Most dives require a boat. The reefs and wrecks are "a stone's throw from shore," but the "shore" adjacent to the best reefs is often formed of jagged, razorlike, ironshore cliffs. Seas along the south coast—locale of the underwater park—are usually dead calm in the morning, but may kick up a three- or four-ft surge in mid-afternoon.

The Curacao Underwater Park, established in 1983 by the Netherlands Antilles National Park Foundation (STINAPA), stretches 12.5 miles from the Princess Beach Hotel to East Point and features 20 dive sites marked by numbered mooring buoys and another 10 unmarked sites. Within the park, divers and snorkelers find crystal-clear water and spectacular, subsea landscapes. The reefs are in pristine condition with many yet to be explored. As diving did not become popular in Curacao until the 1980s when officials realized the potential for additional tourist growth. Before then, the island was promoted solely for honeymoons, sport fishing and sailing.

Although the park's terrain features dramatic coral walls and deep drop-offs, there is excellent diving in the shallow waters with 50-foot

Seal pond at Curacao Seaquarium. To the left, protruding from the water's surface, is the top of the shipwreck, S.S. Oranje Nassau.

brain coral, gigantic sponges, huge, perfectly-formed trees of elkhorn and enormous and lush seafan gardens. Visibility is a dependable 100 feet.

To the west is the (not yet official) Banda Abao Underwater Park with more than 21 outstanding dive and snorkeling sites.

For the very adventurous, the westernmost dive site **Wata Mula**, features a sloping reef and cave frequented by huge moray eels, grouper, nurse shark and rays. This area is diveable only on very calm days and only with an experienced dive guide. Seas at this end of the island are often very rough with strong currents. Yet, visibility and marine life is outstanding. Suggested for experienced divers in top physical condition.

South of Wata Mula is **Mushroom Forest**, the most beautiful of the Banda Abao Underwater Park. This gently sloping reef is highlighted by giant mushroom-shaped elkhorn corals at 50 ft. It is located offshore from Sanu Pretu.

At the end of *Mushroom Forest* is **Playa Lagoen,** a snorkeling beach nestled between two massive rock formations. Snorkelers will find some juvenile fish and small coral heads along the rocks. Be sure to tote a floating dive flag as small fishing boats weave in and out of the area. Energetic divers can swim out about 150 yds to the dropoff.

South of Playa Lagoen, sea turtles and occasional manta are sighted at the **Black Coral Gardens** off Boca St. Martha. Steep dropoffs, 60 to 130 ft, support a colossal, black coral forest. Nearby is **Mike's Place** known for a giant sponge locally known as the "double bed".

Sandy's Plateau (aka *Boka Di Sorsaka*), is part of the marked trail. It can be reached by swimming out from Jan Thiel Bay. It is an excellent spot for novice divers and snorkelers. The terrain is a combination of walls and steep slopes colored with lavender and pink star corals, yellow pencil corals and orange tube sponges. Lush stands of elkhorn coral grow to within 10 ft of the surface. Dense coral flows around an undercut ledge from 10 to 30 ft. Soldierfish, trumpetfish and schools of sergeant majors hover the ledge.

Offshore to the Curacao Seaquarium in Jan Thiel Bay is the wreck of the **S.S. Oranje Nassau,** a Dutch steamer which ran aground here on the Koraal Specht over 80 years ago. Also known as *Bopor Kibra,* Papiamento language for broken ship, this is a shallow dive and a favorite spot for free diving. The seas are always choppy over the wreck. Entry is best from the diveshop docks adjacent to the seaquarium. Check with the divemaster for the day's conditions.

This area is known for outstanding corals. Depths start shallow with large pillar and star corals, seafans, huge brain coral, and gorgeous stands of elkhorn. It then terraces off to a wall starting at 50 ft. Fish life includes swarms of blue chromis and creole wrasses, French angels, barracuda and jacks. Sea conditions are choppy and recommended for divers and snorkelers with some ocean experience.

Jan Thiel Reef, just outside of Jan Thiel Bay, is a fabulous snorkeling site. Lush, shallow gardens at 15 ft are alive with a mass of gorgonians, two-foot, lavender sea anemones, seafans, long, purple tube sponges, pastel star, leaf, fire, pencil and brain corals. Fishlife is superb with walls of grunts, trumpetfish, parrotfish, angels and small rays. Added buoyancy from a snorkeling vest or shorty wetsuit will help you to stay clear of the fire coral. You can swim from Playa Jan Thiel, just east of the Princess Beach Hotel. The beach has changing facilities and is a favorite for picnics. Admission fee.

Piedra Di Sombre is located between Caracas Bay and Jan Thiel Bay. Ideal for snorkeling and diving, the site is a steep wall covered with abundant seafans, seawhips, wire coral, star corals, club finger coral,

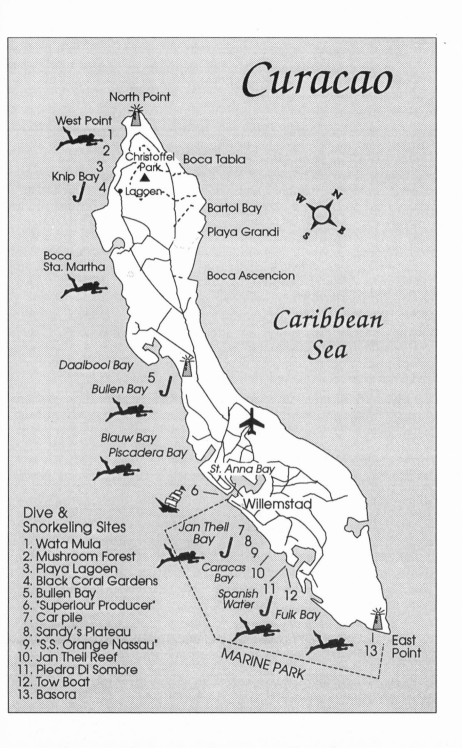

Curacao

North Point

West Point
1
2
Christoffel
Park
3
Knip Bay
4
Lagoen

Boca Tabla

Bartol Bay

Playa Grandi

Boca Ascencion

Boca
Sta. Martha

Caribbean
Sea

Daaibool Bay
5
Bullen Bay

Blauw Bay
Piscadera Bay

St. Anna Bay

Willemstad

6

Dive &
Snorkeling Sites
1. Wata Mula
2. Mushroom Forest
3. Playa Lagoen
4. Black Coral Gardens
5. Bullen Bay
6. "Superiour Producer"
7. Car pile
8. Sandy's Plateau
9. "S.S. Orange Nassau"
10. Jan Theil Reef
11. Piedra Di Sombre
12. Tow Boat
13. Basora

Jan Theil
Bay
7
8
9
10
Caracas
Bay
11
12
Spanish
Water
Fulk Bay

13

East
Point

MARINE PARK

seafans and rows of gorgonians. Depths are from 30 ft to 125 ft. Numerous black corals grow on the wall. Reef residents are lizardfish, black durgons, angelfish and barracuda.

The *Superior Producer* is Curacao's favorite wreck dive. The 100-ft freighter sank in 1977 when her heavy cargo of clothing shifted. The ship is intact and stands upright on a sandy plain at the foot of a steep, coral-covered slope. The wreck is encrusted with orange, red, purple, green and yellow corals and sponges. Clouds of silversides command the wheelhouse; rays and porpoises are frequently sighted. The site has a mooring buoy and is most conveniently reached from a boat, but can be reached by a rugged swim from shore. The closest water-entry point is from the Curacao public swimming pool at the Rif recreation area. Top of the wreck is at 90 feet with sections of the mainmast reaching up to within 40 feet of the surface. Divers are advised to watch the tables as several bounty hunters after the cargo ended up in the island's recompression chamber.

The mooring for **PBH** is in front of the Princess Beach Hotel. This reef starts shallow enough for snorkeling and drops off at 40 ft. Arrow crabs, octopi, and hordes of juvenile fish swim the shallow terrace. Black corals and large grouper are found at depth.

Car Pile, by the Princess Beach Hotel, is an artificial reef constructed from piles of old car and truck wrecks. Depth is 60 to 125 ft. Watch out for jagged pieces of metal and avoid getting under the heaps as the mass is not dependably stable. The wrecks are completely covered over with corals, algae and sponges with resident lobster, crabs and fish. You can reach it by swimming out from the hotel beach. Expect a light to moderate current.

Tow Boat, the favorite shallow dive in the Curacao Underwater Park, is intact, sitting upright on a sandy shelf and can be explored at 15 ft. Tube corals, Christmas trees worms, sponges and sheet corals cover the wheelhouse. Schools of reef fish frolic around the bow. Great for wide-angle photography. Divers can continue down a steep drop off to explore black corals, vase and basket sponges. The wreck is accessible only by boat, a short ride from Caracas Bay.

Choppy seas are usually encountered enroute to **Piedra Pretu**, near the easternmost corner of the coast, but the effort is paid back with exposure to one of the most spectacular reefs in the Caribbean. Massive black-coral trees, huge barrel sponges and dense beds of staghorn and elkhorn adorn a shallow terrace which drops off to a vertical wall. Depths are from 20 to 150 ft. Boat access only.

Basora is the easternmost dive site on Curacao. Much like Piedra Pretu, the area is rich with huge brain and star corals and towering pillar formations. Sheets of star corals drape the wall. Fish life includes monster grouper, sting rays and morays.

Bullen Bay, just north of the park, is an outstanding dive with a protected shallow area for snorkeling and a nice dropoff for diving. Yellow pencil corals and pretty white sea plumes highlight the reef. Average depth is 40 ft.

Klein Curacao (little Curacao) is an uninhabited island about a two-hour boat ride east of Curacao. It is a rugged strip of desolate volcanic rock which plunges into a most spectacular reef. A constant parade of Scorpion fish, red-legged hermit crabs, yellow stingrays, spotted morays, yellow frogfish, eagle rays and huge turtles whistle by the wall.

The shelf drops 100 ft into a blaze of orange elephant-ear sponges, purple tube and rope sponges, black corals, huge seafans and massive boulder corals.

Beaches

Curacao is surrounded by beautiful beaches, from popular hotel beaches to intimate secluded coves. Along the southern coast, there are free public beaches at West Point Bay, Knip Bay, Klein Knip, Santa Cruz, Jeremi Bay and Daaibooi Bay. Knip Bay is the largest and most lovely swimming beach on the island. Snorkeling is good along the adjacent cliffs.

The main private beaches which charge a small fee per car are Blauw Bay, Jan Thiel, Cas Abao, Barbara Beach and Port Marie.

Be careful of the tree with small green apples that borders some beaches. This is the Manzanilla and its sap will cause burns and blisters on wet exposed skin. Its fruit is poisonous.

Dive Operators

Reef and wreck diving and snorkeling trips may be booked through the following operators. Most offer certification courses.

Seascape Divers, on the beach at the Curacao Caribbean Hotel, has fast, comfortable, custom dive boats and ultra-friendly service. ☎ 599-9-625-000 (fax 625-905); divers and snorkelers welcome.

Underwater Curacao,, adjacent to the Seaquarium, at the Lion's Dive Resort is a PADI Five star facility. ☎ 599-9-618-131; fax 613-671. Their

Beach at Curacao Caribbean Resort

double-decker dive boats can easily accommodate large groups. Underwater Curacao's services include round-trip mini-van service from your hotel or cruise ship.

Peter Hughes Diving, at the Princess Beach Resort, offers reef trips and certification courses. ☎ 599-9-614-944; fax 614-131).

Dive and snorkeling trips are also offered by **Dolphin Diving**, at the Curacao Las Palmas Hotel; ☎ 5999-625200, fax 599-9-628181; **Dino Happy Diving, Safari Diving,** ☎ 599-9-688-014; **Divers Way of Curacao,** ☎ 599-9-627-144 (fax 627-632); **Duikschool Landhuis Daniel,** ☎ 599-9-648-400 (fax 648-400); and **Toekan Diving,** ☎ 599-9-612-500.

Travel Packages

Diving is just starting to take off in Curacao with new watersports facilities and dive resorts in the planning stage. A wide range of accommodations are available. Some hotels offer villa-style arrangements and apartments, and there are a wide variety of smaller, more intimate guest houses and inns. Dive/vacation packages including mid-week air fair from the U.S. start at $538. Packages can be booked through the resorts, travel agents, or dive tour operators: **Landfall Productions,** Santa Clara CA, ☎ 800-525-3833, fax 408-983-0677; **Sea Safaris,** Manhattan Beach CA, ☎ 800-262-6670; fax 310-545-1672; **Ocean Connections,** Houston TX, ☎ 800-331-2458/800-364-6232; fax 713-486-8362; **Blue Bonnett Tours,** Miami FL, ☎ 800-334-8582; fax 305-256-9389; 305-256-9389; **Caribbean Adventure Tours,** Atlanta GA, ☎ 800-377-6344, fax 404-952-0656; **Paradise Expeditions,** Lincoln Park NJ, ☎ 800-332-4846, fax 201-696-2335; **Go Diving,** Minnetonka MN ☎ 800-328-5285; **Caribbean Dive Tours,** Marietta GA, ☎ 800-786-3483, fax 404-565-0129.

Accommodations

Curacao Caribbean Resort & Casino is a huge, beachfront hotel with watersports, casino, shopping gallery, tennis, restaurants, beach bar. Dive packages with Seascape Diving. Five minutes from town. Winter rates for four days/three nights with four dives for a double start at $468 per person. For eight days/ seven nights, $938 per person. Includes room, transfers, shuttle bus to and from town, tax, diving, tanks, weights, belts, shorediving, lockers, tee shirt. Reserve through your travel agent or ☎ 800-545-9376 or 203-831-0682; fax 203-831-0817. Write to P.O. Box 2133, Curacao, NA.

Lions Dive Hotel & Marina is a luxurious, oceanfront dive complex adjacent to the Curacao Seaquarium. The resort features a decent restaurant, fitness center and dive shop, Underwater Curacao. Resort and certification courses are available. ☎ 800-451-9376 (U.S.) or 800-468-0023 (Canada). Write to International Travel and Resort Dive Desk, 25 West 39th Street, New York, NY 10018.

The **Princess Beach Resort & Casino** resort overlooks the ocean on a long, white-sand beach. Luxury accommodations, swim-up bar, shopping arcade, restaurant and casino. Dive and snorkeling sites off the beach. Packages. Diving with Peter Hughes. ☎ 800-332-8266 or book through your travel agent.

Las Palmas Hotel, Casino & Vacation Village is less than 400 yards away from the Curacao Underwater Park. This quiet enclave features single rooms or fully-equipped villas in a village setting. A well-equipped dive shop, Dolphin Diving of Curacao is on the premises. Other features are tennis courts, pool, restaurant and mini-market. Packages.

The **Coral Cliff Resort and Beach Club** is nestled in the Santa Marta cliffs on its own private beach. Each unit has a fully-equipped kitchenette and panoramic vistas. Reserve through your travel agent.

Curacao Caribbean Resort & Casino is a huge, beachfront hotel with watersports, casino, shopping gallery, tennis, restaurants. Dive packages with Seascape Diving. Five minutes from town. Reserve through your travel agent.

Holiday Beach Hotel & Casino is located on Coconut Beach facing the Curacao Underwater Park. The 200-room hotel has a complete dive shop, beach, casino, restaurant, open air bar. Rooms are spacious and modern. ☎ 800-223-9815 (U.S. & Canada).

Other Activities

Where ever there is wind and water you are sure to find windsurfing—a cross between sailing and surfing. The area of the Spanish Water Bay at the southeast end of the island is THE spot for testing your board skills.

If you haven't tried it before take a lesson from a pro. The basics can be learned within a few hours from a certified instructor. Experienced boardsailors should head for the Marie Pompoen Area near the Seaquarium. The winds average 12-18 knots, and blow in a left to right direction when facing the water. Check with your hotel's front desk for more information. Sailboards, sunfish sailboats, and jetskis are rented at most of the hotels' watersport centers.

The **Curacao Golf & Squash Club,** near the office for the refinery, offers a nine-hole, oiled-sand course. Stiff trade winds add to the challenge. There are two squash courts which are open all week. ☎ 73590 for reservations.

Horseback riding the beach trails or through the *Kunucu* (countryside) can be arranged through the Ashari Ranch (☎ 86250) or Rancho Alegre (☎ 81616).

In addition to horseback riding, active travelers can jog along the special paved path at the **Rif Recreation Area** *koredor*, a two-mile stretch of palm-lined beachfront about a mile from Willemstad's pontoon bridge.

Deep-sea fishing charters complete with bait and tackle can be arranged for about $50 an hour for a party of four through the marinas at Spanish Water Bay or through the hotel watersport centers. Sport fishing is for marlin, tuna, wahoo and sailfish. Hook and line fishing is allowed in the underwater parks.

Sightseeing

Architecture is the big topside attraction in Curacao. Walking tours of Willemstad and the surrounding countryside are offered by **Old City Tours.** Scheduled departures are on Tuesdays and Saturday at 9 am with pickup by jeep at your hotel. A variety of escorted tours for groups of four or more are offered by Casper Tours, Blenchi Tours and Taber Tours. Arrangements may be booked through most hotels. Taxi tours are about $15 per hour and take up to four passengers.

Many of the hotels offer a free shuttle van to and from Willemstad every half hour until evening. Traffic in town is busy and walking is the best way to see the town. The main town (Punda) area is safe for tourists, but there are occasional robberies. Avoid the long, narrow streets on the outskirts of town. One area is a government-sanctioned, red-light district established to serve transient seamen and is best left unexplored.

Frogfish, Dominica (above) Karen Sabo
Sunset, Bonaire (facing) Jon Huber
Squirrelfish, Dominica (below) Karen Sabo

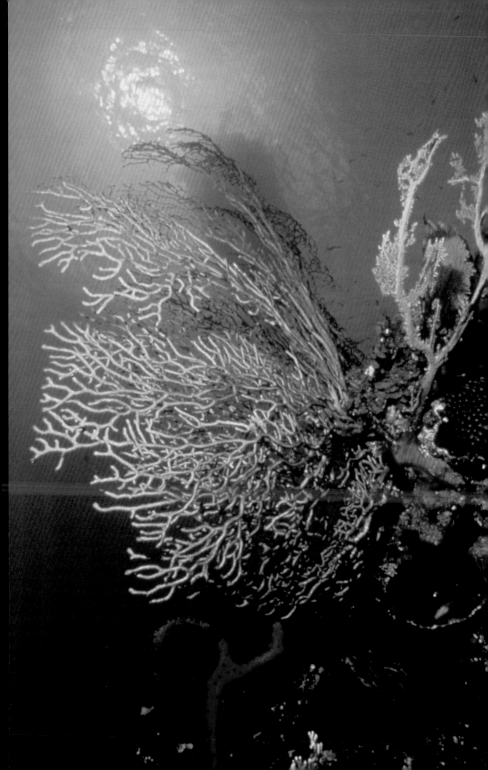

Shipwreck, St. Vincent (above) Karen Sabo
Cayman Wall Dive (facing)
Blue Hole, Belize (below)

Bigeye (above) Jon Huber
Sunset, St. Thomas (facing) Jon Huber
St. Croix, U.S.V.I. (below)

Sea Turtle, Bonaire (above)
First Dive, Humacao, Puerto Rico (facing) Rick Ockelmann
Trunk Bay, St. John, U.S.V.I. (below)

La Parguera, Puerto Rico (above) Rick Ockelmann
Yellow Pencil Coral, Bullen Bay, Curacao (facing) Jon Huber
Squirrelfish in Coral (below) Jon Huber

Vase Sponge, Pigeon Island, Guadeloupe (above) Rick Ockelmann
Snorkeling Malmok, Aruba (facing) Jon Huber
Off St. Vincent (below) Karen Sabo

Stingray City, Grand Cayman (above) Redsail Watersports

Diamond Rock, Saba (below) Joan Borque

French Angelfish, Bonaire (above) Jon Huber

Nisbet Plantation Beach, Nevis (below) Jon Huber

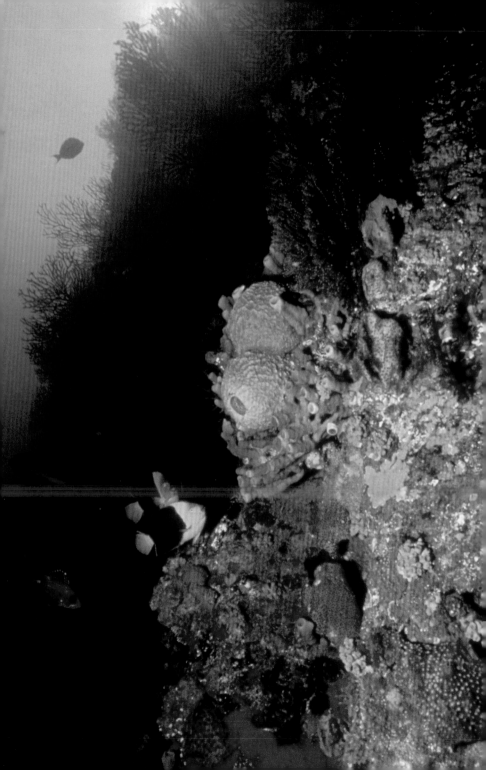

In the 1700s, lavish homes and plantation
houses, were built in the countryside. Go
have assisted in the restoration of many of the
as museums, shops, restaurants and even the
Liqueur Factory.

Landhuis Jan Kock, built in 1650, on the road to W
Bay), is one of the oldest buildings on the island. S
landhuis was restored as a museum in 1960. On Sur
6 pm, Dutch-style pancakes and local specialties an
shop.

Landhuis Brievengat, a Dutch version of the 18th-cent
plantation, was torn down and rebuilt. It now operates as
cultural center, open daily from 9:30 am to 12:30 pm. It is loc
of Willemstad.

The beautifully restored 1700 *Landhuis Ascension*, originally a
house, is a recreation center for Dutch marines stationed on
An open house featuring local music, handicrafts and refresh
held on the first Sunday of the month.

Landhuis Habaai is the only remaining "Jewish Quarter" home bi
early Sephardic settlers. Located in Otrobanda (St. Helena) the planta
home has an authentic cobbled courtyard.

Landhuis Chobolobo is home to the Senior Curacao Liqueur Facto
which distills and distributes the world-famous Curacao liqueur using
the original recipe and distilling equipment from the 1900s.

The popular drink is the result of an agricultural mistake. When Spaniards landed on the island in the early 1500s, they planted hundreds of
orange trees. The arid climate and sparse rainfall did not provide appropriate growing conditions for the citrus crop, and inedible, bitter fruit was
produced. The settlers were not dismayed. They discovered the orange
peel, when dried in the sun, produced an aromatic oil which could be
used to prepare a variety of drinks and foods. Today, the fruit is used to
produce Curacao liqueur. Visitors can tour the factory weekdays from 8
am to noon and 1 to 5 pm to view the process and sample the liqueur.

The island's **Amstel Brewery** manufactures Amstel Beer—the only beer
in the world brewed from distilled sea water. Tours available on Tuesdays and Thursdays at 10:00 am.

In downtown Willemstad, just a few minutes walk from the pontoon
bridge, is a colorful floating market. Scores of schooners tie up alongside

Third Encounter, Saba (Joan Borque/Sea Saba)

ave hut at Christoffel Nat'l Park.

the canal offering fresh fish, tropical fruits, produce, and spices. Docked vessels arrive daily from Venezuela, Colombia and other West Indian islands. Park where you can and walk as traffic is heavy and stopping on the narrow street is tough.

At the western end of the island is **Christoffel National Park** and Christoffel. A protected wildlife preserve and garden covering 4,500 s of land, the park has been open to the public since 1978 and features miles of one-way trails through fields of cactus, divi divi trees and otic flowers. Wild iguanas, rabbits, donkeys, deer and more than 100 ecies of birds inhabit the preserve. If you love roller coasters, you will ve the big rolling hills of this park. Drive slowly. Hiking trails are ery rugged and should be traveled in the cool morning hours.

Walking tours are popular and may be arranged, in advance, through most hotels. Jeeps and four-wheel-drive vehicles are available for rent.

Boca Tabla is the site of a wonderful cave which opens to the sea. You walk the sand path to the cave entrance (signs lead the way) and climb down a path of huge boulders for a spectacular view of waves crashing into the cave entrance. Very photogenic! Because Curacaon's believe women make the ocean angry or more active, a woman may be asked to stay in the cave to liven up the attraction.

So strong is this belief that during a rescue operation off the north shore in 1992, a woman reporter was asked to leave the area so that male divers might do their job more easily.

An even more spectacular natural wonder is **Wata Mula,** a 30-ft-wide crater that tunnels to the open sea. Huge waves crash and recede rhythmically while spewing fountains of froth and rainbows high into the air. Both dramatic and mesmerising, it is a photo buff's delight. Take care if you are driving. The ground is sharp ironshore. The land meets the sea quite abruptly and without warning shoots straight down jagged cliffs into crashing waves. Plus, the area is badly littered with broken beer bottles.

You'll see 20-ft sharks, turtles as big as manhole covers, giant moray eels and more than 400 species of fish, crabs, turtles, anemones, sponges, corals and marine life at the **Curacao Seaquarium.** A "Touch tank" allows

Cave at Boca Tabla opens to the sea

children to pick up starfish, sea urchins and other small sea animals. All species in the 75 hexagonal-shaped aquariums are native to the surrounding waters.

The Seaquarium complex also has two restaurants, plus a magnificent beach and gift shop. It's open daily from 10a.m. to 10p.m. Admission is $5.50 for adults and $2.75 for children under 16.

Other attractions include the **Arawak Clay Factory,** the **Curacao Museum,** the **Hato Caves** near the Hotel Holland, the **Botanical Garden and Zoo,** and numerous old fortresses such as **Rif Fort, Fort Amsterdam** and **Fort Nassau.**

Dining

With culinary influences from more than 40 countries, Curacao offers a wide and wonderful variety of restaurant choices including Dutch, Indonesian, Creole, Swiss, Chinese, French, South American, Indian, Italian and American cuisine. They range from casual eateries to gourmet restaurants, many with spectacular views. Popular fast-food eateries are scattered about the island. Local food is usually chicken, fish or meat in a thin sauce made of onions, peppers and tomatoes with french fries or a biscuit-like pancake.

The **Golden Star Bar and Restaurant,** in town at Socratesstraat 2, is *the* place for goat stew and fungi or other local cuisine at low prices. Hamburgers, sate (skewered meat or fish), bacon and egg sandwiches, sailfish cakes, and fried chicken are on the menu too. Open for lunch and dinner. ☎ 54795-54865.

La Pergola at Waterfort arches in the Punda section of Willemstad is a fine Italian restaurant with lovely views and excellent food. Local seafood, pasta, and steaks. Expensive, but a definite memorable treat. Reservations a must. ☎ 613482. Ask for Simone.

Rumours at the Lion's Dive Hotel is open daily for breakfast, lunch and dinner and features meat dishes and fresh catches of the day. ☎ 617555.

For the charm of a typical Dutch coffee house, with Creole and international dishes try the **Bon Appetit Lunchroom** in the heart of Willemstad's shopping center at Hanchi Snoa. ☎ 616916.

The *Landuis Groot Davelaar* houses the 18th-century **De Taveerne Restaurant & Wine Cellar.** An international lunch and dinner menu also features fine wine and cheeses. Closed Sundays. Reservations. ☎ 370669.

History buffs and romantics will love candlelight dining at the **Fort Nassau Restaurant.** The fort sits high over Willemstad with a 360-degree panoramic view of St. Anna Bay. Both the food and view are spectacular! Open daily from 7 to 11 pm and for lunch Monday to Friday from noon to 2 pm. Prices for lunch average about $15 per person. Dinner entrees (a la carte) are from $22. ☎ 613086/613450.

Fine seafood, from Creole red snapper to Spanish specialties, such as paella mariner, are offered by **El Marinero Seafood** in Biesheuvel, at Schottergatweg Noord 87B. Reservations. ☎ 79833.

Fort Waakzaamheid Bistro is known for its BBQ salad bar and fresh seafood. In Otrobanda, at Berg Domi. ☎ 623633.

For downhome Antillean dishes, there is the **march**—an open-air restaurant where you can choose your lunch from dozens of Curacaoan delicacies cooked up in giant pots. Low, low prices.

In West Punt, stop in at **Jaanchie's Restaurant** for conch stew, goat stew and fried or broiled fish. Located at Westpunt 15. ☎ 640126. This is a beautiful, open-air, garden atmosphere, local restaurant. Local folk artists' work decorate the columns. Very casual, very charming, very special. Excellent local dishes. Average prices.

Fincamar at Lagoen K-27 at West Point is marked by a huge horse sculpture outside. This seafood restaurant is one of Curacao's finest. The back wall is open to scenic views of West Point's towering cliffs. European atmosphere. Prices for dinner entrees start at $18 sans service charges. ☎ 641377.

Fast food fans will find their fill at Breedestraate in Willemstad.

Helpful Phone Numbers

POLICE: ☎ 114

TAXI SERVICE: ☎ 616711

ISLAND BUS SERVICE: ☎ 684733

CAR RENTALS: Budget, ☎ 683198; National, ☎ 683489 or 611644; Jeep Car Rental, ☎ 379044; Love Car Rental, ☎ 690444; 24-Hour Car Rental, ☎ 689410 or 617568.

Facts

Nearest Recompression Chamber: St. Elisabeth Hospital, on the island. ☎ 624900 or 625100.

Getting There: ALM Airlines flies from Atlanta four times a week (Thursday, Friday, Saturday and Sunday), and daily from Miami. Connecting flights are available from most major cities.

Driving: Traffic moves on the right. A. U.S. driver's license is accepted. Rental cars are through Dollar, Budget, Avis, National and Love. Curacao also has an excellent bus system to transport visitors around the island.

Language: The official language is Dutch, but English and Spanish are spoken as well. Most residents speak Papiamento, a blend of Portuguese, Dutch, African, English, French and some Arawak Indian.

Documents: Passports are not required for U.S. and Canadian Citizens. Travelers will need proof of citizenship and a return or continuing ticket. A passport or birth certificate is necessary for re-entering the U.S.

Customs: Arriving passengers may bring in 400 cigarettes, 50 cigars, 100 cigarillos, 2 liters of liquor. There is a duty free shop at the airport.

U.S. residents may bring home, free of duty, $400 worth of articles, including 200 cigarettes, and 1 quart liquor per person over 21 years of age plus $25 worth of Edam or Gouda cheese for personal use.

Airport Tax: For international flights, $10; for inter-island flights, $5.65.

Currency: The guilder, or florin, is the Netherlands Antilles' unit of money. The official rate of exchange is U.S. $1 = 1.77 N.A. florin. However, U.S. dollars and major credit cards are accepted throughout the island.

Climate: Curacao's tropical climate remains fairly constant year round. The average temperature is 80° F and less than 23 inches of rain fall annually, The island is outside of the hurricane belt and its cooling trade winds maintain an average of 15 mph.

Clothing: Snorkelers should bring wetskins or long-sleeve shirts to protect from the sun. Wetsuits are comfortable when making several deep dives, but warm ocean temperatures makes them unnecessary baggage for the average sport diver. Topside dress is casual, lightweight. Topless sunbathing is practiced on some beaches. Jackets are be required for a few restaurants.

Electricity: 110-128 volts, A.C. (50 HZ), which is compatible with American electric razors and blow dryers. Adaptors are not needed. The Lions Dive Hotel has 220 volts.

Religious Services: Protestant, Catholic, Jewish, Episcopal, Seventh Day Adventist.

Additional Information: Curacao Tourist Board, 400 Madison Avenue, Suite 311, New York NY 10017; ☎ 212-751-8266 or 800-332-8266; Fax 212-486-3024.

In Curacao: The Curacao Tourism Development Foundation, 19 Willemstad, Netherlands Antilles; ☎ 011-5999-616000; Fax 011-5999-612305.

Dominica

Dominica, covering 290 square miles, is the largest island in the Windward Chain. Situated between Martinique and Guadeloupe, it is a mountainous island with sheer cliffs on the coasts and volcanic peaks inland. Narrow strips of grey sand skirt much of its perimeter. Ideal for the diver who craves an off-the-beaten-track wilderness adventure, there are no casinos, and no duty free shopping.

Intrepid travelers are lured by the island's sensuous environment and dramatic scenery, both topside and beneath the sea. Its mountainside trails throb with the colors and scents of wild orchids and teas, heliconias, giant ferns, and fruit trees. Cascading waterfalls and wild rivers harmonize with the sounds of exotic parrots and sea birds. Mountain pools simmer from the volcanos seething beneath them. Hillsides, dotted with tiny villages and the ruins of forts and former plantations, climb toward Morne Diablotin, the island's tallest peak with an elevation of 4,747 ft.

Subsea terrain, too, is spectacular with hot springs bubbling up through the sea floor, and shallow wrecks, caves, ledges and walls of critters. Black coral "trees" thrive as shallow as 50 ft.

The island's economic mainstay is agriculture with abundant banana and coconut crops. But the island's outstanding feature is water, with more than 365 rivers, thermal springs, pools, and waterfalls fed by an excess of 350 inches of rainfall per year on its interior and 50 inches on its drier west coast. Thankfully, all of the resorts and dive sites lie off the "dry" western shores.

Most of the 84,000 inhabitants live on the coasts, but 3,700 acres in the northeastern section of Dominica are set aside for the Carib Indian, the island's original inhabitants. The Caribs are fishermen and farmers, canoe builders, basket makers and carvers.

Dive Contributors: Karen & Dennis Sabo, dive instructors and operators of Landfall Productions; Derek Perryman, Dive Dominica.

Roseau, the capital and main city, is built on a flat plain of the Roseau River. It is a busy area which may be seen in its entirety by way of a half-hour walk. Most interesting are some old French Colonial buildings, botanical gardens on the south end and the Old Market on the waterfront where island crafts are offered.

Visitors arriving by cruise ship at the Cabrits National Park, on the northwest tip of Dominica, step off the 300-ft pier and are immediately surrounded by twin waterfalls and a lush garden.

When to Go

The best time to dive Dominica is during the driest season, February through April, though expect the possibility of "liquid sunshine" (aka rain) all year. Whenever you go, plan on doing combat with a ferocious mosquito population, especially at dawn and dusk.

History

Dominica means Sunday in Latin (*Dies Dominica*, day of the Lord). It was named by Columbus for the Sunday he discovered it, Nov. 3, 1493. The island is also called *Waitukubuli* by the Carib Indians, which is translated by some to mean "tall is her body," and by others to mean "land of many battles."

The island was first assigned to its inhabitants, the Carib Indians, in 1660 by an Anglo-French treaty, but later French settlers moved in and established sugar plantations worked by imported black labor which stirred friction between the Caribs, the Brits and the French. Hence, possession passed back and forth between France and Britain during the 18th century. The island gained independence in 1978.

Best Dives and Snorkeling Sites

☆☆☆☆ **Soufriere Pinnacle** rises from the depths of Soufriere Bay to within five feet of the surface. A favorite of macro-photographers, the pinnacle is a cornucopia of crabs, shrimp, lobster, octopi, anemones, starfish, tree worms, and gorgonians. Calm seas and light currents invite all level divers and snorkelers. The site is four miles off the southwest shore—a 15-minute boat ride.

☆☆☆☆ **Coral Gardens**, a short trip from Castaways Beach, is a shallow reef ranging in depth from 15 to 90 ft. Good for diving and snorkeling, the reef is vibrant with corkscrew and pink anemones, arrow crabs, violet Peterson shrimp, flourescent crinoids and flamingo tongue snails. Spotted and green morays eels, sting rays and scorpion fish hide in the shadows.

☆☆☆☆ **Scotts Head Pinnacle** off the southwest tip of the island is a kaleidoscope of brilliant finger sponges, nudibranches, bushy wire corals, sea plumes, crinoids, anemones, and gorgonians over a vertical maze of arches, caves, walls, and ledges. Beware the stinging hydroids!

Fish life is abundant with queen, French and gray angels, mackerel, kingfish, spotted drums, black-bar soldier fish, eels and octopus. The reef starts at 15 ft and drops to great depths. Sea conditions are usually moderate, occasionally rough. Suggested for experienced divers.

☆☆☆ **Scotts Head Drop-Off** lies five miles off Scotts Head, a fishing village at the southern tip of the island. Divers and snorkelers will find large sponges and lavish soft corals along the reef's shallow ledge. The ledge which starts at five ft runs along a wall that drops to 140 ft. Conditions are light to moderate. Good visibility.

☆☆ **Champagne** is a shallow site highlighted by sub-aquatic, freshwater, hot springs which emit a continuous profusion of hot bubbles. A fun dive, it's like jumping into a giant glass of club soda. Near shore with dependably calm conditions, the site covers an area of about 300 square ft. Depths are from the surface to 80 ft, with ten ft the average. The bottom is uninspiring brown weeds ruffled by schools of tiny sprat, reef fish and lobster. Dive or snorkel.

☆☆☆ **Canefield Tug** is a 60-ft wreck lying upright on a sandy bottom. The wreck is intact and acts as an artificial reef attracting colonies of hydroids, anemones, schools of squirrel fish, soldier fish and sergeant majors. The site is four miles from shore at Rivermouth. Visibility varies as do sea conditions. Depths are from 55 to 90 ft.

☆☆☆ **Canefield Barge** is an overturned barge over patches of shallow reef. Depths of five to 40 ft and calm seas make this a good choice for snorkelers and divers. A bevy of small reef fish hover about the wreck. The bottom is vibrant with basket stars, anemones, hydroids and iridescent sponges.

☆☆☆ **Point Guinard Caves**, an area of shallow reefs, grottoes and caves are fun for all level divers and snorkelers. The Caves at 50 ft may be penetrated at 30 ft, but there is rich coral growth in the shallows. It is a great spot for night dives and macro-photography with sea horses, blood stars, octopi, crabs, lobster and hordes of sponges.

☆☆☆☆ **Danglebens Reef,** named for one of the divemaster's ancestors, is a complex of small pinnacles and canyons ending in a deep wall. Average reef depths are 40 to 120 ft. Large barrel and tube sponges, healthy corals, black coral bushes, big grouper and morays delight all levels of divers. Excellent visibility. Sea conditions are light.

Dive Operators

Dive Dominica at Castle Comfort Lodge is a full service dive center. Boats depart at 9:30 for a two-tank trip. Refreshments on board. Friendly staff will wash, rinse and store all of your gear and return it to the boat for the next dive. Shore diving in front of the lodge. Dive/hotel packages (seven nights) from $799, ☎ 800-525-3833 or 809-448-2188; fax 809-448-6088.

Anchorage Dive Centres offers courses, reef, wreck and whale watching aboard two fast boats. Dive-hotel packages from $668. ☎ 800-223-6510 or 809-448-2638; fax 809-448-5680. Write to P.O. Box 34, Roseau, Dominica.

Dive Castaways features personal tours to their own special sights. ☎ 800-223-9815 or 809-449-6244; fax 809-449-6246. Dive-hotel packages from $670. Write to P.O. Box 5, Roseau, Dominica.

Tours

Landfall Productions run by dive instructors and underwater photo pros, Karen and Dennis Sabo, offer all-inclusive, group and individual dive and snorkeling tours to Dominica. ☎ 800-525-3833 or 510-794-1599; fax 510-794-1617. Write to 39189 Cedar Boulevard, Newark, CA 94560.

Paradise Expedition & Trading Co. Ltd packages air, hotel & diving vacations from the U.S. Write to: 6 Lincoln park Plaza, Lincoln Park, N.J. 07035. ☎ 800-468-4748; fax 201-696-2335.

Accommodations

Castle Comfort Diving Lodge is a cozy ten-room inn. Five rooms have ocean-view balconies. All air-conditioned and with ceiling fans. Great meals! Dive packages with Dive Dominica from $750 per day include breakfast and dinner. Reserve through either tour company listed on preceding page.

The **Fort Young Hotel** is a newly rebuilt and refurbished hotel within the walls of the original fort built in 1770. High on a cliff overlooking the Caribbean, the 33-room, ocean front hotel features cable tv, pool, walking

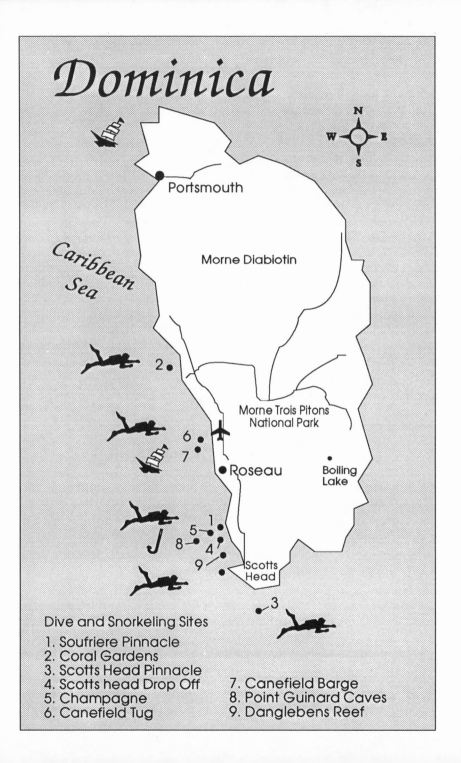

Dominica

Caribbean Sea

Portsmouth

Morne Diabiotin

Morne Trois Pitons
National Park

Roseau

Boiling
Lake

Scotts
Head

2.

6.
7.

1
5.
8.
4
9.

3.

Dive and Snorkeling Sites

1. Soufriere Pinnacle
2. Coral Gardens
3. Scotts Head Pinnacle
4. Scotts head Drop Off
5. Champagne
6. Canefield Tug

7. Canefield Barge
8. Point Guinard Caves
9. Danglebens Reef

proximity to the city, direct overseas dial telephones, restaurant and bar. Neat atmosphere. Dive packages are offered with Dive Dominica from $855 for seven nights, breakfast, ten dives, transfers. ☎ 800-525-3833 or 809-448-5000; fax 809-448-5006.

The Castaways Beach Hotel is a charming, 27-room, waterfront resort surrounded by botanical gardens. Modern, spacious guest rooms have ceiling fans and air conditioning. A beachfront terrace overlooks the sea. Adjacent dive shop. Creole and international cuisine is served at the resort's Almond Tree Restaurant. Casual and quiet. Package tours through Landfall Productions, ☎ 800-525-3833 or 809-449-6244/5; fax 809-449-6246.

Dining

Local specialties include frog legs (mountain chicken), stuffed land crab backs, callaloo soup—made from dasheen leaves and coconut crea—and spicy freshwater shrimps. Restaurants in Roseau serve more familiar dishes too.

Try local specialties at **The Orchard** on the corner of King George V & Gt. George Streets, Roseau, ☎ 44 83051 (closed Sundays) or **La Robe Creole** on Fort St., Roseau, ☎ 82896. **Al's Ice Cream** , 11 Cork Street, Roseau serves 25 flavors, snacks and drinks.

Other Activities and Sightseeing

As with all high altitude areas, be sure to figure strenuous and high-altitude climbs into your dive tables. More than one person has suffered decompression sickness from the combination.

Besides diving there is hiking, canoeing, guided jungle-river tours and rainforest tours. A new coastal road rings the island. Resorts offer windsurfing, water skiing, sailing and tennis.

The favorite topside wonder is **Trafalgar Falls,** just north of Roseau. You can drive to within a 15-minute walk of the 100-ft falls which converge into a lovely pool of granite boulders.

Scotts Head at the southwest tip of the island is a picturesque fishing village offering scenic views of the Atlantic Ocean and Caribbean Sea. It is also the site of the region's first aloe farm.

Heading north, turn left at the village of Soufriere to reach Sulfur Springs where you can see bubbling hot springs of grey mud. Or if you enjoy long hikes, head for **Valley of Desolation** and **Boiling Lake**, east of Roseau where the scenery is absolutely intoxicating.

Emerald Pool in the Central Forest Reserve is a short hike from the road on the northeast side of **Morne Tois Pitons National Park.** Located in the rain forest, the pool is fed by a lovely waterfall.

Boat tours of **Indian River** will bring you close up to exotic birds and plants. Or take the cross-island road to the **Carib Reserve** on the central eastern coast. Native craft shops pave the way. Tours in this region take off from **The Floral Gardens**, (☎ 44 57636) situated at the base of the Tropical Rain Forest bordering the Carib Reserve.

Helpful Phone Numbers

POLICE: ☎ 999

AMBULANCE: ☎ 999

TOURIST BOARD: ☎ 809-448-2351/82186

Facts

Nearest Recompression Chamber: Saba.

Airlines: Reaching Dominica requires a stop in San Juan, Antigua, St. Lucia, St. Maarten or Guadaloupe and, from most European and North American cities, can be reached in a day's journey without an overnight stay. Liat, Air Guadaloupe, Air Martinique and Nature Island Airways are the carriers from the larger islands into Dominica.

Island Transportation: All areas may be reached via bus and taxi services.

Baggage: Only one carry-on bag is permitted and it must fit under your seat. International baggage allowances prevail on flights to Dominica and may not exceed a total of 44 pounds. Baggage in excess of 44 pounds will be charged (depending upon the carrier) around $1 U.S. per pound and flown on a "space available" basis.

Driving: On the left. A local license is required and may be obtained from the airports or at the Traffic Department, High Street, Roseau (Mon. to Fri.). Fees are $20 EC for up to one month. Must be aged 25 to 65 and show a valid driver's license with at least two years experience.

Documents: U.S. and Canadian citizens need proof of citizenship such as passport, voters registration card, or an original birth certificate. A return or onward ticket is also required.

Customs: Banana and coconut fruit, plants and straw materials cannot be brought in. Citrus, coffee and avocado fruit, plants and soil are forbidden.

Currency: The Eastern Caribbean Dollar exchange rate is approximately $2.68 to U.S. $1. Major credit cards are accepted at some hotels and some restaurants, but most purchases and tours require cash in EC dollars.

Language: English is the official language. Creole or French patois is widely spoken.

Climate: Temperatures drop and the chance of showers rise with the elevation. Average temperatures range from 75°F to 90°F. The coolest months are December through March.

Clothing: Lightweight casual cottons are best. Visitors should NOT wear swim suits or short shorts in the streets or stores. A light sweater is suggested for cooler evenings. Pack light—the island is not dressy.

For hiking bring comfortable hiking shoes, light weight raincoat, camera and film, knapsack and shoulder bag, bottled water, hat, sunglasses, sun screen and mosquito repellent.

The water temperature on a deep dive may drop as low as 72°F. Baggage permitting, a shorty or wetsuit jacket is recommended.

Electricity: 220/240 volts, 50 cycles. A converter is necessary for U.S. appliances.

Time: Atlantic Standard Time, one hour ahead of Eastern Standard Time and four hours behind GMT.

Valuables: Lock everything up as you would at home. Avoid taking valuables to the beach.

Departure Tax: $10 U.S.

Religious Services: Roman Catholic, Anglican, Methodist, Pentecostal, Berean Bible, Baptist, Adventist & Baha'i Faith.

Additional Information: *U.S.*, Caribbean Tourism Organization, 20 East 46th St., N.Y., N.Y. 10017-2452. ☎ 212-682-0435; fax 212-697-4258. *England*, Dominica Tourist Office, 1 Collingham Gardens, London SW5 OHW, ☎ 071 835-1937; fax 071 373-8743. *Dominica*, National Development Corp., P.O. Box 73, Roseau, Commonwealth of Dominica, W.I. ☎ 809-448-2351/82186; fax 809-448-5840.

Dominican Republic

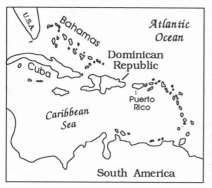

The Dominican Republic shares the Caribbean's second largest island, Hispaniola (between Cuba and Puerto Rico), with Haiti. Located on the eastern half of the island, the Dominican Republic, with an area of 19,376 square miles, is flanked by the Atlantic Ocean to the north and the Caribbean Sea to the south. Its central portion is sculpted by four great mountain ranges with peaks over 10,000 ft. Its coastline varies from rocky cliffs to sandy beaches. Reefs and ancient wrecks surround much of the shoreline.

Santo Domingo on the south Caribbean coast and eastern bank of the Ozama River, is the main port and capital city. Home to more than one million people, it is the oldest city of the New World and professed burial place of its founder, Christopher Columbus. Built in the early 1500's, the city was the first hub of Spanish culture and commerce in the western hemisphere.

One section, about 15 city blocks, has been restored as "Old Santo Domingo" and includes the castle of Diego Colon, Columbus' son and the island's first viceroy. The 22-room castle has been tastefully refurbished with paintings and tapestries to reflect the 16th century. Colonial style shops, galleries and restaurants surround the old city's central plaza.

The main city area is very cosmopolitan and very tourist oriented with 3,498 hotel rooms, several casinos, shopping malls, nightclubs and restaurants. The city boasts the New World's first Cathedral, first University (Santo Thomas de Aquino), first hospital (San Nicolas de Bari), the Monasery of San Francisco, the Ozama Fortress and the world's largest open-air discotheque along its shoreline drive, the Malecon.

When touring Santo Domingo expect solicitations from countless beggars and youthful entrepreneurs pushing shoeshines and other services.

Dive material contributor: Walter Frischbutter, Treasure Divers.

Boca Chica, 31 miles east of Santo Domingo, La Romana, 110 miles east of Santo Domingo and Bayahibe, 125 miles east of Santo Domingo, are the jump-off points for the country's best Caribbean dive and snorkeling sites including La Caleta National Park and the Eastern National Park (Parque Nacional del Este), which encompasses the islands of Saona and Catalina. The marine portion of the parks is a sanctuary to manatees, turtles and waves of passing dolphins. Dependably calm seas and miles of virgin reefs prevail.

Costa Caribe, just west of Boca Chica, is the chief weekend playground for Santo Domingo's million residents. Formerly known as the fishing villages of Juan Dolio and Guayacanes, this beautiful stretch has more than 15 miles of uninterrupted beaches shaded by coconut palms and serviced by first class hotels. It is a half-hour drive from the Las Americas International Airport and under an hour from Santo Domingo, the capital city. Given the close proximity to the capital this area draws crowds on weekends.

On the north coast, the main tourist area stretches from Puerto Plata, a large city and deep-water port, to Cabrera where impressive beaches and coconut groves have lured Europeans for more than 500 years. This area is also a prime whale-watching spot where during winter months (December to March) thousands of humpback whales migrate to an offshore breeding ground. The breeding ground is 50 miles north of the coast, but the herds are spotted enroute as they pass the Samana Peninsula which forms the northeast corner of the Dominican Republic. Reefs and wrecks dot the northern shores, but rough seas frequently rule out diving all but during Summer. Large, modern, upscale resorts skyline the area.

The country's southwest region is the least developed. It is the locale of the largest lake in the Caribbean, Lake Enriquillo, with water three times more saline than the ocean and where the largest American crocodile colony of the New World resides.

Mosquitoes readily announce their presence throughout the coastal areas. Bring and use repellent. We find Autan (sold in the Caribbean) and Deep Woods Off useful. Autan, if you can find it, is the best defense against the tiny gnats, aka no-see-ums, which are out after a rainfall.

The best weather and the fewest mosquitoes exist from mid-December through April, but divers may prefer the summer months when the water is warmer and calmer seas prevail on the north and east coasts. When the skies cooperate, diving along the Caribbean, southeast coast is good year round.

History

Christopher Columbus discovered the island of Hispaniola in December, 1492 when his flagship, *Santa Maria* ran aground on what is now Haiti's north coast. Thirty nine crewmen who were left behind, started the first Spanish settlement in the new world, La Navidad. but, when Columbus returned a year later, the settlement was destroyed and all the crewmen had been killed.

Late in 1493, Columbus established a new colony at Isabela, near Puerto Plata, but abandoned the sight for a better harbor on the south coast, now known as Santo Domingo (originally Santiago de Guzman). Columbus's son, Diego was appointed viceroy and Hispaniola became the hub of Spanish culture and commerce in the New World. After three centuries the Spanish colonizers moved on to exploit Mexico and Peru.

French, Dutch and English explorers settled various parts of Hispaniola during the 1500's and 1600's. As the Spanish settlers congregated around Santo Domino, the north and west coasts were left to buccaneers and foreign settlers who eventually came under the protection of France. In 1697 Spain recognized France's claims to the western third of the island.

The French colony, first known as Saint Domingue and later as Haiti, prospered while the Spanish colony declined. By 1795, Spanish Hispaniola was ceded to France. By 1844, Juan Pablo Duarte established the Dominican Republic as an independent nation, but the nation, under constant Haitian threat asked Spain to reinstate its sovereignty. Fighting between Spain and Haiti continued until 1865 when a strong-willed military dictator, Ulises Heureaux took over. Heureaux was in power until 1897 when he was assassinated.

The early 1900's brought intercession by the U.S. to the violence-torn nation. U.S. occupation brought military rule and economic exploitation by U.S. businesses. The Dominicans resented the U.S. troops and forced their evacuation in 1924.

From 1930 to 1961, the island was ruled by dictator, Rafael Leonidas Trujillo Molina. Trujillo's corrupt form of government left no citizen safe from arrest or degradation by his secret police. Despite the misery he brought upon the people, Trujillo modernized and rebuilt highways, sugar, coffee and cocoa plantations, and by 1947, paid off all of the nation's foreign debts. On May 30, 1961, he was assassinated by his army.

With Trujillo's death, the Dominican Republic attempted to establish a democracy. In 1962, the country held its first free election in 38 years and elected Juan Bosch, a writer and professor. The new government, plagued by unrest and agitation from the upper-class and military, fell to national unrest and a bloodless coup. But, the U.S. alarmed at reports of communist influence stepped in. Military command was then turned over to an InterAmerican Peace Force.

Since then the Dominican Republic struggled through the 1970's worldwide recession which touched off a crisis in the sugar industry, a 1979 hurricane which devastated much of the island and social unrest fueled by crowded cities. The 1980's brought a rising foreign debt and inflation.

With a continued struggle for a better quality of life, the Dominican Republic remains at peace; its golden beaches flaunting the promise of a new era of tourism.

Best Dive and Snorkeling Sites

The best dives and snorkeling sights are off Boca Chica, 30 miles east of Santa Domingo and the marine portion of The Eastern National Park off La Romana, 110 miles east of Santo Domingo. Both marine parks, less than a mile from the shore, display healthy corals in all but the extreme shallows. Large fish are rare as sport fishing is big and reef preservation is new to Santo Domingo. New laws prohibiting spearfishing and coral collecting in the sanctuary have brought back a decent population of tropicals.

There are several good dive sights in La Caleta and along the reefs which start one and one-half miles out from La Romana and follow the coast past Bayahibe to Isla Catalina and Isla Saona. Reef depths range from the shallows to 150 ft. Dive and snorkeling boats leave from the marinas at Boca Chica, La Romana and Bayahibe.

Pristine coral reefs and mini-walls off Bavaro and Punta Cana on the East Coast are subject to wind and current patterns. When seas are calm this is a super diving area.

☆☆☆☆ **Isla Catalina** an uninhabited islet, two and one-half miles off La Romana, was once used as a zoo. Exotic wild birds and monkeys are often sighted along its beaches. The island, surrounded by beautiful reefs which start at 15 ft and drop to 110, is ideal for snorkelers and all levels of divers. The reef, protected from spearfishing and coral collecting, flourishes with walls of tropicals, lobster, sea fans, sea rods, big barrel

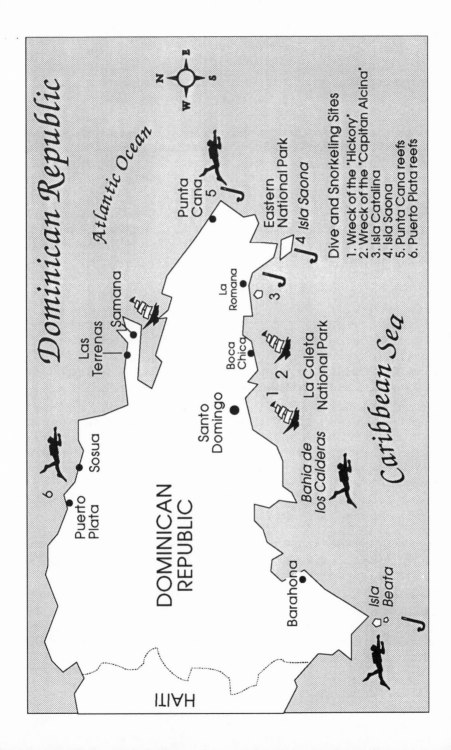

Dominican Republic

Atlantic Ocean

Punta Cana

Samana

Las Terrenas

Sosua

Puerto Plata

Santo Domingo

Boca Chica

La Romana

La Caleta National Park

Bahia de los Calderas

Barahona

Isla Beata

DOMINICAN REPUBLIC

HAITI

Caribbean Sea

Eastern National Park

Isla Saona

Dive and Snorkeling Sites

1. Wreck of the "Hickory"
2. Wreck of the "Capitan Alcina"
3. Isla Catalina
4. Isla Saona
5. Punta Cana reefs
6. Puerto Plata reefs

N E S W

sponges and black corals at depth. Seas are calm with an occasional light current. Excellent visibility though the shallows get kicked up when several snorkeling boats anchor at the same time.

There are no facilities or fresh water on the island but, for the adventurous among you, camping is possible if permission is obtained from the La Romana Naval Station in advance. You need to bring everything with you. At dusk you will be joined by a ferocious mosquito population. Wear and carry as much bug repellent as you can.

☆☆☆ *The Hickory* is a 140-ft wreck, intentionally scuttled in the shallows of La Caleta National Marine Park off La Caleta Beach. Remains of the wreck are found between three ft and 60 ft. The wreck is covered with anemones and hydroids and lots of reef fish—squirrel fish, sergeant majors, and spotted drums. It is surrounded by a pretty reef. Calm seas and 100-ft plus visibility make this spot good for divers and snorkelers.

☆☆☆ Wreck of the *Capitan Alcina* is another ship purposely sunk in La Caleta National Park to attract fish. The wreck sits in a ravine between canyons of the reef. You can reach the top at 75 ft, the bottom at 126 ft. Expect a good reef-fish population, pillar corals, big brain corals, sea rods, plumes, sea fans and deepwater gorgonians. The sea is always fairly calm and currents are mild. Suggested for experienced divers.

When the Atlantic seas are calm (usually summer for a short period) there is additional diving off Isla Punta Cana on the southeast coast, off Sosua and Cabrera on the north coast. Sport fishing and spearfishing in the northern coastal areas have taken a toll on the fish population, but some of the underwater terrain is pretty. Numerous dive shops are found around Puerto Plata.

Dive Operators

Stick with the dive shops associated with the resorts, as most of the Dominican dive shops cater to locals. Certification cards are required to dive in the Dominican Republic.

Treasure Divers at the Don Juan Beach Resort in Boca Chica has one of the finest English-speaking operations in the Dominican Republic. Instructor, Walter Frishchbutter offers reef and wreck trips and cave diving (experienced   cave divers only) off Boca Chica and La Caleta. PADI certification courses. ☎ 809- 523-5320; fax 809-523-4444.

Diver's Cove Dominicano, a PADI training center, is in San Pedro, halfway between Boca Chica and La Romana. Trips and courses. ☎ 809-556-5350 or 809-529-8225.

If you are staying on the north coast, try **Caribbean Marine Puerto Plata**. This PADI center visits the northern wrecks and reefs. ☎ 809-320-2249; fax 809-320-2262.

The resorts listed below either have dive shops or can arrange for dive and snorkeling trips.

Accommodations

A complete list of resorts and rates available from the Dominican Republic tourist office, P.O. Box 497, Santo Domingo, Dominican Republic. ☎ 800-752-1151 or 809-689-3657; fax 809-682-3806.

Don Juan Beach Resort in Boca Chica offers 124 air-conditioned suites, snack bar, restaurant, pool, disco, tennis, dive shop, sand beach, entertainment, baby sitting service, and free parking. Rates are $70 to $100 per day in winter. Book through your travel agent or ☎ 809-687-9157; fax 809-688-5271.

Club Dominicus Beach Resort in Bayahibe is a stone's throw from the reef. This Italian-run beachfront resort offers 340 rooms and all-inclusive packages that include diving, sunfish sailboats, sailboards, three meals daily and nightly calypso shows. Winter room rates are from $70 to $100 per day. ☎ 800-922-4272 or 809-686-8720; fax 809-687-8583.

Casa De Campo is a huge, 7000-acre resort complex in La Romana. It has its own airport and marina, 750 rooms or villas and a variety of sports. The resort appeals more to South Americans and Europeans than Americans and is more geared to snorkelers than divers. But, if you are a snorkeler who is also a trap or skeet shooter, tennis player, horse-back rider, polo player, and artist or golfer, curiosity alone will lure you here. This place has it all including a 16th-century replica of a Mediterranean artist village, Altos de Chavon, and its acclaimed School of Design. For watersports there are glass-bottom, snorkeling, picnic cruises to Catalina Island, 14 pools, miles of beaches—snorkeling off their Minitas Beach, paddle boats, windsurfing. Their "Leisure Time" package, per-person rates for a double in winter (Jan. 8 to April-11) for four days and three nights start at $467 including breakfast daily and transportation on the resort. ☎ 800-854-5405, 305-856-7083 or 809-523- 3333; fax 305-858-4677.

Punta Cana Beach Resort offers a wide choice of accommodations from villas and studios to suites. All air-conditioned with cable TV. Dive shop on premises. Other sports offered are horse-back riding, bicycling, tennis and pool swimming. Features include a beautiful palm-lined beach and disco. Winter rates are from $80 to $90 per day.

Dining

DON'T DRINK THE WATER OR EAT THE SKINS OF RAW FRUIT OR VEGETABLES! Or you might suffer *Caonabo's* revenge, aka "the tourist's disease." The cure, even worse to some than the disease, is *mangu*, a puree of green plantains.

Note: Menu prices are often in Dominican pesos. D$12.50 = US$1.

Italian, Spanish, French and Jamaican restaurants are plastered along the beach roads and the cities. Full course dinners in the tourist areas are about $20 U.S. Much lower prices prevail in the small, local restaurants. Several good restaurants and street vendors are found along the beach road (the Malecon) in Santo Domingo. The vendors' carts steam with sizzling fried pork rinds (chicharones) and meat filled pastries (pastelitos). American sandwiches, snacks, pizza, and salads are offered at the Sheraton's coffee shop. Beer aficionados will enjoy a cold Presidente.

In La Romana you'll find a wide range of restaurants in the Casa de Campo complex. For super views and fresh seafood try **Casa del Rio** in Altos.

Dominican menus typically offer a version of *La Bandera*, a compote of white rice, red beans and stewed meat, usually served with a salad and fried plantains. Regional dishes include fish in coconut milk in Samana and Goat meat in Azua where the goats are fed a daily dish of wild oregano. In Puerto Plata and the south coast, crabs are the favored menu item. A breakfast favorite is *tortilla de jamon*, a hot ham omelet. *Sancocho* is a Dominican stew prepared differently in each region. *Sancocho Prieto* is a black stew made with seven different meats (don't ask which seven).

Other Activities and Sightseeing

If you plan to tour Old Santo Domingo include a stop at **El Alcazar**, Diego Columbus's Castle; **Casa del Cordon,** the first residential house build in Santo Domingo; the **Dominican Monastery**; and the ruins of **St. Nicolas De Bari Hospital.** The remains of Christopher Columbus are believed to be in the **Cathedral of Santa Maria la Menor,** the oldest cathedral in the New World.

In La Romana there is the **Museum of Archaeology** at Altos de Chavon which features exhibits of the Taino Indians, Hispaniola's first inhabitants.

City and mountain excursions are offered from Santo Domingo tour companies. Try ☎ Metro Tours ☎ 544-4580, or Palm Tours ☎ 682-3407.

Additional Reading

For a complete, up-to-date guide to the entire country pick of a copy of *The Adventure Guide to the Dominican Republic* by Harry Pariser (Hunter Publishing) before you go.

Helpful Phone Numbers

POLICE: ☎ 711.

PHARMACY: (Santo Domingo, Los Hidalgos on 27 de Febrero 241) ☎ 565-4848.

DOCTOR: Santo Domingo, Clinica Gomez Patino, Independencia ☎ 701, 685-9131 La Romana, Centro Medico Oriental, Sta. Rosa ☎ 556-2555.

TOURIST BOARD: local, ☎ 689-3657.

INTERNATIONAL AIRPORTS: Las Americas, Santo Domingo, ☎ 549-0450/80; **Herrera,** Santo Domingo, 567-3900; **Punta Aguila,** La Romana, ☎ 556-5565; **Punta Cana,** Higuey, ☎ 686-8790; **La Union,** Puerto Plata, ☎ 586-0219; **Cibao,** Santiago, ☎ 582-4894.

Facts

Nearest Recompression Chamber: Santo Domingo.

Airlines: Direct service is available from U.S. gateway cities and most Canadian and European travel centers. American, ☎ 800-433-7300; American Eagle, ☎ 800-433-7300; Continental, ☎ 562-6688; Air Canada, ☎ 567-2236; Air Aruba, ☎ 541-8766; ALM, Iberia, Lufthansa, Varig, Viasa, Aeropostal, Air France.

Driving: On the right

Documents: Citizens of the U.S., Canada and the Caribbean must have a valid passport and a Tourist Card which costs $10 and may be purchased upon arrival at one of the international airports. Maximum stay is 60 days. Citizens of the United Kingdom may stay up to 90 days with a valid passport.

Customs: You may bring in a liter of alcohol, 200 cigarettes and gift articles with a value of no more than $100. Anyone entering the country with opium, cocaine, coca, cannabis or related drug-making herbs will be fined or imprisoned without bail. You may NOT leave with more than $5,000 U.S. in cash or travelers checks.

Currency: The Dominican Peso. U.S. $1 = D$12.50. The U.S. dollar is not accepted. Change only as much as you think you'll need as most banks won't change back to foreign currency. It is easiest to change currency at the airport. Banks are closed on weekends. Major credit cards are accepted at large establishments, but a surcharge of 3-5% is added on.

Language: Spanish is the official language. People linked to tourism usually also speak English.

Climate: Temperatures along the south coast average 82°F in winter; slightly higher in summer with highs in the 90's.

Clothing: Lightweight. Carry a sweater or jacket for winter evenings. The seashore resorts are informal. Shorts and bare chests are not welcome in the churches. Divers should bring a shorty wetsuit, lightweight wetsuit or wetsuit jacket during winter months. In summer a wetskin or tee shirt suffices.

Electricity: 110-120 volts - 60 cycles, as in the U.S.

Time: Atlantic Standard (Eastern Standard + 1 hour).

Departure Tax: U.S. $10.

Religious Services: Catholic, Evangelical Protestant, Assembly of God, Protestant Episcopal, Seventh-Day Adventists.

Additional Information: *In the U.S.,* ☎ 800-752-1151; *In Canada,* ☎ 514-845-6526 or 416-928-9188. *In Europe* (Madrid), ☎ 341-431-5354 or 01-442-3099; Fax 01-441-7001. Elsewhere ☎ 809-689-3657; fax 809-682-3806; or write Dominican Republic Tourist Board, P.O. Box 497, Santo Domingo, Dominican Republic.

Grenada

Nestled in the eastern Caribbean, Grenada—largest of the three-island nation including Carriacou and Petit Martinique—is the most southerly of the Windward Islands and is the gateway to the Grenadines.

Renowned for its deep, sheltered harbors, the island is a favorite stop-over for private yachts and cruise ships. The hub of mariner activity being the capital city, St. George's, which boasts a superb, horseshoe harbor formed partially from the crater of an extinct volcano.

The island's perimeter is blessed with 80 miles of white-sand beaches. Its coastline stretches out to hundreds of small peninsulas which shelter numerous bays and lagoons. Offshore coral reefs provide home to huge turtles, stingrays, and tropicals. Shipwrecks abound.

Intriguing, too, is Grenada's mountainous terrain. Volcanic in origin, it is thickly wooded and wildly tropical with towering thickets of bamboo, banana plantations, wild orchids, bubbling hot springs and waterfalls—home to butterflies, armadillos, monkeys and exotic cuckoo birds. Fertile soils produce a fragrant bounty of tropical fruits, cocoa, nutmeg, mace, ginger root, thyme, tonka beach, tamarind, turmeric, cinnamon and cloves. Red-roofed houses pepper the hillside.

Carriacou and Petit Martinique retain the idyllic character of early life in the Caribbean. In Carriacou, boat builders still construct and launch sturdy wooden schooners as they have for generations. The brightly-colored boats ply between the islands, carrying passengers and cargo, their huge white sails billowing in the trade wind. Carriacou has great diving and snorkeling reefs off her south and west coasts around White, Mabouya and Sandy Islands.

Contributor: David Macnaghten, Dive Grenada

History

History records Christopher Columbus as the first to sight Grenada in 1498. He named the egg-shaped island Concepcion. Peaceful tribes of Ciboneys and Arawaks first inhabited the island followed by the more war-like Caribs who named the island Camerhogne.

The Caribs were driven by the French to mass suicide in 1651 at the famous "Carib's Leap," located at the northern end of the island where the town of Sauteurs (named after the event—French for "jumpers") now stands.

During the dynastic wars of the 18th century, Grenada changed hands several times between the British and French, until it was finally ceded to the British in 1783. Grenada became independent on February 7, 1974.

The late 1970s brought a Marxist government endorsing the Cuban establishment of a military runway and submarine base on Grenada. Tropical fields were being decimated, the tourist population dwindled and the deteriorating island was crawling with Soviet operatives. In 1984, terrorists took over an American medical school. President Reagan responded by sending in troops and replanting the seeds of democracy. Today, peace and tranquility reign and the island is rebuilding a healthy tourist trade.

Nicknamed the "Isle of Spice," Grenada is one of the last Caribbean islands that actively exports spices. Early spice-cargo ships, to make way for the spices, dropped ballast stone which was used for building houses by the islanders.

Diving and Snorkeling

Grenada dive and snorkeling sites are offshore to Grand Anse Beach, Molinere Point and Dragon Bay, all on the west (leeward) coast.

Diving and snorkeling is weather-dependent. During dry periods the visibility exceeds 100 ft. After a heavy rainfall, run off from the rivers can lower it to 25 ft. Decompression dives are not recommended as there are no chambers in the area.

Good snorkeling from Grenada's shore is possible at the southernmost headland of Morne Rouge Bay and the reef system of Grand Anse. The innermost reef has been destroyed, but a 100-200 ft swim will take you over huge sea fans and beautiful coral heads teaming with fish. Bring a

St. George's horseshoe-shaped harbour.

floating dive flag and stay near to it as many small craft are in the area. A light surge should be expected.

Sandy Island off the southwest coast of Carriacou is surrounded by outstanding reefs and gorgeous beaches. It is among the best snorkeling spots in the Caribbean. You need a boat to get there. Anchorage is south (leeward) of the island (yachtsmen need two anchors to avoid being washed ashore).

☆☆☆ The most adventurous scuba trip is to the *Bianca C*, a 600-ft cruise ship which sank October 24, 1961. Possibly the largest wreck in the Caribbean, the cruise liner, crippled by a boiler explosion, was at anchor for two days, outside St. George's while it burned. It sank as it was being towed by the *HMS Londonderry*, in an attempt to beach it out of the shipping lane. The bottom rests on a sandy plain in 160 ft of water. The top decks at 90 to 120 ft are encrusted with hydroids and have compacted since the sinking. Remains of the internal walls are badly rusted and crumble to the touch.

Because of the depth you are down just 15-17 minutes. Most dives proceed around the stern of the boat, where you can "swim" in the pools with resident barracuda, eagle rays, an occasional shark, huge hawkbill turtles, and large grouper.

Strong currents do occur on the *Bianca*, but die out at 50 feet or so. All divers should have open-water experience before attempting this dive and then only with a qualified, local, dive guide. Dive Grenada dive

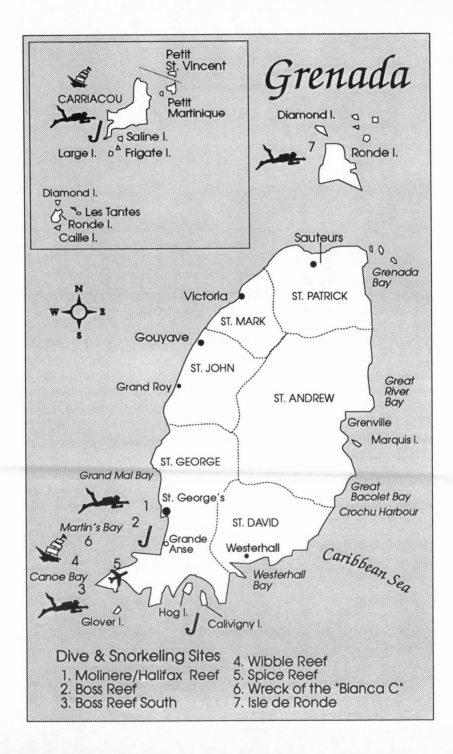

Grenada

Dive & Snorkeling Sites
1. Molinere/Halifax Reef
2. Boss Reef
3. Boss Reef South
4. Wibble Reef
5. Spice Reef
6. Wreck of the "Bianca C"
7. Isle de Ronde

master, David Macnaghten fastens a safety line from the anchor line to the ship. Once everyone is back on the line, it is cast off and you begin your slow ascent to the surface.

☆☆☆ An easier dive and good for snorkeling is **Boss Reef**, a six-mile-long reef, that stretches from Grande Anse Bay to Canoe Bay off the southwest tip of the island. Just a five-minute boat ride from the shore, it extends some 100 feet across and offers numerous dive sites all called "Boss." The reef is a series of coral canyons ranging in depth from 20 to 40 ft with some drop-offs to 60 ft. Fish life is abundant schools of grunts, goat fish, rays, grouper, turtles and barracuda. Seas are usually running a one- to two-ft chop.

☆☆☆ West of Boss Reef is **Wibble Reef**. Most of the dives here are gentle (1 knot) drift dives that take you through vast schools of creole wrasse and chromis. The reef starts at 40 ft and slopes down to 160 ft. Groves of black coral and gigantic sea fans adorn the wall which displays a constantly changing panorama of fish. The bottom is sandy with soft corals, lobster and small critters.

☆☆ **Spice Reef,** just off Pt. Salines, the southwest tip of Grenada, is one of the best spots for snorkeling and shallow dives. The reef drops gradually from 20 to 80 ft. The shallows are home to a vast of array of juvenile fish, octopi, parrotfish, sea fans and finger corals.

☆☆☆ **Isle de Ronde** is a group of tiny, picturesque islands off the north coast of Grenada. They are fringed with virgin reefs that drop sharply down. A profusion of pastel soft corals, sea fans and gorgonians highlight this lovely area. From St. George's, it is a one-hour boat ride to the dive site. Recommended for experienced divers.

☆☆ The **Halifax-Molinere Wall**, is close to shore, making it a favorite night dive. The reef starts at 30 ft and drops down to a sandy bottom at 90 ft. Marine life is splendid with large vase sponges, sea whips, gorgonians, sea fans, finger corals, spotted morays, Spanish hogfish, large French angels, sergeant majors, turtles and rock beauties. Visibility varies with the weather. A day of rough seas and winds may reduce visibility. Expect a light current. Open-water experience is suggested.

Dive Operators

Dive Grenada, at the Ramada Renaissance in St. George's, offers dives and PADI courses for all levels of experience. A dive to the *Bianca C* with all equipment costs $45. Snorkeling equipment is $8 per day. Dive

Grand Anse beach.

Grenada also offers water skiing, windsurfing, cruises, offshore fishing, underwater video and a wide choice of motorized watersports equipment. ☎ 809-444-4371; Fax 444-4800.

Grenada Aquatics Ltd. offers diving, snorkeling and other watersports at Coyaba Beach Resort, Grand Anse Beach. ☎ 809-444-4129.

On Carriacou, **Dive Paradise** offers trips to approximately 30 diving sites in the immediate vicinity and courses for certification. Dive Paradise also has snorkel equipment and underwater cameras. The shop is at the Silver Beach Resort. ☎ 809-443-7337.

Sailing

Day and week-long scuba and snorkeling trips to secluded bays, to Carriacou and the Grenadines may be arranged through Starwind ☎ 809-4403678; 440-2508.

Crewed or bareboat vacation charters may be booked through the Moorings ☎ 800-800-535-728, or write to The Moorings, Ltd., 1305 U.S.19 South, Suite 402, Clearwater FL 34624.

Grenada Yacht Services at St. George's Harbour, has complete marina facilities and charters for week-long or shorter excursions. There are no port dues or fees for visiting yachts. ☎ 809-440-2508-2883.

Accommodations

Grenada is one of the Caribbean's best bargains. Guest-house rooms rent for as low as $12 in summer and $20 in winter. More luxurious cottages are offered for $70 a night. A two-bedroom efficiency can be rented for $340 per week. Hotels average $150 for a double. Several of the hotels may be reserved through the Association office in Grenada. In the U.S.

and Canada, ☎ 800-223-9815 or 212-545-8469; in Grenada ☎ 800-322-1753 or fax 809-444-4847.

The **Ramada Renaissance Hotel** in St. George's is close to diving. It sits on the famous two-mile-long Grand Anse Beach on 20 acres of landscaped tropical gardens. The 186-room resort offers deluxe accommodations—king-sized or extra large twin beds, air conditioning, balconies, direct-dial telephones, color tv, conference facilities. Beachfront open-air restaurant, snack bar, dive shop, pool, beach bar. Rates are deluxe (winter: single $100 double, $158-$183). Major credit cards accepted. ☎ 809-444-4371 or write P.O. Box 441, St. George's Grenada, West Indies.

Coyaba Beach Resort on Grand Anse Beach, a low-rise, 40-room resort, offers a seaview from all rooms, tennis, palm-lined beach, phones, dive shop, two restaurants, balconies, air conditioning. Walking distance from shopping and restaurants. Rates, deluxe—winter: single $100; double, $150.

Siesta Hotel, St. George's, consists of 25 new, studio, one- and two-bedroom luxury apartments. All air conditioned, ceiling fan, kitchen, telephone, TV, balcony, ocean views. Pool, poolside restaurant. Minutes from the airport, golf course and St. George's. Dive shop in walking distance. It is 200 yards from Grand Anse Beach. ☎ 809- 444-4646; fax 809-444-4647. Or write: P.O. Box 27, St. George's Grenada, West Indies.

Secret Harbour Hotel, St. George's Grenada features 20 deluxe suites with large balconies and living area, antique four-poster beds and tiled baths. The resort is owned by The Moorings Inc., the world's largest yacht charter operation. A romantic restaurant overlooks Mount Hartman Bay. ☎ 809-444-4439; fax 809-444-4819. Or write: P.O. Box 11, St. George's, Grenada, West Indies.

Spice Island Inn, in St. George's offers ultra-luxurious beachfront suites with whirlpool bath, spa, or private pool. Dine on your own patio or enjoy sumptuous buffets in the beachside restaurant. All-inclusive rates start at $320 per person in summer; $430 in winter. ☎ 809-444-4258/4423; fax 809-444-4807. Or write P.O. Box 6, St. George's, Grenada, West Indies.

Lance Aux Epines Cottages on the south end of Grenada—about two miles south of Grand Anse beach—has, clean, modern, one- and two-bedroom cottages which are fully equipped and designed for self-catering. Daily maid service. The cottages are on the beach and in walking distance of restaurants and a mini market. Rates for a double are from $55 in summer and winter.

The **Homestead Guest House,** four miles north of St. George's offers four simple rooms for $12 and $14 per night.

Roydon's Guest House, in Grand Anse, offers singles (EP) for $25 per night and $35 for a double.

CARRIACOU

Silver Beach Resort is centrally located for watersports on Carriacou. Ocean front rooms or cottages are between $55 and $105 per night. Dive shop (Karibik) on premises visits over 20 Carriacou sights. ☎ 809-443-7337, fax 809-443-7165 or write Silver Beach Resort, Hillsborough, Carriacou, Grenada, West Indies.

Other Activities

Sunfish sailing, water skiing, jet skiing and wind surfing can be arranged through your hotel or for information call the Tourist Board at 440-3377.

The *Rhum Runner*, based in St. George's harbor, offers water tours for reef viewing, harbor tours, moonlight cruises with barbecues, sails up Grenada's coast, and all-you-can-drink rum-punch cruises complete with live, electronic or steel band music.

Tennis, golf and spectator sports are also on the island. **Secret Harbour, Twelve Degrees North, Calabash, Coyaba, Spice Island Inn** and the **Ramada Renaissance** all have tennis courts. Visitors may also play on the **Richmond Hill** and **Tanteen Tennis Club** courts.

The **Grenada Golf and Country Club** has a nine-hole golf course. Concentration is key for this course, as the view of both the Atlantic and Caribbean waters can be distracting. Cricket, one of the most popular sports on the island, is played on Saturday mornings from January to May at 10 am near St. George's.

A less formal form of sport in Grenada is known as hashing. The sport is a run or walk—whichever one chooses. Participants are guided by special markers through the course, sometimes via Grenada's most hilly topography. Participants must be on the lookout for markers which are purposely put in place to take them off course. Those who make it to the end—and everyone does—enjoy a lighthearted celebration. It is held by the **Hash House Harriers' Club** in various parts of the island every other weekend.

Touring St. George's

Most island tours include and take off from historic St. George's. It is known as one of the most picturesque and truly West-Indian towns in the Caribbean.

For a magnificent vista of all of the city take a hand-rowed "water taxi" across the harbor. Cost is about 50 cents. For $2, a water taxi with motor can be hired.

The original town, Port St. Louis, was established by the French in 1650 on the outskirts of St. George's. The remains of that settlement, which was abandoned in 1706, are now submerged in three to 10 feet of water in the St. George's lagoon. The succeeding town, Fort Royal, was built on the site where St. George's is today. In 1762 it was occupied by the British who gave it the present name.

The center of activity in St. George's is the *Carenage*, or inner harbor. Fishing boats of all sizes and descriptions pull in and out continuously. The adventurous among you may wish to bargain for a trip on one of the fishing boats out to Glover's or Hog island for a day of snorkeling.

At the center of the *Carenage* stands *Christ of the Deep*, a statue given to Grenada by the Costa Cruise Line in remembrance of the hospitality shown the passengers of the *Bianca C* when it burned in the harbor in 1961. Also at the harbor are the post office, public library and small shops selling perfumes, lotions, potpourri, and teas made from the local flowers, spices and herbs. Nearby is the Grenada National Museum which houses archaeological finds, Josephine Bonaparte's marble bathtub, the first telegraph installed on the island in 1871, a rum still, and memorabilia depicting the Indian cultures of Grenada.

Next to the museum on Young Street is Tikal, a boutique carrying crafts and gift items. Nearby the Yellow Poui Art Gallery, just over the crest of the Young St. hill, exhibits and sells local art and sculpture, antique maps and prints.

The Sendall Tunnel takes you to the other side of St. George's: the *Esplanade*, the outer harbor with the fish and meat markets. In back is Market Square, where vendors sell brooms, baskets, fruits and vegetables. Early Saturday morning is the best time to see the market when it overflows with exotic fruits, vegetables and spices.

Stop by St. George's Anglican Church, built on the site of a church originally constructed by monks. Its walls are lined with plaques relating the 18th- and 19th-century history of Grenada.

Forts surround the city. Fort George, which is the oldest, was built by the French in 1705 and Fort Matthew and Fort Frederick were started by the French and completed by the British in 1783. All can be visited. St. George's also has a zoo, botanical gardens, Bay Gardens, and Tower House—the great house of a 1916 plantation filled with island relics, prints, paintings and historic family photos.

Island Tours

Grenada is small enough to be toured in one day. Leaving St. George's to the south coast is Westerhall, a stunning peninsula known for its magnificent homes and gardens. Next, down a dirt road is Bacolet Bay, a wild peninsula on the Atlantic where high surf pounds against miles of uninhabited beaches. Continuing on, **La Sagesse Nature Center** offers hiking trails, wild birds, a banana plantation with guided nature walks, an extensive beach and cafe. Next is Marquis village, the center of a handicraft industry. Nearby, also on the eastern shore is the town of Grenville, Grenada's second city, which is the perfect spot to try the local seafood. Try a bit of barracuda or lambi (conch) at the Seahaven, washed down with mauby—a local drink made from tree bark.

If you tour on a Saturday, be sure to stop by Grenville's large open-air market. This island "bread basket" offers fresh fish, fruits, vegetables, breads, pastries, spices and Grenadian delicacies prepared on the spot. While mingling with the Grenadians doing their weekly marketing, you can stop and watch the expert weavers from Marquis as they ply strips of wild pine into hats, baskets, bags and placemats.

Before leaving the east coast, you can glimpse the old Pearls Airport, which was replaced by the Point Salines International Airport in 1984.

The half-hour ride back through the Grand Etang district zigs and zags through the **Grand Etang National Park.** Dense tropical foliage including bamboo, tree ferns, cocoa, bananas, elephant ears mixed with vistas of the sea make it one of the most beautiful drives in the Caribbean. Stop at the **Grand Etang Visitors Center** in the Forest Reserve which houses exhibits of the area's flora and fauna and videotapes on the island. Nearby is Grand Etang Lake which is the crater of an extinct volcano and, above that, the summit of Mt. Qua Qua (2,372 ft). There are boats for rowing and picnic facilities. Also in this area are hiking trails of varying degrees of difficulty, which wind through the tropical vegetation. Bring pants and a long-sleeved shirt.

The west coast ride north from St. George's takes you past colorful fishing villages set at the foot of the mountains where papaya and breadfruit trees abound. Not far up the coast, a turn off leads to spectacular **Concord Falls.** For the adventurous, a half-hour hike into the interior tropical forest through spice and fruit plantations takes you to a more remote second fall, where the reward is a refreshing swim.

Continuing north along the coast road is Dougaldston Estate where cloves, cinnamon, mace, nutmeg and cocoa are prepared and sorted. The employees will explain how the spices grow, their uses, and show you the large trays where the spices are set to dry before separating.

Close by is Gouyave, a fishing village and the center of the nutmeg industry.

At the northernmost tip are the great cliffs of Sauteurs. Nearby is Levera Beach, a deserted beach ringed by sea grapes and palm trees and the meeting place of the Atlantic and the Caribbean. From here you can sight the Grenadines.

If time permits, take a detour from the coast road to the River Antoine Rum Distillery dating from the 18th century and one of the last enterprises still powered by a water-wheel.

Tours encircling the island run six hours and hit all the high points. City tours run two hours. A special tour for photographers is Photo Safari which includes a professional photographer guide.

Tour Operators

Island tours can be arranged through the following companies:

Arnold's Tours, 444-1167/440-2213; **Barefoot Holidays,** 444-4519/4199; **Capitol Tours,** 444-4557; **Carib Tours,** 444-4363; **Henry Tours,** 443-5313; **Island Tours Ltd,** 440-2906; **McIntyre Brothers Ltd.,** 440-2044; **New Trends Tours,** 444-1236; **Otways Tours,** 440-2558/2423.

Ferry between Carriacou and Grenada

The *Alexia II* and the *Adelaide B* depart Mondays and Thursdays at 10 am, arriving at 2 pm. Fares are $7.50 U.S. each way. One of the boats is available at each port at 10 am. The *MV Edna David* departs Carriacou Sunday 5 pm, arriving Grenada at 8:30 pm.

Dining

Where better to eat than the "Isle of Spice"? Grenada has all the fresh ingredients and an intriguing culinary heritage influenced by the French, British and the East Indians, all of whom spent time on her shores where

28 varieties of fruit, countless vegetables, 22 kinds of edible fish, and 12 spices are harvested.

Grenada's bounty is apparent at Saturday's market in St. George's and Grenville. Farm women sitting under umbrellas tempt you with bananas, papayas, oranges, yams, plantains, exotic roots and vegetables and fresh spices. Coconut water quenches your thirst and fish cakes appease your appetite.

Eating is a favorite pastime, and quantities are copious, especially at a totally authentic Grenadian meal. With fish stew, curried chicken or lambi (conch), you'll be treated to a plate brimming with rice and pigeon peas, plantain, yam or sweet potatoes. Or try *Oil Down*—breadfruit and salt pork steamed gently in coconut milk, covered with callaloo leaves (like spinach)—with an appetizer of cold, red-pepper soup. (Breadfruit was brought to Grenada on the *Bounty* from Tahiti. Captain Bligh left one tree in St. Vincent and one in Grenada as an economical means of feeding the slaves.) Wash it all down with local Carib beer, Grenada Wine Cooler, or mauby, a popular drink made from tree bark.

Bread and rolls are baked in each hotel's kitchen—and each baker creates his own variation. Fudge-ladies stroll St. George's streets with their wares in cloth-covered baskets.

Dining in Grenada is West Indian informal, characterized by open settings and a view of the sea. In St. George's proper, **Delicious Landing** on the Carenage offers great views, seafood and island drinks. Also on the Carenage, **Rudolf's** offers a pub-like setting for fish and chips and lobster "as-you-like-it." **The Nutmeg,** with its second floor harbor view, has delicious turtle soup and curried lambi.

In Belmont, a five-minute drive south from St. George's, internationally-praised **Mama's** serves some 21 to 25 dishes "family style." There is no menu—just the best and freshest offerings bought and prepared in the small kitchen. From lobster and callaloo soup to fresh fish, chicken, manicou or tatou (armadillo), and other entrees, to a wide variety of salads and vegetables. Exotic ice cream finishes the meal.

Spice Island Inn holds weekly Grenadian buffets to the sounds of a steel band. The chef at **Secret Harbour Hotel** serves his delicacies amid island antiques—a giant marble chess set and Empire-style chaise lounges. For those wanting a different ethnic cuisine, try **Coconuts Beach,** a French restaurant on Grand Anse beach; for Italian, there's the **Ristorante Italia;** the **Bird's Nest** for Chinese food; and **Tropicana** for Grenadian/Chinese dishes.

During a day tour of Grenada, lunch at Betty Mascoll's plantation great house, **Moren Fendue,** near Sauteurs, offers a buffet of Grenadian specialties, including Betty's famous pepper pot.

While out on the town "feteing" as the islanders call their version of partying, remember that the word "grog" (grand rum of Grenada) originated on this friendly isle.

Grenada's spice baskets, filled with everything from whole nutmegs and cloves to saffron or bay leaves, make an ideal souvenir for as little as $2 (U.S.). You might even find a recipe book tucked among the spices, so that you can recreate a fete of your own.

Helpful Phone Numbers

POLICE: ☎ 911/440-2244/3999

HOSPITAL: ☎ 440-2052

AIRLINES: **LIAT,** ☎ 440-2796/7; **BWIA,** ☎ 440-3818/9; **British Airways,** ☎ 440-2796/7; **American Airlines,** ☎ 444-2222.

COAST GUARD: ☎ 440-2852. Stands by on Marine channel 16 VHF 8 am-4 pm.

FACTS

Nearest Recompression Chamber: Barbados, Trinidad
(AVOID DECOMPRESSION DIVES—no chambers are close enough for an emergency)

Airlines: BWIA flies from Grenada to Aruba, Canada, Caracas, Curacao, Frankfurt, London, New York, Miami (daily), Stockholm and other European cities. LIAT connects with international airlines—British Airways, BWIA, Air Canada, American Airlines, Air France, Lufthansa—in Barbados, St. Lucia, Trinidad, Martinique and Antigua. American Airlines flies from America through Puerto Rico. ALM flies between Curacao and Grenada.

LIAT has daily flights to Carriacou and other islands in the Caribbean.

Airport: Point Salines International Airport is located on the southwest tip of Grenada.

Driving: On the left. You must produce a bonafide drivers license to the local traffic department.

Documents: British, American and Canadian citizens do not need passports for visits not exceeding three months providing they have two documents proving citizenship, one with a photograph—i.e., an expired passport or drivers license with photo plus a birth certificate or voters registrations cards, and an onward or return ticket. For all other nationalities, a valid passport is required. However, any traveller in transit in Trinidad en route to or from Grenada requires a valid passport for their transit stop.

Customs: There is no restriction on the amount of foreign currency brought into Grenada. Clothing and dive gear are also admitted freely, as long as they are for personal use.

Currency: East Caribbean Dollar (EC$) at a rate of EC$1 to U.S. $.37.

Credit Cards: Major credit cards are accepted by some hotels, but not by car rental companies and shops. Travelers checks are accepted everywhere.

Language: English

Climate: The year-round average temperature is 80 ° F and rainfall averages 78 inches. Peak rainfall is in summer and late fall.

Clothing: Bring a wetskin or shorty wetsuit in winter. For land, casual light-weight. For hiking the rainforest, bring sturdy shoes with nonslip soles, a long-sleeved shirt and long pants—cotton or a coolweave fabric. Swimwear and very short shorts are not welcome in the city streets, stores or hotel restaurants or bars.

Electricity: 230 volts, 50 cycles. A.C. transformers and adapters are needed.

Time: Eastern Standard

Tax: A departure tax of $9.25 U.S. for adults; $3.70 U.S. for children.

Religious Services: Catholic, Anglican, Presbyterian, Methodist, Scots Kirk, Seventh-Day Adventist, Jehovah's Witnesses, Islam, Christian Scientists, The Baha'i Faith.

Additional Information: Grenada Board of Tourism, Suite 900 D, 830 Second Avenue, New York NY 10017; in the U.S. ☎ 800-927-9554. In Grenada 809-440-2279.

Guadeloupe

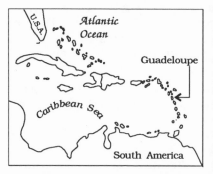

Atlantic Ocean

Guadeloupe

Caribbean Sea

South America

Touted by Jacques Cousteau as "one of the world's ten best diving spots," Guadeloupe combines the cultural and cosmopolitan charm of a European vacation with fabulous diving on reefs untouched by all but a minimal group of discriminating dive-travelers. Named for Our Lady of Guadeloupe by Christopher Columbus in 1493, this charming, French island is blessed with miles of white-sand beaches and spectacular sub-sea attractions.

Guadeloupe is actually two main islands connected by a bridge across the River Salee and several out islands. From the air it resembles the wings of a butterfly. Basse-Terre, the western wing, is mountainous, highlighted by the still-active volcano, Mt. Soufriere. Travelers touring this portion of the islands will find tropical rain forests, bamboo trees, hot springs, postcard waterfalls, and a profusion of tropical flowers, fruits, almond and palm trees. Grande-Terre, the eastern wing of Guadeloupe, is flat, dry, and home to modern resorts, beautiful swimming beaches, fields of sugar cane and unlimited topside tourist attractions.

The prime dive-vacation attraction is Pigeon Island, located just off the central western coast of Basse-Terre. Pigeon Island is a mountain in the sea whose base is surrounded by miles of dense coral reefs. It was the site of the film, *The Silent World*.

Residents of Guadeloupe are extremely friendly and kind to tourists. Still, non-French-speaking divers visiting Guadeloupe should pick up a French phrase book and familiarize themselves with the language. English is NOT widely spoken; even the grunts grunt with a French accent. Also, divers and snorkelers must bring their own equipment, except for tanks and weights. European adapters, if needed, are widely available.

Topless sunbathing, scuba and swimming is *de rigueur* on Guadeloupe.

Area contributors: Richard Ockelmann and Beth Ann Molino, BDC; Myron Clement, French West Indies Department of Tourism, Guy Genin of Chez Guy Diving; Raphael Legrand, Directeur, Auberge de la Distillerie Hotel; Florence Marie, Relais du Moulin Hotel.

Best Dives and Snorkeling Sites

Pigeon Island, composed of volcanic stone and scrub trees, lies off the western coast of Basse-Terre, the western wing of Guadeloupe. The area consists of two land masses, North Pigeon and South Pigeon. The waters surrounding it come under French Government protection as an Underwater Natural Park—the Cousteau Marine Sanctuary.

☆☆☆☆☆ **North East Reef.** The northeast side of North Pigeon Island is a superb wall dive. Beginning at the surface, the wall drops 40 ft to a shelf then slopes down to 70 ft and finally plunges steeply to 140 ft. The wall is carpeted with lacy soft corals, tube sponges, plate corals, and large pillar-coral formations. Residents include huge groupers, puffers, lobster, big French angels and throngs of small critters—arrow crabs, feather dusters and tube sponges. The seas are usually calm, visibility more than 100 feet. Recommended for both novice and experienced divers.

☆☆☆☆☆ **North Side Reef** You'll find superb seascapes for photography on the north side of North Pigeon Island. Huge clusters of tube sponges, some six feet tall, and enormous green and purple sea fans grow on the ledges and outcrops of the wall. The reef begins in the shallows and drops off to a maze of small canyons and outcrops. Divers are befriended by large gray snappers. They are tame and may be handfed. Large curious barracuda circle overhead; trumpet fish and damsels adorn the lush thickets of coral. Star and brain corals abound. North Side Reef is a super dive for novices as well as experienced divers. Seas are calm, visibility excellent.

☆☆☆☆ **West Side Reef,** off North Pigeon Island, is everyone's favorite. The wall begins at the surface, drops to a shelf at 25 ft, slopes down to 40 ft. then drops off sharply to the bottom at 140 ft. As in all of the Cousteau Marine Sanctuary the corals here are vibrantly alive with color and create a dramatic landscape. Large brain coral heads and gardens of soft corals thrive. Fish life is abundant. Inhabitants of the reef include large hog snappers, trumpet fish, and parrotfish. Photo enthusiasts are drawn to the gigantic orange sponges and teal sea fans. Calm seas invite divers of all experience levels to this site.

☆☆☆ **Rock Canyons,** located off Iles de Saintes, a small group of islands just south of BasseTerre, is a large maze of narrow rocky coral alleys and caves. Its walls, riddled with endless nooks and crannies, provide shelter for sea cumbers, bristle worms, tree worms, arrow crabs, sea horses,

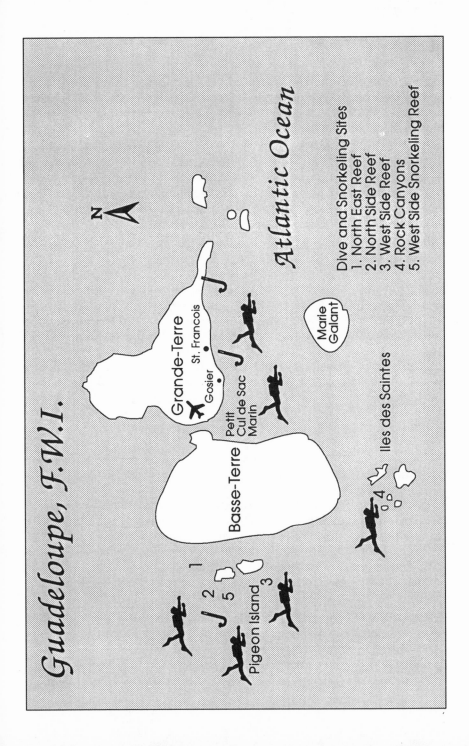

octopi, lobster, eels and an ever-present mob of grunts. Huge formations of rare pink corals color the area. The canyon entrance starts at 10 ft then drops to a sandy bottom at 45 ft. Tricky surface surges and currents make this pick for experienced divers.

☆☆☆☆☆ **Pigeon Island's West Side Reef** is the best snorkeling area in the Cousteau Marine Sanctuary. Its shallow walls ruffle with enormous feather dusters, sea plumes, sea rods, huge sea fans and sponges. Barrel sponges (large enough to camp in) thrive among clumps of elkhorn and enormous brain corals. Puffer fish and unusual golden moray eels are inhabitants. Expect calm seas and exceptional visibility.

Additional snorkeling and diving sites are found among the lagoons and bays of Les Saintes, the east coast of BasseTerre, and off-shore Gosier (the south coast of Grande Terre). Check out Mouton Vert, Mouchoir Carre, and Cay Ismini. They are close by the hotels in the bay of Petit Cul de Sac Marin, near Riviere Salee, the river separating the two halves of Guadeloupe. North of Salee is another bay, Grand Cul de Sac Marin, where the small islets of Fajou and Caret also offer decent diving. St. Francois Reef on the eastern end of the south shore of Grande-Terre is a good snorkeling reef as is Ilet de Gosier, off Gosier. Diving is a young sport on Guadeloupe and every dive-explorer has a unique opportunity to find a new "best dive" of his/her own. New sites are discovered every day.

Dive Operators

Chez Guy, directly opposite Pigeon Island on Malendure Beach in Bouillante on Basse-Terre, with another on Les Saintes. Operator and master diver Guy Genin has three fast comfortable boats for daily dive and snorkeling excursions to Pigeon Island. The boats have wide hydroplanes which double as diving platforms. This operation boasts 60 complete sets of equipment. Rates: $30 per dive, including transfer from hotel. Chez Guy also offers a one-week, all-inclusive package for $590 which includes two dives per day, equipment and accommodations with breakfast and dinner at Guy's guest house, the Auberge de la Plongée. ☎ 590-98-8172; fax 590-98-8358.

The Nautilus Club, which faces Pigeon Island from the beach at Malendure, specializes in diving excursions. Their four boats carry 14 passengers. ☎ 590-98-8569; fax 590-90-2187.

Les Heures Saines is a modern PADI and NAUI dive center facing Pigeon from Rocher de Malendure. Five instructors, Dominique Derame, Francois Aubry, Pascale Esptripeau, Frederic Aragones and Louis Galbiati escort daily dives and night dives. Single dives are $40. Les Heures Saines also has two dive lodges: Le Paradis Creole, with one week at $840 for meals, accommodations and ten dives, and Les Bungalow-Villas at $520 for the same. ☎ 590-98-8663; fax 590-95-5090.

Aqua-fari Club is based at La Creole Beach Hotel in Gosier, a bustling resort area 15 miles east of Point-a-Pitre, Guadeloupe's largest city. Divemaster Alain Verdonck offers guided wreck dives and excursions to nearby coral reefs and Pigeon Island (a one-hour drive). Prices range from $36 to $64 dollars depending on the dive site. A 10-dive package is available; it includes airport to hotel transfer, welcome cocktail, bus trip to Pigeon, two dives a day and one night dive, and cocktail party. ☎ 590-84-2626.

Another well-organized watersports center is Nauticase at the Hotel Salako, ☎ 590-84-2222.

Accommodations

Rates are U.S. (See also dive operators)

If your tongue doesn't curl comfortably around conversational French, head for one of the bigger hotels where English is spoken. Or if getting to know people is one of the reasons you travel, stay at a Relais Creole, a small family-owned inn. Most of the hotels are situated on Grande-Terre (one-hour drive to Malendure). Among the small hotels close to Pigeon Island on Basse-Terre are Raphael Legrand's charming 12-room **Auberge De La Distillerie** at Tabanon near Petit-Bourg. This fully air-conditioned inn is a short ride from Pigeon Island dive operators. ☎ 590-94-2591; fax 94-1191. The adjacent restaurant, Le Bitaco, is popular with the locals and noted for Creole dishes. Freshwater pool.

La Sucrerie du Comte has opened on the site of an old rum distillery. With 26 comfortable bungalow rooms, La Sucrerie is by the sea at Ste-Rose in the north of the western wing of Basse-terre. Rates are $134 for two people in a bungalow with breakfast; lower from January 6 to April 12. ☎ 590-28-6017. Write to: Comte de Loheac, Sainte-Rose 97115, Guadeloupe, FWI.

Relais du Moulin, near Sainte Anne on Grande-Terre, is marked by a sugar-mill tower which serves as the office. This small resort features 20 air-conditioned bungalows set in a bougainvillea garden, a tennis court, pool and stables. The beach is a half mile away. The hotel has a fabulous West Indian restaurant and a snack bar at the pool. Entertainment.

Combination hotel and sailing vacations are offered. Relais du Moulin is about an hour's drive from Pigeon Island. Rates are $145 to $178 for a double. ☎ 590-88-2396. Reservations through your travel agent.

La Creole Beach Hotel is located on the beach at Gosier. It was once a Holiday Inn and the rooms are large and well appointed. The Aqua-Fari Dive shop on premises offers tours to the coral reef surrounding Gosier Island as well as excursions to Pigeon Island. Introductory dives. Rates for a double are $160 to $290. Packages available. ☎ 590-90-4646; fax 90-6060.

Meridien Guadeloupe is just east of Gosier at St. Francois. This is a four-star deluxe beachfront resort with 272 rooms. Despite the boom in tourism, the town of St. Francois manages to retain its fishing village look. On the road east of it are any number of beachside bistros serving lobster and seafood. Rates are $283 to $417 for a double. Dive shops here offer daily trips to the off shore reefs of Grande-Terre and excursions to Pigeon Island.

Other Activities

Sailboats, crewed or bareboat, are plentiful. For rentals or tours try Vacances Yachting Antilles at Marina Bas-du-Fort, Pointe-A-Pitre. ☎ 90-82-95. Full-day picnic sails on the trimaran, *La Grande Voile* (☎ 84-4642), or catamaran, *Papyrus*, can be arranged through your hotel. ☎ 90-9298.

Sightseeing

Hiking through Basse-Terre's Parc Naturel takes you along well-marked trails through tropical rain forests to waterfalls, mountain pools, and La Soufriere, a 4,813-ft volcano and the park's most famous site. You'll also find exhibits on the volcano, coffee, the sea, and the forest. Hiking brochures are available from the Guadeloupe Tourist Office (address below). Horseback riding along the beaches can be arranged at Le Relais du Moulin (☎ 88-23-96). Those who can dive all day and still party all night will find Guadeloupe's cities alive with dancing and entertainment.

Shopping

Local craft items, such as dolls, jewelry, furniture or souvenirs are made from fruit, wood, sea-shells, stone, and leather and are widely available in the town shops. Art galleries and antique dealers are found in Gosier, Pointe-a-Pitre, and other cities.

Dining

Guadeloupe is a gourmet's delight. Top restaurants and hotel dining rooms offer classic French and Caribbean cuisine. Though the island is French it is also decidedly Creole, and Creole eateries are gaining enormously in popularity. Some are beachside cafes, some are in-town bistros, and several are little more than the front porch of the cook's home. On Malendure Beach, Basse-Terre, check out **Chez Loulouse,** noted for Chef Loulouse's crayfish sauce Americaine. This is a small native seafood eatery in a simple setting. ☎ 98-70-34. In Gosier, try **Le Bassignac** on the Beach Road (*Route de la Plage*). Seafood specialties in a comfortable beachside setting.

FACTS

Nearest recompression chamber: Located in Pointe-a-Pitre, Grande-Terre.

Getting there: Connections from Miami on Air France and from San Juan; take American Eagle (800-433-7300). Inter-island flights can be arranged at Le Raizet Airport. Water ferries to Iles Des Saintes are available from the city of Basse-Terre or Trois Rivieres on the south coast.

Island Transportation: All major car rental agencies are at the airport. Reservations should be made before arriving in Guadeloupe to insure getting a car. Bus service in Mercedes vans is available between cities. The cities are clearly marked on the outside.

Driving: Right side of the road. The main roads between major cities are clearly marked. A wonderful tourist map is available from the tourist office in Pointe-a-Pitre.

Documents: For stays of up to three months Canadian and U.S. citizens require a return ticket and two forms of I.D.— either a passport or proof of citizenship such as a birth certificate or voter's registration card with some type of photo. A passport is recommended. British citizens require a passport.

Currency: French franc. 6.5FF = $1.00 U.S.

Climate: Temperatures range from 75 to 85° F. Water temperatures are warm year round so you won't need a wetsuit, although a wetskin or 1/8 inch shortie wetsuit is comfortable in mid-winter.

Clothing: Casual light clothing. Most beaches are topless.

Equipment required: Bring all of your own SCUBA gear except for tanks and weights. Most operators have Scubapro tanks which do not require any special regulator adaptor.

Electricity: European adaptors required.

Time: Atlantic Standard (EST + 1 hr).

Language: French, local Creole dialect.

Tax: A service charge of 10 to 15 percent is included on most hotel and restaurant tabs.

Photography: Fast, reliable film processing is not yet available. Take your own film and have it processed after returning home.

Religious Services: Catholic, Protestant, Jewish.

Additional Information: French West Indies Tourist Board, 610 Fifth Avenue, NY NY 10020. ☎ 212-315-0888.

The Bay Islands

Honduras

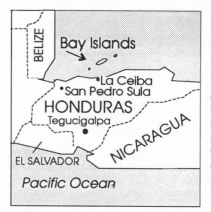

Located between 12 and 40 miles off the coast of Honduras, the Bay Islands are a remote outpost set in the middle of the world's second largest barrier reef. The islands are mountainous jungles rimmed with a sparkle of coconut palms and white sand set against an azure sea. Inland, fragrant almond, mango, cashew, mandarin orange and breadfruit trees shade the cliffs and provide food and shelter to iguana, parrots, snakes, deer and wild boar.

Roatan, the largest of the 70-island chain, is the most populated with 30,000 residents and the most developed. It is where you'll find the most dive resorts and creature comforts. Next in size is Guanaja which is surrounded by its own barrier reef. Third in size, and a newcomer to this "dedicated-dive-resort" group is Utila. The Cayos Cochinos, a mini cluster of small fishing-village islands boasts one dive resort on their biggest island, Cochino Grande.

The smaller islands are uninhabited or sparsely populated. Most do not have roads. Phones and faxes are newcomers. Surrounding reefs are impressive with brilliantly-colored sponges and corals, towering pinnacles, walls, tunnels, wrecks and caves. Visibility and water clarity are superb. Big turtles, grouper, rays, eels, and pelagics proliferate despite an active fishing industry. And snorkelers discover their own special paradise in the small patch reefs that dot the shallow bays throughout the entire area.

Contributors: Alvin Jackson, Roatan; Linda Fouke, Bayman Bay Club, Guanaja; Ray Jones, Coco View Resort.

And while everyone in the Bay Islands speaks "dive" fluently, the predominant language is English. On the mainland, however, Spanish is spoken.

Plan on an entire day to reach the Bay Islands from the U.S. The islands are close to Honduras' coastline, but the mainland airport at San Pedro Sula is 160 miles away. Some flights depart La Ceiba which is closer. Connections are often erratic. Luggage sometimes is late. Sand fleas and no-see-ums are a nuisance and make their presence known as soon as you arrive. Apply repellent beforehand.

History

Evidence from shreds of pottery and pre-Columbian remains indicate the early presence of Lanca, Mayan and Payan Indians on the Bay Islands. Columbus is credited with their latter-day discovery in 1502.

During the early 1500's, the Spaniards, in their manic quest for gold and precious gems, brutally attacked and enslaved the Bay Island Indians. Finally, during the mid-1500's, the Indians revolted. One chief, Lempira, put up such a fierce offensive, it took thousands of Spanish troops to kill him. Lempira has since been declared a national hero and the currency of Honduras is named for him.

Following that conquest, word of Spanish treasure ships lured pirates from Jamaica and the Caymans to set up a base at Port Royal, Roatan. Tales of jewels and stashed treasures hidden on the island abound.

Best Dives and Snorkeling Sites

Roatan

☆☆☆☆☆ **West End Wall** which encompasses **Peter's Place and Herbie's Place** is great for diving and snorkeling. The reef starts at the shore and extends out 20 yards where the wall drops off sharply from a ledge at 15 feet. Visibility often exceeds 100 ft. Fishlife is superb with schools of horse-eye jacks, permits, and schoolmaster. Seas are calm with an occasional light current. No spearfishing.

Guanaja

☆☆☆☆☆ The **Bayman Drop and Pinnacle** are wall dives off the north shore. The top of the wall is between 10 and 40 ft. The Pinnacle rises

from 135 to 50 ft at the top where you'll find large barrel sponges, azure vase sponges, gorgonia and black coral. DO NOT ENTER THE CRACK AT 70 ft. Large black coral trees are found at 80 ft. Good for diving and snorkeling. No collecting or spearfishing.

☆☆☆☆ **Pavilions** is a series of blind tunnels and pillar corals and out croppings between 30 and 60 ft. Soft corals and sponges dominate the shallows. Beware of the fire coral which seems hotter here than other parts of the Caribbean. The site is off Michael's Rock around the point next to the Bayman Bay Club. Good for diving and snorkeling.

☆☆☆ **Waterfall Reef** is the site of a huge black coral tree growing off the wall at 45 ft. Top of the dive is five ft. Waterfall is nice for photography with numerous overhangs, bushy corals, anemones, big vase sponges and lots of fish. Good for all-level divers and snorkelers.

☆☆☆☆ *Jader Trader* is a 200-ft wreck lying on its right side at 90 ft off the southwest side of Guanaja. Big morays, schools of silversides, turtles and barracuda are in residence. Seas average two to four ft with a light current. Always good visibility. For experienced divers.

Additional dives along Guanaja's barrier reef are **Eel's Garden** off the Bayman Bay Club shore; **Black Rock Canyons**, a maze of tunnels and canyons; **Jim's Silverlode** a sheer wall off southwest cay with huge sponges and soft corals; **The Cut**, a narrow, sandy cut through shallow coral that branches out into caverns and tunnels.

Utila

Utila is fringed by yet-unnamed, virgin reefs, caves and canyons. Wildlife is exceptional, with turtles, eagle rays, southern sting rays, schools of Atlantic spade fish and tropicals.

Barbaretta

☆☆☆☆ **Barbaretta Wall** off Barbaretta Island, a favorite snorkeling-picnic spot between Guanaja and Roatan, is a wonderland of barrel sponges and soft corals. The wall stretches for a mile.

Pigeon Cays

☆☆☆☆ Pigeon Cays are a small cluster of islands surrounded by shallow, protected reefs, all perfect for snorkeling.

Dive Resorts

Each resort offers dive services. Group and individual tours from the U.S. are offered by **ICS Scuba and Travel,** ☎ 800-722-0205; **Rothschild Travel Consultants,** ☎ 800-359-0747; **Tropical Travel,** ☎ 800-451-8017 or 713-367-2286; fax 713-298-2335; and **Innerspace Adventures,** ☎ 800-833-SEAS. A 7% hotel tax is added.

Utila

Utila Lodge is a two-story, eight-room inn. Rooms are air conditioned and overlook the sea. Dive shop on premises. Packages for seven nights, six days diving are $700 per person. Included are three meals daily, three boat dives per day, two night dives, tanks and weights, belts, unlimited fills for shore dives and airport transfers.

Roatan

Anthony's Key Resort was the first dedicated dive resort in the Bay Islands. The resort features beachside and reefside rustic cabins. Packages offered at $900 per person, per week, include three meals daily, three boat dives daily, unlimited shore dives, and horseback riding. The Institute for Marine Sciences is on the grounds of the resort and features dolphin swims. ☎ 800-227-DIVE or 305-858-DIVE.

Coco View Resort, on the southside peninsula, is a group of oceanside bungalows, two-story cottages and cabanas which are built over the water. Standard rooms each have one double and one twin bed. Bungalows have two rooms, each with a kingsize bed.

Rates for a winter dive package are $725 per person, double occupancy, for seven nites in either a cottage or cabana and include three meals daily, beach barbecues, taxes, transfers from the airport, two two-tank boat dives daily, unlimited shore diving and night diving. Non divers pay $625. Great wall dives are a stone's throw from the beach bar. Nearby is a 140-ft tanker wreck, *Prince Albert*, in 25 ft of water. Disabled access. ☎ 800-282-8932 or 904-588-4158; fax 904-588-4158.

Fantasy Island Beach Resort sprawls across its own 15-acre island off Roatan's south coast. A small bridge connects the resort to the main island. Built in 1989 by local entrepreneur, Albert Jackson, the resort's 73 guest rooms are luxurious with air conditioning, phones, refrigerators, full baths and cable TV. There is a full-service dive operation on premises with a fleet of 42-ft custom dive boats. Excellent shore diving and snorkeling. Package rates for seven nights in a standard room with six days of diving, three meals daily, service charges, airport transfers in Roatan and use of kayaks, sailboats and Hobie Cats are $896 per person, double occupancy. Rates drop between Sept. 15 and Dec. 15 (hurricane season). ☎ 800-6-ROATAN or 813-835-4449.

Romeo's Dive & Yacht Club is on the south end of Roatan on Brick Bay. Standard rooms, some air-conditioned, have porches facing the sea. Restaurant and lounge. The dive shop has a fleet of 40-ft custom boats. Winter rates for a dive package for seven nights from $650 per person, double occupancy. Includes three boat dives daily, three meals per day, transfers, two night dives, use of kayaks and paddle boats. Pool. ☎ 800-535-DIVE or 305-633-1221; fax 633-1102 or write to P.O. Box 350683, Miami FL 33135.

Roatan Beach House Rentals are offered for $625 per week for a two-bedroom, four-guest modern home. Marine packages available. ☎ 414-582-4806. Fax: 011-504-1016.

Guanaja

Bayman Bay Club is a beautiful, waterfront lodge. Guests stay in cottages on a hillside overlooking the reef. The resort features a dive shop, restaurant, gameroom and clubhouse. Spacious rooms are cooled by ceiling fans and sea breezes. Sea-kayak dive adventures and guided hikes to the island's lovely waterfall are offered. Great snorkeling is right off the resort's 300-ft dock. Dive packages are $775 ($725 for nondiver) and include three meals daily, two boat dives daily, unlimited shore dives, one night dive, hiking tips and use of kayaks. ☎ 800-524-1823; Fax 011-504-454179. Write to Terra Firma, 11750 N.W. 19th Street, Fort Lauderdale FL 33323.

Nautilus Beach Resort is a charming, Georgian-style, six-room resort on a 1,000-ft beach. Some rooms are air-conditioned. A full-service, PADI dive shop on premises offers basic and advanced courses and operates a 27-ft Delta dive boat. Oxygen. Dive packages are $560 per week, per person for a double including a two-tank morning boat dive and one-tank afternoon boat dive daily, three meals per day, airport transfers, unlimited fills for shore dives. ☎ 800-535-7063 or 512-863-9079.

Posada Del Sol is a luxurious, Spanish villa resort on 72 acres of oceanfront greenery and, except for two small villages, is the only developed area on the southeast shore. It has an excellent restaurant, bar, pool and tennis court. Rooms are luxurious and spacious. Three 42-ft dive boats whisk guests to 50 moored dive sites. Packages at $900 per diver, double, include three meals daily, two boat dives daily, one night dive, unlimited shore diving, round-the-island cruise, weights, beach barbecue, and airport transfers on Guanaja. Handicapped access. ☎ 800-642-3483 or 407-624-3483; fax 407-624-3225.

Casa Sobre El Mar is a small, family-run hotel built on concrete piers over the reef. The effect is like staying on a live-aboard that doesn't rock. Comfortable rooms have private baths and are cooled by sea breezes. Weeklong packages are $595 per person year round and include three boat dives daily, unlimited 24-hour-per-day, front-door or back porch diving and three meals daily. ☎ 800-869-7295 or direct 011-504-45-4269. Write to Casa Sobre el Mar, Pond Cay, Islas de la Bahia, Honduras, Central America.

Cayos Cochinos

Plantation Beach Resort, formerly a pineapple plantation, on Cochinos Grand, is a delightful 10-room, beachfront resort. Guests stay in chalets crafted of solid Honduran mahogany, each with private bath, ceiling fans, and either one king or two twin beds. Rooms are clean and simple. Great diving and snorkeling is a giant stride off the beach. All-inclusive, seven-night packages are $750 per person. Transfers not included. ☎ 800-628-3723 or 713-973-9300; Fax 713-973-8585. Write to 8582 Katy Freeway, Suite 118, Houston TX 77024.

Note: If your flight arrives after 4:00 pm on day of arrival or departs before 8:00 am on day of departure, an overnight on the mainland will be necessary at a cost of approximately $40 per room.

Live-Aboard

The **Bay Islands Aggressor** is a seven-cabin, 18-passenger, air-conditioned luxury yacht that visits all the best dive sights off the Bay Islands. A week stay costs $1,495 per person. Pick up is from Roatan. ☎ 800-348-2628 or write to P.O. Drawer K, Morgan City LA 70381.

Sightseeing and Other Activities

A lack of roads on all but Roatan makes exploring on your own difficult and taxis there are very expensive. Check with your hotel for transportation. Some resorts offer water-taxi service or have kayaks for getting around the bays. The mainstay of apres-dive activities are fishing, bird watching, hiking and other water sports.

Facts

Nearest Recompression Chamber: Roatan, Bay Islands. Air evacuation is possible from some other areas.

Getting There: The best days to travel are Friday and Saturday. *From Miami,* American Airlines (800-433-7300) has daily flights to San Pedro Sula, Honduras. *From Houston,* Continental Airlines to San Pedro Sula with a stop in Tegucigalpa. *From New Orleans,* TAN SAHSA flies to La Ceiba, Honduras. Islena Airlines flies to the Bay Islands every day but Sunday from Tegucigalpa, San Pedro Sula and La Ceiba to Guanaja. TAN SAHSA flies from San Pedro Sula to Roatan. Water taxis are sent by the one-island resorts to pick you up.

Precautions: Register your cameras and electronic gear with customs before visiting Honduras. Do not bring drugs, plants or flowers into or out of the country.

Language: English on the Bay Islands, Spanish on mainland Honduras.

Documents: A passport, visa, and onward ticket is required to enter Honduras.

Health: Vaccinations are not required. Check with your own doctor for health precautions. Drinking water comes from mountain wells on the islands. Ask about the water before drinking. Pack a diver's first-aid kit for sea stings and bug bites. (Sea sting kits are sold in many U.S. dive shops). Buy all your sundries and cosmetics before you leave home.

Currency: The lempira (L). L2 = U.S.$1.

Climate: Hot and humid. March and April are the hottest months. Island resorts are on the sea and cooled by the trade winds. Rain clouds crop up most afternoons during Summer and Fall. Coolest months are January and February. Water temperature averages 80° F year round.

Clothing: Shorts and tee shirts, jeans and sneakers. Long sleeve shirts and long pants are good for mountain hikes and protection from bugs or sunburn. Snorkelers should wear protective clothing from the hot sun. Divers will find a lycra suit comfortable for deep wall dives.

Electricity: Most resorts have 110 volts, but some have 220. Carry an adaptor to be sure.

For Additional Information: Contact the resorts direct, the tour operators listed under "Dive Resorts" or your local travel agent.

Jamaica

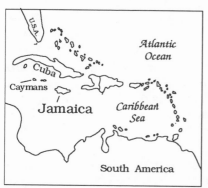

Jamaica's first tourists arrived in the late 1800's by banana boat, a brainstorm of New England sea captain, Lorenzo Down Baker who fell in love with this mountainous island of delights. By the turn of the century banana exports grew and Jamaica became one of the trendiest vacation spots in the world.

Today most tourists arrive by jet and cruise ship. In all, 1.3 million tourists arrive each year to experience Jamaica's diverse watersports, mountain vistas, vibrant night life and duty-free shopping.

At 4,411 square miles, it is the third largest island in the Caribbean after Cuba and Puerto Rico. Geographically, it is a cornucopia of scenic wonders with miles of soft, sand beaches and lush greenery along the coasts, and high mountains inland. Overall, the terrain is very mountainous with half of the land rising above 1,000 ft. The highest point, Blue Mountain Peak, soars to 7,500 ft—higher than any in the eastern half of North America. Hundreds of wild rivers and plunging waterfalls crisscross the mountains and moisten the fertile valleys which produce some of the world's most outstanding coffee, fruits, flowers and vegetables. The flatter southern coast can look like the African savanna or Indian plains, and has alternating black and white sand beaches as well as mineral springs.

Offshore reef tracts provide a bounty of dive and snorkeling sites. Many are a short swim from the beach. Wall dives predominate as Jamaica's north stretch of reef tract edges the Great Cayman Trench. A ledge of shallow reefs stretch around the island's perimeter. Depths range from extreme shallows to awesome depths.

Almost everything imaginable grows in Jamaica's sensuous environment. Marine scientists have identified more than 50 species of sponges

Contributors: Theo Smit, Poseidon Divers; Donna Oliver, Dynamic Travel; Linda Jacobson.

on the surrounding reefs. In the heyday of the British Empire, flowering and fruit trees were brought from Asia, the Pacific and Africa, evergreens from Canada, roses and nasturtiums from England. The breadfruit was sent from Tahiti, first by Captain Bligh on the *Bounty*. In return, Jamaica's native pineapple was sent to Hawaii and its mahogany to Central America. There are varieties of orchids, bromeliads and ferns in Jamaica that are native to nowhere else and fruits like the Bombay mango that don't flourish anywhere else.

The island's 2.4 million permanent residents are a mix of African, European, Afro-European, East Indian, Afro-East Indian, Chinese, Afro-Chinese—and every known combination of races that bespeak the island's heritage. Most are black; many are shades of brown. Together they blend into a most unique culture steeped in magical rituals, legends and customs.

Religion is an important force. The vast majority is Christian, but there are communities of Jews, Hindus and Moslems. The Church of Jamaica, formerly the Church of England, has the largest membership. Rastafarianism commands a large following.

Jamaicans speak English and speak it eloquently, but with their own musical lilt and with some words which are a survival from West African languages.

When Jamaicans speak Patois, a blend of English and African, the discussion may be almost incomprehensible to the visitor at first, but after a while you catch the rhythm and pick up some expressions—*BEN*, Weh yuh ben deh? (Where have you been?); *NUTTEN*, Minuh hab nutten. (I don't have anything.); *YEH-MON (Yes, man.)* –spoken as a greeting and an agreement.

Proverbs and place names express the vitality of Jamaica talk: for "mind your own business," there is "cockroach no business inna fowl-yard"; for being corrupted by bad companions, "You lay down wid dawg, you get up wid fleas" and for the pretentious, "The higher monkey climb, the more him expose."

Jamaica also boasts a broad variety of birds, both native and migratory, from the tiny bee hummingbird and its cousin the "doctor bird' (whose longer-tailed profile is the logo of Air Jamaica) to the mysterious solitaire with its mournful cry. Divers visiting the north coast will meet the kling-kling—a shiny black Antillian grackle who shares breakfast toast. A hike through the highest mountains may be rewarded by a sight of *papillio homerus*, one of the world's largest butterflies, also a native.

History

When Columbus sighted Jamaica on his second voyage in 1494, he recorded in his log: *"The fairest land ever eyes beheld...the mountains touch the sky"*

The Spanish never fully settled Jamaica, but they stayed long enough to kill off the peaceful, resident Arawak Indians through forced labor, mass executions and European diseases.

Spanish colonists raised cattle on Jamaica and shipped lard (manteca) from a north coast port today called Montego Bay. Jamaica became a provisions stop for ships headed to Central America in search of gold. In the century and a half of their rule, the Spaniards made two introductions which became pivotal to Jamaica's future: they brought in sugar cane and slaves from Africa to cultivate it.

In 1509 the Spaniards established New Seville as the capital, near the modern town of Ocho Rios. Today, the foundations of New Seville are being excavated and a search continues for the remains of two ships which Columbus left beached nearby.

By 1655, the British conquered the island driving the Spaniards from their new capital of St. Jago de la Vega (now Spanish Town) to Cuba.

For nearly 200 years fortunes were built on sugar plantations with slave labor. Corruption became commonplace. Buccaneers were encouraged to operate from Jamaica, attack the treasure ships of Spain and France and capture territory. A young indentured laborer from Wales called Henry Morgan rose to become Jamaica's Lieutenant Governor and prospered as one of history's best-known pirates. His home base, Port Royal, on a peninsula outside today's capital, Kingston, was considered "the richest, wickedest city in Christendom," until one hot afternoon in 1692 when an earthquake tumbled most of it beneath the sea. Today, Port Royal and her treasures are covered by a dense reef. When winds are calm the site makes an interesting dive.

Magnificent plantation houses like Rose Hall and Greenwood rose above the cane fields. A spirit of independence among the planters and slaves took root during the early 1700's. For the slaves, there was the presence of the Maroons, descendants of the escaped slaves of the Spaniards, who called them "cimarrones" (runaways); they lived in the mountains, defied the British troops, served as a magnet for other runaways and periodically staged rebellions until a treaty in 1739 gave them a measure of local autonomy which they still retain today.

The planters, too, were rebellious. When the 13 American colonies declared independence from Britain, the Jamaica House of Assembly voted to join them.

Slavery ended in 1834. Economic chaos followed and Jamaica's Assembly voted away its traditional independence and became a full colony of England. Jamaica remained a British colony until August 6, 1962 when the Union Jack was lowered and the black, green and gold flag of the independent nation of Jamaica was raised.

Despite the loss of slave labor, Jamaica's rich farmlands prospered and indirectly launched its tourism industry when the banana boat captains began carrying North American vacationers.

Jamaica also expanded citrus exports, including new hybrids like the ortanique and the "ugly fruit." Rum became the principal export and a new overseas market was found for Jamaican ginger in a product called ginger ale. Pimento was exported under the name 'allspice' and Jamaica Blue Mountain coffee became a premium brand worldwide.

During the 1970's Jamaica supplied nearly two-thirds of the U.S. needs for aluminum from the island's rich bauxite (alumina) deposits. With the current collapse of that market, Jamaica is restructuring an economy where tourism and modern agriculture take a bigger place in the support of the nation.

When to Go

The best months to dive Jamaica are December through May, the dry season. June through November brings chance of a hurricane though July and August are often dry.

DIVING

Offshore diving is most prominent along the north and west coasts of the island, particularly in Negril on the leeward western tip which is sheltered from high winds and waves. Montego Bay, Runaway Bay and Ocho Rios follow in popularity. Despite many sites being a short swim from shore, diving on your own is prohibited. You must be accompanied by a guide from the Association of Diver Operators.

Marine Park regulations are as follows: 1) Always stay at least two ft above the reef. 2) Don't touch or stand on the coral and don't take souvenirs. 3) Don't wear gloves.

Also, it is illegal to buy or possess coral and turtle products. There is a closed lobster season from April till June 30.

Best Dives and Snorkeling Sites

NEGRIL

Negril has three reef areas with most interest between 50 and 70 feet. Seas are dependably calm and the visibility often exceeds 100 ft.

☆☆☆ **The Throne** is a 50-ft wide cave at a depth of 65 ft. which you enter from the top at 40 ft. Its walls are carpeted with soft corals and huge yellow sponges hang from ceiling to floor. There is a 12-ft by three ft chute at the back of the cave with fine growths of black coral. Eels, octopi, turtles, sting rays, barracuda, reef fish, and an occasional nurse shark inhabit the cave.

☆☆ South of The Throne is a shallow reef area known as **Awee Moway.** Local dive guides have tamed resident stingrays which you may pet if you approach them slowly. Eagle rays come by at night. Depths are 20 to 50 ft. Seas are calm.

☆☆ **Coral Gardens** is a shallow dive and snorkeling area near the shore. Elkhorn, staghorn, brain and star coral form the reef. Fish life includes filefish, angels, triggerfish and fairy basslets. Starfish and anemones are along the base.

☆☆ **Airplane Wreck** at 70 ft is in Bloody Bay off the Sandals resort beach. The wreck, an intentionally sunk Cessna, attracts numerous fish and is beginning to cover over with sponges and corals.

MONTEGO BAY

Montego Bay is Jamaica's first marine park. Depths vary from waist deep to a ledge at 30 ft and vertical drops to 100 ft. The shallow reefs show signs of wear from storms and crowds of snorkelers, but the deeper scuba sites are fairly lush with big tube sponges, sea whips and good sized fish. Seas are usually the calmest in the morning.

☆☆ **Airport Reef** has expansive coral fingers and gullies at depths of 25 to 35 ft. The reef is in Montego Bay. Throngs of small fish, blue chromis, trumpet fish, tangs and parrot fish inhabit the area. Visibility varies from 60 to 80 ft.

☆☆☆ **Widowmakers cave** is named after the cave in James Jones Novel, "Go to the Widowmaker." The wall starts at 40 ft and slopes down to a

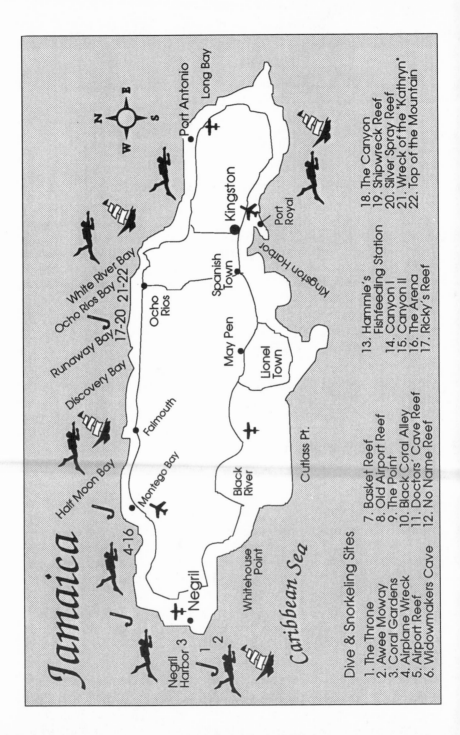

Jamaica

Half Moon Bay

Port Antonio

Long Bay

N E W S

Kingston

White River Bay

Port Royal

Ocho Rios Bay 17-20 21-22

Spanish Town

Runaway Bay

Discovery Bay

Ocho Rios

May Pen

Kingston Harbor

Lionel Town

Falmouth

4-16

Montego Bay

Black River

Cutlass Pt.

Negril Harbor 3

Whitehouse Point

Negril

Caribbean Sea

Dive & Snorkeling Sites

1. The Throne
2. Awee Moway
3. Coral Gardens
4. Airplane Wreck
5. Airport Reef
6. Widowmakers Cave
7. Basket Reef
8. Old Airport Reef
9. The Point
10. Black Coral Alley
11. Doctors' Cave Reef
12. No Name Reef
13. Hammle's Fishfeeding Station
14. Canyon I
15. Canyon II
16. The Arena
17. Ricky's Reef
18. The Canyon
19. Shipwreck Reef
20. Silver Spray Reef
21. Wreck of the "Kathryn"
22. Top of the Mountain

cave at 80 ft. You swim into the cave till you reach a wide chimney which exits up onto a beautiful shallow reef.

Copper sweepers crowd the cave as do parrot fish, king fish, Creole wrasses and barracuda. Black corals, sea feathers, sponges and long gorgonians cover the wall. Seas vary. Currents are usually light. Boat dive.

☆☆☆ **Basket Reef** starts in 50 ft with a sheer drop to 150 ft. Named for huge barrel sponges which adorn the ledge, the reef is extremely photogenic. Expect a light current. A short boat trip.

☆ **Old Airport Reef** is a shallow reef with lots of fish and corals at 15 ft and small caves and crevasses at 35 ft. A good second dive. A boat dive. Good for snorkeling and diving.

☆☆ **The Point** is a drift dive with an average current of two knots. Bermuda chub, rays, occasional hammerhead shark, barracuda, big angelfish, and parrot fish seem to fly past a static display of crimson sponges, long lacy corals, slender gorgonians and anemones growing on the wall. Depths are to 3,000 ft.

☆☆ **Black Coral Alley** is a narrow canyon landscaped with bushy black coral trees. The canyon starts at the base of a coral-covered seamount. Swim around the pinnacle to spot crabs, tubeworms, sea cucumbers, urchins and octopi hiding in the ledges and crevices. Depths are from 40 to 65 ft. Visibility about 80 ft.

☆ **Doctors Cave Reef** is a shallow dive opposite Doctors Cave Beach. Depths average 25 ft. This spot is ideal for beginners—completely sheltered from the afternoon wind and waves. The reef is mostly elkhorn clumps with some brain and star coral heads. Small, friendly reef fish scurry about. Visibility varies from 40 to 60 ft. Boat access.

☆☆ **No Name Reef** is straight out from Doctors Cave. The reef is pretty, with yellow and purple seafans, tube and barrel sponges, lacy corals, gorgonians and patches of finger coral.

Shore Dives

The following sites are accessible from the jetty at Chalet Caribe, just west of Montego Bay. Currents are normally very light though winter storms blowing from the north will make entry difficult or impossible. Before entering the water check with the dive shop for rules on diving the marine park. Cave and tunnel dives should be attempted only by experienced cave divers.

Poinciana Resort, Negril

☆ **Hammie's Fishfeeding Station** came about in 1981 when dive shop owners, Theo and Hammie Smit, started a private marine sanctuary. The site is now part of the Montego Bay Marine Park. Friendly fish will pose for pictures. Check with dive guide for appropriate fish rewards. Depth is 25 ft.

☆ **Canyon I** is a cave/tunnel dive out past the fish feeding station. There is an entrance to the cave at the edge of the reef at 30 ft. Exit at 70 ft. Rare orange sponges grow in the tunnel. Next to Canyon I is **Canyon II**, a hangout for spiny and rock lobsters, schoolmaster snappers and an occasional nurseshark.

☆ **The Arena** is about 250 yards from the jetty. This shallow reef is bowl-shaped, resembling an amphitheater with walls of coral. The walls slope to 70 ft. where two tunnels lead to more caverns with abundant black coral and big barrel sponges. There is a neat, old anchor at the top of the reef. Turtles and eagle rays are common dive buddies.

RUNAWAY BAY

☆☆ **Ricky's Reef** is a huge reef complex with gigantic lavender and yellow tube sponges, thick growths of lacy soft corals, bush corals, orange tube corals, cactus corals, lettuce corals, and stony corals. Most interest is at 90 ft. For experienced divers.

☆☆ **The Canyon** cuts between two walls covered with dense growths of sea rods, sea plumes, sea whips, tube sponges, feather corals, bush corals, and mesh sea fans. Depths are from 35 to 100 ft. Expect a rendezvous with curious angel fish, sergeant majors, trumpet fish, barracuda and an occasional nurse shark. For experienced divers.

☆☆ **Shipwreck Reef** is a shallow reef shot through with caves and crevices. The dive is in front of the Ambience Jamaica resort. An old freighter at 15 ft houses spotted morays, schooling fish and barracuda. An occasional visit by a turtle adds interest. Average depth is 30 ft. Nice for snorkeling or diving.

☆ **Silver Spray Reef** is another shallow garden with a good deal of fish and nice soft corals.

OCHO RIOS

☆☆ **Wreck of** *The Kathryn* was a Canadian mine sweeper acquired by Jamaica many years ago and used as a cargo vessel and later as a fishing vessel. In 1991 it was acquired by Fantasy Divers and Water Sports owners who sunk it to create a new dive and fish breeding spot. The ship sits in 50 ft of water. It's located a mile east of the mouth of the White River off the coast of St. Mary.

☆☆ **Top of the Mountain** is a sea mount at 60 ft decorated with orange sponges, bushy corals, and gorgonians. At 75 ft a cave leads inside the pinnacle. Visibility averages 70 ft.

Dive Operators

NEGRIL

Negril Scuba Centre offers reef trips, night dives, cave dives and underwater photography rentals. Repairs. Dive pages for ☎ 809-957-4425; fax 809-957-4425. Write to P.O. Box 49, Negril, Jamaica.

Sundivers Negril Ltd. is a PADI five star center at the Poinciana Beach Hotel which offers reef trips and specialty courses, custom underwater videos. ☎ 809-957-4069; fax 809-957-4069.

Blue Whale Divers offers boat and shore dives. ☎ 809-957-4438.

MONTEGO BAY

Poseidon Divers is a PADI facility with two locations. One at Marguerites' Restaurant near Doctor's Cave Beach offers boat dives and courses.

Videos and guided snorkel trips can be arranged. At Chalet Caribe Hotel all diving is done from shore. Courses available. ☎ 809-952-3624; fax 809-952-3079.

Scuba and snorkeling reef tours are offered by **Jamaica Scuba Divers,** located at the Half Moon Hotel in St. James. ☎ 809-953-2211; fax 809-953-2731.

Tango Divers specialized in 35 mm photo courses and drive-and-dive trips for divers and snorkelers. They also operate an 18-ft boat. ☎ 809-952-2452; Fax 809-952-6271. Write to Suite M81, 17 Humber Ave., Montego Bay, Jamaica.

Fisherman's Inn watersports center offers diving, snorkeling, fishing and sailing plus dockage for visiting yachts. It is located in Falmouth, a few miles east of Montego Bay. Hotel packages. Handicapped divers program. ☎ 809-954-3427; fax 809-954-3427.

OCHO RIOS

Fantasea Divers, located at the Sans Souci Hotel & Spa, is a PADI international training facility. The shop has a certified Handicapped Scuba Association instructor on staff. Several instructors are trained in American Sign Language for communication with the hearing impaired. Trips range from shallow reefs and caves to deep walls and drop-offs and to the *Katharine* described above. Most sites are ten minutes by boat. ☎ 809-974-5344. Dive/hotel packages.

Sea and Dive Jamaica has three dive boats and offers morning and afternoon dives, snorkeling trips, hotel packages, rentals, repairs, oxygen. ☎ 809-974-5762; fax 809-974-5762. Write to 74 Main Street, Ocho Rios, Jamaica.

Resort Divers Ltd. offers PADI specialty courses, reef trips, night diving and wreck diving aboard four dive boats. Underwater camera rental, gear rental. ☎ 809-974-5338; fax 809-974-0577.

Princess of the Sea Water Sports Ltd. take divers and snorkelers out on two fast boats. Specialties include underwater video service, resort courses. ☎ 809-974-1480; fax 809-974-0574.

Barlovento is a 72-ft sailing yacht which explores remote reefs and hidden beaches. Dive or snorkel. Day sails only. Compressor on board. ☎ 800-562-7273 or 809-974-1518; fax 809-974-5362.

Accommodations

The all-inclusive resorts following usually include airport transfers, all meals, drinks, dive trips, equipment, and tips. Scuba courses are extra and require a medical certificate from home. Rates subject to change. All rates in U.S. dollars based on double occupancy.

Wholesale and retail dive/hotel tours are offered by **Rothschild Travel Consultants,** ☎ 800-359-0747, and **ICS Scuba and Travel,** ☎ 800-722-0205 or 516-797-2132.

NEGRIL

Poinciana Beach Hotel spreads across 1,000 ft of Negril's seven mile beach. This 130-room, full-facility resort offers air-conditioned rooms with private balconies, good facilities for children, entertainment, selected free watersports, tennis, gym, pool, jacuzzi, satellite TV. Dive packages with Sundivers are from $750 in winter for five nights and six days and include tanks, air, weights, guide and boat trip. Add $15 per day for BC's and regulators. Add $130 for unlimited day diving. Non-divers pay $622. Summer rates drop to $626 for a diver and $498 for a non-diver. ☎ 800-468-67728 or 809-957-4069; fax 305- 749-6794. Write to P.O. Box 16003, Plantation FL 33318.

Negril Scuba Center offers low price accommodations from $290 for seven days and six nights. ☎ 800-848-DIVE or 809-957-4425.

Rock Cliff Hotel is a charming resort with shore diving from the dock and Sundivers on premises. Packages. ☎ 809-957-4069 or 800-359-0747. Write to Sundivers, Lighthouse Road, Negril, Jamaica.

Hedonism II is an all-inclusive resort for couples and singles only. Features are luxurious rooms and suites, five bars, a clothing optional island with swim-up pool bar, laser karaoke, indoor game room with satellite TV, sauna, arts & crafts centers. Sports include scuba, water-skiing, snorkeling, windsurfing, sailing, kayaking, water trikes, tennis, fitness center, squash, bicycles, golf and horseback riding. Rates for three nights start at $690 per person in winter, $625 in summer. ☎ 800-859-SUPER. In the U.K., ☎ 0992-447420.

Grand Lido is another adult-only, all-inclusive resort scattered over 22 acres in Negril. Features include nine bars, clothing-optional beach, games room, tennis, 24-hr. food and drink Club Houses. Sports include scuba, snorkeling, kayaking, sunfish sailing, wind surfing, and water skiing. Rates per person for three nights start from $950 winter, $830 summer, ☎ 800-859-7873 or 809-957-4010; fax 809-957-4317.

Sandals Negril is yet another all-inclusive resort which caters to couples only. Facilities include two pools, swim bar, scuba center, satellite TV and disco. Rates for a couple for six nights are from $2,530, winter. ☎ 800-SANDALS; fax 305-667-8996. Write to Unique Vacations, 7610, S.W. 61st Ave., Miami, FL 33143.

Negril Inn is a smaller, 46-room, all-inclusive resort which allows anyone 13 years or older. Rates of $160 winter, $130 summer, per person, per day include one dive per day, transfers from Montego Bay, meals, accommodations, drinks, except champagne, entertainment, sports. ☎ 800-NEGRIL or 516-261-1800; fax 516-261-9606.

Those who prefer sleeping under the stars may pitch a tent at Lighthouse Park on the beach. Contact the Jamaica Tourist Board for details (☎ 800-233-4582).

MONTEGO BAY

Caribe Blue Beach Hotel is a bed & breakfast inn offering three nights and five dives from $200. ☎ 809-953-2180; fax 809-953-2550 or write P.O. Box 610, Montego Bay, Jamaica.

Sandals Montego Bay is an all-inclusive resort for couples. See Sandals Negril for details.

FALMOUTH

Fisherman's Inn & Dive Resort, a 30-minute drive east of Montego Bay, is a dedicated dive resort located on a phosphorescent lagoon at Oyster Bay. Designed and built by divers for divers, the resort features modern, spacious, air-conditioned, waterfront rooms, a good restaurant, poolside bar. Their dive boat, the *Jamaica Queen*, a 42-ft custom yacht, is fast and comfortable. Dives sites are a five-minute ride from the resort dock. Rates for seven nights, eight days in winter are $711 per person for a double (non-diver pays $435) and includes room, one two-tank dive plus one, one-tank dive daily, including tank and weight belt, breakfast and dinner daily, airport transfer, beach shuttle, lounges and beach towers. Summer rates drop to $611 for a diver and $365 for a non-diver. ☎ 800-247-0475 or 809-954-3427.

Trelawny Beach Hotel is a beachfront, family resort. With the exception of lunch and liquor, moderate rates include meals and watersports. Book through your travel agent or direct ☎ 809-954-2450; fax 809-954-2173. Write Box 54, Falmouth, Jamaica.

OCHO RIOS

Boscobel Beach is an all-inclusive resort for families that offers scuba and snorkeling as part of the price. One child under 14 per adult (in parents' suite) can stay for free. Additional children under 14 stay for $50 per day. A Super Nanny program teaches kids to reggae, tie-dye a tee shirt, play with animals in the petting zoo, work in the computer lab, snorkel, play tennis, video games, collect shells and build sand castles. There is even a "Kiddy cocktail" party. Rooms and suites are luxurious. Rates per person start at $795 for three nights in winter, $690 in summer. ☎ 800-859-SUPER.

Dining

Credit cards are accepted at most resorts and large restaurants, but expect to pay cash at the smaller establishments.

Inexpensive = under $20

Moderate = $20 to $35

Expensive = $35+

Jamaica's blend of cultures has exploded in a world of culinary adventure. From the island's first inhabitants, the Arawak Indians, through the Spaniards and the Africans, an early mix of spices and secrets were born. Later, under English rule in the 17th century, Yorkshire pudding, meat pies and hot cross buns were added to an already diverse menu. Variations like the Jamaican pattie (seasoned meat baked in a flaky savory crust) took their place.

During the 1800's Chinese and East Indian indentured laborers added their culinary treasures. Indian curry quickly became the pillar of several of Jamaica's favorite dishes, from meat to seafood and vegetables.

Pimento, or Allspice, is indigenous to Jamaica. One of its most famous uses is for "jerked" pork, chicken or fish which can be sampled at dozens of jerk pits island wide.

Go lightly with the island's favorite seasoning, Pickapeppa Sauce, a fiery concoction of mangos, tamarinds and hot, hot peppers.

NEGRIL

You'll find "Rasta Pasta" and other Jamaican specialties at low prices in Negril at **Paradise Yard** (☎ 957-4006), **Cosmo's, Pamela's Country Restaurant, Miss Nellie's Chicken Lavish,** and **De Buss.** For French cooking, **Cafe au Lait** is a must (☎ 957-4471). **The Negril Yacht Club** serves excellent Chinese food.

Be sure to spend one night at **Rick's Cafe** for sunset watching, light meals and drinks. It's on the tip of Negril's West End. ☎ 957-4335. No credit cards.

MONTEGO BAY

Great seafood, steaks and rum punches are served at **Pier 1** off Howard Cook Blvd. Moderate to Expensive. Or for more casual dining, try **Marguerite's Beer Garden** on Gloucester Avenue. Specials include fried fish, lobster and cheeseburgers (☎ 952-2452).

Stop at the **Pork Pit** for spicy hot jerk pork and Red Stripe beer. Inexpensive. It's next to the Fantasy Hotel by the airport. Cash only.

For very elegant dining with a spectacular view of the town and harbor try **Richmond Hill** (☎ 952-2835) or the **Diplomat** (both expensive).

OCHO RIOS

Jamaican-Italian (really) cuisine has found the perfect home at **Evita's** in Ocho Rios where the "Rasta Pasta" is a must try. The menu offers 15 other pasta specials, excellent fish, steak or pork dishes. Evita's is set in an old plantation house overlooking the bay. Moderate. (☎ 974-2333.)

Almond Tree offers excellent native cuisine and atmosphere. Overlooks the sea at 83 Main St. Moderate to Expensive. (☎974-2813)

Sightseeing and Other Activities

NEGRIL

Negril is the most quiet area of Jamaica and one of the loveliest. Building codes have kept the highest structure "no higher than the highest palm tree." Most activities are water-related and can be arranged through the dive shops.

Getting around Negril is easy. You can rent a car, bicycle, or canoe, or just stroll along the beautiful seven-mile beach. Among the interesting buildings to visit is the 19th-century Courthouse of Lucea, and the clock tower modeled after the helmet once worn by the German Royal Guard. The clock itself was made in 1817; it keeps perfect time, and is tended by a family that has had the job for over a hundred years.

At Kenilworth, on the highway that leads to Montego Bay (an hour away), are the ruins of a sugar factory and distiller—one of the best examples of early industrial architecture in Jamaica.

Evening entertainment in the form of reggae, calypso and rock music is best at Rick's Cafe, Arthur's Golden Sunset and Kaisers.

MONTEGO BAY

This second largest city in Jamaica offers many attractions, from architecture and museums to natural scenic beauty. **The Cage**, an 18th-century jail for slaves and runaway seamen, is in the center of the city and houses a small museum. **St. James Parish Church**, built 1775-1782, is regarded as one of the finest churches in Jamaica. **The Bird Sanctuary** at Anchovey features "Doctor Bird" hummingbirds, one of 24 species found only in Jamaica. A trip into the interior on the **Hilton High Day Tour** gives a taste of country farm life, a ride in a hot-air balloon, and exposure to a different Jamaica: the mysterious cockpit country, and blond Jamaicans whose ancestors came long ago from Germany.

A ride on the **Appleton Express** is a "traveling-in-style" experience. Once used for official travel by the Governor of Jamaica, this train has been converted into an all-day special coach very popular with visitors. It chugs its way some 40 miles into the interior, stopping at the **Appleton Rum Distiller** and **Ipswich Caves**, and also makes two stops for passengers to buy custom-made clothing—one to select fabric and style on the way inland, one to collect the finished product on the way home.

Montego Bay offers duty-free shopping for liquor, china, glassware, perfumes, cigars, English cashmeres and a variety of crafts. There are also several art galleries, including the **Gallery of West Indian Art**, which are worth a browse.

Montego Bay's nightlife is varied. Three different once-a-week events deserve special consideration: The Cornwall Beach Party; an Evening on the Great River—a torchlight ride in dugout canoes followed by dinner, dancing and entertainment; and MoBay Monday Night Out—lots of music, food and drink in a street festival setting. Discos throughout the city provide reggae to rock.

OCHO RIOS

Ocho Rios is the central point of a magnificent region that includes both deserted and developed beaches, fern-clad cliffs and breathtaking waterfalls. Tranquil, yet stimulating, it evolved from a center of Spanish cultural influence to a modern Caribbean resort area.

Ocho Rios may well be the most photographed area in the West Indies. Shaw Park Gardens on the high ground affords spectacular vistas of the coast. Dunn's River Falls, over 600 feet high, is considered the Niagara of the Caribbean. Fern Gully offers a spectacular, curving three-mile journey through a world of tropical ferns, including the 30-ft-tall Fern Tree and more than 550 other native varieties.

Several excellent plantation tours give an introduction to Caribbean farming. "Firefly," the mountaintop house where Noel Coward lived and is buried, is open to visitors. There are the excavations of the 16th-century Spanish ruins of New Seville and, of course, there is Discovery Bay, which today features historic **Columbus Park**. The Cukka Cove Equestrian Center offers several scenic horseback trails.

At night the larger hotels offers shows and dancing. Romantics should find time for a torchlit canoe ride on the White River with a spectacular Island fest and entertainment on the beach below.

PORT ANTONIO

Port Antonio is a playground of the world's elite—from royalty and movie stars to captains of industry, commerce and politics. It has also been the selected backdrop of Hollywood producers for several feature films. For many years, Port Antonio was a well-kept secret hideaway of Clara Bow, Bette Davis, Errol Flynn, Ginger Rogers and J.P. Morgan.

Orchids, bananas, tree-ferns and palms grow along the roadside around this quiet port town. Elegant villas nestled in the hills and along the seacoast are a contrast to old abandoned mansions, historic forts, waterfalls, and caves.

Sightseeing in Port Antonio is relaxing. There is **Fort George** overlooking the two harbors, with 10-ft-thick walls and cannons pointed out to sea. The once glorious **Folly Mansion** is now a legendary ruin.

In contrast, the **Errol Flynn Plantation**, is well-tended and prosperous. A harbor cruise which leaves from the town dock covers many of Port Antonio's points of interest.

Water-lovers can choose between an icy-cold dip in Somerset Falls, and snorkeling, scuba diving and swimming in the "bottomless" Blue Lagoon (actually 180-ft deep). Or they can get carried away down the Rio Grande in a 30-ft bamboo raft, guided by a licensed Jamaican raftsman.

For those who like to explore, there are **Nonsuch Caves** with fossils, coral formations and remnants of an early Arawak Indian community. East of Port Antonio is **Reach Falls**, one of the most spectacular waterfalls in all of Jamaica.

KINGSTON

Kingston, Jamaica's capital city, is the largest English-speaking city south of Miami.

Set against a backdrop of the Blue Mountain range, Kingston is a busy, well-populated, cosmopolitan city. It is the cultural center as well. The **National Gallery of Jamaica** and **the Institute of Jamaica** offer an exciting view of Jamaican culture, including the most complete collection of the country's art to be found anywhere.

MANDEVILLE

The inland town of Mandeville is considered the most English town in Jamaica; many of its original buildings of early 1800's vintage remain. Outside Mandeville are bauxite mines and a production facility, which are open for touring. Nearby is the famous **Picakapeppa factory** where the popular Jamaican hot sauce is produced.

Helpful Phone Numbers

POLICE: ☎ 119

HOSPITAL: Montego Bay, Cornwall Regional Hospital, ☎ 952-5100; Ocho Rios, St. Ann's Bay Hospital, ☎ 972-2272.

Facts

Nearest Recompression Chamber: The Marine Lab at Discovery Bay.

Getting There: Donald Sangster International Airport in Montego Bay is the best entry point for the dive-resort areas. American Airlines ☎ (800-433-7300) offers direct service from New York. Air Jamaica ☎ (800-523-5585) flies from Miami, Atlanta, Philadelphia, Los Angeles, Orlando, Baltimore and New York. Continental ☎ (800-231-0856) flies from Newark; BWIA from San Juan; Northwest ☎ (800-447-4747) has daily flights from Minneapolis and Tampa.

Precautions: Avoid touring the off-the-beaten-track areas of the cities, especially at night. The dive-resort areas listed are fairly quiet, but ragged natives pandering *ganja* (marijuana) may approach you.

Driving: On the left. Rental cars are scarce in season. Be sure to arrange for a rental car in advance of your trip. Hertz ☎ (800-654-3131); Avis ☎ (800-331-1212); Dollar ☎ (800-800-4000); and National ☎ (800-227-3876). Renters must be 21 and have a valid driver's license and a major credit card.

Language: English and "Patois" (Jamaican Creole words and speech patterns used by most of the population).

Documents: Visitors from the U.S. or Canada must show proof of citizenship such as a birth certificate with raised seal or a passport and a return ticket. British visitors must have a passport and a return ticket.

Customs: Visitors are prohibited from bringing in drugs, fresh fruit, flowers, meat or rum. Firearms or ammunition are prohibited.

Airport Tax: $10 U.S.

Currency: The Jamaican dollar. The exchange rate fluctuates daily, depending on the foreign exchange markets. The current rate stands at U.S.$1.00 = JA$22.00.

Climate: Average annual air temperature is 82°F. Water temperature ranges from 80 to 90°F. Wetsuits are not necessary, but a lycra suit is comfortable in winter.

Clothing: Lightweight, casual. Hiking shoes for visiting the "mist forests."

Electricity: Varies with the hotel. Some have 110 volts/60 cycles and others 220. To be safe carry a converter for your appliances.

Religious Services: Protestant, Catholic, Jewish, Rastafarian.

For Additional Information: Contact the Jamaica Tourist Board. ☎ 800-233-4582. *In New York*, 801 Second Avenue, 20th Floor, New York NY 10017, ☎ 212-856-9727, fax 212-856-9730. *In Miami*, 1320 S. Dixie Highway, Suite 1100, Coral Gables FL 33146, ☎ 305-665-0557. *In Los Angeles*, 3440 Wilshire Boulevard, Suite 1207, Los Angeles, CA 90010, ☎ 800-421-8206 or 213-384-1123. *In Canada*, Mezzanine Level, 1110 Sherbrooke St., West, Montreal, Quebec, Canada H3A 1G9, ☎ 514-849-6386. *In The U.K,*. 111 Gloucester Place, London W1H, 3PH; ☎ 071-224-0505; fax 071-224-0551.

Puerto Rico

Puerto Rico's beautiful beaches, cosmopolitan cities and abundant man-made attractions pale in comparison to the pristine coral reefs that surround three fourths of its coastline. Coupled with first-class hotels, easy access from the U.S., affordable dive-accommodation packages, and a choice of rural or urban settings, it is gaining in favor as an all-around vacation spot for Caribbean divers. The farthest east in the Greater Antilles chain, this 110-by-35-mile island is surrounded by the Atlantic Ocean to the north, the Caribbean to the south and three main out-islands—Vieques and Culebra to the east, and Mona to the west. Three and one-half million people inhabit the mainland, with about one million in the San Juan metropolitan area.

The island's terrain ranges from palm-lined beaches on four coastlines to rugged mountain ranges, gently rolling hills and deserts. There are 20 designated forest reserves in Puerto Rico and an additional six proposed reserves. The most notable are the 28,000-acre El Yunque rain forest near San Juan, part of the Caribbean National Forest and the only tropical rainforest in the U.S. Forest Service; the Guajataca Forest, with 25 miles of trails through karst reserves—an area of huge, moonscape craters and caves; and the Guanica Forest Reserve, a dry forest with the largest number of bird species on the island. There are also two Phosphorescent Bays, one off La Parguera on the southwest coast and one off the island of Vieques.

Diving and snorkeling is along the Continental Shelf which surrounds the island on the east, south and west coasts. Underwater terrain is diverse with shallow reefs off Humacao on the east coast, caves and wrecks off Aguadilla on the west coast, and dramatic walls at The Great Trench, which starts in the Virgin Islands, stretches the entire length of Puerto Rico's southcoast and winds up at Cabo Rojo on the west coast.

Contributors: Gareth Edmondson-Jones; James Abbott, Coral Head Divers; Cathy Rothschild, Rothschild Travel; Jose E. Rafols, Aquatica Underwater Adventures; Efra Figueroa, Parguera Divers; Rick & Lisa Ockelmann.

Marine life is exciting with manatees in the brackish mangrove areas, pelagics at Mona Island (50 miles southwest), and all species of sea turtles at Culebra. In winter, migrating humpback whales travel the Mona Passage off the west coast. Dolphins are frequently spotted off the eastern shores. Towering soft corals grow to 20 ft in some spots.

History

Cave drawings indicate that people lived on Puerto Rico for more than 2,000 years before Christopher Columbus claimed it for Spain in 1493. Back then it was known as Borinquen and inhabited by several Indian tribes including the Taino Indians. The Spaniards renamed it San Juan for St. John the Baptist, but later changed it to Puerto Rico, which means "Rich Port."

Ponce de Leon, seeker of the Fountain of Youth, was the first governor in 1508. During the next three centuries, settlers defended the island from the French, the Dutch and English—traditional enemies of the Spanish empire. Following the Spanish-American War in 1898, Spain ceded the island to the United States. Puerto Ricans became U.S. citizens in 1917, held their first gubernatorial elections in 1948, and adopted Commonwealth status in 1952.

Puerto Rico, the Caribbean's most industrially developed island is a major producer and exporter of manufactured goods, pharmaceuticals and high technology equipment. Since the 19th century, Puerto Rico has been a major exporter of rum and today approximately 83% of the rum sold in the U.S. comes from Puerto Rico.

Best Dives and Snorkeling Sights

EAST COAST

Diving off Puerto Rico's east coast centers around Fajardo, Humacao and the offshore islands of Icacos, Palominos, Palminitos, Monkey Island, Vieques and Culebra. Outstanding features are towering soft corals, walls, dramatic overhangs and abundance of fish. Many of the mainland dive sights are close to shore, but the best are about a 20-minute boat ride. Depths are from 35 to 100 ft. Shore diving and snorkeling is possible off Fajardo, but freshwater runoff near the shore clouds the water and lowers visibility. Spearfishing and coral collecting are prohibited.

Seafan at The Reserve, Humacao

☆☆☆ **The Reserve**, a 20-minute boat ride from Humacao, is a spur-and-groove reef that appears like rivers of white sand between coral canyons. The reef is vibrant with towering pillar coral, large star-and brain-coral heads ruffled with sea rods, spiny sea fans and slender tube sponges. Nurse sharks, stingrays, spotted and green morays and tropicals inhabit the ledges and overhangs of the reef. Seas average two to four ft. Depths average 50 to 80 ft. Water temperature ranges from 82° to 90°F. Divers should have some experience.

☆☆☆☆ **Basslet Reef**, one mile from Humacao, is a small wall with overhangs, caves and swim-throughs. It is frequented by hawksbill turtles, nurse sharks, and enormous angelfish. Most of the reef is formed of mushrooming pillar corals rippled by a healthy display of sea plumes and sea rods. Dolphin visit the area during early summer and spring. Top of the wall is at 60 ft. Usually no current, but expect three-to five-ft surface swells. Basslet Reef is a 15-minute boat ride from Palmas Del Mar docks.

☆☆☆☆☆ **The Cracks** is a section of subsea cliffs ripped apart by an earthquake. The results are an intriguing maze of chasms and fissures where throngs of fish and lobster hide out. Small caves and coral buttresses drop down to a sandy bottom. Dramatic photo opportunities. Depths are from 50 to 80 ft. For novice and experienced divers only. Seas run three to five ft.

☆☆☆☆ **Monkey Reef** is a five-minute boat trip from Palmas Del Mar docks. The reef is an expanse of sloping hills covered over with acres of soft corals and sponges. One area slopes to a sandy bottom where you will find large, friendly southern sting rays, spotted eagle rays and thousands of shells. The other side is ledges and overhangs where you never know what to expect. Depths range from 20 to 50 ft and it is excellent for novice and experienced divers.

☆☆☆ **La Jolla Ridge** is a small coral wall one mile from shore. A healthy display of soft corals, sea whips, sea fans and throngs of schooling fish starts at 40 ft and plunges down to 80 ft. Ledges, overhangs and swim-throughs are home to every imaginable sea creature. A spectacular night dive when the area becomes a ballet of basket stars. Recommended for novice and experienced divers. Seas average two to four ft.

☆☆☆ **The Grotto**, a spur and grove reef four miles from Palmas Del Mar docks, is a memorable dive experience with small caves, overhangs and swim-throughs inhabited by crowds of copper sweepers, fairy tailed basslets and blue chromis. Good for all level divers.

☆☆☆ **The Drift** is a gently sloping hill covered on one side with giant sponges, sea rods and whips. As you glide over the top you approach a valley of swim-throughs and ledges frequented by moray eels, lobsters, queen and French angels, and nurse sharks.

CULEBRA AND VIEQUES

Trips to out islands, Culebra and Vieques take off from Humacao or Puerto del Rey Marina at Fajardo, north of Humacao. Puerto del Rey is the largest marina in the Caribbean with 700 deepwater slips and service facilities. For ferry schedules ☎ 809-863-0705. If you wish to ferry an automobile you must reserve space a week in advance.

Culebra is a mini archipelago with 23 offshore islands situated mid-point between Puerto Rico and St. Thomas. Shallow coral reefs surround the entire area. A favorite snorkeling and photo spot is Culebrita where there is also a lighthouse. The main five-mile-long island, home to 2,000 people, is a National Wildlife Refuge known for its white sand beaches, sea bird colonies (boobies, frigates, and gulls) and as a nesting ground for all species of Caribbean sea turtles (leatherback, green, hawksbill and loggerhead). The turtles nest from April through July. (National Wildlife

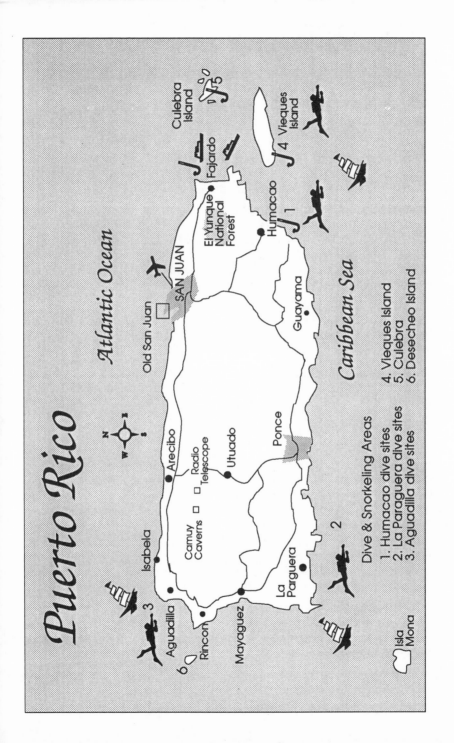

Puerto Rico

Atlantic Ocean

Caribbean Sea

Old San Juan
SAN JUAN
El Yunque National Forest
Fajardo
Culebra Island
Vieques Island
Humacao
Guayama
Ponce
Arecibo
Radio Telescope
Camuy Caverns
Utuado
Isabela
Aguadilla
Rincon
Mayaguez
La Parguera
Isla Mona

Dive & Snorkeling Areas
1. Humacao dive sites
2. La Parguera dive sites
3. Aguadilla dive sites
4. Vieques Island
5. Culebra
6. Desecheo Island

Refuge 809-742-3291.) Expeditions for turtle watching are conducted by Earthwatch, a non-profit organization.

VIEQUES

Vieques is a popular camping island for locals and day trip for east coast divers and snorkelers. Known for its beautiful beaches, two thirds of the island is owned by the U.S. Navy with a small section still used for military operations and manuvers. The rest is rural.

Shallow reefs and dropoffs lie within one mile of the shoreline. Many are in less than 50 ft. with some very shallow areas. Sea conditions, sometimes rough, vary with the wind. Swells on the leeward side average two to three ft. Vieques subsea highlights are walls, caves, giant barrel sponges, healthy fish populations, and a magnificent phosphorescent bay. Beach dives are possible off the West end at Green Beach with reef depths from ten to 25 ft.

Two towns, Esperanza and Isabel Segunda, serve Vieques" 8,000 residents. Accommodations are available at Casa Del Frances (809-741-3751) near Esperaza.

Vieques is a 30-minute boat trip from Fajardo or Humacao. Or by air via Sunaire Express from San Juan's international airport (about $50 round trip).

East Coast Dive Operators

Coral Head Divers (CHD) at the Palmas Del Mar Resort is an English-speaking PADI and NAUI Pro Facility offering personalized dive adventures. CHD is owned and operated by Captain Jim Abbott, an awarded (Platinum Pro 5000) and accomplished dive instructor with 20 years experience. Jim has pioneered the pristine dive sites off Puerto Rico's south coast and personally escorts most of the dives. Hundreds of return customers can attest to Jim's reputation as "the most gracious dive host in the Caribbean"—dive boats are never overcrowded and he personally looks after each divers safety and enjoyment.

CHD visits 24 sites, all within five to 20 minutes from the dock. For those of you whose favorite après-dive activity is more diving, the shop also rents ocean kayaks suitable for carrying a tank out to a nearby islet for additional diving or snorkeling.

CHD carries state-of-the-art equipment including dive computers which are provided at no extra charge to divers who do not have their own. Pure

Courtesy Coral Head Divers.

Dive boat "Elegance," Humacao

air is provided through an electric-powered fill station with water separators and filters—all excellently maintained.

The shop has two dive boats, a six-passenger, 26-ft dive boat, for nearby sites and a 44-ft, custom dive yacht, *Elegance* for trips to Monkey Island or Vieques. CHD is one of the best-equipped operators in the Caribbean with more than 100 sets of hypoallergenic masks, snorkels and fins of all sizes and designs. Reservations required. ☎ 809-850-7208; 800-635-4529. Write to P.O. Box CUHF, Humacao, Puerto Rico 00792.

Dive and snorkeling tours aboard the *Fiesta*, a 48-ft trimaran and weekly live-aboard charters are offered by **Caribbean Marine Services** on Culebra. ☎ 809-742-3555; fax 809-742-0036.

East Coast Accommodations

NOTE: Paradores are country inns that offer quality lodging near places of great natural beauty, historical monuments and points of interest.

Palmas del Mar, located 40 miles southeast of San Juan, is a beauiful 2,700-acre luxury resort with three miles of sandy beach. Rooms feature air conditioning, cable tv, phones, and Caribbean decor. Sports facilities include 20 tennis courts, an 18-hole golf course, five swimming pools, fitness center, and equestrian center. Water sports include sailing, deep-sea fishing, snorkeling and diving. Coral Head Divers is on the grounds. Rothschild Travel offers discounted dive/accommodation packages from the U.S. starting at $217 for three nights (double), four boat dives, transfers, taxes and service charges. ☎ 800-359-0747. Contact the hotel at 809-852-6111; fax 809-852-2230. Write to P.O. Box 2020, Humacao, Puerto Rico 00792.

Hotel Parador La Familia Inn, at Las Croabas, Fajardo, offers air- conditioned rooms with TV, refrigerator and bath. Restaurant and pool on premises. ☎ 800-359-0747 or 809-863-1193.

SOUTH COAST

Dive trips off the south coast originate in Ponce, Puerto Rico's second largest city or La Parguera, a sleepy fishing village known for its famed Phosphorescent Bay—one of four bio-luminescent bodies of water in the world. It is also home to the University of Puerto Rico's Marine Science Facility.

A two-and-one-half-hour drive from San Juan airport, La Parguera is not yet heavily populated by tourists. Accommodations are modest, local attractions and other activities are limited.

Best Dives and Snorkeling Sites

Ponce Caja de Muertos (coffin Island), Cayo Ratones, Cayo Caribe and Cayo Cardon form a crescent barrier reef from Ponce west to Tallaboa. All are a 20-minute boat ride from Ponce. Shore dives are possible off Coffin Island, a park administered by the Department of Natural Resources. Depths are from 15 to 40 ft.

☆☆☆ LA PARGUERA WALL DIVES:

There are no shore dives. The best sites are along a 20-mile wall that edges the Great Trench from La Parguera to Ponce. Recommended for advanced divers, depths on the wall vary from 50 to 100+ ft. Visibility exceeds 150 ft. Currents, if any, are light. Seas average one to two ft. Boat trips are all 45 minutes to an hour long.

Snorkeling is not particularly good in this area...limited to boat trips along a few shallow reefs and exploring the mangrove roots which shelter countless fish and invertebrates.

Black Wall is a vertical wall which starts at 60 ft and drops down to depth. Divers encounter lots of schooling fish, green morays, big crabs, deep-water black gorgonians, and good coral heads.

Hole in the Wall at 120 ft, as the name implies, is a hole where divers can swim through and come up in 100 ft of water.

Hai Lite are deep water trenches with valleys of schooling grunts and squirrel fish. Beautiful barrel and giant tube sponges. Lavender trumpet-fish.

Grunts Valley, like Hai Lite, is a hangout for myriads of grunts, yellow-tail, snapper, squirrel fish.

Eel Garden is a mildly sloping wall down to a big sand patch at 90 ft where hundreds of garden eels are found.

Cylinders is a sharp sloping wall named for huge gas cylinders dropped by a cargo ship 20 years ago. The cylinders are covered with corals and sponges.

Fallen Rock is a huge rock in the middle of a Y-shaped trench. The walls are sheer with lots of schooling fish, big barrel sponges and gorgonians. The adjacent trench is so congested with traveling fish the locals nick-named it "L.A. Highway." Expect the unexpected!

☆☆ LA PARGUERA INNER-REEF DIVES

Depths on the inner reef, a 10-minute boat ride, range from 6 to 30 ft. Good for novice divers.

The Playground is the site of the Parguera Divers Bubble Bell. You fill the bell with fresh air from your tank and experience a mini underwater habitat for two. You can talk, kiss, eat or hangout under it. Two big French angelfish will hover close and play in your bubbles.

Barracuda City at 50 ft. is a dense forest of staghorn and elkhorn corals packed with clouds of the silvery fish for which it was named. While encountering one or two barracuda on any Caribbean reef is scarcely noteworthy, this spot can be downright unnerving. Exciting photo possibilities for those who dare!

Hog Heaven I, II, III is a newly discovered, triple-site reef off La Parguera with a fascinating complex of coral caves, holes and canyons. It was named by local divemaster, Efra Figueroa who, upon first diving the area, met a colossal hogfish. The big hogfish is gone, but sightings of nurse shark are common.

The Pinnacles are coral formations estimated to be 5,000 years old. They appear like giant mushrooms with holes and caves. This is spot for marine invertebates—octopi, sea horses, arrow crabs, basket sponges and more.

The Forest is a mass of towering soft corals growing across rocky canyons. Many critters and fish. Expect a light surge.

Additional similar dive and snorkeling sites off the south coast are **1990, The Star, Aquarium, Manhattan, Coral Garden, Sponge Garden,** and the *Margarita* **Wreck.**

South Coast Dive Operators

Paraguera Divers Training Center is a PADI and NAUI instruction facility offering certification, dive master, rescue and medic courses. Snorkeling, jet skis, wind surfing, mangrove-trail tours, Phosphorescent Bay trips, fishing and boat rentals can be arranged. Open water referrals accepted for PADI and NAUI. Major credit cards and traveler checks accepted.

This English/Spanish speaking dive center is owned and operated by Captain Efra Figueroa who personally escorts most dives. His background is impressive with 23 years of diving all over the world as: a U.S. Navy diver, a University of Puerto Rico Marine Sciences instructor and recompression chamber operator, Sea Grant Program consultant for marine advisory services, co-director for seven NAUI ITC's (Instructor Training Courses), and certified instructor for PADI, NAUI, CMAS, SSI, ARC, MEDIC-FIRST AID since 1976. Efra also has a degree in zoology and animal science. ☎ 809-899-4171; fax same. Write to Parguera Divers, P.O. Box 514, Lajas, Puerto Rico 00667.

Marine Sports & Dive Shop in Ponce visits Coffin Island. ☎ 809-844-6175.

South Coast Accommodations

Parador Villa Parguera faces Phosphorescent Bay and is next door to the dive dock. This parador (small hotel) features waterfront rooms with private terraces. There are 52 rooms, a fine restaurant and bar, plus pool. Dive/accommodation packages start at $284 per person for two nights. ☎ 800-359-0747 or 212-662-4858. Write to 900 West End Ave. Suite 1B,

New York, N.Y. 10025. Hotel direct: ☎ 809-899-7777. Route 304, La Parguera, Lajas, PR 00667.

Parador Posada Porlamar has 19 air-conditioned rooms with kitchen facilities and charming gardens. The dive dock for Parguera Divers is directly in front of the hotel. Dive/accommodation packages start at $83 per person for three nights. ☎ 800-359-0747 or 212-662-4858. Write to 900 West End Ave., Suite 1B, New York N.Y. 10025 or ☎ 800-899-4015.

WEST COAST

Diving centers around Aguadilla named for a natural spring which for centuries served as a watering place for Spanish sailors. Pretty beaches shaded by coconut palms stretch from Rincon, south of Aguadilla to Crash Boat Beach, north of Aguadilla. Visibility and water temperature along Puerto Rico's west coast sites are best during Spring and Summer—March through November. Sea conditions are rough and suggested for advanced divers only. Beach dives are possible at Crash Boat Beach, though visibility is often clouded by freshwater runoff.

☆☆☆ **Yellow Reef** is a pyramid-shaped sea mount that starts at 15 ft and drops to 85 ft. Coral caverns, arches and a 10-ton anchor make it uniquely interesting. Average depth is 60 ft. The bottom is sandy and dotted with other pinnacles. Big schools of amberjacks (200 +) are always about, as are queen angels, rock beauties and nurse shark. Big star coral heads, orange cups and big barrel sponges prevail. This area is wind-dependent—wiped out for diving if swells exceed four feet.

☆☆☆☆☆ **South Gardens—Desecheo Island** located 13 miles offshore is being considered for a marine sanctuary. This popular west-coast dive features a huge fish population, immense barrel sponges, giant sea fans (six-ft across) and shallow depths. Sting rays and turtles are frequently sighted. Dives are off the protected southwest tip of the island where you can explore an unknown wreck or a cave at 25 ft. Snorkelers will be encircled by curious fish along the rocky shore. Star, brain and staghorn corals form the shallow reef.

☆☆☆ **Airplane Wreck** is a B-29 Bomber that went down in 1949. Huge grouper patrol its coral-encrusted wings, propellers and landing gear. The wreck sits at 115 ft., on a sandy bottom surrounded by rocky ledges. Visibility is around 80 ft. Possible strong surface currents make line descent and ascents a must. Hordes of lobster hide in the surrounding rock ledges. This is a decompression dive with a mandatory (by the dive operator) stop at 15 ft. For advanced divers only.

MONA ISLAND, a remote, uninhabited island 50 miles off the southwest tip of Puerto Rico, is a six-hour boat trip from the mainland across rough water or a half-hour flight from Mayaguez. The trip and stay are a rugged adventure, but the intrepid nature lovers are rewarded with colonies of seals, sea birds, colorful marine life, 200-foot cliffs and dazzling white beaches. Virgin dive sites average 80-ft depths. Camping overnight is permitted, but most visitors arrive by boat for day visits. Some cabins are available. Contact Department of Natural Resources, ☎ 809-722-1726.

West Coast Dive Operator

Aquatica Underwater Adventures is a PADI/NAUI instruction center offering referrals, open water, advanced and rescue courses, dive and snorkeling trips. C card and log book requested. Repairs and rentals. English-speaking dive master and captain, Jose E. Rafols is Coast Guard certified to operate a 100-ton vessel. Dive boats depart from Aguadilla or Joyuda Beach. ☎ 809-890-6071; fax same. Write to: P.O.Box 350, Ramey, Aguadilla, PR 00604.

West Coast Accommodations

Tours below may be booked by your travel agent.

Parador El Faro is a modern inn with 32 comfortable guest rooms. Dive-hotel packages through Rothschild Travel start at $115 per person for three nights. ☎ 800-359-0747 or 212-662-4858. Write to 900 West End Ave. Suite 1B, New York, N.Y. 10025.

Joyuda Beach Hotel is a beachfront property offering 52 tastefully decorated guest rooms. The dive-boat pier is a short walk away. Joyuda Beach on Cabo Rojo is a quaint fishing and resort community with more than 20 great seafood restaurants. Dive packages for three nights start at $127 per person. Book through your travel agent or Rothschild Travel. ☎ 800-359-0747 or 212-662-4858. Write to 900 West End Ave. Suite 1B, New York, N.Y. 10025.

Mayaguez Hilton, at Mayaguez, just north of Cabo Rojo, has 145 luxurious guest rooms and suites with full amenities. Two fine restaurants, bar, dance club, casino, olympic pool, and three tennis courts. Dive-hotel packages start at $265 per night per person. ☎ 800-359-0747 or 212-662-4858. Write to 900 West End Ave. Suite 1B, New York N.Y. 10025.

Dining

Puerto Rico boasts some of the finest restaurants in the Caribbean, offering international dishes from Spain, France, Italy, Germany, Mexico, Argentina, and the Orient. Traditional Puerto Rican cuisine offers an interesting mix of Spanish, Creole and native Indian influences. Some of the island's best restaurants are *mesones gastronomicos* (gastronomic inns), located outside the San Juan urban area and featuring local cuisine at reasonable prices.

EAST COAST

Anchor's Inn in Fajardo serves steaks and seafood. Located on Route 987, Km 2.7 (863-7200). For French and international cuisine try **DuPort** on Route 3, Km 51.3 (860-4260) Major credit cards. In Humacao tasty fish and lobster dinners are offered by **Daniel Seafood** at 7 Marina (☎ 852-1784), major credit cards; or **Paradise Seafood** on Route 3 at Km 75 (☎ 852-1180).

SOUTH COAST

For steaks and seafood in Ponce, stop in at **Lydia's** on Ramal 52, Km 255 (☎ 844-3933) major credit cards; or **Pito's** on Route 2, Cucharas (☎ 841-4977) major credit cards.

WEST COAST

Cabo Rojo has an abundance of good seafood restaurants. Try **Perichi's** on route 102, Km 14.3 (☎ 851-3131) credit cards accepted; or **Brisas del Mar** on Route 308, Pto. Real (☎ 851-1264), major credit cards accepted.

Caracol in Aguadilla offers international and seafood favorites. It's on Route 107, KM 2 (☎ 882-8000)

Sightseeing

Visitors to Puerto Rico will find many attractions, especially in the capital city of San Juan. The seven-square-block area of Old San Juan, named a National Historic Zone in the 1950s, is chock-a-block with interesting museums, churches, forts, restored homes, restaurants, boutiques, art galleries, sidewalk cafes and some of the most authentic examples of 16th and 17th century Spanish colonial architecture in the western hemisphere. The peaceful countryside, "out on the island," offers Spanish colonial towns, 15 picturesque country inns (paradores puertorriquenos), great seaside restaurants, beautiful beaches, and dramatic mountain scenery.

OLD SAN JUAN. Founded in 1521, Old San Juan is the oldest capital city under the U.S. flag. Among the many landmark sites are **El Morro**, constructed by the Spanish from 1540-1586 to protect the San Juan harbor from invasion by Sir Francis Drake; **La Fortaleza**, the official home and office of the governor of Puerto Rico, built in 1540 and the oldest executive mansion in continuous use in the New World; **Casa Blanca**, built in 1523 as the residence of the family of Ponce de Leon, the first governor of the island and today housing a Taino Indian museum and a Ponce de Leon family museum; the **Pablo Casals Museum** which houses memorabilia of the famous cellist who lived in Puerto Rico for the last 20 years of his life; and the **San Juan Cathedral**, one of the oldest places of Christian worship in the Western Hemisphere.

PONCE. Puerto Rico's second largest city is just 90 minutes by car south of San Juan. Since 1988, more than 500 historic buildings dating from the mid 1800s to the 1930s have been meticulously restored. The **Ponce Art Museum**, designed by Edward Durell Stone, is the most extensive in the Caribbean. Founded by former Governor Luis A. Ferre, the museum houses more than 1,000 paintings and 400 sculptures, and is noted for its late Renaissance and Baroque works. Ponce is also well known for its 1883 red and black firehouse, traditional town square, and pre-Columbian **Tibes Indian Ceremonial Park**, the oldest Indian burial ground in the Antilles. Nearby is **Hacienda Buena Vista**, a recently restored 19th-century coffee plantation and grain mill which is now open to the public as a museum.

SAN GERMAN. This quaint Spanish town's **Porta Coeli Church**, built in 1606, is the oldest church still intact under the U.S. flag. The town itself, located in the southwest corner of the island, still retains much of its original Spanish colonial architecture and charm.

ARECIBO OBSERVATORY. Two hours from San Juan on the north coast in the town of Arecibo, which dates to 1556, is the world's largest radar-radio telescope, equal to the size of 13 football fields. Here scientists from Cornell University and the National Science Foundation study the planets and distant galaxies by gathering radio waves from space.

THE RIO CAMUY CAVE PARK. Opened in December 1986, this 300-acre park is one of Puerto Rico's most fascinating sightseeing attractions and is located near the Arecibo Observatory. The caves have been hailed by experts as one of the world's most spectacular cave systems with one of the world's largest underground rivers.

EL YUNQUE, 35 miles east of San Juan, is a vast 28,000-acre rain forest in the Luquillo Mountains. Some 100 billion gallons of rain fall each year on over 240 varieties of tree and flower species. It is the only tropical rain forest in the U.S. Forest Service.

LAS CABEZAS DE SAN JUAN NATURE RESERVE. Opened in March 1991, this 316-acre nature reserve encompasses seven different ecological systems including: forest, mangroves, lagoons, beaches, cliffs, offshore islets and coral reefs. Visitors may tour the reserve's nature center and 19thcentury working lighthouse, *El Faro*, which offers views of distant Caribbean islands. Contact: The Conservation Trust, ☎ 809-722-5834. Las Cabezas is a 45-minute drive from San Juan.

INDIAN CEREMONIAL PARKS. Two sites on the island showcase Puerto Rico's Indian heritage. Located near Ponce, **Tibes Indian Ceremonial Park** is the oldest Indian burial ground uncovered in the Antilles. The site has seven ceremonial ball courts, two dance grounds and a re-created Taino Indian village. A museum displays Indian ceremonial objects, jewelry and pottery.

Located in Utuado, **Caguana Indian Ceremonial Ball Park** was built by the Taino Indians for recreation and worship some 800 years ago. Stone monoliths, some etched with petroglyphs, rim several of the ten ball courts which were used for a game which some historians believe was the forerunner to soccer.

FESTIVALS. Each town honors its patron saint during the year. Catholic in origin, the festivities have combined many African and Spanish customs. The fiestas usually take place at the town's central square and can last up to 10 days. They include processions, games, local food, music and dance. Folkloric festivals are held year-round in many of Puerto Rico's cities and towns. Some celebrate the coffee harvest. Others showcase flower exhibitions, musical competitions and local crafts displays.

Other Activities

Watersports. Puerto Rico offers visitors hundreds of beaches on 272 miles of coastline and just about every water sport imaginable. "Balnearios" (public beaches) offer lockers, showers and parking at nominal rates. Closed on Mondays, Election Day and Good Friday. For information about overnight stays ☎ 809-722-1551 or 721-2800.

Fishing. Puerto Rico hosts many deep-sea fishing tournaments, in which 30 world records have been broken. The island's annual Billfish Tournament is the world's largest consecutively held tournament of its kind. Deep sea fishing boats can be chartered in San Juan, Fajardo, Humacao, Mayaguez and other towns. Lake fishing for largemouth bass, peacock bass, sunfish, catfish and tilapia is also popular. For more details, contact the Department of Natural Resources at ☎ 809-722-5938.

Horseback Riding. The island's palm-lined beaches are inviting settings for horseback riding. Riding instruction and/or trail riding can be arranged through the Palmas del Mar Equestrian Center or the Hacienda Carabali.

Camping. There are several camping facilities on the island. For information, contact the Parks & Recreation Association in San Juan, ☎ 809-721-2800.

Racing. El Comandante, Rt. 3 km. 15.3 at Canovanas, is an ultra-modern racetrack where thoroughbred races are held Sundays, Wednesdays, Fridays and holidays at 2:30 p.m. year round.

Tennis courts and golf courses proliferate.

Shopping

Puerto Rico has duty free shopping at the Luis Munoz Marin International Airport and several factory outlets in Old San Juan. Traditional as well as contemporary items can be purchased in Old San Juan and out on the island, including santos (small religious figures hand carved from wood by generations of local artisans), cuatros (handmade guitars) and mundillo (bobbinlace). Local art, rum, hand-rolled cigars, and casual to elegant fashions are also sold.

Facts

Nearest Recompression Chamber: Roosevelt Roads U.S. Navy Base ☎ (809-865-2000). The base is on the easternmost point off Ceiba between Fajardo and Humacao.

Getting There: *By Air* - Major airlines including American ☎(800-433-7300), United and USAir fly into San Juan from most major U.S. cities. American has service to Aguadilla from Miami. American has made the Luis Munoz Marin International Airport its hub for all flights from the U.S. to other Caribbean destinations, Europe and Latin America. International carriers include Air Portugal, British Airways, BWIA, Iberia, LACSA, LIAT, Lufthansa and Mexicana. *By Cruise Ship* - San Juan is the largest home-based cruise port in the world. 24 vessels use San Juan as their home port, and each year new cruise ships either originate or call at the port. In 1993, cruise ships brought more than one million cruise passengers to San Juan.

Island Transportation: *By Road* - Taxis, buses and rental cars are available at the airport and major hotels. All taxi cabs are metered, but they may be rented unmetered for an hourly rate. "Publicos" (public cars) run on frequent schedules to all island towns (usually during daytime hours) and depart from main squares. They have fixed rates. The "Ruta Panoramicas" is a scenic road meandering across the island offering stunning vistas.

By Ferry and Boat Service - Ferries shuttle passengers to and from Culebra and Vieques at reasonable rates. Car transport is available on some. San Juan's harbor can also be crossed by the Catano ferry to the Bacardi Rum plant's free tours.

Driving: On the right. Distance markers are in kilometers.

Customs: U.S. citizens do not need to clear customs or immigration (Other citizens do). On departure, luggage must be inspected by the U.S. Agriculture Department, as laws prohibit taking certain fruits and plants out of the country.

Entry Requirements: Since Puerto Rico is a commonwealth of the United States, no passports are required for U.S. citizens. Visitors do need a valid driver's license to rent a car. If you are a citizen of any other country, a visa is required. Vaccinations are not necessary.

Pets: Dogs and cats may be brought to Puerto Rico from the U.S. with two documents: a health certificate dated not more than ten days prior to departure showing that the animal is disease free and certified by an official or registered veterinarian; a certificate of rabies vaccination, dated not more than 30 days prior to departure, authenticated by the proper authorities.

Currency: The U.S. dollar is legal tender and credit cards are widely accepted. Several foreign exchange offices are available in San Juan and at the airport for the benefit of international travelers.

Climate: Temperatures average in the mid-80's on land and underwater. During winter and on deep dives a light wetsuit is recommended. The rainy season is April to November, but most days have some sunshine. The south coast receives much less rainfall than the north.

Clothing: Lightweight, casual. Bring a light jacket for mountain hikes in winter.

Electricity: 110V AC 60 cycles, same as U.S.

Time: Puerto Rico operates on Atlantic Standard Time, which is one hour ahead of Eastern Standard Time and the same as Eastern Daylight Savings Time.

Language: Spanish is the official language, although many people speak English, which is taught from kindergarten to high school level.

Taxes: The airport departure tax is included in the price of the airline ticket, and there's a 6% government tax at all hotels. Gratuities in restaurants are not included in the bill but 15% is the usual tip.

Publications: A free monthly magazine, *Que Pasa*, is available in English. The *San Juan Star* is the daily English-language newspaper.

Religious Services: The majority of Puerto Ricans are Catholic, but religious freedom for all faiths is guaranteed by the Commonwealth Constitution. Catholic services are conducted throughout the island in both English and Spanish. There is a Jewish Community Center in Miramar and a Jewish Reform Congregation in Santurce. There are English-speaking Protestant services for Baptists, Episcopalians, Lutherans, Presbyterians and inter- denominational services.

For Additional Information:

PUERTO RICO TOURISM COMPANY OFFICES

575 Fifth Avenue, New York, NY 10017, ☎ 212-599-6262 or 800-223-6530

3575 West Cahuenga Blvd., Suite 560, Los Angeles, CA 90068 ☎ 213-874-5991

200 S.E. First St., Suite 700 Miami, FL 33131 ☎ 305-381-8915.

67-69 Whitfield St., London WIP 5RL, United Kingdom ☎ (07-1) 436-4060

In Canada, ☎ 416-969-9025.

Paseo de la Princesa, Old San Juan PR 00901 ☎ 809-721-2400

Saba

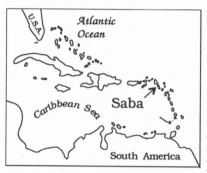

Located 30 miles off the coast of St. Maarten, Saba is a tiny, five-mile-square mountain that rises almost vertically to 3,000 ft. Once an active volcano, it is an island of paradoxes—a Caribbean hideaway without a single beach, with a road that engineers insisted couldn't be built, and with a capital called "The Bottom" that's on top of a mountain. The smallest of the Netherlands Antilles, Saba rises from the sea like the nose of a friendly dolphin breaking the water's surface.Its cliffs rise sharply from the blue Caribbean, culminating in mist-shrouded 2,855-foot Mount Scenery.

Tiny white villages cling to the sides of the mountain—Hell's Gate, Windwardside, St. John's, The Bottom—linked by a road that dips and soars, curves and backtracks like a giant roller coaster. Visitors arrive at one end of the road or the other since it begins at the airport and ends at the pier.

Diving is superb, with most reefs, walls, ledges and pinnacles within 100 yards of shore—most five or six minutes by boat. With little fishing, less than 1,000 divers per year and a government long-active in marine management, fish life is spectacular. Water clarity is too. The sea floor is a dense, heavy black sand—not prone to silting or clouding the water. A constant wash of open-ocean currents supports a rich growth of soft and hard corals on submerged lava rocks and pinnacles. And it is one of the few destinations left in the Caribbean where you can still find huge turtles and grouper.

If arriving by air, the first sight of Saba may surprise you as your Windward Airways' STOL (Short Take-off and Landing) aircraft swoops down to Juancho E. Yrausquin Airport's mini runway. You may at first think it is a matter of visual perspective, that perhaps you are still quite

Contributors: Joan Borque, Sea Saba; Bill Wilson McQueen, Wilsons Dive Shop; Mike Meyers, Saba Deep.

high. In fact, the runway measures just 1,312 ft. Nonetheless, touchdown is gentle. The airstrip stretches along Flat Point, one of the few level areas on the island. From here, the road rises in 20 serpentine curves to the village of Hell's Gate which, despite its name, nestles in the shadow of the island's largest church.

Swinging through groves of feathery tree ferns and past terraced banana plantations, the road continues on to Windwardside, a toylike village astride a saddle of land connecting Mount Scenery and Booby Hill. Its tiny houses, sparkling white under bright red roofs, are laced with wooden gingerbread. The narrow streets meander between stone walls enclosing miniscule yards that frequently contain the graves of previous owners. It is not unusual to find a doorside gravestone draped with the family's laundry drying in the sun. With level space so limited, the ingenious Sabans have converted every available square inch to some use.

Mini shops with such eye-catching names as "Around the Bend" and "Green Shutters" are tucked in among the cottages. Most carry Saba's unique "Spanish Work," a form of airy linen drawnwork created by generations of Saban wives awaiting the return of their sailor husbands.

Leaving Windwardside, the highway snakes its way past Kate's Hill, Peter Simon's Hill and big Rendezvous to the village of St. John's. From this point, you can see St. Eustatius floating on the southern horizon.

The road continues climbing, then swoops down to The Bottom, Saba's capital and, with 350 of the island's 950 inhabitants, her largest town. The village did not get its name, as is often stated, because it is set in the bottom of a volcanic crater—it isn't. The name is a corruption of the Dutch words "De Botte," meaning "The Bowl." A look at the surrounding hills tells why.

From The Bottom, the road makes its final descent, corkscrewing down to Fort Bay and the cruise ship pier.

When to Go

The best visibility is during winter, though seas can be rough outside the leeward side of the island. Summertime brings warmer 80° water with plankton blooms and lowered visibility, but a tremendous amount of fish life. Water temperature varies from 76° in February to 82° in October. Sea conditions vary. The island is round, with no natural harbors and a very small leeward side. Seas are usually calm, but tropical storms can rule out many dive sites.

History

Saba's discovery is credited to Cristopher Columbus, who first sighted the island in 1493. It remained sparsely inhabited by the Caribs until a group of Englishmen shipwrecked on Saban shores in the early 1600's. Later, in the 1640's, the Dutch built a community at Tent Bay. With nearby bountiful fishing grounds, Saba became a desirable property to several nations. Overall, the island changed hands 12 times, being claimed by the British, Spaniards, French, and, lastly in 1816, the Dutch. Sovereignty changed hands fewer times than on St. Maarten or St. Eustatius because the Sabans, taking advantage of the unique topography, pelted aggressors from above with rocks and boulders. Saba has always been English-speaking—influenced by early English missionaries and settlers.

Because of the island's largely vertical terrain and unapproachable coastline, roads, taxis, airports and even electricity came relatively late to the Saban scene.

Until 1934, Saba had no telephones. Work on "the road" began in 1938, but the first automobile did not arrive until 1947. The Leo A Chane Pier at Fort Bay was built in 1972. Approaching the island in Saba's early days meant riding the crest of a wave onto a rocky beach at Ladder Bay. Flights of steps carved by hand from volcanic rock connected one village to another. Two hundred steps rose from the small landing stage at Fort Bay to The Bottom, 900 more linked the capital to Windwardside, the island's second largest village.

Everything, from pianos to prelates, was hoisted up these stairs. Twelve men were needed to manhandle a Steinway from the Bay to The Bottom; four men and a sedan chair to tote a visiting bishop up the steep stairs.

Without roads, wheeled vehicles were, of course, useless; Sabans walked or rode tiny donkeys. During World War II, tales of the wondrous "jeep" reached local ears and thoughts that, perhaps, here at last was a vehicle that could conquer the precipitous Saban landscape. Officials were prompted to construct a road from Fort Bay to The Bottom. . .just in case.

Even not-so-old timers reminisce about the arrival of the island's first car—a second-hand jeep—in March, 1947. The novelty was swung over the side of a freighter that arrived every month from Curacao, eased onto two longboats, hauled through the surf and finally deposited at the foot of the Fort Bay road.

When the ignition key was turned, however, nothing happened; the shipper had forgotten to have the engine overhauled. Hurried consultations were held and the ship's engineer was summoned ashore. A few adjustments, a couple of stout whacks with a wrench and the engine sprang to life. Minutes later, the jeep roared into the capital, pursued by the entire junior population shouting "donkey on wheels!" Today, about 200 cars negotiate "the road."

When electricity finally reached the island in 1963, it was a sometime thing—from 6:00 p.m. till midnight. Not until 1970 was electric service extended to 24 hours a day.

SABA MARINE PARK

The Saba Marine Park (SMP) was established in 1987 "to preserve Saba's Marine resources for the benefit and enjoyment of the people, in perpetuity." The project was funded by World Wildlife Fund-Netherlands, the Prince Bernhard Fund, and the Dutch and Saban Governments.

The park encompasses the entire island and includes the waters and the seabed from the highwater mark down to 200 ft. and two offshore seamounts. It was set up by Dutch marine biologist, Tom van't Hof, who also established successful marine parks in Bonaire and Curacao.

Park officials maintain a system of mooring buoys and administer the Saba Marine Park Hyperbaric Facility, a four-person recompression chamber operated by a staff of trained volunteers.

Visitors to the marine park are charged a "dollar-a-dive" to help maintain the park and facilities. Spearfishing and collecting of any marine animals are prohibited. Divers must use proper bouyancy control and must not sit or stand on the corals. Anchoring on corals is prohibited. Vessels entering the park are advised to contact the marine park office on VHF channel 16 for directions on anchoring. For additional information Write to Saba Marine Park, Fort Bay, P.O. Box 18, The Bottom, Saba, Netherlands Antilles.

STAY SAFE

Saba's altitude and any strenuous climbing—even from the dock back to your hotel room—must be considered when calculating the diving tables. Without careful planning, both the altitude and strenuous activity may bring on decompression sickness.

Dr. John Buchanan, co-author of *Guide to the Saba Marine Park*, suggests people climb Mt. Scenery "... only if their dive tables or dive computers say that it is O.K. for them to fly...."

Saba dive guides will help you plan each dive safely. All dive sites have permanent moorings with submerged lines for descents, ascents and

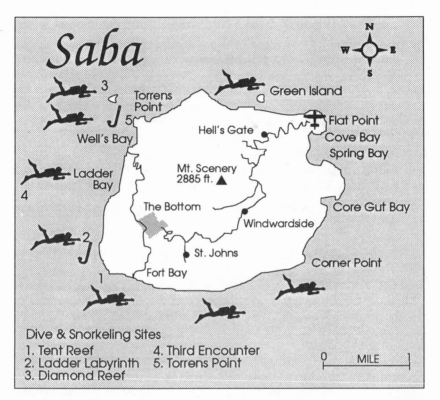

Saba

N
W—✧—E
S

3 ⌇ Torrens
Point
5⌇
Well's Bay

Green Island

Flat Point
Cove Bay
Spring Bay

Hell's Gate

Ladder
Bay
4

Mt. Scenery
2885 ft. ▲

The Bottom

Core Gut Bay

Windwardside

2⌇

St. Johns

1
Fort Bay

Corner Point

Dive & Snorkeling Sites
1. Tent Reef   4. Third Encounter
2. Ladder Labyrinth   5. Torrens Point
3. Diamond Reef

0   MILE   1

Resort and certification courses. Owner Mike Myers is a NAUI and PADI certified instructor.

Accommodations

Accommodations may be reserved through your travel agent, direct or packaged through the dive shops listed above.

Captain's Quarters, a former sea captain's home, is set into the hillside at the base of Mt. Scenery in Windwardside. Its 10 rooms are clustered around a pool and outdoor bar, all overlooking the Caribbean. Each room has private bath and balcony; some with unusual antiques. Island cuisine is served in the indoor/outdoor dining area. Winter rates, per-person, double occupancy for accommodations and diving: seven nights/10 dives, $1,016 (non-diver, $582); summer $752 (non-diver, $348). Reservations for a package may be made with one of the dive shops or through your local travel agent. ☎ 599-4-62201 Write: Captain's Quarters, Windwardside, Saba, NA.

Julianas is a group of eight, bedroom units, one apartment and a separate two-bedroom cottage built in 1989. Owners, Franklin and Juliana Johnson, are local residents who maintain the property. Grounds are landscaped with tropical flowers and plants. Pool, cafe, open for breakfast and lunch. Each room has an ocean view. ☎ 599-4-62269. Write: Juliana's Windwardside, Saba, NA.

Scout's Place in Windwardside is a cheerful, low-budget, 10-room property with pool and restaurant. Packages with Saba Deep. ☎ 599-4-62205 or 212-545-8469. Write: Scout's Place, Windwardside, Saba, NA.

Private homes with dive packages are available through Saba Real Estate, P.O. Box 17, Saba, NA ☎599-4-62299; fax 599-4-62415.

Other Activities and Sightseeing

Saba nightlife is limited to stargazing and swapping dive stories. Restaurants serve as the town meeting places. Diving, hiking and birdwatching are the mainstay of daytime activities. Hiking, though strenuous, is exceptionally pleasant as there are no mosquitoes or biting insects. If your dive computer says it's all right to fly and you are in excellent physical condition you may want to climb Mt. Scenery. The hike takes about 90 minutes. On the climb you'll pass through several types of tropical vegetation. At 1,600 feet the rain forest is enveloped in clouds. Wildlife includes lizards, iguanas, hummingbirds and treefrogs.

Directional signs and interpretive signboards have been placed along many of Saba's trails. Pick up a copy of the *Saba Nature Trails* brochure at the Tourist Office to help you plan your hikes.

There are a few craft and souvenir shops in Windwardside and The Bottom offering local Saban threadwork, a lacy embroidery applied to linens, hand-woven fabrics, silk-screened clothing and Saba Spice, a 151-proof rum.

Dining

In Two Deep Restaurant, upstairs at Saba Deep complex in Fort Bay, is open for breakfast, brunch, lunch and dinner. Menu offers "New England" style omelettes, chowders, salads and sandwiches.

The Captain's Quarters Hotel Restaurant in Windwardside offers three meals daily, American and West Indian, ☎ 46-2201. Or try local fish specialties for lunch or dinner in 130-year-old Cranston's Antique Inn in The Bottom, ☎ 46-3218. Sharon's Ocean View Bay and Restaurant in Hell's Gate. Great views!

Cantonese culinary creations are at Saba Chinese Restaurant, ☎ 46-2268 and Chinese Family Restaurant, which also features satellite TV—both in Windwardside.

Pizza and burgers are served at Guido's, ☎ 46-2230 in Windwardside.

Local delights, including curried goat and soursop ice cream, are served at the Sunset Restaurant ☎ 46-3332 in The Bottom, Lollipops in St. John's, ☎ 46-3330 or the Brigadoon Restaurant in Windwardside, ☎ 46-2380.

Facts

Nearest Recompression Chamber: Saba Marine Park Hyperbaric Facility at Fort Bay.

Airlines: International flights connect through St. Maarten via Windward Island Airways (WINAIR). There are also connecting flights between Saba and St. Eustatius.

Ferry: *Style,* a 52-ft luxury commuter craft departs Great Bay Marina in St. Maarten on Wed, Fri and Sun for Saba. Returns to St. Maarten at 3 pm. The ride takes 45 to 60 minutes.

Driving: On the right. Rentals are available through Johnson's Rent A Car or your hotel. Beware of hairpin turns, pothoes and bumps along "the road."

Seaport: A deep water pier accommodates ships at Fort Bay. Anchorage for yachts at Ladder Bay and Wells Bay.

Documents: U.S. and Canadian citizens require official proof of citizenship—passport, voter registration card, or birth certificate and a return or onward ticket.

Customs: No customs.

Currency: Netherlands Antilles Guilder. US dollars accepted everywhere. Credit cards are NOT widely accepted.

Language: Dutch is the official language, but English is widely spoken.

Climate: Air temperature is from 78°F to 82°F year round. Winter evenings may cool to 60°F. Rainfall is 42 inches per year.

Clothing: Casual, lightweight. Sweater or light jacket suggested for winter evenings. Light wetsuit or wetskin recommended, especially during winter months when water temperature drops to 75°F.

Electricity: 11 Volts, 60 cycles (220 volts on request).

Time: Atlantic Standard (Eastern Standard + one hour).

Departure Tax: US $2 within NA, US $5 elsewhere.

Religious Services: Limited.

Additional Information: Saba Tourist Information Office, 271 Main Street, Northport, NY 11768. ☎ 516-261-7474; fax 516-261-9606.

St. Eustatius (Statia)

St. Eustatius is a speck of land about 38 miles south of St. Maarten, six miles north of St. Kitts, and 17 miles south east of Saba. It is one of the lesser-known islands in the eastern Caribbean—so small and with a name so long that it is often deleted from maps. A part of the Netherlands Antilles, this eight-square-mile territory is home to a population of 1,800.

Statia's profile is distinct with a flat plain in the center, sharp, green hills at the north end, and The Quill, a 2,000-ft, extinct volcano, covering most of the south end. The Quill is noted by geologists as having an almost perfect cone shape. Inside its crater is a magnificent, tropical rain forest of towering mahogany trees, wild bananas, air plants and trailing vines festooned with wild orchids and flowering air plants. Wood doves and sulfur-yellow butterflies flutter the shadows, and at full moon, torch-bearing Statians hunt scuttling land crabs.

Steep, limestone cliffs interspersed with a few stretches of black sand beach dominate the island's western coast. Its eastern shores shelve into a wide strip of dark sand and pebbles. There are few roads, and donkeys are still used for exploring rocky, inland trails. Offshore lie the remains of more than 200 shipwrecks.

Beautiful shallow reefs, highlighted by giant, golden sea fans and lush, soft corals, skirt the ballast stones and rubble of sunken, 17th-century wooden trading ships. Now dive and snorkeling sites, they are all close to shore—at most, a few minutes by boat.

A leisurely stroll through the narrow, cobblestone streets of Oranjestad, Statia's capital and only village, reveals the grey-stone and yellow-ballast brick walls of historic buildings dating back to the 1600's and the now-restored Fort Oranje (pronounced "oh-rahn-ye") .

The fort, perched on the cliffs overlooking Oranjestad Bay, was the scene of the first salute to the U.S. colors back in November 1776. Nearby, the ruins of an 18th-century synagogue and graveyard, and a Dutch Re-

Contributor: Mark Padover, marine biologist & former Dive Statia instructor.

formed Church nestle among the pink and yellow homes of today's Statians. This area is Upper Town, the uphill section of town.

From the center of the village, just past a monument erected in honor of Queen Wilhelmina's Golden Jubilee, the stone-paved Fort Road zig-zags down to Lower Town, once the Caribbean's most bustling port.

In the mid-1700s Lower Town stretched for two miles along the Bay. Warehouses, taverns, slave markets and merchants' stalls lined the double roadway. The lively traffic, both licit and illicit, made St. Eustatius the richest port in the West Indies. Today, gentle-faced donkeys browse among its ruins.

Sheep and cows graze on small farms and pastures outside Oranjestad. On the opposite side of the island, surf tumbles onto a long strand where beachcombers find a treasure of shells, glass floats and sun-bleached driftwood.

Overall, the island is perfect for vacationers seeking an unhurried, peaceful haven. There is virtually no crime on the island. Everyone is safe walking the streets at night. Doors are rarely locked and the people are extremely friendly. When an elderly resident of St. Eustatius was asked if many tourists visited the island, the old gentleman looked hurt. "My dear sir," he replied, "we don't have tourists on Statia, we have guests!"

And, Statians do have a knack for making "guests" feel welcome. Passersby exchange greetings in the narrow streets; young boys offer to lead newcomers to hunt for the island's favorite treasure—blue "slave beads"—found no where else in the Caribbean.

When to Go

Visibility is best in winter, though seas occasionally get rough. Summer brings calm seas, warmer water and more fish. Water temperature varies from 76° in February to 82° in October.

History

Statia played a key role in America's war for independence. It was a major trans-shipment point for European arms and supplies intended for George Washington's troops. Muskets and gunpowder, frequently shipped in casks marked "Tea," were stored in yellow brick warehouses that stretched for a mile along the Bay. From there, blockade runners in swiftly moving brigantines would carry the supplies to the ports of Boston, New York, and Charleston.

It was on November 16, 1776, that the cannons of Fort Oranje roared forth the first official salute to the American colors by a foreign power. The armed American merchant ship *Andrew Doria* sailed into the harbor and fired a 13-gun salute to the Dutch flag fluttering above Fort Oranje. Commander Johannes de Graaff, sympathetic to the cause of the rebels to the north, ordered the cannons of the fort to return the courtesy with an 11-gun salvo. By this act he unwittingly set in motion events that would bring to a violent end the age of prosperity on Statia.

De Graaff's salute turned out to be the world's first official recognition of the sovereignty of the rebellious colonies, though he was obviously unaware of its historic importance. Getting wind of it, however, the British were understandably infuriated.

By 1781, the situation had become desperate for the British. Not only was the war going badly for George III's troops in North America, but the stream of supplies passing through St. Eustatius was unabated despite a British blockade. Turnabout came on February 3, 1781, when British Admiral George Brydges Rodney attacked what he called "this nest of vipers."

Storming ashore with 650 troops he demanded the surrender of the Dutch garrison and began systematically looting not only the well-stocked warehouses, but the personal possessions of the merchants as well. In all, he destroyed the harbor and ransacked the town while accumulating five million pounds' worth of booty. Rodney also kept the Dutch flag flying above the ramparts of the Fort, thereby luring more than 150 ships into his trap. Less than a year later the British troops were expelled from the island by the French.

Today, the island is an autonomous part of the Netherlands and is self-governing. But on each anniversary of DeGraaff's salute the island band strikes up *The Star Spangled Banner*, as the American flag is hoisted to the top of the flagpole in the center of the compound.

Sunken Treasure Hunting

The remains and treasures of 17th- and 18th-century sailing ships are played up in many Statia dive articles, but the island's real treasures are her lovely shallow reefs. The ships' wooden hulls rotted away centuries ago. What's left are some wonderful old anchors and piles of stone ballast where small fish play hide and peek.

A few sites have, in fact, given up treasures of jewels and exotic pottery, but any charted wrecks not yet salvaged are buried in the sand and would require extensive and expensive excavation work to uncover. Plus, if a diver happens upon an intact artifact, it must go to the St. Eustatius Historical Foundation. Treasure hunting is discouraged—metal detectors are prohibited as is "fanning" of the bottom to find artifacts. Exceptions which divers may keep are fragments of clay pipe stems or bowls and blue beads (slave beads). Uninhabited shells and broken pieces of dead coral may also be taken.

Best Dives and Snorkeling Sites

There are approximately 20 dive/snorkel sites around Statia ranging from extreme shallows to 130 ft. Visibility often exceeds 100 ft with water temperatures averaging 80°F. Divers must dive with a buddy, stay within the no-decompression limits, have a pressure gauge, depth gauge, flotation device and timing device. C cards are required.

☆☆☆☆☆ **Caroline's Reef** is a spectacular site in the center of southern reef complex. Several long ledges meet forming a circular hub. Big barrel sponges, tube sponges, sea fans, brain coral, sea whips and volcano sponges adorn the tops of the ledges. Hoards of small critters are in residence—blennies, lightbulb tunicates, pistol shrimp in their corkscrew anemones, lavender cleaning shrimp, cleaning gobies and arrow crabs. Big angels are common as are rock beauties, barracuda, scrawled file fish, Bermuda chub, butterfly fish, sharptail eels and groupers. Nurse sharks and turtles cruise the area.

The hub is a keyhole in the coral, about 18 inches in diameter. Used as shortcut by fish traversing one side of the ledge to the other, it also serves as an excellent photo-subject frame. Maximum depth is 65 ft. Recommended for novice and experienced divers.

☆☆☆ **False Shoal**, outside of Kay Bay off the southwest shores, is an unusual formation of huge boulders that rise from the bottom at 25 to 30 ft to within a foot of the surface. Coral cover is minimal, but fish life is superb with big congregations of tiger groupers, French and queen angels, several species of parrot fish and swarms of reef fish. Good for snorkeling and novice divers.

☆☆☆☆ **Anchor Reef** is named for an enormous anchor hooked under a ledge. The anchor is seven feet across and 14 ft long with an 18-inch ring. It is surrounded by a pretty reef with a colorful array of elephant-ear, moose antler, green-, lavender-, and red-vase sponges. Cracks and crevices reveal feather dusters, shrimp anemones, barber shrimp, and gorgonians. Bushy sea whips, sea plumes, and sea fans decorate the ledges. Maximum depth is 60 ft.

☆☆☆☆☆ **Dropoff**—the southernmost dive on Statia and the most dramatic wall starts at 85 ft and drops vertically to about 130 ft. The face of the wall is a collage of mountainous star coral, black wire corals, and sponges. Enormous French and queen angels, Nassau and tiger grouper, black durgons, spotted eagle rays and occasional reef sharks and hammerheads frequent the area. For experienced divers.

☆☆☆ **Barracuda Reef** is a 700-ft-long mini wall at 45 ft that drops to a sand pit at 70 ft. A 12-ft long, five-ft wide, coral-encrusted anchor earmarks this site. As the name implies, schools of barracuda frequent the area as do some more unusual creatures. On one occasion a friendly humpback whale cruised smack into a group of snorkelers and hung out with them for 15 minutes. (Whale season on Statia is from December to mid-March). Healthy soft corals, a host of invertebrates, reef fish, spotted morays, stingrays, and nurse sharks typify the area. Recommended for all level divers.

☆☆☆☆ **Outer Crooks Reef** is a pretty, shallow reef, five minutes by boat south of the city pier. The reef's ledges form a V shape which might stand for variety as every imaginable hard and soft coral thrives within its bounds. Fish life, too, is diverse with schools of smallmouth and striped grunts, black durgons, blue head wrasse, coneys, rock hinds, banded and four-eyed butterflyfish, rock beauties, blue tang, bar jacks, damsels, fairy basslets, princess parrots, queen parrots, stoplight parrots, Spanish hogfish, sharknose gobies, spotted drum, honeycomb cowfish, burrfish, and huge porcupine fish—some over three-ft long.

There are also secretary blennies. It takes a sharp eye to spot these tiny fish, but if you can, try watching them for a few minutes. You'll see them dart out for food that's drifting by, then quickly shoot tail first back into their holes. They are unafraid of divers and make great subjects for close-up photography.

Invertebrate life includes flamingo-tongue snails, small crinoids, corkscrew anemones, giant anemones, pistol shrimp, pederson shrimp, thor shrimp, feather dusters, fire worms, crabs and spiny lobster. At night, divers have spotted rare, copper lobsters and orange-ball anemones.

Outer Crooks is a best pick for getting reacquainted with the water and your gear after a long dry spell. Also, a great spot for night dives. Snorkeling. Maximum depth, 40 ft.

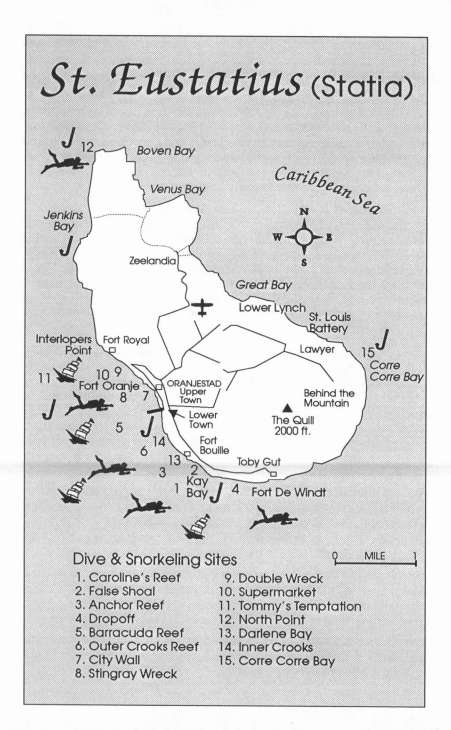

St. Eustatius (Statia)

Boven Bay

Venus Bay

Caribbean Sea

Jenkins Bay

Zeelandia

Great Bay

Lower Lynch

St. Louis Battery

Interlopers Point

Fort Royal

Lawyer

Corre Corre Bay

Fort Oranje

ORANJESTAD
Upper Town

Behind the Mountain

The Quill
2000 ft.

Lower Town

Fort Bouille

Toby Gut

Kay Bay

Fort De Windt

Dive & Snorkeling Sites

1. Caroline's Reef
2. False Shoal
3. Anchor Reef
4. Dropoff
5. Barracuda Reef
6. Outer Crooks Reef
7. City Wall
8. Stingray Wreck
9. Double Wreck
10. Supermarket
11. Tommy's Temptation
12. North Point
13. Darlene Bay
14. Inner Crooks
15. Corre Corre Bay

0   MILE   1

☆☆ **City Wall** is 40 yards out from shore in front of Dive Statia and the hotels in Lower Town. The rock wall parallels the shore from 75 yards south of the Golden Era Hotel to the pavilion at Smoke Alley. The wall was the old sea wall for Lower Town back in the days of sailing ships. Storms, erosion, a freak earthquake and wave action have since repositioned the shoreline and the wall underwater. The top is at six ft, the bottom at seven to 13 ft. In many areas the wall is folded or crumpled, forming deep crevices where fish and creatures stand guard. There is not much coral cover, but reef fish are plentiful and invertebrate life is good. Watch out for sea urchins. The deepest point of the wall is 12 ft. Suggested for snorkeling and warm-up dives.

☆☆☆ **Stingray Wreck** is one-half mile offshore in Oranjebaii. Named for a great number of stingrays in residence, the site has been studied by William and Mary University and found to be the remains of a Dutch trading ship that went down in 1768.

The sea moss beds at the south end of the wreck attract hawksbill turtles and flying gurnards. Average depth is 50 ft.

☆☆☆ **Double Wreck** is a colorful dive, five minutes from Oranjebaii. Two wrecks, one on top of the other, are overgrown with red-vase sponges and giant anemones. Bring your dive light to see the colors. Basket starfish curled into balls rest inside the sponges during the day. Patches of sea grass double as conch beds for four different species. The most common is the queen conch; the most rare, the rooster conch. At night, helmet conchs crawl out of the sand. Empty conch shells are often taken over by giant hermit crabs scavenging for food. Mantis shrimp, spotted snake eels and flying gurnards are curious residents. The northern wreck is littered with centuries-old, broken bottles and pottery shreds. Good for scuba, all levels.

☆☆ **Supermarket**, just outside of Double Wreck, is another dual wreck site. The remains are encrusted ballast which is overgrown with branching corals, barrel and vase sponges, and plumes. A number of stems and bowls from old clay pipes—some dating back to the 1600s—have been unearthed by the shifting sands. But, remember, no fanning the bottom and anything intact goes to the museum.

Fish life includes cottonwicks, queen triggerfish, scorpionfish, stingrays, coneys, parrotfish, chalk bass and an occasional hawksbill turtle. Conchs reside in the sandy patches off the wreck. Depth is 70 ft.

☆☆☆☆ **Tommy's Temptation** is a photographer's delight. A 15-minute boat ride from town, this site is a lava finger that runs parallel to shore and just over a mile and a half straight out. The top is at 70 ft and the bottom at 100 ft. Soft corals and coral rubble umbrella the sides of the finger. The big attractions are the mega-sized, old anchors hooked under the ledge. They average seven ft across and 14 ft in length with hawsers (the rings the ropes were tied to) about 18 inches in diameter.

Hundreds of schooling great barracuda, black margates, grouper, triggerfish and French angels sail by the ledges. This is also a good place to see turtles. If you spot one, stay still. Dive guide and contributor, Mark Padover reports frequent advances on the turtles' part when the divers are motionless. "If you charge them, they get scared and vanish at lightening speed."

Currents often rule out a dive to this area, but when sea conditions are calm, and currents light this is a super spot for intermediate to advanced divers. If the ocean isn't flat, the dive site is a bad choice.

☆☆ **North Point** is an outstanding dive and snorkeling site at the north point of the island. The bottom slopes off steeply from shore bottoming out in sand at 70 to 100 ft. The area is strewn with huge boulders, some up to 40 ft tall. The boulders are covered with corals, sea fans and gigantic barrel sponges—up to five ft across. Fishlife is extraordinary. On one dive expect to see schoolmasters, black margates, hogfish, whitespotted filefish, blue tangs, rock beauties, sergeant majors and squirrel fish. Huge two-ft French and gray angels swim by. Spotted eagle rays and reef sharks cruise the area. Good for all experience levels.

☆☆ **Darlene Bay** is excellent for snorkeling when the seas are calm. The dive (or snorkel) boat anchors in a sandy area offshore of the shallow reefs or will drift with you as you swim among lava outcrops and fingers. Maximum depth is 20 ft. The lava and corals come up to the surface in the south end of the bay. Good fish life—turtles, sea fans, sea whips and branching corals.

It is easiest to reach this site by a five-minute boat ride. It is a most difficult hike for a shore entry with large rocks and loose gravel to negotiate, but if you are rugged... you can reach it by heading south along the coast for half an hour after passing the ruins of Crooks Castle.

Additional good snorkeling is found at **Inner Crooks**, just north of Crooks Castle (max. depth, 18 ft); **Jenkins Bay** (max. depth, 25 ft) on the northwest corner of the island; and **Corre Corre Bay** (max. depth, 40 ft), opposite town on the Eastern shores.

Dive Operator

Dive Statia is a full-service, PADI training facility and NAUI PRO facility offering courses from introductory through instructor, and guided reef and wreck trips. Their boats range from inflatables to a 31-ft cabin boat. Every dive is accompanied by a certified instructor or dive master. Rental gear and dive/accommodation packages are offered. ☎ 011-599-3-82435; fax 011-599-3-82539. Write P.O. Box 491938, Fort Lauderdale, FL 33349 or P.O. Box 158, St. Eustatius, NA.

Accommodations

Statia hotels add a 15% service charge and 7% government room tax unless otherwise stated. Dive/accommodation packages may be arranged through the dive operator. Accommodations are most easily reserved through your travel agent. Note: St. Eustatius and Saba are marketed jointly in the U.S.A. and offer dual-destination packages that include dives, accommodations and more. For information write to Tourist Office, 271 Main St., Northport, NY 11768.

The Golden Era Hotel, within walking distance of the dive shop, offers 20 air-conditioned rooms on Oranje Bay, pool and seaside restaurant. Rates start at $88 per night, per room for a double. Book through your travel agent or arrange through dive shop.

The Old Gin House in Lower Town is a faithful reconstruction of an 18th-century, cotton-gin factory. Six of the rooms are oceanside with balconies over the water. This cozy resort features a renowned five-star gourmet restaurant plus an open-air breakfast and lunch cafe. Dive package rates are moderate: seven nights/ten dives for $800; six nights/eight dives for $665; and five nights/six dives for $530. Non-diver package rates are about 50% less. Packages include accommodations, welcome cocktail, airport and diving transfers, continental breakfast daily, guided boat dives, tanks and weights, pre-dive slide presentation, après-dive beverage, tax and hotel service charge. Group rates available. For nature, historical and exercise buffs, the hotel offers a year-round hiking / walking package that includes 15% off E.P. rates, welcome drink, and a series of tour maps featuring historical sites, mountain trails and island paths. ☎ 516-261-7474 or see your travel agent.

Talk of the Town, with eight standard and efficiency rooms and its own restaurant, is located five minutes from Statia's airport—a 20-minute walk from the dive shop. Dive package rates for a double, per diver include seven nights/ten dives for $670 or six nights/eight dives for $550. Includes accommodations, airport and diving transfers, welcome cocktail, breakfast daily, boat dives, tanks and weights.

Dive Statia also arranges dive packages for those preferring to stay at Statia's apartment and villa properties. For additional information contact the St. Eustatius Tourist Information Office, 271 Main Street, Northport, NY 11768. ☎ 516-261-7474.

Other Activities and Sightseeing

Swapping dive stories, nature hikes, historic walks, and hunting for blue slave beads highlight a visit to Statia.

Historical Sites

In spite of British Admiral Lord Rodney's savaging of the island in 1781, numerous historical buildings remain, from large monumental structures to small workers' homes. Many are currently being restored in Upper Town.

Among those are Fort Oranje and Fort de Windt, The Historical Foundation Museum, old ruins at Oranje Bay and remains of *Honen Dalim*, the second oldest Synagogue in the Western Hemisphere.

Blue Bead Hunts

Remnants of a curious past, these five-sided, blue-glass beads were used to buy and sell slaves during the 17th and 18th centuries, as well as to reward the slaves. Upon accumulation of enough beads a male slave could buy freedom or a woman. The woman was priced by the number of beads that fit around her waist. Today, to some, a heavy woman is still considered more valuable than a thin one.

Beads are most often found on the beach between the end of the city pier and the ruins of Crooks Castle, headquarters of the slave trade way back when.

HIKING TRAILS

Be sure you are OK to fly on your dive tables before climbing The Quill. Hiking Statia is strenuous. Certain trail conditions are often slippery and dangerous. Hikers should be properly attired and in good physical condition. Trails are marked with numbered signposts. Pick up a trail guide at the tourist office in the airport or at the Historical Museum (☎ 2288).

The most exhilarating trails lead along the rim and down through the rainforest-covered crater of the Quill. The main trail starts at Welfare Road (south end of Oranjestad) at a telephone pole marked "Quill Track 1" (nos. 1-20). This trail brings you up the mountain to the rim of the volcano. It is a strenuous hike and may be slippery in places. The climb up takes about 45 minutes; down takes 30.

Dining

The Old Gin House in Lower Town features gourmet steak and seafood dishes. Advanced reservations. ☎ 599-38-2319. Major credit cards are accepted.

The Golden Era specializes in West Indian, International and Creole cuisine. Sunday night buffet. At the sea in Lower Town. ☎ 599-38-2345.

The Chinese Restaurant on Prinseweg 9 serves West Indian and Chinese food. NO credit cards. ☎ 599-38-2389.

Talk of the Town serves West Indian, international and local dishes, sandwiches and ice cream. All major credit cards accepted. ☎ 599-38-2236 or 599-38-2681.

The Cool Corner in the heart of Oranjestad serves a tasty cross between West Indian and Chinese cuisine. ☎ 599-38-2523.

Sunny's Place on the Oranjestraat serves sandwiches and tasty local dishes. ☎ 599-38-2609.

Super Burger, also on the Oranjestraat, specializes in burgers, all types of sandwiches, chicken and fries.

L'Etoile is a brightly decorated cafe note for the spiciness of its *pastechis* (deep-fried turnovers stuffed with meat). Local specialties. Located on Heiligerweg. ☎ 599-38-2299. No credit cards.

Helpful Phone Numbers

POLICE: ☎ 599-38-2333

HOSPITAL: ☎ 599-38-2211 or 599-38-2371

AIRPORT: ☎ 599-38-2361

TOURIST BOARD: ☎ 599-38-2433

USA TOURIST OFFICE: 516-261-7474; Fax 516-261-9606

Facts

Nearest Recompression Chamber: Saba, 17 miles away.

Airlines: Windward Island Airways (WINAIR) connects daily from Princess Juliana Airport, St. Maarten. Flight time is 20 minutes. Passengers from the U.S. and Saba are considered "in-transit" and do not need to clear immigration in St. Maarten.

Driving: On the right.

Seaport: Gallows Bay.

Documents: U.S. and Canadian citizens need official proof of citizenship—a valid passport, birth certificate or voter registration card. Others need a passport or alien registration card. You need an onward or return ticket.

Customs: No customs.

Currency: Netherlands Antilles Guilder. American dollars are accepted everywhere on the island.

Language: Dutch is the official language; English is widely spoken.

Climate: Air temperature is from 78°F to 82°F year round. Winter evenings may cool to 60°F. Rainfall is 45 inches per year.

Clothing: Casual, lightweight. Light wetsuit or wetskin suggested during winter.

Electricity: 110, 60 cycles (same as U.S.).

Time: Atlantic Standard (Eastern Standard + one hour).

Departure Tax: U.S. $2.00.

Religious Services: Limited.

Additional Information: St. Eustatius Tourist Information Office, 271 Main St., Northport, NY 11768, ☎ 516-261-7474; fax 516-261-9606.

St. Kitts & Nevis

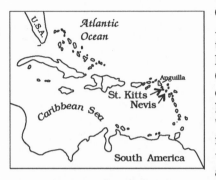

Cradled between St. Maarten and Antigua in the Eastern Caribbean, the sister islands of St. Kitts and Nevis call themselves "The Secret Caribbean," but the way tourist accommodations have expanded in the last 10 years, the islands won't be "secrets" too much longer. New tourist interest, sparked by Princess Di's visit in 1993, has brought world-wide attention to the area's unique natural beauty and subsea wonders. And a change in government planning has set the island's sights on increased tourism.

Physically beautiful, the islands are a patchwork of rolling, green mountains surrounded by miles of unexplored, shallow reefs, swim-through caves and grottoes. More than 400 ship wrecks, dating back to the 1600s, lie below their clear waters. Narrow strips of black and gold sand beaches skirt much of the coasts.

St. Kitts is an oval-shaped landmass that stretches out into a long, narrow peninsula extending like a guitar handle from its southeastern corner. Formed from volcanic eruption, its central area is a rugged mountain range, whose highest point is the dormant volcano, Mount Liamuiga, at 3,792 feet. Tropical forests, ridges and waterfalls at the high elevations contrast with its lowlands where spacious and fertile valleys produce an abundance of sugar cane, sea-island cotton and peanuts. Most of the beaches are black volcanic sand, though white sandy beaches can be found along the southeast peninsula of Frigate Bay and Salt Pond. Overall, the island is 23 miles long, covering an area of 68 square miles.

On the seaboard lies Basseterre, the capital, with a population of about 15,000. Its ambience is decidedly old-world Caribbean with an informal produce market and rows of weather-beaten, pastel buildings along the

Contributors: Tim Bedford; H.V. Pat Reilly; Kenneth Samuel, Kenneth's Dive Centre; John Yearwood, Oualie Beach Hotel; Ellis Chaderton, Julian Rigby, Scuba Safaris Ltd.; Auston MacLeod, Pro Divers; Gary Pereira, Turtle Beach Club; Jennifer Woods, Caribbean Explorer.

The Circus, Basseterre, St. Kitts

waterfront. Narrow streets lead from the town pier to a four-block, made-for-tourists area known as the "Circus," a town square, or actually town circle, dominated by a tall, grandfather clock, where three streets converge in the center of town.

Old sugar plantations on both islands have been transformed into wonderfully stylish inns. These classic "great houses," once the homes of the plantation owners, sit high in the foothills of the volcanic mountains that dominate the skylines. Surrounding the great houses are the remains of old windmills where the sugar cane was crushed, and the boiling houses where the sweet liquid was processed. Before the "around-the-island" narrow-gauge railroad was completed in 1926 to transport the cane to the central sugar factory in Basseterre, each plantation was a kingdom unto itself, growing, cutting, crushing, boiling and selling sugar. The down side of that free enterprise was air pollution. During the boiling season, the tall, stone smokestacks on more than 50 estates would belch smoke into the atmosphere for 18 to 20 hours a day. To eliminate the problem, the government purchased the sugar-producing land and began transporting the cane to a central boiling house in Basseterre.

The majority of plantation owners sold their great houses to entrepreneurs who refurbished them as delightful inns. Most are furnished with a potpourri of antiques or West Indian furnishings.

Separated from St. Kitts by a two-mile strait known as the "Narrows" lies Nevis, the sister island Columbus named for its mountainous resemblance to the snow-capped "Nieve" peak of Spain. Dubbed *Queen of the Caribees*—by 17th- and 18th-century European visitors for its therapeutic hot springs and fertile soil, this island encompasses 36 square miles of spectacularly beautiful land. The tip of the island's dominant central peak, usually encircled by clouds, rises into an almost perfectly formed

American Eagle at Golden Rock Airport, St. Kitts

cone of 3,232 ft. The capital city and only town is Charlestown, with a population of 1,200.

The terrain of Nevis encompasses numerous fertile hillsides and stretches of narrow golden sand beaches. Most of the inhabitants are vegetable and coconut farmers.

Low-cost ($8 US) passenger ferries operate daily once or twice a day from Basseterre, St. Kitts to Charleston on Nevis. The trip takes about 45 minutes. Air service at $100 for a four-passenger twin is also available. The ferries run twice a day and are not synchronized with airline arrivals. It is often difficult to make the connection. Be sure to call or write to the tourist board for a ferry schedule before planning a trip to Nevis. Phone numbers and addresses are at end of chapter.

Diving

Diving is diverse with ledges, mini walls, white holes teeming with fish, caves and drift diving in some areas. Most reefs on the Atlantic side and offshore on the Caribbean side are pristine with monster-sized sea fans and sponges growing over piles of lava rocks. Regularly visited reef and wreck sites are on the sheltered Caribbean side of the islands and in the

View of St. Kitts from Oalie Beach, Nevis

cut (the Narrows) between Nevis and St. Kitts, but trips to the Atlantic where the mysterious white holes lie and large pelagics are encountered may be arranged when seas are calm.

St. Kitts offers the most dive sites with alternate sheltered areas on the Caribbean side when the seas are rough on the Atlantic side or at the Narrows. Nevis dive sites are more vulnerable to swells when the winds are high, even on its the Caribbean side, but currents are usually light and the sites are spectacular. Average visibility is 80 to 100 ft. with exceptional water clarity at the cut and offshore Caribbean and Atlantic reefs. Water temperature is 80 to 85 degrees year round. Depths for scuba range from 30 to 90 ft, the average depth at 50 ft. Certification, referrals and resort courses with PADI and NAUI instructors are offered. The average boat trip to a dive site takes 15 minutes. Following rainy periods, freshwater runoff from the mountains will lower visibility on the close-in reefs and wrecks, especially off Basseterre. Coral collecting and spear fishing are prohibited only off Turtle Beach on the southeast (guitar handle) peninsula of St. Kitts.

Be sure to let the boat captains know if you prefer to dive a sheltered area as the diver population is tiny—diving is new on these islands— and some of the captains who double as fishing guides are more apt to want to share their best spots rather than the calmest.

Stay shallow and keep a close eye on your bottom time. The nearest recompression chamber is on Saba, a 15-minute flight from St. Kitts airport. But getting to that airport and arranging for a flight may take the good part of a day or more. Avoid exhausting mountain hikes and climbs after a dive or you risk the shaken soda bottle effect (see page 245, Saba chapter).

When to go

The best weather is from December to April though air and water temperatures are good for diving year round and reduced-rate dive packages are offered between May and December. The best months for diving the Caribbean side are April and May. June through mid-November brings the most rain and a chance of a hurricane. Late December brings the "Christmas wind" which churns up the seas.

History

First named *Liamuiga*—The Fertile Isle—by the Carib Indians, St. Kitts was renamed "St. Christopher" by discoverer, Christopher Columbus in 1493 who, apparently, was so taken by its beauty he honored it with the name of his patron saint. The name was later shortened to St. Kitts.

Latter day historians equate St. Kitts with its most notable site, Brimstone Hill, a spectacular 18th-century fort turned national park and nicknamed the "Gibraltar of the West Indies." An architectural and engineering marvel, the fortress spreads across 40 acres on a bluff 800 ft above the sea.

Settled in 1623 by Sir Thomas Warner, St. Kitts was the first island in the West Indies to be colonized by the English. The French, under D'Esnambuc, colonized another part of the island in the following year.

During the 17th century, intermittent warfare was waged between the French and British settlers. In 1713, St. Kitts was ceded to Britain by the Treaty of Utrecht. Fighting over possession of the island occurred for the last time in 1782, when the French captured the British fortress of Brimstone Hill. Later that year, the British were victorious over the French in a battle off the island of Dominica and regained possession of St. Kitts in 1783 under the terms of the Treaty of Versailles.

Nevis was colonized in 1628 by British settlers living in neighboring St. Kitts. Like its sister island, Nevis suffered stormy attacks from both the French and Spanish throughout the 17th and 18th centuries. On September 19, 1983 St. Kitts and Nevis gained independence

Best Dives of St. Kitts and Nevis

Dive sites in the cut and around the southeast peninsula are shared by both islands' dive shops. Caribbean sites off Basseterre are most often dived by Kenneth's.

Note: The "sunken city of Jamestown" on Nevis, reputed to be washed away by a hurricane, is listed in at least one guide as a great dive.

Scuba Safaris Dive Shop, Oalie Beach, Nevis.

Unfortunately it is nonexistent, more myth than fact. There is some small mention of it in historical records, but if it exists on the sea floor, no diver has discovered it. Historians feel that Jamestown simply fell into disuse as marshlands moved over it.

☆ **Turtle Bar Reef** off the unpopulated southwestern tip of the St. Kitts, is a spur and groove reef growing over a rocky bottom. Pillar corals and sea plumes rise from a rocky bottom which slopes from 15 ft down to 65 ft. Seas are always calm. The shallows are a good dive for novices and snorkelers. Ten-minute boat ride from the Turtle Beach Watersports Center, 20 minutes from Basseterre.

☆☆☆☆ **Monkey Reef** is two and one-half miles off the peninsula and Nevis, a longer boat ride than most, but worth the trip when seas are calm for the wonderful array of fish and invertebrate life including blackbar soldierfish, coneys, shark, barracuda, turtles and rays. The reef is a labyrinth of small caves, canyons and ledges ablaze with pink-tipped anemones, orange tube sponges, encrusting sponges, mounds of club finger corals, and seafans. Big barrel sponges. Excellent visibility. Average depths are from 45 to 60 ft. Suggested for experienced ocean divers only. Sea conditions are often choppy with four- to six-ft swells.

☆☆☆ **Coral Gardens** is a hilly reef off Oalie Beach, Nevis, typified by huge pillar coral formations and gigantic barrel sponges. It is a good place to spot big turtles, schools of spade fish, nurse sharks, rays, remoras, lobster. Depths are from 50 to 80 ft. Seas average three to four ft with little current. Excellent visibility. For experienced divers only. Ten minutes from Scuba Safaris.

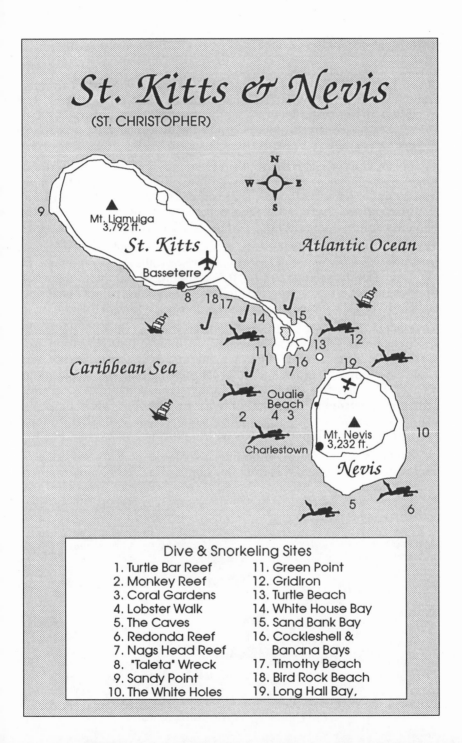

St. Kitts & Nevis

(ST. CHRISTOPHER)

N
W · E
S

Mt. Liamuiga
3,792 ft.

St. Kitts

Atlantic Ocean

Basseterre

Caribbean Sea

Oualie
Beach

Charlestown

Mt. Nevis
3,232 ft.

Nevis

Dive & Snorkeling Sites

1. Turtle Bar Reef
2. Monkey Reef
3. Coral Gardens
4. Lobster Walk
5. The Caves
6. Redonda Reef
7. Nags Head Reef
8. "Taleta" Wreck
9. Sandy Point
10. The White Holes
11. Green Point
12. Gridiron
13. Turtle Beach
14. White House Bay
15. Sand Bank Bay
16. Cockleshell &
    Banana Bays
17. Timothy Beach
18. Bird Rock Beach
19. Long Hall Bay,

☆☆☆ **Lobster Walk** is inside Coral Gardens, about one and a half miles from Oalie Beach, Nevis. The dive is similar to Coral Gardens, but inhabited by numerous lobster. Depths start at 70 ft and drop to 110 ft. Experienced ocean divers only. Visibility and water clarity is outstanding Expect some swells.

☆☆☆☆ **The Caves** off the southwestern coast of Nevis are a series of large caverns formed of ancient lava flows. The once-molten tubes are now home to schools of grunt, snapper, chubs, stingrays, nurse sharks and black tip reef sharks. Huge, 200-lb. turtles and rays have been spotted here. Maximum depth is 40 ft. Good for all levels of diver and snorkeler.

☆☆☆☆☆ **Redonda Reef,** off the southern end of Nevis, is a wilderness area—an extensive series of caverns, and mini walls just beginning to be explored. Depths average 60 to 70 ft. Sea conditions vary with the wind. Spectacular visibility and marine life. It is a 45-minute or longer boat ride. Seas must be exceptionally calm for the dive boats to visit this site.

☆☆ **Nags Head Reef** is at the southernmost tip of St. Kitts where the Caribbean and Atlantic meet. About a 55-minute boat ride from Basseterre, 10 minutes from Turtle Beach, this area is THE place for spotting eagle rays, huge stingrays and other large pelagics. Even whales occasionally blast by. This site is weather dependent, sometimes rough and with strong currents, suggested only for experts. But, when the sea is calm, it is good for novice divers. Depths range from 25 to 110 ft. The reef is a mix of mini-walls and canyons with superb and varied marine life.

☆ *Taleta* **Wreck** sank in 1985 off the west coast of St. Kitts and lies in 50 ft of water. A quick boat ride from Basseterre, it is one-half mile offshore

Pro Divers' off Turtle Beach, St. Kitts

Dive boat leaves Kenneth's Dive Center, Basseterre, St. Kitts.

surrounded by coral rubble. Its steel hull attracts schooling fish, barracuda and lobster. The wreck is subject to murky conditions after a storm.

☆☆☆☆ **Sandy Point** is the photographers' favorite with huge barrel sponges, lavender seafans, gorgonians and orange, elephant-ear sponges. A mini-wall and canyon, depths range from 45 to 100 ft. Unfortunately this site is a long trip for both St. Kitts dive operators and is visited only on request by groups who are then bussed to the site (15 miles north of Basseterre) where they rendezvous with the dive boats.

☆☆☆ **The White Holes**, off the Atlantic side of Nevis, are clear, sandy hollows packed with fish and surrounded by coral. Depths range from 15 to 45 ft. Fishlife and visibility are incredible, but the seas are often rough and the trip uncomfortable. On a calm day, this is an exceptional dive.

☆☆☆ **Green Point**, off the Caribbean side of the southeast peninsula on St. Kitts, is alive with black corals, big barrel and tube sponges and a variety of soft corals. Abundant lobster and fish. A 15-minute trip from either St. Kitts dive shop. Twenty-five minutes from Nevis. Depth is 50 ft. Sea conditions are always calm. Good for all level divers.

Another Atlantic dive is ☆☆☆☆ **Grid Iron**. This reef starts at New Castle Airport on Nevis and extends out past Booby Island and the north shoreline of St. Kitts. It is an undersea shelf that rises to within 15 ft of the surface. The shallows support a dense growth of well-formed elkhorn stands, fan-shaped hydroids, colonies of giant brain coral, yellow and orange tube sponges, barrel sponges, elephant ear sponges, and plate corals. There are plenty of fish including blue tangs, French angelfish, porcupine fish, chubs, lobster, scrawled filefish, and yellowtail. Sea conditions vary. High winds and currents may rule out the area, but when conditions are favorable it is a spectacular dive and snorkeling site.

Snorkeling

Note: All St. Kitts and Nevis beaches are open to the public. Access in some cases is through hotel property.

NEVIS

☆☆ **Longhaul Bay** has good snorkeling on the inner side of the barrier reef off Nisbets Plantation. The water is shallow and visibility quite good. The beach is gorgeous. Get there by driving down to the beach at Nisbets Plantation Inn (near the airport) and walk south along the beach. Facing the sea, turn right and follow the shore to the last jetty. Experienced snorkelers should go outside the jetty, swim out to the reef and turn right to find a protected inner reef. Novice snorkelers will find many fish among the rocks closer to shore inside the last jetty. The current will bring you back to the Nisbet beach bar which serves cool drinks and an excellent lunch! Always calm inside the barrier reef. A wonderful spot for swimming and picnics too.

ST. KITTS

☆☆ **Turtle Beach.** Facing the cut, walk to your left along the beach and swim out about 20 yards to the reef where you'll find the beginning of Ballast Bay Reef. Turtle Beach is a watersports facility at the end of the southeast peninsula. Signs lead the way. Snorkeling gear may be rented from Pro Divers on the beach. Turtle Beach Bar & Grill serves drinks and lunch from 12:00 p.m. to 5:00 p.m.

☆ **White House Bay** is the first dirt road to your right as you reach the Great Salt Pond Area. You'll know it by the two sections of tugboat sticking out of the water. If the road is muddy, you may have to park near the main road and walk part of the way back. Choose the dirt road to the left. Lots of fish and corals are around the wreck which was washed ashore by Hurricane Hugo in 1989. Depths range from shallow to 25 ft in the bay.

☆☆ **Sand Bank Bay** is the first turn off to your left before reaching the Great Salt Pond area. The Bay is on the Atlantic side and subject to waves on windy days. Walk to your right along the cove and swim over to the rocks where there are a bevy of beautiful reef fish.

☆☆ **Cockleshell & Banana Bays** are one bay south of Turtle Beach. To reach it drive straight to the end of the scenic drive. There is a construction sight with framework for an unfinished hotel at the end of the road. Park next to it and walk toward the old Cockleshell Hotel (devastated by Hurricane Hugo) on the bluff. Directly in front of the bluff is a pretty reef. Watch out for fire coral. Both bays are calm with good visibility. Beautiful, white sand beaches skirt the area. At press time the hotel property was sold to Sandals for a future resort.

☆ **Timothy Beach Resort**, just south of Basseterre, has a small reef off the beach. Shallow depths.

☆☆ **Bird Rock Beach Hotel**, just outside Basseterre on the Caribbean, has a narrow strip of jet-black sand at the bottom of its property. Just off the shore are several rocks and a pretty reef which drops off enough for a shallow dive. Always calm, never a current. Decent visibility. Reach the area by boat or by climbing down the three steep flights of stairs behind the multi-terraced hotel. On the climb back up you'll find cold drinks and meals at the hotel's open-air restaurant.

Dive Operators

Prices for a two-tank boat dive range from $70 to $80 U.S. and include all the equipment, if desired.

St. Kitts

Kenneth's Dive Centre on Bay Road East, Basseterre, offers full PADI certification programs, rental gear and two fast dive boats. Owner Kenneth Samuel has been diving St. Kitts for more than 20 years and is an expert on the reefs and wrecks, tides and currents. Friendly service is provided by a professional staff. Comfortable, roomy, twin-hull, twin-engine, flat-bottom dive boats tour the Caribbean sites around Basseterre. Trips to the cut and Monkey Reef on request. ☎ 800-359-0747 or 809-465-2670; fax 809-465-7723.

Pro Divers is based at Turtle Beach on the Southeast Peninsula. This PADI instruction center, owned and operated by Auston MacLeod, offers dive packages and dive/accommodation packages with Ocean Terrace Inn which provides guests with daily shuttle service to the beach. All gear rentals, Nikonos camera and strobe rentals. The shop offers a full range of services, resort courses and PADI certification (open water to assistant instructor). Reef tours aboard a fast 30-ft twin-engine dive boat. Pro Divers circles the peninsula and always visits the best sites. When the wind is too high on the Atlantic, they dive the cut. When weather rules out the cut the dive boats go around the bend to the Caribbean and a

Beach at Nisbet Plantation, Nevis

protected cove. Pro divers also rents gear for beach dives. No spear fishing in this area. ☎ 809-465-3223; fax 809-465-1057.

MV Caribbean Explorer is a live-aboard which departs from St. Maarten and tours St. Kitts and Saba. The yacht has nine air-conditioned cabins, and is fully equipped for scuba, underwater photography and video. ☎ 800-322-3577 or write to Jennifer Woods, 10 Fence Row Drive, Fairfield, CT 06430. The *Explorer* visits some of the outer Caribbean reefs that are out of range for the dive shops.

Nevis

Dive uncrowded and unhurried Nevis with **Scuba Safaris** at the Oualie Beach Hotel. Owner Ellis Chaderton is a NAUI instructor offering personalized cave, wreck, and reef dives to **The Caves, Monkey Shoals** and **Redonda Bank,** noted for hammerheads, dolphin and whale sightings. ☎ 800-359-0747 or 809-469-9518; fax 809-469-9619.

Snorkeling Tours

Day-sail snorkeling tours aboard a sleek, 70-ft catamaran are offered by **Leeward Islands Charters.** ☎ 809-465-7474. Glass-bottom catamaran sails with beach barbecue and snorkeling tops are through **Sunset Cruises** at Jack Tar Village. ☎ 465-8224. Or try **Tropical Tours** on Canyon Street, Basseterre, for customized tours.

Travel Tours

Air/hotel/dive packages from the U.S. are offered by **ICS SCUBA and Travel,** ☎ 800-722-0205, and **Rothschild Travel,** ☎ 800-359-0747.

A chaperoned camp-type scuba and/or snorkeling program for "mature teenagers" is offered by **Island Tours,** 149 Frederick Pl., Bergenfield NJ 07621, ☎ or fax 201-385-4960.

CEDAM International offers scientific and educational expeditions to St. Kitts. Write to World Headquarters, One Fox Road, Croton on Hudson, NY 10520, U.S.A. ☎ 914-271-5365.

Accommodations

A list of all accommodations including rooms in the historic inns (most are not air conditioned), apartments, and guest houses is available from the tourist board. See details at end of chapter.

Dive packages including room (double occupancy), airport transfers, tax, service charge and 10 dives are offered by the following resorts (a 7% government hotel tax is automatically included on all hotel bills):

ST. KITTS

Ocean Terrace Inn (OTI), perched on a hill overlooking the capital city of Basseterre and its snug harbor, is a multi-terraced resort owned by native Kittitian, Colin Pereira. Modern guest rooms are air-conditioned, have satellite TV and tubs with showers. The inn features two bars, two pools and a jacuzzi. OTI is headquarters for Pro Divers. Packages available. ☎ 800-223-5695 or 809-465-2754; fax 809-465-2754.

Diving and snorkeling guests are shuttled by mini-van from the hill-top resort to the dive boats.

Timothy Beach Resort, three miles from Basseterre on Frigate Bay, offers modern, air-conditioned suites with mountain or bay views, pool, bar, open-air restaurant. Dive trips with Kenneth's Dive Centre depart from the hotel beach. Summer rates per person (May 15 to Dec. 13) start at $649. Winter, $700. Packages with Kenneth's includes two-tank dives daily. ☎ 800-858-5375 or 809-465-8597; fax 809-465-7723.

Sun' N Sand Beach Villas are one- and two-bedroom air-conditioned cottages with kitchenettes. Located on Atlantic Beach in the Frigate Bay area with a golf course, restaurants and casino nearby. Baby sitters (on request), pool, restaurant, mini mart, gift shop, TV. Studio apartments have one queen-size bed and a kitchenette. ☎ 800-223-6510 or 809-465-8037/8; fax 809-465-6745.

St. Christopher Club is a waterfront hotel and condo resort with casino. All sports facilities nearby. In Frigate Bay on Atlantic beach, five minutes from the Caribbean. Winter dive packages are from $985 per person, double occupancy for seven nights. Diving with Kenneth's. ☎ 800-359-0747.

Bird Rock Beach Hotel is high on a bluff overlooking Basseterre with a panoramic view of the Caribbean. The inn has 24 deluxe rooms and two-story cottages complete with TV and telephone. Divers and snorkelers are bussed to waiting dive boats. Gear may be stowed at the dive shop. The hotel features an excellent, adjacent restaurant, pool, coffee shop, bar. Winter rates for seven nights start at $1,065 per person, double occupancy.

NEVIS

Oualie Beach Hotel, Nevis is headquarters for dive vacations on Nevis. Located on the beach in a sheltered cove on the leeward side of Nevis, the hotel offers standard and deluxe rooms and studios. The 22-room beachfront hotel features screened verandas overlooking the water and nightly sunsets. All rooms have ceiling fans and telephones. A few are air-conditioned and have cable tv. Studio rooms have full kitchens and a queen-sized four-poster bed and can connect to other rooms to form suites. The restaurant is open for breakfast, lunch and dinner. Informal and friendly. Winter rates with diving are from $730 per person; summer, from $610. Winter rates for a standard room only are $130 for a double, summer $90. Studios with kitchens start at $170 per day. Dive packages are offered with adjacent Scuba Safaris, currently the island's only dive center. Children under 12 are free with parents. Nice swimming beach. ☎ 800-255-9684 or 809-469-9176; fax 809-469-9176.

Nisbet Plantation Beach Club is by far the most picturesque spot on Nevis. Built as a sugar plantation in 1778, the resort is situated on a mile-long white sand beach on the island's reef-protected north shore. Units are housed in 13 duplex cottages with spacious bedrooms, showers and enclosed screened patios. All have small fridges, hairdryers (a rarity on these islands), tea and coffee making facilities, and telephones. Cooled by ceiling fans. The club's gourmet restaurant is outstanding and worth getting a package for. Packages (no diving) include deluxe accommodations, breakfast, afternoon tea, and gourmet dinner each evening, car rental for two days, gratuities and taxes—summer, from $849 per person; winter from $1,149 per person. ☎ 800-344-2049 or 809-469-9325; fax 809-469-9864.

The Mount Nevis Hotel on the slopes of Mt. Nevis offer breathtaking views of St. Kitts and the Caribbean. Air-conditioned, modern rooms have 11-channel cable TV, VCRs, phones and private balconies. Suites with kitchens are available. Restaurant, pool, shuttle to beach. Dive packages for a double are from $1,210 per person in winter; $960 in summer. ☎ 800-359-0747 or 809-469-9373/4; fax 809-469-9375.

Sightseeing and Other Activities

ST. KITTS

Among the sporting activities are golfing (18-hole international championship course at Frigate Bay and a nine-hole course at Golden Rock, St. Kitts), tennis, horseback riding along the beaches of Friar's Bay and Conaree Beach. Traveling on land is done by taxi, auto, moped or bicycle. Or you can venture through town by horse and carriage. Taxis are expensive and allowed to jack up their rates at night. Be sure to have the published rates in hand and note the hours they are in effect. Taxis with T 's on the license plates mean the driver is able to recite the local history and give sightseeing tours. Cars can be rented for rates starting at $30 per day.

Tours of St. Kitts start at Basseterre and "The Circus," an area patterned after London's famous Piccadilly Circus. Its centerpiece is a memorial to Thomas Berkeley. Surrounding it are a few craft boutiques, restaurants and galleries. Souvenir shops offer locally hand-screened fabrics, straw and coconut products, and jewelry fashioned from conch shells and volcanic rocks—many "Made in St. Kitts., Batik clothing and fabrics crafted on the island are found below the Ballahoo Restaurant on "The Circus" at **Island Hopper**. From town, rent a car or taxi and travel north along the west coast island road. You'll pass several former "great houses," some newly converted into restaurants or shops. Continue to **Old Road Bay**, the island's first capital city. Near the English colony Carib drawings are sketched on the boulders. A short distance away is **Romney Manor**, the home of **Caribelle Batik** where local artists apply colorful designs onto fabric with wax and dyes.

Continue to **Brimstone Hill**, a national park and fort which spreads over 40 acres above the sea and offers glorious views of St. Kitts and surrounding islands. The fort, which took over 106 years of slave labor to build, is connected to a museum displaying photos and memorabilia honoring those who fought here.

Heading north from the fort brings you to **Sandy Point**, once headquarters for the Dutch tobacco industry.continue along the island road, around the island past miles of sugar cane fields until you come to the **Black Rocks**, rugged cliffs formed of ancient lava flows from Mt Liamuiga. A left will head you to the Frigate Bay area, the site of luxury hotels, casinos, and the yacht club.from here head up the mountain on the new scenic road out through the uninhabited **South East Peninsula** and **The Salt Ponds**, habitat to vervet green monkeys, herons, sea turtles and wild deer. The ponds are a source of salt to the islanders.

The scenic road winds, dips and soars through seven miles of the most gorgeous, lush, green mountains and breathtaking, ocean views on earth. On the Atlantic side there are panoramic views of waves crashing against rocky cliffs and washing over secluded, golden beaches and snorkeling coves. Rounding the mountains brings the turquoise Caribbean and distant mountains of Nevis into view. Near the end is the Great Salt Pond. Watch for monkeys and, near the ponds, cows crossing the road.

Hikes into the rainforest, windsurfing, deep sea fishing, horseback riding, sunset cruises, and historic tours are easily arranged through the resorts or individual operators. Rainforest tours, cave tours, volcano tours and plantation tours are offered by **Greg's Safaris**, ☎ 465-4121/22, or **Kriss Tours**, ☎ 465-4042.

NEVIS

If you arrive on Nevis by boat, you can walk to Charlestown. You'll first encounter the **Cotton Ginnery** still used to gin cotton and **Market Place** where local merchants sell fresh fruits, spices and seafood. But the most interesting sites in town are the **Nevis Philatelic Bureau** which offers beautiful color plates of marine life, historic aircraft and space subjects, and local flora—unique souvenirs, all suitable for framing and the **Nevis Museum and Hamilton House**, birthplace of statesman and first Secretary of the U.S. Treasury, Alexander Hamilton.

Heading north on the coast road past Oualie Beach you'll come to **Newcastle Pottery** where centuries-old methods create natural red pottery—from small ashtrays to flower pots and the coalpots used by many villagers. The best prices on the pottery are at the factory.

South of town turn left across from the Esso station to find the **Bath Hotel and Spring House**, once THE grand hotel and health spa of the Carib-

The Baths, Nevis

bean. Much of the original structure was destroyed by an earthquake in 1950, but visitors can enjoy a mineral bath or just stick a toe in and tour the hotel.

Horseback riding and rain forest walks may be arranged through the hotels.

Dining

Local seafood, lobster dishes, and West Indian cuisine highlight St. Kitts and Nevis menus. Fast food and pizza shops are found in towns. Menu prices are in EC (East Caribbean Dollars), worth about $2.70 to a U.S. dollar. When you are quoted a price in "dollars" ask which one. Credit cards are NOT widely accepted. (Prices below are in U.S. dollars)

ST. KITTS

Fisherman's Wharf, on the harbor in Basseterre, offers fresh seafood and local dishes. Seating is on a broad deck a few inches over the water, much like eating on a yacht that doesn't rock. Great views of Basseterre at night. Don't miss the pumpkin fritters. Informal. Open for dinner nightly, and for lunch on weekends. Entrees from $5 to $15. ☎ 465-2695.

Roses, just off the Bay Road south of Basseterre, serves gourmet fish and local dishes. This place is tricky to find, but worth the effort. When the road ends, turn left at the basketball court. Drive down the block toward the water. Once in the parking lot, walk down the stairs and left to find the restaurant. Artsy menu.

The Ballahoo, center of town, Basseterre at the Circus, open Mon- Sat, serves seafood and local dishes. Open 8 a.m. to 11 p.m. ☎ 465-4197.

J's Place at the foot of the Brimstone Hill Fortress serves sandwiches and cold drinks. Open Tues-Sun from 11 a.m. to 11 p.m. ☎ 465-6264.

PJ's Pizza Bar and Restaurant is an Italian and vegetarian restaurant that features pizza, sandwiches and Italian dinners. Eat-in or take-out. Entrees from $5 to $16. ☎ 465-8373.

Sundae Best on the scenic Atlantic side of Frigate Bay offers the best in banana splits, and ice cream sundaes, sandwiches, and snacks. Open Sun-Thurs, noon to 7 p.m., Fri and Sat, noon to 9 pm. ☎ 465-6171.

NEVIS

Oualie Beach Hotel, open daily from 7am to 11pm, serves breakfast, lunch and dinner. Enjoy West Indian cuisine in an informal atmosphere at the water's edge. Excellent broiled lobster and pineapple mousse. Moderate prices. No credit cards. ☎ 469-5329.

Unella's Waterfront Bar & Restaurant serves refreshing tropical drinks, sandwiches, local and seafood dishes, including curried lamb, spare ribs and conch, at reasonable prices. By the ferry pier on the waterfront in Charlestown. ☎ 469-5574.

Nisbet Plantation offers elegant settings, excellent service and taste-tempting creations such as chilled avocado & apricot soup, marinated salmon over asparagus mousse with caviar-stuffed quail eggs, amberjack with hollandaise sauce or sumptous, meat dishes. Expensive. Meals average $55 U.S. per person without drinks, plus tax and an "optional" tip. If you are staying at Nisbet, be sure to get the money-saving meal package which includes breakfast, afternoon tea and gourmet dinners nightly. ☎ 809-469-9325.

Helpful Phone Numbers

POLICE: ☎ 465-2241

HOSPITAL: ☎ 465-2551

TOURIST BOARD: St. Kitts ☎ 809-465-4040; Nevis ☎ 469-5521

FERRY BOAT: ☎ 465-2521

Facts

Nearest Recompression Chamber: Saba, a 15-minute flight from St. Kitts. Avoid decompression dives. Getting from the dive boat to the airport and arranging for air transport may be dangerously time consuming. Exercise extreme caution while diving.

Getting There: American Airlines (800-433-7300) is the main carrier with direct flights from major U.S. cities to San Juan connecting to American Eagle which serves Golden Rock Airport, St. Kitts. Other North American and international carriers have direct flights to San Juan, Antigua and other Caribbean islands that connect with American Eagle, BWIA, LIAT, and Windward Islands Airways to and from the island of St. Kitts. Golden Rock Airport on St. Kitts can handle wide-body jets, while Newcastle Airport on Nevis can accommodate smaller twin-engined, prop aircraft. Daily ferry service connects Basseterre to Charlestown. Several cruise lines stop at St. Kitts.

Driving: Traffic moves on the left. A local license is required and can be obtained from the Police Traffic Dept for about $10 US. Rental car steering wheels are on the left also.

Language: English

Documents: Passports are required of all visitors except U.S. and Canadian citizens who may use a voter registration card or original birth certificate.

Airport Tax: Departure tax of $8 U.S or $20 EC.

Currency: East Caribbean dollar (EC) $2.70 = $1 U.S.

Climate: Average temperate of 79°F. Annual rainfall is 55 inches.

Clothing: Casual, lightweight clothing. Beach attire, short shorts, bikinis or bare chests are NOT ALLOWED in public places—town, restaurants or shops. Snorkelers should wear wetskins or long-sleeve shirts to protect from the sun. Wetsuits unnecessary though a shortie or wetskin is nice for winter diving and when making several deep dives. On land, wear casual lightweight clothing.

Electricity: 230 volts, 60 cycles A.C. Some hotels have 110 volts, A.C. Transformers and adapters are generally needed.

Religious Services: Adventist, Anglican, Baha'i, Baptist, Catholic, Church of God, Jehovah's Witnesses, Moravian, Methodist, and Pentecostal. Contact hotel desk for details.

Additional Information: *In the U.S.*, St. Kitts & Nevis Tourist Board, 414 East 75th St, N.Y. 10021, ☎ 212-535-1234; fax 212-879-4789 or 1464 Whippoorwill Way, Mountainside, NJ 07092, ☎ 908-232-6701 *In Canada*: 11 Yorkville Ave., Suite 508, Toronto, M4WIL3, ☎ 416-921-7717; fax 416-921-7997. *In the U.K.*, 10 Kensington Court, London W8 5DL, ☎ 71-376-0881. *In St. Kitts and Nevis*: Department of Tourism, Church St., P.O. Box 132, Basseterre, St. Kitts, W.I., ☎ 809-465-2620/4040, fax 809-465-8794.

St. Lucia

Saint Lucia (pronounced loo'sha) is the second largest of the Windward Islands. An independent state, the 238 square-mile island is about 1,300 miles southeast of Florida, 24 miles north of St. Vincent and 21 miles from Martinique.

Mountainous and scenic, the island is characterized by Morne Gimie, the highest peak at 3,145 ft and two spectacular, ancient forest-covered volcanic cones—Gros Piton (2,619 ft) and Petit Piton (2,461 ft)—that rise abruptly from the sea near Soufriere, an old colonial town on the west coast. Nearby, hot sulfurous springs bubble and spout steam from muddy, black craters. Lush jungle-like vegetation covers much of the island and seems to grow as you pass through it.

St. Lucia's coast is lined by miles of beautiful beaches interspersed with sheer volcanic cliffs that dive straight into the sea where they are covered with a blaze of orange and yellow corals and sponges. Most diving and snorkeling is off Anse Chastanet and Soufriere Bay, both sheltered coves on the island's southwest corner. Within 150 ft of their shorelines lies a 30-mile-long coral reef on a shelf at ten- to 30-ft depths. Farther out are shallow caves and a sheer wall. Beyond the coves, strong currents mandate drift diving. The entire area is protected as a marine park.

St. Lucia is heavily populated. Her 160,000 people are mostly African or mixed African and European descent. English is the official language, although there is also a local patois that owes much to early French domination of the island. One third of the population resides in Castries the capital and deep water port.

Contributors: Karoli Kolcuoglu, Durand Berg

The economy is agricultural with bananas as the main export crop. Cocoa beans, coconut oil, and copra (dried coconut) also are exported. Industries include rum making, fishing, and brick manufacturing.

There are two airports, Hewanorra International at the southern tip of the island and Vigie in the north. Since the island's road system is bad, try to fly into the airport closest to your resort. American Airlines serves both airports.

In summer, bug repellent is necessary from the moment you step off the plane.

When to Go

Dive St Lucia from January to April, the dry season. The rainiest months are May through August. Annual rainfall varies from 55 inches on the south coast to 140 inches in the interior. Air temperatures average 80 F.

History

No one is certain when St. Lucia was discovered or by whom though some credit Christopher Columbus in 1502. The British tried to settle the island in 1605 and 1638, but were driven off with fierce attacks by the native Carib Indians. French claims to the island were confirmed by a treaty with the Caribs in 1660. St. Lucia subsequently changed hands several times before being captured by the British in 1803 and ceded to them by the Treaty of Paris in 1814. From 1838, it was part of Britain's Windward Islands administrative group.

On Feb. 22, 1979, St. Lucia attained full independence. The British monarch continues to be head of state and to be represented by a governor general, who appoints the prime minister. Parliament consists of a Senate and House of Assembly, and there is a supreme court.

Best Dives and Snorkeling Sites

☆☆☆ **The Wreck of** *Lesleen M* is a 165-ft freighter sunk by the Department of Fisheries in 1986 to create an artificial reef. The wreck is intact, lying upright at 65 ft. Its hull, covered with soft corals, slender tube sponges and hydroids, provides shelter to many juvenile fish. Divers can explore the pilot house at 35 ft. It is possible to explore inside the hold and in the engine room. Good visibility.

☆☆☆☆ **Anse Chastanet Reef** is off the Anse Chastanet Hotel. There are three distinct dive areas. New divers and snorkelers enjoy a nice shallow area with a small cavern, sponges, large brain and boulder corals at depths of five to 25 ft. A resident school of squid are joined by goat fish, a frog fish, parrot fish, chromis and wrasse.

Farther out the reef slopes off to a wall which plummets to 140 ft. Most dives are at 50 to 60 ft where the coral ledges sparkle with ruby sea whips, pink anemones, lacy corals, teal vase sponges, and crimson rope sponges. Crabs, lobster, trumpet fish, peppermint-stick lobster, blackbar soldier fish, brown chromis, batfish, peacock flounders, flying gurnards, moray eels, and margates inhabit the area.

Below 100 ft are larger fish, black corals and porcelain-like plate corals.

☆☆ **Anse la Raye Reef** is a slope covered in huge boulders near the wreck of the *Lesleen M*. The shallow areas have lots of colorful fire corals, while deeper there are iridescent vase sponges, huge barrel sponges and bushy soft corals. Schools of jacks, Bermuda chub and spotted drums frequent the area.

☆☆☆ **Fairyland** is outside the Anse Chastanet cove and always done as a drift dive. Subject to occasional strong currents, this area has outstanding visibility and vibrant corals. The plateau slopes from 40 to 60 ft and is strewn with huge boulders. Finger corals, anemones and lavender tube sponges attach to the rocks with plenty of nooks and crannies for fish and invertebrates.

☆☆☆☆☆ **Pinnacles** are four spectacular seamounts that rise from the depths to within a few feet of the surface. These coral-covered subsea cliffs are a macro-photographer's dream—alive with octopi, feather dusters, arrow crabs, seahorses, squid, and shrimp. Cleansing currents nurture big barrel and vase sponges and a lattice of soft corals—sea plumes, sea whips and sea fans. Lots of fish. Black corals at depth.

☆☆☆ **Piton Wall** at the base of Petit Piton falls from the surface to hundreds of feet below. Sea whips, gorgonians, big feather dusters give way to a profusion of fish. Strong currents possible. Experienced divers only.

☆☆☆ **Superman's Flight** is a 15-minute boat trip across Soufriere Bay to the base of the Petit Piton Mountain which was used as a setting for the film Superman II. Strong currents make this an exciting drift drive. You'll "fly" the wall underwater. Good fish life and excellent visibility.

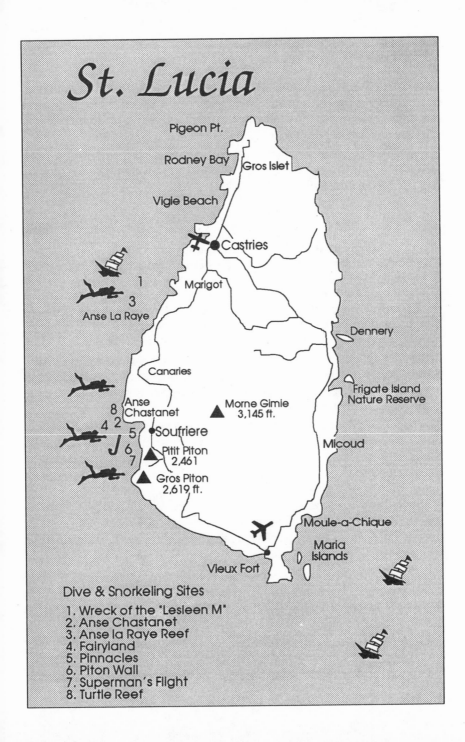

St. Lucia

Pigeon Pt.

Rodney Bay

Gros Islet

Vigie Beach

Castries

1

Marigot

3

Anse La Raye

Dennery

Canaries

Frigate Island
Nature Reserve

Anse
Chastanet

Morne Gimie
3,145 ft.

8

4 2

5

Soufriere

6

Pitit Piton
2,461

Micoud

7

Gros Piton
2,619 ft.

Moule-a-Chique

Maria
Islands

Vieux Fort

Dive & Snorkeling Sites

1. Wreck of the "Lesleen M"
2. Anse Chastanet
3. Anse la Raye Reef
4. Fairyland
5. Pinnacles
6. Piton Wall
7. Superman's Flight
8. Turtle Reef

☆☆ **Turtle Reef** is a crescent-shaped shoal north of Anse Chastanet Bay. the top at 40 ft drops to over 150 ft. Divers enjoy spectacular pillar coral and barrel sponges in the shallows. Lots of crustaceans, squid, parrotfish, starfish and soft corals.

When occasional calm seas occur off the southeast coast you can dive two wrecks—an airline and a freighter. But more often than not rough seas and strong currents rule them out as safe sites.

Dive Operators

Scuba St. Lucia is a PADI five-star training facility located at Anse Chastanet. The seven-instructor shop offers introductory and advanced open-water and rescue courses plus specialty courses in marine life identification, underwater navigation, drift diving, wreck diving and UW photography. E-6 processing and photo rentals are available. Five custom dive boats. Hotel-dive packages with Anse Chastanet Hotel. ☎ 809-459-7000 or 809-459-7355. Write to P.O. Box 7000, Soufriere, St. Lucia, W.I.

Buddies Scuba at Vigie Marina, Castries, is a full-service PADI facility. Buddies offers resort courses and reef and wreck tours. Six- dive packages are available. ☎ 809-45-25288 or 809-45-27044. Write to Buddies Scuba, Vigie Marina, Castries, St. Lucia, W.I.

The Moorings Scuba Centre at Club Mariner, Marigot Bay offers reef and wreck dives, camera rental, instruction and night dives. ☎ 809-451-4357.

Accommodations

St. Lucia has a wide range of accommodations for all budgets, some as low as $30 US per night. Space dictates we list only those with or near dive facilities, but a complete list is available from the tourist board offices listed at end of chapter.

For apartment or private home rentals contact: **Happy Homes,** P.O. Box 12, Castries, St. Lucia; **Caribbean Home Rentals,** P.O. Box 710, Palm Beach, FL 33480; or **Tropical Villas,** P.O. Box 189, Castries, St. Lucia, ☎ 809-452-8240.

Anse Chastanet Beach Hotel (pronounced "ants-shas-tan-ay") is the islands' premier dive resort. It is named for one of the French aristocratic families who settled on the island during the 18th century, the Chastanet family who originated in the Bordeau region. "Anse" is antique French for "Bay."

Anse Chastanet is a beautifully scenic resort set amidst a lush 400-acre plantation edged by a secluded, quarter-mile-long, soft-sand beach. Some of the resort's 48 rooms are scattered on a hillside, others are beachside. All rooms have fridges, electric tea/coffee makers, wall- mounted hair dryers, clay tile or tropical hardwood floors, private showers, AC and ceiling fans. Scuba St. Lucia is a part of the resort. Snorkeling and shore dives are possible from the resort beach. Dive-hotel package rates for a double, with meals, start at $2,798 (Dec. 20 to April 15). For a single from May 16 to Oct. 31 dive-hotel package rates start at $1,029 without meals. All packages include seven nights accommodations, airport transfers, six days of diving (two tanks), weights, local plantation tours and beach towels. Night dives may be substituted. Non-divers' rates, no meals, start at $849 in summer. MAP supplement is mandatory during the high season. Group packages available. ☎ 809-459-7000; fax 809-459-7700. Telex: 0398/6370. Write to P.O. Box 216, Soufriere, St. Lucia, W.I.

Club Med at Vieux Fort on the southern tip of the island, offers all-inclusive dive vacations—meals, six nights accommodations, two dives daily and one, night dive starting at $800 per person. Club Med accepts only NAUI and PADI certifications, but will give others a free resort course and related certificate that may be used at other clubs. Rates for children accompanying adults start at $600. Age 12 and over may take a certification course for $175. The resort offers all water sports plus horseback riding, tennis, golf, and other activities. Mini club for children. For reservations ☎ 1-800-CLUB-MED.

Marigot Bay Resort is nine miles from Vigie Airport and Castries on picturesque Marigot Bay. The resort features 47 villas set in the hillside around the bay and marina. Cottages rent from $90 per day in summer and $140 per day in winder. A hillside house is offered from $115. The Moorings dive shop is on the premises. Scuba packages are $975 per person between April 16th and December 19th; $1,205 from Dec. 20 to April 15. Price includes seven nights in a cottage with kitchenette, breakfasts and dinners, complimentary snorkeling, small-boat sailing and more. Dives can be replaced with a skippered day sail on a 43-ft yacht, an island tour or a windsurfing lesson. Bareboat or crewed charters are on Beneteau 39s to Morgan 60s. For current rates and reservations ☎ 1-800-334-2435 or 813-538-8760; fax 813-530-9747. In St. Lucia ☎ 809-451-4357; fax 809-451-4353.

Dining

Menu prices are in EC. $1 EC = $2.70 U.S. Credit Cards are NOT widely accepted. Prices following are in U.S. dollars.

Fast-food lovers will find good burgers, salads and pizza at two **Peppino's Pizza** locations: in Castries on upper Bridge Street and in Gros Islet at the north end of the island. All available for take out. No credit cards. ☎ 452-3942.

Natural Cafe on Chaussee Road on the outskirts of Castries serves vegetarian food, soy meals and Caribbean dishes. ☎ 452-6421.

Rain is in a century-old mansion at Columbus Square, Castries and features a courtyard, sidewalk bar and balcony, all in the tradition of a Somerset Maugham novel. Open for breakfast, lunch, and dinner. Entrees are from $10 to $25 ☎ 452-3022.

Dasheene in Soufriere is on a 1,300-ft ridge in a lush setting. Good Creole and seafood dishes. Open seven days for breakfast, lunch and dinner. ☎ 459-7850. Reservations.

For chargrilled steaks, ribs and fresh seafood try the **Charthouse** overlooking Rodney Bay (northwest corner). Entrees start at $15 U.S. ☎ 452-8115.

Tuesday evenings are beach barbecue nights at **Anse Chastanet**. Festivities begin at the hotel at 7:30 pm. Each Friday night in **Gros Islet,** also known as "The Village" there is an all-out street party with music, dancing, food and loads of local color. It can get rowdy.

Sightseeing

St. Lucia has a dreadful road system which has popularized helicopter tours. But, if you don't mind spending three hours to travel 30 miles, a driving tour of the west coast affords breathtaking views of the bays, mountains, rain forests, and surrounding countryside. The road is tough to negotiate, with muddy, crater-sized potholes, occasional landslides, hairpin turns, marauding chickens and goats.

Starting at the southern tip of St. Lucia is Moule a Chique Peninsula, marked by a lighthouse. From here you can see St. Vincent and the Grenadines. Heading north along the west coast brings you to the **Sulfur Springs**, billed as the world's only drive-in volcano. A walk through takes you past steaming hot sulfur springs and bubbling mud craters. An ever-present smell of rotten eggs usually makes this a quick stop.

Just north of the springs is the 18th-century village of Soufriere, the island's breadbasket where local fruits and vegetables are grown. It is also the island's deepest harbor accommodating large cruise ships and freighters.

The **Soufriere Estate** offers tours where you can learn about the harvesting and processing of copra (dried coconut meat yielding oil) and cocoa. Adjacent to the estate are the **Diamond Falls and Mineral Baths** where you can take a "therapeutic" hot dip and enjoy the surrounding gardens.

Take the dirt road (very slowly) south of town for spectacular views of the Pitons.

Continuing north brings you to **Anse-la-Raye**, a fishing village where dugout canoes are made. Beyond lies **Mt. Parasol** and **Mt. Gimie**. From here the road winds and dips through banana country to **Marigot**, a world-famous yacht harbor and resort community. There are two hotels and restaurants.

The road from Marigot to Castries curves and bends sharply with the rugged terrain through miles of banana plantations.

When you reach **Castries** take the John Compton Highway to the center of town where you'll find duty free shopping, a busy port. Behind the city is **Morne Fortune**, the "Hill of Good Fortune." A scenic drive up the Morne begins on Bridge Street. From the top are splendid views of the countryside and **Fort Charlotte**, an 18th-century French fort.

From Castries you can cross the island to the Atlantic coast or head north to Gros Islet, a sleepy fishing village and **Pigeon Island National Park** with 40 acres of forts, ruins and caves that are reputed to still hold pirate treasure. Beyond Pigeon Island lies **Cap Estate** covering 1,500 acres of fine beaches, secluded coves and a gold course.

Full- and part-day water excursions are offered down the island's western coast. Most offer snorkeling and lunch.

The windward, Atlantic coast is home of the **Frigate Island Nature Reserve**. A one-mile walk encircles the park area and takes you to a lookout where you can view outlying islets. During the summer the area is a nesting site of the Frigate birds and timid boa constrictors. Half-day tours may be arranged by the National Trust (425-5005). Avoid swimming in the Atlantic. Strong currents and powerful waves make it dangerous.

Offshore to **Vieux** on the south tip is the **Maria Islands Nature Reserve** which houses unique grass snakes and ground lizards, plus many species of birds. Tours may be arranged when its open.

Guided hikes in the Pitons and into the rain forest are offered by the Forest Service (☎ 452-3231 or 452-3078).

Helpful Phone Numbers

POLICE: ☎ 999

ST. JUDE'S HOSPITAL: Vieux Fort, ☎ 454-6041

VICTORIA HOSPITAL: Hospital Road, Castrie, ☎ 452-2421

Facts

Nearest Recompression Chamber: Guadeloupe ☎ 011-590 828888 Dr. Dramor; ☎ 011-590-829880, Dr. Serina.

Getting There: American Airlines (☎ 800433-7300) has service from Miami, New York and other gateway cities with a stop in San Juan. BWIA (800-327-7401) flies direct from New York and Miami. Air Canada (☎ 800-422-6232) flies from Montreal and Toronto with connections through Barbados. LIAT connects with other Caribbean destinations.

Island Transportation: Car rentals: **Avis, Vide Boutielle** (☎ 809-45-24554/22700; fax 809-45-31536); **National,** Gros Islet (☎ 809-45-28721; fax 809-45-28577); **Dollar,** Reduit (☎ 809-45-20994) and **Budget,** Marisule (☎ 809-45-20233/28021; fax 809-45-29362).

Cab service is readily available from Hewanorra International Airport at the south end of the island. Taxis are unmetered and unregulated. Be sure to ask the cost *before* getting in the cab and whether it is in EC or U.S. dollars.

Driving: You must be 25 or older and hold a valid driver's license. Buy a temporary St. Lucian license for $11 at the airport or police headquarters on Bridge St in Castries. Steering wheels are on the right. Driving is on the left. Drivers should exercise extreme caution while negotiating St. Lucia's rugged mountainous roads and hairpin curves.

Documents: Citizens of the U.S., U.K. and Canada must produce proof of identity. Passports are suggested, but a birth certificate with a raised seal and some form of photo ID will suffice. Visitors must have onward tickets.

Currency: The Eastern Caribbean dollar which is exchanged at the rate of $1 US to $2.70 EC ($2.60 in hotels and stores). U.S. and Canadian dollars are accepted.

Credit cards accepted in many stores, but not all restaurants. Check when making reservations.

Climate: In winter temperatures are between 65°F and 85°F. Summer between 75° and 95°. Summers are rainy. Light wetsuits are suggested for winter diving.

Clothing: Lightweight and casual. Some of the fancier restaurants at the hotels in Castries require a jacket and tie.

Electricity: 220. Adapters are required.

Time: Atlantic Standard (EST + 1 hr.)

Language: English.

Tax: An 8% government tax is added on to accommodations. A service charge of 10% is added by restaurants and hotels. Note: hotels often calculate the taxes and charges in the rates.

Religious Services: Most of the island is Catholic, but Anglican, Methodist, Baptist, Seventh-Day Adventist, and Jehovahs Witness faiths are also represented.

For Additional Information: Contact the St. Lucia Tourist Board: *In New York*, 820 Second Ave., New York NY; ☎ 212-867-2950; fax 212-370-7867. *In Canada*, 151 Bloor St West, Suite 425, Toronto, Ontario, Canada M5S 1S4; ☎ 416-961-4317. *In London*, 10 Kensington Court, London W8 5DL, England; 044-71-937-1969; fax 044-71-937-3611. *In St. Lucia*, P.O. Box 221, Castries, St. Lucia, ☎ 809-45-24094/25968; fax 809-453-1121..

St. Maarten/St. Martin

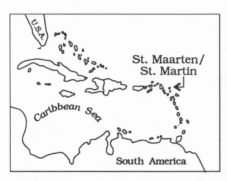

St. Maarten/St. Martin is one of the most well-suited spots for experienced divers and snorkelers or non-divers to share a vacation. The island is surrounded by extremely shallow reefs, perfect for snorkeling or learning to dive. There are some areas suitable for children. For the more experienced diver, there are advanced reef, cave and wreck sites off the south coast. The island is also a jump-off point for day trips to three neighboring "best dive" islands—Saba, St. Eustatia, and Anguilla—where advanced reef, wall and wreck dives await.

It is the largest of the Dutch Windward Islands, though still compact enough to stay on one end and easily explore the other. The north half (St. Martin) is French, the south half (St Maarten) is Dutch. It is the only island shared by two governments.

The island's dual personality, coupled with its reputation as the gourmet capital of the Caribbean, exciting nightlife, duty-free shopping, endless watersports and extraordinary scenery have contributed to its popularity as a prime vacation spot. The bustling tourist population may seem too busy for the devout naturalist, yet, given half a chance, this island's beautiful beaches and endless creature comforts can seduce, surprise and entertain just about anyone.

Residents of this small West Indian island point proudly to more than 300 years of peaceful co-existence. They are fond of describing their 37-square-mile island as "the smallest bit of real estate in the world shared by two countries—and." they are quick to add, "probably the friendliest".

Contributors: Tom Burnett, Trade Winds Dive Center; Dominique & LeRoy French, Ocean Explorers

A single border monument bracketed by a pair of flags stands beside the road connecting Philipsburg and Marigot, the Dutch and French "capital villages." There are no real boundaries or borders.

History

St. Maarten/St. Martin was discovered by Christopher Columbus on November 11, 1493. Though Spain claimed the island, it was deserted in 1648 when the Spaniards no longer needed a Caribbean base. The Dutch commander of St. Eustatius promptly sent Captain Martin Thomas to take possession. Thomas found French troops who, after a few skirmishes, signed a treaty dividing the island between France and Holland. Legend portrays a Frenchman and a Dutchman walking around the island from opposite ends to see how much territory each could earmark for his side in one day.

Unfortunately, that early agreement didn't last as long as the legend, and St. Maarten changed hands 16 times before becoming permanently Dutch.

During the 17th and 18th centuries, fishing, sugar plantations, and salt harvesting became the base for the island's economy. By the middle of the 18th century, however, the tiny nearby island St. Eustatius began to overshadow St. Maarten/St. Martin in prosperity. Farms on St. Maarten/St. Martin supplied grapes for the tables of wealthy Statian merchants.

St. Maarten/St. Martin remained little noticed by the outside world until Princess Juliana Airport opened in 1943. With the end of World War II, American and European travelers, eager for an unspoiled Caribbean getaway, began to discover the island. In 1947, St. Maarten's first hotel, the Sea View, opened.

The decades following 1960 brought an increase in tourism. Today St. Maarten/St. Martin is one of the most popular vacation spots in the Caribbean.

Diving

The best dive and snorkeling sites are about a mile offshore and must be reached by boat.

The Windward side of St. Maarten, extending from Philipsburg up the coast to Dawn Beach is known for brilliant rock formations and a moon hole from the impact of a meteor. The Leeward side of St. Maarten has scattered coral heads.

Bobby's Marina (Left) & Great Bay Marina, Philipsburg

Off the northeast coast of St. Martin, dive sites include Ilet Pinel, a small out-island good for shallow diving, Green Key, a prolific barrier reef and Flat Island (also known as Ile Tintamarre), for sheltered coves and sub-sea geological faults. To the north, Anse Marcel is a good choice.

Best Dives and Snorkeling Sites

☆☆☆ **Wreck of the *Proselyte*** sits off the south coast of St. Maarten in 50 ft of water. Remains include three 14-ft long anchors, cannons, ballast bars and brass barrel hoops from the powder kegs. Divers still find square nails and spikes. Schools of sergeant majors, hordes of angelfish, yellow tail snappers and grunts inhabit the wreck with an occasional sighting of and eagle ray or grey reef shark. The ship, first named *Jason*, began her 31 years afloat as a Dutch war frigate at Rotterdam, Holland. She was taken over by a mutinous crew in 1796 and given to the British. The ship sank in 1801 after striking a submerged reef.

The reef surrounding the *Proselyte* is pretty with stands of elkhorn and soft corals. Reef depths are from 15 to 45 ft. A swim behind the reef reveals two new wrecks, a 30-ft sailboat and a 100-ft steel barge, sunk in 1989.

Seas average three to four ft. No spearfishing or coral or shell collecting. Good for novice divers.

☆☆ **The Alleys** and **Cable Reef** are a two-reef complex just east of the *Proselyte* wreck. Maximum depth is 65 ft. The reefs are riddled with small caves crowded with fish and lobster. Besides the usual parade of tropicals there are a few nurse sharks, an occasional hammerhead, eagle rays and turtles. In winter, the barracuda population quadruples. Coral rubble interspersed with sea fans and gorgonians carpet the bottom. Visibility varies with sea conditions from 50 to 100 ft. This area is recommended for novice divers when the seas are calm. Expect two- to four-ft swells. No spearfishing or collecting.

☆☆ **The Maze** is a huge shallow reef off Little Bay Beach on the south tip of St. Maarten. Top of the reef is 20 ft, bottom at 50 ft. Elkhorn corals predominate. There are a number of mini caves and arches. One section of The Maze, a hangout for hundreds of barracuda, has been dubbed **Barracuda Alley.**

☆☆☆☆ **One Step Beyond** is a seven-mile boat ride off St. Maarten's southeast tip. High winds often rule this area out, but when seas are calm it is a great dive with huge eagle rays, sharks, turtles, big morays, schools of grunts, spadefish, and pretty fields of soft corals. The reef is a big hill which branches into coral arches and swim- throughs. Expect three- to four-ft seas on the calm days. Maximum depth is 90 ft. Average visibility is 80 to 100 ft. Suggested for experienced divers only.

☆☆☆ **Fish Bowl Reef** is between One Stop Beyond and Cable Reef off the southeastern corner of the island. Abundant in fish life, this spot is one of the prettiest reefs in the area. Besides a mass of tropicals, huge nurse sharks, stingrays and barracuda are found in the ledges and caves. Depths are between 40 and 60 ft. Good for novices. Visibility varies from 60 to 100 ft. No spearfishing or collecting.

Snorkelers and novice divers will find some shallow reefs and wrecks off the northern and western coasts. **Creole Rock** with depths from ten to 25 ft is off the town of Grand Case on the French Side. Seas are always calm with no currents and visibility usually good. Small tropical fish are plentiful.

Long Bay Reef is close to shore at Long Bay off the western peninsula. This is a good choice when the outer reefs are weathered out. Watch for occasional currents. **French Reef** is close to shore off Cole Bay on the south coast. With depths from 12 to 25 ft, this protected reef is a good choice for beginners. Lots of tropicals.

Beach snorkeling is possible off Pointe Plum on the western peninsula, Mullet Bay, the point between Lay Bay and Cole Bay, the point between Cay Bay and Little Bay and off Dawn Beach on the east coast.

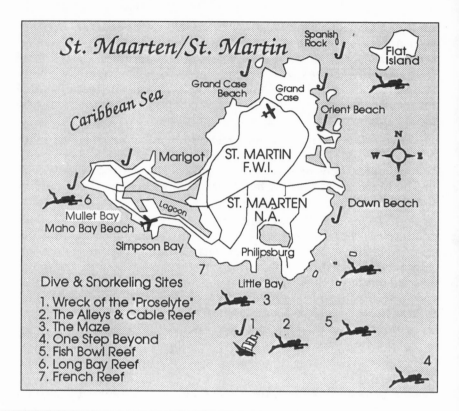

St. Maarten/St. Martin

Caribbean Sea

Spanish Rock

Flat Island

Grand Case Beach

Grand Case

Orient Beach

Marigot

ST. MARTIN F.W.I.

ST. MAARTEN N.A.

Dawn Beach

Mullet Bay

Maho Bay Beach

Lagoon

Simpson Bay

Philipsburg

Little Bay

Dive & Snorkeling Sites

1. Wreck of the "Proselyte"
2. The Alleys & Cable Reef
3. The Maze
4. One Step Beyond
5. Fish Bowl Reef
6. Long Bay Reef
7. French Reef

Dive Operators

ST. MAARTEN

Ocean Explorers Dive Center is on a quiet beach on the south coast at Simpson Bay. It is owned and operated by LeRoy & Dominique French, long time residents of St. Maarten who personally escort tours aboard a fast, 26-ft Robalo dive boat. A maximum of seven divers per trip are taken. Ocean Explorers provides stab jackets with auto inflators, 80 cu. ft tank, regulators with high pressure gauges, and wet suits. The shop has been appointed a NAUI Dream Resort. C-cards required. Resort and certification courses available. ☎ 011-599-5-45252. Local 45252. Yachts may contact the shop on VHF 16.

Leeward Islands Divers at the Simpson Bay Yacht Club offers PADI, SSI, CMAS and HSA'S certification, and resort courses, dive tours to reefs and wrecks, live-aboard sail charters, snorkeling trips, deep sea fishing. Dive/hotel packages are offered from $399 per person, double occupancy for five nights at the Treasure Island Hotel & Casino, five dives, transfers, breakfast daily. ☎ 011-599-42262; fax 011-5995-42262. Local ☎ 42262. Dive guides speak English, French, German, Dutch, Italian and Spanish.

Trade Winds Dive Center is on the dock at Great Bay Marina, Philipsburg near Chesterfield's Restaurant. The shop visits the south coast dive areas with a 25-ft Mako and a 27-ft, ridged-hull, Avon inflatable powered by twin 120-hp outboards. PADI certifications available. Introductory lessons are taught in calm Mullet Bay. ☎ 011-599-5-54387; from the French side 03-54387. Local 54387.

Maho Watersports is on the beach at the Mullet Bay Resort on the western peninsula. The shop offers PADI courses, resort courses, trips. Cost per dive is $45 with equipment provided. ☎ 011-599-5-54387; from the French side 03-54387. Local 54387.

ST. MARTIN

Lou Scuba Club at the Laguna Beach charges $45 per dive. PADI and CMAS courses. Dive packages are available. ☎ 590-872258; fax 590-8-72014.

Blue Ocean at Le Pirate in Marigot is a PADI and CMAS operation offering trips and courses. ☎ 590-8-78973; fax 590-8-72636.

Accommodations

St. Maarten/St. Martin resorts are not geared specifically towards scuba. Hotel/air packages are offered by tour operators and travel agents. Money-saving, dive-travel packages for groups and individuals are offered by ICS Travel. ☎ 800-722-0205; fax 516-797-2132. Write to 5254 Merrick Rd. Suite 5, Massapequa, NY 11758.

Laguna Beach Hotel is a charming 60-room resort on Nettle Bay, between the sea and lagoon, five minutes from Marigot. Guest rooms are air conditioned and spacious, each with a large balcony, refrigerator, safe, private bath, French and American T.V. by satellite. Restaurant, pool, lagoon beach, tennis courts. Lou Scuba Club on premises. ☎ 800-722-0205; fax 516-797-2132.

Grand Case Beach Club is a condo resort on the beach at Grand Case. All 62 air-conditioned studios and suites have balconies or patios and kitchenettes. Ocean-view rooms are $145 for two in winter; garden-view rooms are $120. Diving is nearby and can be arranged at the desk. ☎ 800-223-1588 or 011-590-875187. Write Box 339, Grand Case 97150, St. Martin.

ST. MAARTEN

Mullet Bay Resort is a 600-room hotel on Mullet Bay. Rooms and suites are air conditioned with color T.V. and kitchens. The resort has fresh and saltwater pools, golf, a shopping arcade and the Maho Watersports dive shop on premises. Book through your travel agent or ☎ 800-325-0446. Write to Box 309, Philipsburg, St. Maarten, NA.

Great Bay Beach Hotel & Casino is a 300-room hotel on the beach at the edge of Philipsburg. Recently renovated rooms have marble baths, air conditioning, and phones. The resort features a casino, restaurants, a discotheque, shopping arcade, two pools, entertainment and tennis. Tradewinds Dive Shop on premises. ☎ 800-223-0757.

Pelican Beach Resort & Casino on Simpson Bay offers air-conditioned suites and rooms with color tv, ocean views, kitchens. There is a dive shop on premises and five pools, jacuzzis, restaurant, shopping arcade, marina and health spa. ☎ 800-327-3286.

Dining

St. Maarten/St. Martin has more than 150 restaurants featuring a wide variety of international cuisine. Here are a few favorites.

The Turtle Pier Bar & Restaurant in Dutch St. Maarten offers a unique dining experience. The entire restaurant is surrounded and enclosed in an outdoor nature preserve, where aquatic animals and birds live in their own habitats and entertain guests. Giant turtles, parrots, monkeys and rabbits live amid tropical gardens. The restaurant is known for its beef ribs, a popular dish throughout the island. The Turtle Pier Restaurant is on Simpson Bay on the Airport Road. Local ☎ 52230. Moderate to expensive.

The Grill & Ribs Co. at two Dutch-side locations on Front and Old Street and Simpson Bay Road next to the Pizza Hut, is a locals' favorite for ribs, burgers and chicken. Meals average $12. Open from 11:00 a.m. to 11:00 p.m. ☎ 24723. No credit cards.

Key Largo is a great place for dining on conch chowder, swordfish and fresh scallops in an Art Deco setting. The restaurant features a dance floor

Secluded Cove, St. Maarten

Courtesy St. Maarten Tourist Office

on the beach. It's located at Grand Case Beach on the French side. Credit cards accepted. ☎ 878158

Jean Dupont overlooks the Marigot Marina. Menu features classic French cuisine. Moderate prices. ☎ 877113.

Frigate on the lagoon at Mullet Bay is the island's only steak house—"where the beef is". Good seafood too! ☎ 52801, ext. 1583.

Pizza Hut is on Airport Road. ☎ 53210.

Sightseeing and Other Activities

For guided sightseeing tours try **St. Maarten Sightseeing Tours,** ☎ 22753.

You can get a good bird's-eye view of St. Maarten from **Fort Willem** in Philipsburg, but walk up to it rather than drive as the road is fairly treacherous.

The new, three-acre **Sint Maarten Zoo and Botanical Gardens** are on the Arch Road in Madame Estate on the Dutch side. The collection focuses on plants and animals of the Caribbean area, including a large reptile collection. Open Mon.-Fri., 9am- 5pm, weekends 10:00a.m. to 6:00 p.m.☎ 22748.

Windsurfing instruction and rentals are offered at the Little Bay Beach Hotel, Mullet Bay Resort and the Dawn Beach Hotel. Jet-skiing, water-skiing, parasailing, sailing, horse-back riding and deep-sea fishing can be arranged through hotel activity desks.

Casino gambling is offered by many hotels on the Dutch side.

The Mullet Resort has an 18-hole championship golf course designed by Joseph Lee which stretches along the shores of Mullet Pond and Simpson Bay Lagoon.

Helpful Phone Numbers

POLICE: Dutch side, ☎ 522222; French side, ☎ 855016

AMBULANCE: Dutch side 522111; French side, 875006.

PHARMACIES: Central Drugs, Philipsburg, ☎ 522321 or Mullet Bay Drug Store ☎ 542801, ext. 342.

Facts

Nearest Recompression Chamber: SABA (30 miles from the south coast)

Getting There: Major carrier service is available to St. Maarten. American Airlines (800-433-7300) has daily non-stop service from New York, Miami and San Juan. Continental offers daily service from Newark; BWIA serves St. Maarten twice weekly from Miami; Prinair has daily service from Puerto Rico; ALM from Aruba, Curacao and Bonaire. Air Guadaloupe uses Esperance airport, a small domestic strip on the French side in Grand Case.

Driving: On the right. Major car rental offices are at the airport.

Language: English is widely spoken though Dutch is the official language of St. Maarten and French is the official language of St. Martin.

Documents: U.S. citizens need a passport or original birth certificate with the raised seal. Canadian and UK citizens must have a valid passport and an onward ticket.

Customs: None, but luggage is checked for illegal drugs and contraband.

Airport Tax: $10.00 per person over two years of age.

Currency: On the Dutch side, the Netherlands Antilles Florin or Guilder. FL 1.77 = $U.S. 1. On the French side, the Franc (F) 5.30F = $U.S.1.

Climate: Mean temperature is 80°F year round; 45 inches rainfall annually.

Clothing: Lightweight, casual.

Electricity: 110 volts, 60 cycles.

Religious Services: Roman Catholic, Adventist, Anglican, Baptist, Jehovah's Witness, Methodist.

For Additional Information: Contact the St. Maarten Tourist Bureau, 275 Seventh Ave., New York NY 10001; or the French West Indies Tourist Office, 610 Fifth Ave, New York NY 10020, ☎ 900-990-0040. There is a $.50 charge for the 900 number.

Saint Vincent and The Grenadines

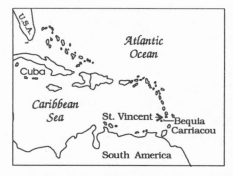

St. Vincent and The Grenadines, a multi-island nation in the eastern Caribbean, is known to just a few discriminating divers and snorkelers, but sailors have been enjoying her sheltered coves, beautiful beaches and harbors for centuries.

The islands' capital and chief port is Kingstown on St. Vincent, the main island at 18 miles long and 11 miles wide. St. Vincent is also the most densely populated island with 100,000 residents. Its topography is mountainous with black and white sand beaches looping most of the coastline. The north end is a mix of jagged peaks and gentle slopes, dominated by La Soufriere, an active volcano and the highest point reaching 4,048 ft. (1,234 meters). It erupted last on Good Friday, the 13th, April 1979 causing extensive damage to farmlands, houses and roads.

The Grenadines are 32 small islands and cays strung out like emerald stepping stones between St. Vincent and Grenada. All but two, Carriacou and Petit Martinique, are a part of this nation. Many are uninhabited or the site of a single estate or resort. A favorite for many yachtsmen and divers are the tiny, uninhabited Tobago Cays, a five-island national park celebrated for its translucent waters and adjacent Horseshoe Reef—a magnificent snorkeling area.

The larger Grenadine islands include Bequia (beck-way), Carib for "Island of the Clouds," Canouan (Can-o-wan), Mayreau (My-row), Mustique, Union, and Carriacou. All are postcard-perfect, fringed in part by soft, white-sand beaches, and towering palm trees. Dive trips take off from St. Vincent, Bequia, and Union Island, a tiny, three-by-one-mile-long rock 40 miles south of St. Vincent.

Also tiny Palm Island and Petit St. Vincent are world class, one-resort islands offering guests luxurious, jungle hideaways.

Contributors: Dennis and Karen Sabo, Landfall Productions; Bill Tewes, Dive St. Vincent.

Intrepid divers, snorkelers, birdwatchers and hikers are slowly expanding the small tourist population, but the country's economy is chiefly agricultural with exports of bananas, arrowroot, coconuts, cotton, sugar, cassava and peanuts.

Two main airports, one at Arnos Vale on St. Vincent's south coast, and another on Bequia, nine miles south of St. Vincent, serve the area. The most direct air service from the U.S. is through Barbados. Mustique Airways offers excellent inter-island service.

When to Go

The dry season is from December to April. Average rainfall on the coastal areas is 60 inches. The climate is tropical, tempered by the trade winds, with a mean temperature of about 80°F (27°C).

Insects are a problem year round, especially for hikers. Pack plenty of bug repellent.

History

St. Vincent was first sighted by Christopher Columbus in 1498 when it was populated by Carib Indians. It changed hands between the British and the French during the 17th and 18th centuries until 1763, when it was ceded to the British crown in perpetuity. In 1969 St. Vincent became an associated state of the United Kingdom. The northern Grenadines from Bequia to Petit St. Vincent were administered by St. Vincent, while Carriacou and islets south of it were governed by Grenada. On Oct. 27, 1979, Saint Vincent and the Grenadines became an independent monarchy within the Commonwealth of Nations.

Best Dive and Snorkeling Sites

Underwater landscapes are distinctive with canyons, caves, ledges and grottoes carved into with mountain-sized boulders. Black corals are found at much shallower depths than normal.

ST. VINCENT

Dive sites are off the southwest corner of the island. Sea conditions are generally calm. Strong currents which maintain outstanding water clarity occur in some areas. Private boaters should check local conditions before diving or snorkeling.

☆☆☆☆ **Bottle Reef**, located off a point under Fort Charlotte near Kingstown, is a wall and reef dive named for a huge collection of antique rum and gin bottles tossed down from the fort during the 18th century. Reef fish, including huge tarpons and morays, abound. Swim round the point of the wall to spot tuna, amber jacks, and bonito. Immense sea fans, towering gorgonians and sponges shelter hermit crabs, octopi and mini critters. Bottle Reef is suggested for all level divers and experienced snorkelers. Sea conditions range from calm to choppy depending on the wind.

☆☆☆ **Turtle Bay Reef** near Bottle Reef is a shallow wall brimming with giant gorgonians, sponges, club finger, and star corals. Masses of fish swarm the area. Crabs, turtles, huge spotted eels and rare, yellow frogfish are frequently spotted. Average reef depth is 30 ft. with shallow areas for snorkeling. Good for novice divers. Visibility exceeds 80 ft. Seas are calm.

☆☆☆☆ **The Wall**, 200 yards off the western shore, starts with a shallow ledge at 18 ft then slopes off into a stream of monster-sized boulders. Countless fish and mini critters hide in the crevices and cracks. Big basket sponges bedeck the mammoth rocks. Large numbers of snappers, copper sweepers, squirrel fish, grunts, barracuda, and kingfish inhabit the reef. Black coral trees are found at depth. Average scuba depths are from 45 to 90 ft. Good for all level divers and experienced snorkelers.

☆☆☆☆☆ **New Guinea Reef**, just ten minutes from Dive St. Vincent's dock, is a reef and wall dive that drops down from a beautiful cove of orchids and lush vegetation. The dive starts at 40 ft in a kaleidoscope of pastel gorgonians and finger sponges at the base of a sheer cliff. Purple, and orange sea fans, some eight ft across, dwarf divers. A cave at 80 ft shelters hard and soft black corals which bloom in shades of yellow, pink, green, white and red. Sea horses, large schools of reef fish, big angels and morays inhabit the ledges and overhangs. A great dive! Good, too, for advanced snorkelers. Seas usually calm.

☆☆☆ **The Wrecks** refer to the rubble, anchors and cannons of two old wrecks in Kingston Harbor, and the nearby *Seimstrand*, an intact 120-ft freighter in 80 ft of water. All attract huge groupers, rays and eels. Better for diving than snorkeling, but the clear water gives good views to snorkelers. Sea conditions are calm.

☆☆☆☆☆ **The Gardens** is a spectacular, shallow reef located 15 yds from the shoreline, just north of Kingston. Frogfish, hordes of angelfish, creole wrasse, gray snapper, kingfish, parrots and soldierfish crowd a profusion of soft, club and finger corals. Big boulders, brain corals, and colonies of iridescent yellow tube sponges cover the bottom. Perfect for shallow dives and snorkeling. Seas are calm. Boat access.

BEQUIA

Bequia's leeward side is a marine park protecting eight miles of pristine reefs. Ferry and air service is available from St. Vincent.

☆☆☆☆ **L'Anse Chemin,** a 30-minute trip from Admiralty Bay, is a drift dive. Healthy corals and a big fish population popularize this spot. Seawhips, feather corals, orange-cup coral, lettuce and brain corals, blue sponges and mauve seafans envelop the rocky bottom. As many as 20 flamingo tongues may be attached to one seafan. Fish life is superb with large parrotfish and groupers, queen triggerfish, queen and French angels, spotted and juvenile drums, gray snapper, Spanish mackerel, tuna, creole wrasse and schooling reef fish. Nurse shark are seen beneath the ledges of the reef. Depths range from 60 to 90 ft.

☆☆☆ **Ship's Stern** is a maze of swim-through tunnels, pinnacles, caverns and grottos all lavish with a thick cover of lacy corals, gorgonians and sponges. Big groupers and schooling fish abound. The site is a five-minute boat ride from the dock at Admiralty Bay. Depths are between 40 and 90 ft. Seas are calm.

☆☆☆ **Northwest Point,** a five-minute boat ride from the dock, is a seascape of coral buttresses. Throngs of squirrel fish, margate, trumpetfish, parrotfish, morays, chromis, grunts and creole wrasse are in residence. Micro life is abundant with corkscrew anemones, flamingo tongues, flaming scallops, arrow crabs, neon gobies, barber shrimp and octopi. Seas generally calm. *The* spot for night dives.

☆☆ **West Cay,** off Bequia's southernmost tip, is the meeting point of the Atlantic and Caribbean. Mixing currents make this an exciting wall/drift dive and the best place to spot huge grouper, reef sharks, turtles, durgons, jack and spadefish. Photogenic with big sponges and dramatic overhangs. Depths are from 15 to 115 ft. For experienced divers.

☆☆ **Wreck of the** *M.S. Lirero.* This 110-ft freighter was scuttled in 1986 to create an artificial reef. She sits upright in 60 ft of water, covered over with red and yellow sponges and soft corals. The hull may be penetrated.

OUT ISLANDS

Dive trips to Union Island, Tobago Cayes, Petit St. Vincent, Palm and Mayreau take off from Union Island.

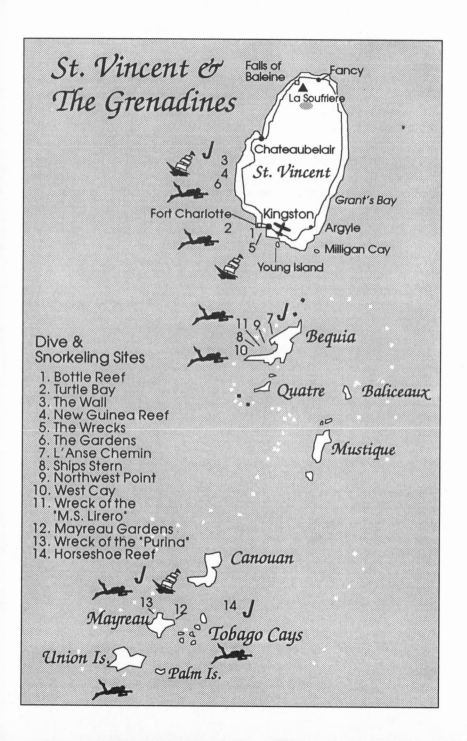

St. Vincent &
The Grenadines

Falls of Baleine

Fancy

La Soufriere

Chateaubelair

St. Vincent

Grant's Bay

Fort Charlotte

Kingston

Argyle

Milligan Cay

Young Island

Bequia

Dive & Snorkeling Sites

Quatre   Baliceaux

1. Bottle Reef
2. Turtle Bay
3. The Wall
4. New Guinea Reef
5. The Wrecks
6. The Gardens
7. L'Anse Chemin
8. Ships Stern
9. Northwest Point
10. West Cay
11. Wreck of the "M.S. Lirero"
12. Mayreau Gardens
13. Wreck of the "Purina"
14. Horseshoe Reef

Mustique

Canouan

Mayreau

Tobago Cays

Union Is.

Palm Is.

☆☆☆ **Mayreau Gardens,** a 20-minute boat ride from the dock at Union Island, is a sparkling forest of branching and plate corals. Tornedos of fish, stingrays and exotic fish drift with you as the current carries you along the walls and channels of this colorful reef. Average depth is 60 ft.

☆☆☆☆ **Wreck of the** *Purina* is a 140-ft merchant trawler which went down in 1918 off Mayreau Island. Intact, the wreck at 40 ft is the center of activity for communities of yellow tail, huge French and grey angels, spotted morays, barracuda, nurse shark, squirrel fish and sergeant majors.

☆☆☆☆☆ **Horseshoe Reef** which skirts four islands in the Tobago Cays is one of the top five snorkeling spots in the Caribbean. Despite the remote location, it is populated by as many as 70 boats per day. Visibility is exceptional—you can see the reef and fish just peering down from a boat. Depths range from the surface to 80 ft. Gigantic seafans, gorgonians, and barrel sponges highlight the reef. Throngs of angelfish, grunts, big parrotfish and grouper cluster about.

Dive Operators

Dive/travel packages can be arranged through Landfall Productions. ☎ 800-525-3833 or 510-794-1599; fax 510-794-1617. Write to 39189 Cedar Boulevard, Newark CA 94560.

ST. VINCENT

Dive St. Vincent is located on the southern tip of the island opposite Young Island. Owner Bill Tewes, a NAUI, PADI, CMAS instructor, offers personalized, scuba and snorkeling trips to best reef and wall dives around St. Vincent. Resort and C-Card courses. Bill is an outstanding underwater photographer. He and his work appear on St. Vincent postage stamps. ☎ 809-457-4714 or 809-457-4928; fax 809-457-4567. Write to P.O. Box 864, St. Vincent, West Indies.

Mariners Watersports Center a short distance from Dive St. Vincent offers reef trips and charter sailboat tours. ☎ 809-458-4228. Write to P.O. Box 639, St. Vincent, West Indies.

BEQUIA

Dive Bequia is on the beach at the Sunny Caribbee Plantation House Hotel. Owner, New Jersey born Bob Sachs, offers personalized tours aboard a 22-ft Mako. ☎ 809-458-3504; fax 809-458-3612.

Sunsports Diving Bequia at the Gingerbread Complex, offers three trips daily to nearby dive sites. ☎ 809-458-3577.

UNION

Grenadines Dive at the Anchorage Yacht Club tours the Tobago Cays and other southern Grenadine dive and snorkeling spots. ☎ 809-458-8138. Write to Glenroy Adams, Grenadines Dive, Union Island, St. Vincent & the Grenadines, West Indies.

Snorkeling excursions aboard a 60-ft catamaran are offered by Grenadine Tours, ☎ 809-435-8451.

Accommodations

Rates listed are for winter and are based on double occupancy.

Money-saving accommodation/dive travel packages for groups, individuals and agents are offered through Landfall Productions. ☎ 800-525-3833 or 510-794-1599; fax 510-794-1617. Write to 39189 Cedar Boulevard, Newark, CA 94560.

ST. VINCENT

Coconut Beach Inn at Villa Beach in Kingston is a tiny inn with an excellent open-air bar and restaurant. The garden patio extends to the water's edge. Black-sand beach. Dive St. Vincent picks you up on the hotel beach. Per person, package rates are from $695 for seven nights and 10 dives with transfers and breakfasts. Non-diver pays from $325. Major credit cards. ☎ 800-525-3833 or 809-458-4231. Write to Indian Bay, Box 355, St. Vincent, West Indies.

The Umbrella Beach is a 10-room hotel adjacent to Dive St. Vincent. Rooms are simple with ceiling fans, private bath. Porches overlook the gardens or waterfront. Each unit has a fully-equipped kitchen. Low per person package rates for seven nights, 10 dives are from $565. Includes transfers. Non-divers pay $245.

The Grand View Beach Hotel at Villa Beach is a plush 12-room resort set in a renovated plantation house on eight tropical acres. The dining room has a great view of the neighboring islands. Tennis, pool, fitness center. Good snorkeling off the beach. Transportation is provided to Dive St. Vincent's dock. Rates with diving during the high season are from $1,215 per person for seven nights and ten dives. Non-divers pay from $845.

Prices drop dramatically during summer. ☎ 800-525-3833, 800-223-1108, or 809-458-7421.

Young Island is a short 200-yard hop by boat from the southern tip of St. Vincent. This 25-acre tropical-garden island offers 29 individual cottages featuring king or twin beds, a refrigerator, ceiling fan and private patio. Life is ultra casual. Packages offer an optional two nights aboard one of the resort's 44-ft sailing yachts, complete with captain and cook. No children under five years accepted between Jan. 15 and March 15. Diving is with Dive St. Vincent's. Snorkelers walk to the reef! Breakfast, lunch and dinner are included in seven-night dive packages. Rates per person for seven nights, 10 dives are from $1,940 for superior rooms (nearest the beach) in the high season, from $1,230 in summer. Room rates with breakfast and dinner (double) are from $410 per day. Deluxe and luxury accommodations at higher prices. For dive packages ☎ 800-525-3833. Hotel only ☎ 800-223-1108. In the UK, 0800-373742. In St. Vincent, 809-458-4826. Write to P.O. Box 211, St. Vincent, West Indies.

Blue Lagoon is for sailing enthusiasts and yacht owners. About 15 minutes from the airport, this is where you can charter a sailing cruise or chat with yacht owners. Rooms are spacious. Beach bar and pool. ☎ 800 631-1593, 800-526-4789 or 809-458-4308. Write to Box 133, St. Vincent, West Indies.

BEQUIA

From St. Vincent you can reach Bequia by Mustique Airways or ferry. The nine-mile ferry ride takes 70 to 90 minutes. Trips depart the main dock in Kingstown. Direct flights from Barbados are available.

Frangipani, on the shore of Admiralty Bay, accommodates guests in eight hillside, garden cottages built of stone and hardwood. Units have two beds, modern bath, ceiling fan and sun deck over the bay. Bar and excellent restaurant on premises. Adjacent to Sunsports Dive Center. Per person rates are from $775 for seven nights/10 dives. ☎ 800-525-3833 or 809-458-3255.

The Gingerbread Complex is on Admiralty Bay and adjacent to Sunsports Dive Center. The complex is three apartments, a restaurant, and boutique. Good for an extended stay. apartments have large porches, full kitchens and modern baths. Divers pay $665 for seven nights, 10 dives. Non-divers pay $305. ☎ 800-525-3833 or 510- 794-1599. Write to 39189 Cedar Boulevard, Newark, CA 94560.

Plantation House offers 25 pastel cottages, each with a private veranda, king or twin beds, ceiling fan and stocked mini bar. Resort features a sunken pool lounge, open-air dining room and weekly entertainment. Divers pay $1,450 each for seven nights and 10 dives--includes breakfast and dinner. Non-divers pay $1,030. Add 17% government tax/service charge. Dive Bequia is on the resort beach. ☎ 800-525-3833, 809-458-3425, or 212-599-8280. Write to Box 16, Admiralty Bay, Bequia, St. Vincent, West Indies.

Petit St. Vincent is a private 113-acre island touted as the Caribbean's most luxurious and romantic hideaway. Accommodations are in 22 cottages, each with spectacular views. Each cottage has a living room, bedroom, bathroom and patio. Meals are served in the main pavilion, at your cottage, or on the beach if you wish. Diving is provided by Grenadines Dive with pickup at the resort's dock. Dive packages are offered from $2,645 per person—breakfast, lunch and dinner included and round trip transfer from Union Island airport. Add 15% tax. ☎ 800-525-3833, 800-654-9326, or 809-458-8801. No credit cards. Closed September and October.

UNION

Sunny Grenadines Hotel is a very simple, inexpensive place to stay (under $60 per night—room only). Guest rooms are in two-story, stone cottages with twin beds and small porches. Kitchen units available. ☎ 809-458-8327.

Anchorage Yacht offers comfortable cottages at the marina. ☎ 809-458-8221. Expensive.

Dining

French Restaurant adjacent to the Umbrella Hotel is one of the finest and one of the most expensive in the islands. The restaurant features its own lobster/crab pool from which guests select their entree. Menu specialties are charcoal grilled lamb chops, or beef tenderloin in garlic butter, crepes, curried conch and steamed fish in a green pepper sauce. Reservations needed in season. ☎ 809-458-4972.

Join the locals at **Lime N Pub**, two doors down from the Umbrella Beach Hotel. Specials are pumpkin, lobster and callaloo soups, veal, chicken, steak, burgers and pizza. No credit cards. Moderate.

Chicken Roost serves Caribbean-style burritos (rotis), pizza, fish sandwiches at three locations; across from the airport, in downtown Kingstown, and in the Villa area across from Young Island. No credit cards. Inexpensive. 809-456-4939.

Bounty on Halifax Street in Kingstown offers inexpensive steaks, *rotis* and homemade ice cream. No credit cards.

Young Island, directly across the channel from the French Restaurant features a super barbecue and steel band on Saturdays (approx. $20 per person). Call for the Young Island water taxi from the phone at the dock adjacent to the French Restaurant. ☎ 458-4826.

Basil's in the Cobblestone Inn, a converted 1800's sugar warehouse, offers a buffet lunch, seafood pastas, lobster and excellent French wines. On Bay St in Kingstown. ☎ 457-2713. Expensive.

BEQUIA

Credit cards are not accepted. Most restaurants close on Sundays.

Mac's Pizzeria seen on *Lifestyles of the Rich & Famous* serves a world class lobster pizza, tangy pita sandwiches and mouth watering brownies and lime pie. It's on the beach at Port Elizabeth. Call for reservations. ☎ 458-3474. No credit cards. Moderate.

Other diver-dinner favorites are **Old Fig Tree** overlooking the harbor, **Port Hole** in Port Elizabeth for great rotis, **Harpoon Saloon** for a cold drink and **Daphne's** for home cooking.

For a special treat try **Le Petit Jardin** in Port Elizabeth. ☎ 458-3318. No credit cards. Expensive.

Sightseeing and Other Activities

Prime topside sightseeing attractions are on St. Vincent, the most popular being the **Botanical Gardens.** Located north of Kingstown on the west coast, the 20-acre gardens are the oldest in the Western Hemisphere, established for growing herbs, spices and medicinal plants.

Garden paths wind through passion flowers, breadfruit, ironwood, and blooming jacaranda trees; sealing wax palms (a sticky gum taken from the base is used for sealing envelopes), coconut, avocado pears, huge mahogany, nutmeg, cocoa and fragrant ylang-ylang, trees—oil from the ylang-ylang is used to make perfumes. The oldest tree sprouted about 1765.

Rugged hiking trails crisscross St. Vincent's 33,000 acres of forest. The nicest are the **Vermont Nature Trails** in the upper part of the Buccament Valley, directly north of Kingstown—home to a community of 100 parrots which may be spotted early mornings or late afternoons.

Fort Charlotte, named for the wife of King George III, is only a few minutes drive from Kingstown. Situated on a 600-ft ridge, the fort is complete with a moat and drawbridge to the mainland. Visitors enjoy panoramic views of the Grenadines from the old gunner ports.

Baleine Falls is reached by boat and a short hike through a rocky stream. Wear boat shoes or aqua socks and plan on most of a day for the trip (approximately a one-hr boat ride arranged through either dive shop) which includes snorkeling and diving stops. Rum punch and lunch are usually a part of the deal. The falls which would befit a Hollywood set are 60 ft high and drop into a deep crystalline pool. They are located on the northwest coast near the northern tip of the island.

Shop for batiks, tie-dyed sarongs, and crafts in **Kingstown**—a charming port town with cobblestone sidewalks, old stone buildings and a cluster of three churches.

Helpful Phone Numbers

Note: The small islands do NOT have phones.

POLICE: 457-1211

HOSPITAL: 456-1185

PHARMACIES: *Kingstown*, Reliance 456-1734 or Deane's 457-1522; *Bequia*, 458-3296.

Facts

Nearest Recompression Chamber: Barbados

Airlines: From the U.S. American Airlines (800-433-7300) connects with LIAT (809-457-1821) and Mustique Airways (800-223-0599 or 800-526-4789) in Barbados. Mustique flies from Barbados to St. Vincent, Bequia, Union, and Mustique. Other carriers with connecting flights are BWIA, British Airways, Air Canada and Air France.

Island Transportation: Taxis and buses are available at the airports.

Driving: On the left. A temporary license is required and costs about $9 U.S. Rental cars are available on St. Vincent at the airport. Johnson's U-Drive is at ☎ 458-4864.

Documents: U.S. and Canadian citizens must have a passport and onward ticket.

Currency: The Eastern Caribbean Dollar exchange rate is approximately $2.68 to U.S. $1. Major credit cards are accepted at large hotels and restaurants on St. Vincent. With some exceptions, cash is necessary on the Grenadines.

Language: English is spoken everywhere.

Climate: Average air temperature is 86°F; water, 80°F.

Clothing: Very casual. Pack light. Bring sneakers or light hiking shoes if you plan to hike the trails. Aqua socks are good for mucking about the shallows.

Electricity: 220 volts, 50 cycles. Bring an adaptor.

Time: Atlantic Standard (EST + 1 hr.)

Departure Tax: $20 EC ($7 US).

Religious Services: Catholic, Methodist.

Additional Information: *In the U.S.,* 800-729-1726, fax 212-949-5946, 801 2nd Ave. 21st floor, New York, N.Y. or 214-239-6451, fax 214-239-1002. *In Canada,* 100 University Ave., Suite 504, Toronto, Ontario M5J 1V6. *In the U.K.,* 071-937-6570.

Tobago

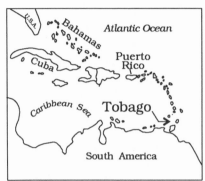

Tobago (to-ba-go), the "Robinson Crusoe Island," is Trinidad's small sister island. Separated by 22 miles of sea, both islands lie about seven miles off Venezuela's coast. Tobago sits on the South American continental shelf at the southernmost tip of the Lesser Antilles arc. It has a land area of 116 square miles (300 sq. km) and a mountainous interior with a central backbone known as Main Ridge that runs most of its length. Pigeon Peak, its highest point, reaches 1,700 ft (518 meters).

The hillsides and lowlands are dotted with thatched cottages, each with an array of prayer flags on bamboo poles. Most of the people live on lower ground and are fishermen or farmers. The northwestern, Caribbean coast is ribboned with smooth beaches fringed by palms, breadfruit, mango and banana trees.

Inland jungles support exotic wildlife and luxuriant vegetation including flowering trees such as the crimson immortelle, pink poui with large bunches of trumpet-shaped flowers, its cousin the yellow poui, and the purplish queen of flowers (pride of India). There are more than 700 species of orchids. The country's national flower is the chaconia, or wild poinsettia. Among the animal species are 60 kinds of bats, rodents such as the agouti and spotted paca (lappe), the pig-like peccary, the armadillo, the caiman (related to alligators), many types of snakes (including poisonous ones), and a great variety of birds and butterflies. This is the only place outside New Guinea where birds of paradise exist in their wild state.

The main tourist areas are Scarborough, the capital, and along the Caribbean coast between Plymouth and the island's southern tip.

Contributors: Suzette Braun; Finn Rinds, Man Friday Diving; John K. Darwent, Keith Darwent, Tobago Marine Sports; Sean Robinson, Daphne Moffat, Tobago Dive Experience.

About half of Tobago's 40,000 people are of black African descent including those of mixed race, 40% have South Asian ancestry (the "East Indians") and the remaining are of European or Chinese descent. Many languages are spoken, but English is the official and common medium of communication.

DIVING

Diving Tobago is adventure diving at its best. It's not just a visual experience but a delight in sensations for the entire body and spirit. There are drift dives, "flights" through churning cuts, holes swarming with huge pelagics, monster coral forms, caves, grottoes, fish and more fish. For the diver grown weary of the ordinary, it is therapeutic.

Tobago's best dive areas are nurtured by fresh and saltwater currents which attract an ever-present population of manta rays, huge turtles, dolphins and sharks. Many sites are drift dives though less spectacular, calm, shallow-reef areas exist for snorkeling and novice and casual divers. The most famous spot, but not necessarily the most interesting is Buccoo Reef off the island's northwest corner.

When to Go

December through June brings the best visibility and the fewest mosquitoes. Rainfall is heaviest from July to November, although it occurs in every month. Yearly precipitation varies in different parts of the islands but almost everywhere averages at least 50 inches (1,270 mm). The islands are south of the normal hurricane belt.

The climate of the country is tropical, with little seasonal variation in temperature but with a significant contrast between day and night readings. Northeast trade winds moderate the heat.

History

Christopher Columbus discovered Trinidad in 1498, but never mentioned Tobago. The island later made up for this neglect by changing hands more frequently than perhaps any other Caribbean island. For two centuries, the Dutch, English, and French fought for control. The Treaty of Amiens gave Tobago to France, but the island was ceded to Great Britain in 1814. For a while the island was declared neutral territory. This, however, made it irresistible to pirates and Tobago turned into such a dangerous outpost of rogues that in 1762 the British invaded just to clear them out.

Subsequently, a prosperous sugar industry developed on the island and "as rich as a Tobago planter" became a familiar saying.

In 1976, Trinidad and Tobago severed its ties with the British crown and in 1980 Tobago was granted limited autonomy, exercised through its new House of Assembly.

Tourism increased greatly after World War II, becoming the country's second-largest industry as fast air service brought the islands within easy reach of North America. Tobago was discovered by tourists seeking a quiet, unspoiled tropical island.

Best Dive and Snorkeling Sites

Fresh water overflow from the Orinoco and the Amazon rivers is carried past the south and east coasts of Tobago by the Guyana Current. This mix of salt and freshwater nutrients produces massive plankton blooms that support a huge range of marine life. Many deep-sea fish are found much closer to the surface here than normal.

Manta rays, turtles and dolphin are the star attractions, with a splendid supporting cast of huge, silvery tarpon, spotted eagle rays, stoplight parrotfish, queen angels, electric eels, durgons, squid, jewfish, lizard fish, spadefish, triggerfish, occasional black tip sharks, and hammerheads. Little Tobago is also a haven for every imaginable critter including multi-colored barber shrimp, banded shrimp, arrow crabs, spider crabs, Christmas trees and feather worms, slugs, nudibranchs and urchins. One diver reports three sightings of a whale shark.

The main areas for diving are off Speyside around the out islands—Little Tobago, Goat Island; off the north coast around the islets known as The Sisters; and off the southern tip of the island.

The best snorkeling areas are along the Caribbean coast at Arnos Vale Bay, Englishman's Bay, Castra Bay, Fort James, Courtland Bay, Buccoo Bay, Store Bay and off Speyside at Tyrells Bay.

SPEYSIDE MARINE AREA DIVE SITES

All of the reefs in this area fringe the out islands. There is a prevailing northerly current and most dives are drift dives. Check with dive shops before diving or snorkeling on your own. Water temperature averages 82°F year round.

☆☆☆☆☆ **Manta City**, on the north side of Little Tobago, is *the* single most popular dive in Tobago. As the name implies, it is where manta rays

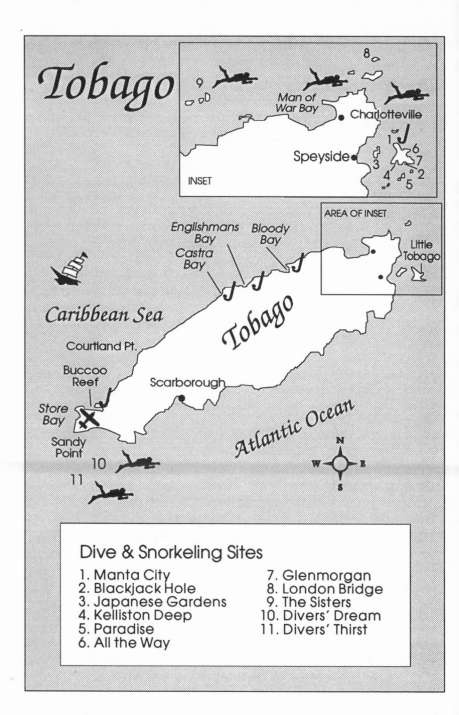

Tobago

INSET

Man of War Bay

Charlotteville

Speyside

8

9

1
6 7
3
4 2
5

AREA OF INSET

Englishmans Bay
Castra Bay
Bloody Bay

Little Tobago

Caribbean Sea

Tobago

Courtland Pt.

Buccoo Reef

Scarborough

Store Bay

Sandy Point

Atlantic Ocean

10

11

N
W   E
S

Dive & Snorkeling Sites

1. Manta City
2. Blackjack Hole
3. Japanese Gardens
4. Kelliston Deep
5. Paradise
6. All the Way

7. Glenmorgan
8. London Bridge
9. The Sisters
10. Divers' Dream
11. Divers' Thirst

are most commonly seen. Several of the mantas are used to interacting with divers and will approach to play. Avoid the temptation to hitch a ride as you may inadvertently harm the animal. Other residents are big French angels, urchins, crabs, blue tangs, jacks, damselfish, sharpnose puffers, and barracuda. Dive depths range from the extreme shallows near the shore to 50 ft. The bottom is a magnificent landscape of boulders and big rocks with good growth of star, brain and flower corals. Large barrel sponges and tube sponges are found at depth. The rays are usually spotted along the edge of a drop off. Seas are generally calm with an occasional surge. The shallows are suitable for experienced snorkelers and novice divers. Unparalleled photo opportunities.

☆☆☆Blackjack Hole, also off the south shore of Little Tobago, is a gentle slope allowing divers to choose their own depth preference. A beautiful dive with loads of fishlife, as well as loads of corals, big and small. Peek interest on the reef is between 45 and 90 ft. The surface is calm, protected by the nearby island. Currents, if at all, are gentle.

☆☆☆ Japanese Gardens, off the western tip of Goat Island, is another manta-watch point. The reef's rich and varied soft corals take on a flower-garden appearance with a landscape of odd shapes, colors and patterns. The surface is usually choppy, but there is little or no current below except at the center of a reef where you will catch a good "flight" for some minutes through a narrow canal. The first part of the dive is on a slope, and the last part is in an area with big reef-boulders and reef-patches on a sandy bottom. Sunlight reflecting in the sand adds a lot of color to the dive. Angels, grunts, moray eels, and parrots are always about. Divers select depths for their skill level—30-60 ft or 50 to 100 ft for the very experienced.

☆☆☆☆ Kelliston Deep is the site of the biggest recorded brain coral head in the world—16-ft wide and 12-ft high! The reef is off the southwest tip of Little Tobago. It starts at shelf between 30 and 50 ft. then slopes down to a sandy bottom at 120 ft. Typical reef fish are abundant with occasional sightings of nurse sharks and manta. The outer edge starts at 50 ft. This beautiful area is designated to become a marine reserve.

☆☆☆ Paradise is an almost circular arena with a sandy bottom. The site is off an islet just south of Little Tobago. You enter at the edge of a hole, go through a narrow canal, around a corner and over an edge. Above you heavy wave action forms clouds and clouds of white foam, and right under the white foam drift loose schools of tarpons four- to eight-ft long. A magnificent sight. Nearby and a part of this dive is a gently sloping reef

Manta Ray

with lots of coral and fishlife. Suggested experience level depends on sea conditions. Average depth is 60 ft.

☆☆ **All the Way** is a playground of gigantic boulders—a secretive dive where you don't know what's around the next corner. The reef slopes are a marvelous seascape rich with coral and sponge growth. Depths average 40 to 50 ft. "All the Way" is off the northeast tip of Little Tobago.

☆☆☆ **Glennmorgan** lies in a sheltered area off the eastern coast of Little Tobago. Soft corals and slender tube sponges color the canyons and walls of the reef. Average depth is 60 to 80 ft. Seldom any current. Expect to meet white-tip sharks and other pelagics. Suggested experience level depends on sea conditions. Often calm.

CARIBBEAN DIVE SITES

☆☆☆ **London Bridge**, at St. Giles Island off the northern tip of Tobago, is a rugged dive on a good day. St. Giles is a small rocky island, a natural bridge with a hole going through both above and beneath the surface—like a bridge. As you enter the hole you experience a venturi effect and are whirled through by a rush of water. Exhilarating! The depth in the hole is 30-40 ft and the rest of the dive is normally at 60 ft. Maximum depth is 110 ft. Fishlife is superb with 30-lb. parrot fish, huge green morays, lobster, schools of tarpon and pelagics between the walls, boulders and narrow gabs. Big sponges, sea fans and corals. For experienced ocean divers except on extremely calm days.

☆☆ **The Sisters** are a group of small islands off Bloody Bay on the northern coast. The site is a 30 to 45 minute boat ride over choppy seas, but if you crave a dramatic wall dive with huge pelagics, it's worth it. The wall is strewn with big boulders and rocks. At times you might find current and at times you might find surge. For experienced divers.

SOUTHEAST DIVE SITES

Water temperature on this Atlantic side is about 79°F. Dives on the Atlantic side are drift dives with strong currents and some surge. Currents often run in one direction on the surface and the opposite way at depth with occasional upwellings and downwellings. Not suggested for the timid or inexperienced diver.

☆☆☆☆☆ **Diver's Dream** is an awesome stone formation with towering fissures, cracks, canyons and caves packed with an incredible wealth of fish and crustaceans. Once in the "Dream" you'll encounter giant vase sponges measuring six feet across, and finger corals that are 10 feet high. Large schooling reef fish mingle with black-tip sharks, nurse sharks, huge turtles, barracudas, and mantas. Surface conditions are calm with gentle rollers. Always a drift dive with a one to three-knot current. Recommended for experienced drift divers.

☆☆☆☆ **Diver's Thirst** is a mix of rock and reef which forms an amphitheater populated by big groupers, black tip sharks, eagle rays and midnight parrot fish. Maximum depth is 45 ft. Always a drift dive. Surface conditions are light. Experienced drift divers.

Dive Operators

All Tobago dive operators require a C-card and request a logbook. Rates for a two-tank dive average $50. Note: Prices subject to change.

Man Friday Diving is at Man-O-War Bay, Charlotteville, near Speyside. Danish owner and dive manager Finn Rinds tours the best sights around Little Tobago and the northeastern spots. He is personal friends with a few mantas too! The PADI/NAUI shop has storage lockers and equipment rentals. Finn whisks divers out to the reefs aboard a 28-ft custom dive boat. Dive packages can be arranged with Blue Waters Inn at Speyside or Man-O-War Bay cottages. ☎ 809-660-4676; fax 809-660-4676. Write to Man Friday Diving, Charlotteville, Tobago, West Indies.

Tobago Dive Experience is located at the beautiful Grafton Beach Resort on the northern Caribbean coast. Dive master Sean Robinson, offers trips to all the Caribbean spots and around the south tip to the rugged Atlantic sites. This NAUI/PADI shop offers basic and advanced courses, dive equipment and photo rentals. Also personalized videos. ☎ 809-639-0191; fax 809-639-0030. Write Tobago Dive Experience c/o Grafton Beach Resort, Black Rock, Tobago, West Indies.

Tobago Marine Sports Ltd is at the Crown Reef Hotel, Store Bay. Operated by Keith Darwent, this full-service PADI Shop offers all courses and—around the southeast tip of Tobago—Caribbean and Atlantic dives. Contact Keith or John Darwent at 809-639-0291. Write to P.O. Box 300, Crown Reef Hotel, Store Bay, Tobago.

Jane Boyle's **Tobago Scuba Limited** at Charlotteville caters to the beginner as well as the experienced diver. Packages, including accommodations at home-like cottages at Charlotteville or Speyside with meals for a week, start at $800 per person. Book in writing at least 30 days in advance. Ms. Boyle requests a 30% deposit. No phone. Write to Tobago Scuba Limited, Charlotteville, Tobago, West Indies.

Dive Tobago Limited at Pigeon Point is Tobago's oldest dive operation. It caters to the beginner and advanced diver. Resort courses, $60. One-tank dive with equipment supplied, $30. ☎ 809-639-2266/2385. Write to P.O. Box 53, Scarborough, Tobago, West Indies.

Accommodations

Dive accommodation packages are offered by Scuba Voyages starting at $670 per person for a double. ☎ 800-544-7631.

Grafton Beach Resort in Black Rock is the island's leading hotel. Situated on the Caribbean, this 100-room, luxury resort is set amidst five acres of tropical splendor. Features are a swim-up bar, pool, air-conditioned squash courts, gym, restaurant, palm-lined beach, entertainment, dive shop and an 18-hole golf course nearby. Guest rooms are have air conditioning, cable TV, private bath and mini fridge. ☎ 809-639-0191; fax 809-639-0030. Dive package tours are offered by Scuba Voyages for seven nights and 10 dives are from $809 per person for a double ($465 for non divers). ☎ 800-544-7631.

Arnos Vale Hotel in Plymouth on the Caribbean is too hilly for lugging dive gear, but perfect for snorkelers, with a protected reef a stone's throw from the beach. The hotel offers 32 romantic white stucco cottages set on

Manta City, Off Little Tobago

a hillside overlooking the sea. Facilities include gift shop, pool, bar, restaurant. Rooms only are $90 per day off-season plus 15% tax. ☎ 809-639-2881; fax 809-639-4629.

Cocrico Inn at Plymouth offers 16 low-priced rooms. This family-owned inn has a restaurant, bar, pool and gift shop. Rates for a room start at $45 plus tax. Walking distance to the beach and bird sanctuary. ☎ 809-639-2961; fax 809-639-6565. Write to P.O. Box 287, Plymouth, Tobago, West Indies.

Mt Irvine Bay Hotel is a 64-room, two-story complex with 42 adjacent cottages on the site of a 17th-century sugar plantation. It is located on the south end of the Caribbean coast. Beaches are across the street. Facilities include a pool, restaurant, spa, tennis and meeting room. Rates for a double are from $140 per day. ☎ 809-639-8871; fax 639-8800. Write Box 222, Tobago, West Indies.

Turtle Beach Hotel at Plymouth is just 15 minutes from the airport on Courland Bay. Rooms have private bath, air conditioning, balcony or patio overlooking the beach. Beach bar, small pool, Creole Restaurant. Entertainment. ☎ 809-639-2820; fax 809-639-1495. Write P.O. Box 201, Plymouth, Tobago, West Indies.

Blue Waters Inn, Batteaux Bay, Speyside is at the heart of the Speyside Marine area. Rustic and rural, it is a haven for nature lovers, far away from the tourist area in its own private bay with 46 acres of grounds.

Snorkel from the beach. The inn has 28 guest rooms and four cottages. All are cooled by ceiling fans. Dive shop on premises. Rates for a double are from $64. With meals add $32 per person per day. Cottages are from $110 for two persons, and from $170 for four people. ☎ 809-660-4341, 809-660-4077; fax 809-660-5195.

Man-O-War Bay Cottages near St. Giles and Little Tobago Islands are for nature lovers and bird watchers. Far from the tourist area, the Caribbean-side cottages are part of Charlotteville Estate, a 1,000-acre cocoa plantation 36 miles from the airport. The cottages are plain and simple, each with one to four bedrooms with twin beds, kitchenette, shower, jalousie windows. No A/C. (Air temperature averages 82°F year round.) ☎ 809-660-4327; fax 809-660-4327. Write to Charles and Pat Turpin, Charlotteville Estate, Charlotteville, Tobago, West Indies.

Dining

Curried crab and dumplings highlight Tobago's menus along with fish and lobster dishes prepared with callaloo (like spinach), coconut and cornmeal. Peas and rice are a frequent side dish.

The Village at Kariwak Village in Crown Point offers island atmosphere and a fabulous Creole menu. Fresh seafood and fruit concoctions are special. ☎ 809-639-8442. Moderate.

The Corico Inn in Plymouth offers fabulous seafood dishes in simple surroundings. At North and Commissioner St. ☎ 809-639-2661. Prices are moderate.

The Blue Crab in Scarborough is a tiny spot offering lunches daily and dinner on Wednesday and Fridays. Fresh fish and local vegetables are prepared with island spices. ☎ 809-639-2737.

Sightseeing and Other Activities

A two-hour drive from Scarborough, the capital, to the northern tip of Tobago will lead you through most of the sightseeing spots on this tiny, rural island.

While in **Scarborough** visit the **Botanic Gardens,** the 18th-century **Fort King George** and the **National Fine Arts Gallery and Museum.** The fort commands a magnificent view of southern Tobago and the Atlantic coast.

Pigeon Point is the island's most famous beach, with offshore **Buccoo Reef.** A stop at **King's Bay Waterfall** is a necessity for the photo buff. It's about 20 miles from Scarborough along the Windward road to Charlotteville. Bring your bathing suit for a dip in the natural pool at the base of the falls.

Two of Tobago's loveliest spots are **Argyll Waterfall** near Roxborough on the north end of the Atlantic coast and **Courland Bay** on the leeward coast, named for early settlers from Latvia.

Diving and bird watching dominate the sports scene, but golfers will enjoy the **Mt. Irvine Golf Course** (☎ 639-8871) founded in 1892. Windsurfing is big off Speyside (☎ 660-5206) and horseback riding is offered at the **Palm Tree Village Beach Resort** (☎ 639-4347).

Helpful Phone Numbers

POLICE: ☎ 999; 622-5412

MEDICAL HELP: ☎ 623-2951

FIRE, AMBULANCE: ☎ 990

SCARBOROUGH HOSPITAL: ☎ 639-2551

Facts

Nearest Recompression Chamber: Trinidad

Getting There: BWIA (☎ 800-327-7300) has frequent flights to Piarco Airport, Trinidad, from New York, Miami and Toronto with connections to Tobago via LIAT. American Airlines (☎ 800-433-7300) flies from major U.S. gateway cities to Trinidad with connections via LIAT.

Island Transportation: Taxis are very expensive in Tobago. If you drive, rent a jeep at Sweet Jeeps (☎ 639-8533), or Tobago Travel (☎ 639-8778) or a car at Hill Crest Car (☎ 639-5208) at the Crown Point Airport, R.L. Rattan Car Rental Service (☎ 639-8271), Singh's Auto (☎ 639-0191) at the Grafton Beach Hotel or Toyota Rent a Car (☎ 639-7495). Some of the roads are narrow and muddy during spring and summer.

Driving: On the left. A valid license is required.

Documents: Passport valid for length of stay.

Currency: The Trinidad and Tobago dollar (TT$) is fixed at 4.25 to one U.S. dollar. There are TT$35 to the pound sterling and TT$3.7 to the Canadian dollar. U.S. dollars are not officially currency. Credit cards are widely used in tourist areas.

Climate: Average water temperature is 78°F. Air temperature averages 85°F. Humidity is high with frequent showers, especially from June to December. Biting insects are a problem.

Clothing: Ultra casual and lightweight. Long-sleeve shirts, long pants and closed shoes are best for hiking the rainforest trails. Light wetsuit suggested for deep dives. Snorkelers should wear protective covering from the midday sun.

Security: Avoid walking alone at night; don't stop if flagged down while driving, Use hotel safes, lock cars and hotel rooms. Avoid wearing flashy jewelry.

Electricity: 110 and 220v, 60 cycles.

Time: Atlantic Standard (EST + 1 hr.)

Tax: 15% is tacked on to hotel rates. A departure tax of TT$50 must be paid in local currency. A 10% tip is expected at restaurants.

Religious Services: Catholic, Protestant.

For Additional Information: The Trinidad and Tobago Tourism Development Authority—*In the U.S.*, 330 Biscayne Blvd., Suite 310, Miami FL 33132 ☎ 800-232-0082; or in New York, 25 W 43rd St., Suite 1508, New York, NY, ☎ 212-719-0540. *In the U.K*, European Business Center, Suite One, 7th floor, 113 Upper Richmond Rd, London SW15 2TL, ☎ 081-780-0318; fax 081-780-0319. *In Canada*, 40 Holly St., Suite 102, Toronto, Ontario M4S 3C3, ☎ 416-486-4470 or 800-268-8986.

United States Virgin Islands

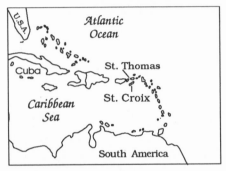

Discovered by Columbus in 1493, the United States Virgin Islands (U.S.V.I.) comprise three main islands—St. Croix, St. John and St. Thomas. Each has a distinct personality and flavor, and since they are close together you can choose one island as your vacation base and still catch the fun of the other two. These islands offer the diving and snorkeling vacationer an enormous variety of reefs, wrecks and drop-offs, all in crystal-clear water protected from strong currents and heavy seas.

The U.S.V.I. lived under six different flags before becoming an American territory. This varied background is reflected in the islands' architecture and ambience. Wander through old Danish arcades covered with tropical flowers in the historic town of Christiansted on St. Croix; visit Bluebeard's Castle on St. Thomas; or stroll around the partially restored ruins of the Annaberg Plantation on St. John.

ST. CROIX

St. Croix, the largest of the U.S.V.I., plays host to over 50,000 visiting snorkelers and divers per year, the main attraction being Buck Island National Park—the most famous snorkeling spot in the world. Scuba divers will find their share of reefs, walls and wrecks to dive.

Picturesque St. Croix, once a Danish territory, is known for its easy lifestyle and warm hospitality. The streets of Christiansted, its tiny capital, are lined with 18th-century buildings in pastel pinks, blues and

Contributors: Monica Leedy, Barker Campbell & Farley; Luana Wheatley, Virgin Rhythms; Michelle Pugh, Dive Experience.

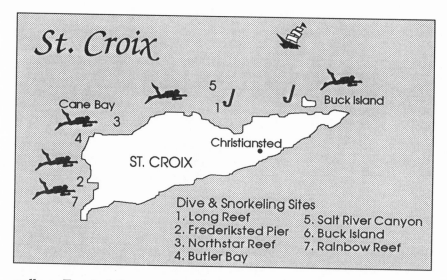

St. Croix

Cane Bay

Buck Island

Christiansted

ST. CROIX

Dive & Snorkeling Sites
1. Long Reef
2. Frederiksted Pier
3. Northstar Reef
4. Butler Bay
5. Salt River Canyon
6. Buck Island
7. Rainbow Reef

yellow. Tropical flowers greet the visitor everywhere. At night shops, restaurants and clubs vibrate with reggae music and island hospitality.

The small town of Frederiksted is laced with wide tree-shaded streets that lead to a lovely waterfront with arcaded sidewalks. After a devastating fire in 1878, Frederiksted was rebuilt in the Victorian style. Flowering vines now cling to the balustrades of the gingerbread frames the Cruzans built over the Danish masonry. Much of the best diving and snorkeling around St. Croix is accessible by beach entry. The waters off St. Croix are home to Hydrolab, an underwater habitat used for experiments by NOAA (National Oceanic and Atmospheric Administration).

Best Dives of St. Croix

☆☆☆☆ **Long Reef,** on the outskirts of Christiansted harbor, is a nice shallow site, ideal for snorkeling and for novice divers. The reef slopes gently from 30 ft to an average depth of 50 ft, reaching 80 ft at some spots. As you swim down the terraces you'll be joined by French angels, parrotfish, rays, turtles, morays, octopi, lobsters and goatfish. A docile nurse shark is frequently sighted here. The reef is shot through with hundreds of small caves and crevices, habitat to hundreds of species of fish and ocean critters. Huge brain and elkhorn corals decorate Long Reef.

☆☆☆☆ **The Frederiksted Pier** is the ultimate night dive at St. Croix. Its underwater pilings are carpeted with a mix of red, yellow and orange sponges, feathery, amber tube worms, and soft and hard corals. Macro photographers are enticed by seahorses, octopi, baby morays, juvenile fish, brittle stars, puffers, parrotfish and tube anemones. Take your dive light. Entrance to the dive site is by climbing down a ladder from the pier. Be sure to see the Harbor Master at the pier, C-Card in hand, before entering the water. ☎ 772-0174. Diving is prohibited when a ship is in.

☆☆☆☆☆ **Northstar Reef** is a spectacular wall dive at the east end of Davis Bay. This dive is recommended for intermediate or experienced divers. Beach entry is possible, but most divers opt for boat access because of the rocky terrain. The wall is covered with beautiful staghorn thickets and brain corals. At 50 ft, there is a sandy shelf that leads to a cave where a huge green moray hides out. Huge anchors typify Northstar, a one-time port for 18th-century sailing ships. The marine life here is superb, featuring schools of tropical and open water fish, turtles, morays and eagle rays. Frequent dolphin sightings are reported. Expect some current.

☆☆☆ **Butler Bay,** located just north of the Frederiksted Pier on the west shore, is the site of three ship wrecks: the 170-ft *Rosaomaira* which sits in 100 ft of water; the 140-ft *Suffolk Maid*, an old fishing trawler which can be seen at a depth of about 90 ft; and the *Northwind*, a retired tugboat at about 60 ft. The wrecks are part of an artificial reef system made up of old cars and trucks, music boxes, typewriters, and a vast array of other items. All three wrecks are havens for goat fish, groupers, snappers, hogfish, parrotfish, turtles, rays, and angel fish. This site is recommended for intermediate to experienced divers.

☆☆☆ **Salt River Canyon** features two distinct dives, one on each side of the deep, submerged canyon formed by the outflow to the Salt River. **Salt River East** is famed for the schools of bigeyes and grunts that congregate in front of the massive orange elephant ear sponges and black corals that decorate the precipice. **Salt River West** plunges from 40 to more than 130 ft. Plate corals cascade down the reef slope to stands of large purple tube sponges.

When seas are calm, it is an excellent spot for novices. Visibility, normally good, may decrease during stormy weather.

Diving on your own is possible at Cane Bay, Davis Bay and Butler Bay. Visibility close to shore is weather-dependent and will decrease when a lot of rain and wind churn the bottom. Tanks and other equipment may be rented at any of the dive shops.

Christiansted Harbor, St. Croix

Best Snorkeling of St. Croix

☆☆☆☆ **Buck Island Reef,** off the north coast of St. Croix, is the world's only underwater national park. A snorkelers' paradise, this 850-acre park was established by President John F. Kennedy as a national monument and recognized by National Geographic as one of the 10 most beautiful spots in the world.

Protected from the invasion of spear fishermen and developers, Buck Island remains exactly as it was when Kennedy swam there. As in most national parks, Buck Island has rangers, only here they sport swim trunks and patrol in power boats. There are also the standard park guide markers, but at Buck Island they stand at a depth of 12 ft, embedded in the sands of the ocean floor.

Each day, catamarans, trimarans, sloops, and yawls unload what the islanders call "the wet set." The Buck Island welcoming committee includes green parrotfish, snappy sergeant majors, grouper, rainbow-striped angel fish and the silvery Bermuda chub.

Beginners and experienced snorkelers alike can experience this underwater fantasy in an unusually safe atmosphere. The reefs of Buck Island lie only 100 yds off the coast and no trail is more than 15 ft deep.

As snorkelers enter the park, they are startled to see a blue and white welcoming plaque shimmering below the surface. One marker (number eight) located next to an unusual round coral full of veins inquires, "What would you name this coral?" The next marker says "You are right. Brain Coral." Arrows and signs guide the swimmer along the underwater trail and give the precise names of coral and other growths below the surface. More than 300 species of fish are identified, just as other national parks describe their attractions. One species that audibly demands attention is the small striped grunt, a fish that can be clearly heard underwater.The National Park Service maintains a careful watch, but one familiar park rule—Don't Feed the Animals—does not apply here. Swimmers can feed the fish as often as they like. Grouper, a favorite fish to hand-feed, come readily at the slightest beckoning.

Since the reef park is strictly non-commercial, you are advised to rent gear before heading out. Whether you're coming from St. Thomas, St. Croix or St. John, you can obtain equipment readily on all three islands.

And getting there is half the fun. Most hotels on St. Croix offer a shuttle service to Christiansted, where you can select almost any kind of boat imaginable.

Dive Operators of St. Croix

Dive Experience is located at the Club St. Croix in Christiansted. Owner Michelle Pugh is a diver-medic instructor as well as a PADI instructor. This PADI five star facility offers all certifications including a four-day certification, a resort course, rentals, photography equipment . Dive Experience offers boat dives around the island and will shoot personalized videos. Hotel and dive packages are available. ☎ 800-635-1533, 809-773-3307 or write # 1 Strand Street, Christiansted, St. Croix, U.S.V.I. 00820.

Dive St. Croix in Christiansted offers wall and wreck diving trips, night dives, Buck Island trips, camera rentals, resort through certification courses, and accommodation package tours with several different resorts. ☎ 800-523-3483 or 809-773-3434; Fax 809-773-9411. Write to 59 Kings Wharf, Christiansted, St. Croix, U.S.V.I. 00820.

Virgin Island Divers is located at the Pan Am Pavilion in Christiansted. All certification ratings and rentals. Beach dives, boat, night and wreck dives from custom dive boats. ☎ 809-773-6045 or write Pan Am Pavilion, Christiansted, St. Croix, U.S.V.I. 00820.

Anchor Dive Center is a PADI five star IDC training facility. Resort to instructor courses. Located at the Salt River Marina, they are three minutes from Salt River Canyon. ☎ 809-778-1522 or 800-532-3483. Write to P.O. Box 5588, Sunny Isle, St. Croix, U.S.V.I. 00823.

Cruzan Divers, Inc. offers boat, beach and pier dives plus wall and reef dives. Resort, rescue, dive master and advanced courses. ☎ 800-352-0107 or 809-772-3701. Write to 12 Strand St., Frederiksted, St. Croix U.S.V.I. 00840.

Sea Shadows is in Cane Bay and at Kings Wharf. Owners Libby Wessel and Steve Fordyce are beach diving specialists. The shop also operates two dive boats that tour all the sites around St. Croix.

Scuba Tech at the Salt River Marina is a full-service dive facility. Accommodation packages available. ☎ 800-233-7944 or 809-778-9650; write P.O. Box 5339, St. Croix, U.S.V.I. 00820.

Accommodations

St. Croix offers a wide range of luxury resorts, villas, condominiums, inns and guest houses. Like the neighboring British Virgin Islands, the waters around the U.S.V.I. are excellent for sailing. Many visiting divers combine a week of bare boating or live-aboard sailing with sub sea exploring. The following resorts cater primarily to divers.

Divi St. Croix Beach Resort is a magnificent beach-front hotel complex located on Grapetree Beach. All 86 guest rooms and suites are air-conditioned, and each has a private terrace or balcony with ocean views. Features are a large freshwater swimming pool, restaurants, lounge, beach bar, tennis courts, and conference facilities. Dive packages are arranged with Dive St. Croix. ☎ 800-367-DIVI or write to Divi Hotels, 54 Gunderman Rd., Ithaca NY 14850.

The Buccaneer Hotel in Christiansted also offers packages with Caribbean Sea Adventures. The Buccaneer is a sprawling resort with three beautiful beaches, three restaurants, a spa, shopping arcade, eight tennis courts, an 18-hole golf course and all water sports. ☎ 800-223-1108 or 809-773-2100; write P.O. Box 800, Waccabuc NY 10597.

The Royal Dane Hotel is a restored Danish town house on the harbor in Frederiksted. Dive packages with Cruzan Divers. ☎ 809-772-2780 or write 13 Strand Street, Frederiksted, St. Croix, U.S.V.I. 00840.

Condo and Villa Rentals

The Waves At Cane Bay, P.O. Box 1749, Kingshill, St. Croix, U.S.V.I. 00850. ☎ 809-773-0463.

Dining

The U.S. Virgin Islands is considered the mecca of haute cuisine in the Caribbean. From the islands' rich mixture of cultures—Spanish, French, English, Danish, Maltese, Dutch and American—its pungent local spices and fresh tropical fruits, local chefs create dishes to dream about. So many fine restaurants have opened up within the last five years,we can only give a hint of the many options.

The Buccaneer Hotel's **Brass Parrot** on St. Croix promises a feast to remember. Situated just 20 minutes outside of historic Christiansted, the restaurant combines a taste of past glory with a stunning modern decor. The Haitian chef prepares fine continental cuisine with a touch of the islands. Specialties include conch with hot lime sauce; Shrimp Bahia, giant shrimp sauteed in garlic butter and topped with brandy and pineapple liqueur; or a rack of lamb carved at your table. In a more informal setting, diners will enjoy the lively **Club Comanche Restaurant**, located on the second floor of an old Danish town house in Christiansted. Favorites here are cucumber soup, steak tartar, or roast chicken with oyster stuffing. For dessert try key lime pie.

The Wreck Bar on Hospital Street is the place for West Indian atmosphere. Opens for dinner 4:00 pm Mon- Sat. Specials are fish and chips, fried shrimp and beer batter onion rings. Entertainment includes crab races and guitar music. Cash only.

Banana Bay Club features exotic breakfast omelets and pancakes. Local favorites for lunch and dinner are conch fritters, fried shrimp, fish or chicken fingers, fresh fish and conch chowders. Yummy desserts. Steel drums after 6:30. Major credit cards welcome. ☎

ST. JOHN

St. John, the smallest and most verdant of the U.S.V.I., is truly the most "virgin." The island is an unspoiled sanctuary of natural beauty and wildlife. Two thirds of the 28-square-mile island and most of its stunning shoreline comprise the Virgin Islands National Park, part of the U.S. National Park system. Here nature flaunts her majestic mountains, emerald valleys and lush tropical vegetation. St. John is the best choice for beach front camping.

Best Dives of St. John

The best dives of St. John are in the out islands, Congo Cay and Carvel Rock. Shallow dive sites are found around the south shores of Reef Bay and west shores of Cruz Bay.

☆☆ **Congo Cay** is a favorite dive site for dive boats based at St. John and St. Thomas. It is a rocky islet located between them. Visibility is usually good. As with many of the small cays, the rocky submerged areas are home to large schools of fish. The coral mounds, some of which have been beaten up by the sea, are decorated with soft corals and brightly colored sponges. Currents are occasionally strong .

☆☆☆ **Carval Rock** is a short boat ride from the north end of St. John. Try this dive only if weather and sea conditions permit; recommended for very experienced divers because of strong currents sometimes encountered. The attraction here is the schools of very large fish and eagle rays. The submerged part of the rock is covered with sponges, gorgonians, basket stars, and false corals.

☆☆ **Fishbowl Reef**, just south of Cruz Bay is a nice shallow dive for novices and snorkelers. Divers swim along ledges sparkling with beautiful elkhorn and staghorn coral. Soft corals undulate in the shallows. Small reef fish hide in the crevices.

Best Snorkeling Sites of St. John

Half-day and full-day snorkeling excursions by boat are available, or you can explore outer reefs and shipwrecks,.

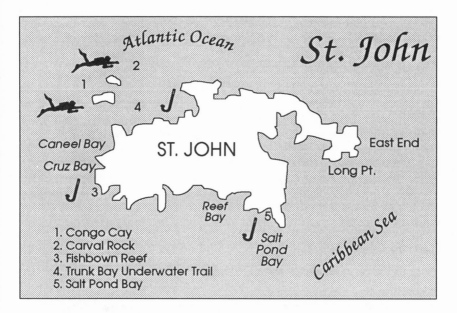

Atlantic Ocean
St. John
2
1
4
Caneel Bay
ST. JOHN
East End
Cruz Bay
Long Pt.
3
Reef
Bay
5
1. Congo Cay
2. Carval Rock
3. Fishbown Reef
4. Trunk Bay Underwater Trail
5. Salt Pond Bay
Salt
Pond
Bay
Caribbean Sea

☆☆☆ **Trunk Bay** on the north shore of the island has a clearly marked underwater trail, with abundant soft and hard corals, yellowtail, damsel fish, and occasional turtles. The reef is shallow and is just off beautiful Trunk Bay Beach. Top-side here is great for snapshots. Average depths, ten to 15 ft.

☆☆☆ **Salt Pond Bay** at the southeast end of the island is never crowded and is blessed with ample shade trees. A pretty, shallow reef stretches from both points of the bay offering snorkelers a full day's worth of adventure. Hordes of fish swarm the reef.

Dive Operators

Coral Bay Watersports Center offers diving rentals, snorkeling gear, sailing, windsurfing, fishing, and parasailing. ☎ 809-776-6857 or write 14 Emmaus, Coral Bay, St. John, U.S.V.I..

St. John Watersports Inc. offers rentals and dive trips. ☎ 809-776-6256. Or write P.O. Box 431, Cruz Bay, St. John, U.S.V.I. 00830.

Cinnamon Bay Watersports Center, located at Caneel Bay Resort, operates a 42-ft custom dive boat complete with compressor. Dive trips are offered to the outer islands (cays) and reefs. Day trips to the *R.M.S. Rhone* can be arranged for groups. Dive packages with Caneel Bay Resort are available. ☎ 809-778-8330. Write to P.O. Box 720, Cruz Bay, St. John, U.S.V.I. 00831.

Accommodations

Caneel Bay Resort occupies a 170-acre peninsula that adjoins the Virgin Islands National Park. There are 171 guest units in low-profile buildings scattered about the grounds, three restaurants, seven white sand beaches and seven tennis courts. The resort is known for the gardens where over 500 tropical plant species grow. Divers may combine a week with Little Dix Bay resort on Virgin Gorda (transfers handled by resort) or sailing on Hinckley yachts ranging in size from 40 to 50 ft. ☎ 800-223-7637 or see your travel agent.

Campgrounds

Camping is popular on St. John. Be sure to take your own gear.

Cinnamon Bay Campground, P.O. Box 720, Cruz Bay, St. John, U.S.V.I. 00830. ☎ 800-223-7637 or 809-776-6330. Dive packages available, windsurfing and sailboat rentals.

Maho Bay Camps, P.O. Box 310, St. John, U.S.V.I. 00830.

ST. THOMAS

St. Thomas is the second largest of the U.S.V.I. and site of their capital, Charlotte Amalie. Provincial yet cosmopolitan, modern yet rich in history, St. Thomas can be seen in a day. Divers should save an afternoon for shopping. Duty-free prices and keen competition make St. Thomas a bargain hunter's dream. In the narrow cobblestone streets and arcades of Charlotte Amalie you'll find designer shops housed in 200-year-old restored warehouses which were once full of molasses and rum. For those content to idle away some topside-time, St. Thomas boasts sugar-white beaches. It is in these calm sands that St. Thomas's history, rich and tumultuous, lies hidden. The sheltered coves once harbored some of the most blood-thirsty pirates in Caribbean history.

The architecture and people of St. Thomas reflect the island's many-cultured past. Dutch, French and Spanish historic sites sit side-by-side with contemporary resorts that offer all the amenities of a modern vacation. Those mixing scuba diving and sailing will find several yacht-charter companies operating from St. Thomas.

Though some beach entry diving exists here, the prettiest reefs and clearest waters are found around the outer cays. Some dive shops offer trips to the wreck of the *R.M.S. Rhone*. Cruise ship visitors will find an abundance of snorkeling opportunities.

Best Dives of St. Thomas

☆☆☆ **French Cap Cay** is well south of St. Thomas, but worth the long boat trip for both divers and snorkelers. This reef complex displays an enormous array of corals, caves, tunnels, and a spectacular sea mount. Visibility is often unlimited. The reef teems with fish, rays and critters. Beautiful lavender, orange, and yellow vase and basket sponges grow on the walls, interspersed with orange and red corals and unblemished stands of elkhorn. A light current is usually encountered here.

☆☆ **Capella Island** just east of Little Buck Island is flanked by a lush reef at 25 ft. Divers swim down through coral-encrusted canyons to a beautiful rocky garden of basket sponges, soft corals and pillar coral. The visibility, often excellent, is weather-dependent. Fish life is abundant.

☆☆ **Saba Island**, a short boat trip from the St. Thomas's harbor, is a favorite one-tank dive. Depths are 20 to 50 ft.

Trunk Bay, St. John

Charlotte Amalie Harbor, St. Thomas

Best Snorkeling Sites

☆ **Coki Beach,** adjacent to Coral World, on St. Thomas' north shore is a favorite beach dive and snorkeling site. The reef ranges in depth from 20 to 50 ft. Divers join schools of snappers, French and queen angels, and an occasional baby shark. The reef has small coral arches and recesses, a favorite hiding place for small fish, sea turtles and stingrays. Star coral, sponges, crinoids, and rock are abundant.

☆☆☆ *Cartanser Senior,* a 190-ft wreck, sits off Little Buck island in 35 ft of water. It is filled with schools of squirrel fish, morays, angels, butterfly fishes, sergeant majors, and damsels, all of whom are accustomed to being hand fed and will approach you looking for a snack. Visibility is often good here.

☆☆☆ **French Cap Cay** has the best visibility for snorkeling and free diving photography (see description on preceding page). The reef shallows have large sea fans, antler coral, and elkhorn thickets.

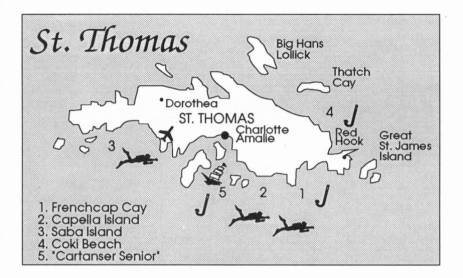

1. Frenchcap Cay
2. Capella Island
3. Saba Island
4. Coki Beach
5. "Cartanser Senior"

St. Thomas Dive Operators

Aqua Action at Secret Harbour Beach Hotel features custom tours to area sites. Accommodation packages. ☎ 809-775-6285 or write Red Hook, Box 15, St. Thomas, U.S.V.I. 00802.

Chris Sawyer Diving Center has three locations, one at the Stouffer Grand Beach Resort at Coki Beach, American Yacht Harbor and the main operation at Compass Point Marina. The shops offer resort courses as well as PADI and NAUI scuba certifications. All gear, including underwater photo equipment, is available for rental. A fast 42-ft dive boat shuttles divers to all the best dives around St. Thomas and its outer islands. ☎ 809-775-7320. Write to 6300 Estate Frydenhoj, St. Thomas, U.S.V.I. 00802.

Caribbean Divers at Red Hook has boat dives and PADI certification classes. ☎ 809-775-6384.

St. Thomas Diving Club at the Bolongo Bay Beach Club, specializes in dive and snorkel excursions to local and neighboring BVI sites. ☎ 809-776-2381.

Virgin Island Diving School. If you're arriving by cruise ship, Virgin Island Diving School will pick you up at the dock, take you diving, and drive you back to the ship. Resort courses and scuba certification lessons are available. Boat and beach diving for novices and experienced divers around St. Thomas and the outer cays. ☎ 809-774-8687 or write P.O. Box 9707, St. Thomas, U.S.V.I. 00801.

Dean Johnson's Caribbean Diving Institute is located on Mandalh Rd. near the Mahogany Run Golf Course. The school offers resort to dive-master courses, photo lessons and trips. ☎ 809-775-7610 or write P.O. Buccaneer Mall 106-208, St. Thomas, U.S.V.I. 00802.

Accommodations

Bolongo Bay Beach Club offers diving packages with the on-premises St. Thomas Diving Club. Bolongo Bay also packages combination vacations with live-aboard cruises to the BVI. Three days and two nights minimum—sailing or motor yacht. The resort has 77 air-conditioned, beachfront units with telephone, color TV, kitchens and balconies. Nightly entertainment by steel band and calypso singers. The resort is the island's leading sports facility with four tennis courts, a Sunfish sailboat fleet, snorkeling, volleyball and board games. Informal atmosphere. Children welcome. Beach bar. ☎ 800-524-4746 or 809-775-1800 or write 50 Estate Bolongo, St. Thomas, U.S.V.I. 00802.

Stouffer Grand Beach Resort is a deluxe beachfront resort located at Pineapple Beach on the east shores of St. Thomas. It has 315 rooms, all air conditioned, two pools, three restaurants, entertainment, and TV. It offers dive packages in cooperation with Chris Sawyer Diving Center. ☎ 3571 or write P.O. Box 8267, St. Thomas, U.S.V.I. 00801.

Live-Aboards

Virgin Islands Charter Yacht League will rent you a sailing yacht and teach you how to sail. On some yachts crew includes a divemaster; some also have compressors aboard. Others arrange rendezvous with dive boats. ☎ 800-524-2061 or 809-774-3944. Advance reservations suggested.

Regency International Yacht Charters offers dive vacations aboard crewed, 40- to 100-ft yachts. Scuba instruction available. ☎ 800-524-7676, 809-776-5950 or write 5200 Long Bay Rd, St. Thomas, U.S.V.I. 00802.

Sightseeing and Other Activities

The U.S.V.I. provide opportunities for a wide variety of activities. Check with your hotel or the tourist newspapers (available everywhere) for historic tours, rum factory tours, golf, tennis, deep-sea fishing, bird walks, day sails, visits to the new national park on Hassel Island, parasailing, and board sailing. Check nightclub listings for broken bottle dancing, fire eating, limbo dancing, steel bands, and island entertainment acts. Be sure to see a performance of the Mocko Jumbis on their 17-foot stilts or the Mungo Niles Cultural Native Dancers and Musicians. The dancers, ranging in age from 20 to well over 70, swirl and twirl in their bright red and white floral-motif costumes to the sounds of Quailbay or "scratch" music. For schedules call the Reichhold Center on St. Thomas at 809-774-9200 or Island Center on St. Croix at 809-778-5272.

Dining

The rich history of the U.S.V.I. is reflected in the wonderful restaurants. You can dine on the finest continental cuisine or sample exciting local dishes. Check the tourist newspaper for complete listings.

Hotel 1829 was built by a sea captain and completed in the year of its name. This is a formal restaurant with an interior resembling an Italian villa. The chef specializes in rack of lamb and various pasta dishes. Located in the heart of the harbor. ☎ 809-776-1829.

Blackbeard's Castle is an old observation tower built on a scenic hilltop in Charlotte Amalie. Gourmet seafood is served weekdays at lunch and dinner. ☎ 809-776-1234.

The Chart House, located in Frenchtown's historic Villa Olga, serves dinner on a lovely terrace. The favorite here is the 40-dish salad bar. Entrees include ribs, chicken, fish and shrimp. ☎ 809-774-4262.

Tonga Reef is on the shore at the Carib Beach Hotel. Diners are served by torchlight beside a glimmering waterfall. Specialties are native fish, steaks and seafood. Entertainment. ☎ 809-774-2525.

Sparky's Waterfront Saloon on Charlotte Amalie's waterfront is open day and night for snacks, sandwiches, burgers and conch fritters. ☎ 809-774-8015.

FACTS

Nearest Recompression Chamber: St. Thomas.

Getting There: There are daily direct flights from the U.S. mainland, via American Airlines (800-433-7300) and Continental. Other airlines serving the newly expanded Cyril E. King Airport are Sunair and Air Anguilla.

Inter-island connections can be made by ferry, seaplane shuttle or one of the island airlines. U.S. citizens must carry a passport if also traveling to the BVI.

Island Transportation: Taxi service is readily available on all three islands. Taxi rates are determined by law and those rates are available from your driver. Bus service and tours are available on St. Thomas and St. Croix. Car rentals: ABC Auto Rentals, Avis, Budget, Hertz.

Driving: Traffic keeps to the left on all three islands. A U.S. driver's license is required.

Customs: U.S. residents are entitled to take home $800 worth of duty-free imports. A 5% tax is levied on the next $1,000.

Currency: U.S.$, travelers checks, major credit cards. No personal checks accepted.

Climate: Year round temperatures vary from 76 to 82° F.

Clothing: Casual, lightweight, with sweaters for winter; jackets and ties needed for some resorts and eating establishments.

Electricity: 110V AC 60 cycles (same as U.S.)

Time: Atlantic Standard, which is one hour earlier than Eastern Standard.

Language: English.

Taxes: No sales tax. 7.5% hotel tax. Service charge may apply at some restaurants.

Religious Services: All denominations.

For Additional Information: ☎ 800-USVI-INFO (8784-4636). United States Virgin Islands Division of Tourism, P.O. Box 6400, Charlotte Amalie, U.S.V.I. 00804. *In New York,* 1270 Avenue of the Americas, NY, NY 10020, 212-582-4520; Fax: 581-3405.

What About Sharks?

Sharks have generated more sensational publicity as a threat to divers than any other animals, even though their bites are among the least frequent of any injuries divers sustain. Two opposing attitudes seem to predominate: either irrational fear or total fascination.

Nowhere is this fascination more apparent than the "JAWS" exhibit at Universal Studios in Orlando, Florida where people wait in long lines for the opportunity to be drenched, buffeted and threatened by a huge, relentless great white shark.

Paul Sieswerda, collection manager of the New York Aquarium, warns divers about taking either approach to this honored and feared species. Common sense and a realistic understanding of the animals should be used, he says, adding that "anything with teeth and the capability of biting should be treated with the same respect we give to any large animal having potential to inflict injury." The vast majority of sharks are inoffensive animals that threaten only small creatures; but some sharks will bite divers that molest them. Included are such common forms as nurse sharks and swell sharks. These animals appear docile largely because they are so sluggish, but large individuals can seriously injure a diver when provoked. Sieswerda cites an incident with a "harmless" nurse shark as the cause of 22 stitches in his hand—the result of aquarium handling.

The answer to "What about sharks?" from dive masters is usually a shrug of the shoulders. Experience tells us that most sharks are timid animals. Fewer than 100 serious assaults by sharks are reported worldwide each year with the average being closer to 50. Less than 35 % of these are fatal. Statistics isolating attacks on divers alone are not available, but they would be far fewer than 50. A majority of those few fatal attacks on man are not cases of the infamous great white shark biting the diver in two; they are by four- or five-foot sharks causing a major laceration in an arm or leg. Loss of blood due to lack of immediate medical attention is usually the cause of death.

Overplaying the danger is equally unrealistic. Encounters with dangerous sharks by divers on shallow reefs or shipwrecks are rare. Divers interviewed for this book who have sighted dangerous shark all report the same thing—getting a long look at a shark is tough. When a shark encounters man, it tends to leave the area as suddenly as it appeared.

Sharks are largely pelagic animals found out in deep open water. In general, dangerous sharks are not found in shallow areas where most novice sport diving takes place— certainly not on shallow snorkeling reefs. Most dive guides agree. They would change their line of work if they thought a huge set of jaws were awaiting them on each day's dive.

So use common sense. Avoid diving in areas known as shark breeding grounds. Avoid spearfishing and carrying the bloody catch around on the end of the pole. If you do see a shark and are uncomfortable about its presence, leave the water. Above all do not corner or provoke the shark in any manner.

One crowd of bathers in Miami, fearful after seeing a well-known shark terror movie, clubbed a baby whale to death in the surf, thinking it was a shark. Our favorite shark danger story comes from Florida divemaster, Bill Crawford. A young diver begged to see a shark in the water. Finding one presented quite a problem. The area was largely shallow reefs so shark sightings were rare indeed. Thinking hard, the divemaster remembered a big old nurse shark who could be found sleeping under a ledge on one of the outer reefs. She had been there for years totally ignoring the daily stampede of divers and snorkelers. So he took the young man to that spot and, as luck would have it, there was the shark. Upon seeing it sleeping under the ledge, the young diver became frozen with fear. In a wild panic he backed into a wall of coral putting his hand deep into a hole where a big green moray eel lived. The nurse shark, true to its calm reputation just kept sleeping. But the moray, incensed at the intrusion, defended its home by sinking its sharp teeth deep into the diver's hand.

Photo by Jon Huber

"Jaws" at Universal Studios, Orlando, Florida.